PENGUIN BOOK

THE EMERGENCY

David C. Unger has been an editorial writer at *The New York Times*—where he writes about foreign policy, international economics, and military issues—for more than thirty years and a member of the paper's editorial board for twenty-four years. He is a member of the Council on Foreign Relations and teaches courses in American foreign policy at the Bologna Center of The Johns Hopkins University Nitze School of Advanced International Studies.

TheEmergencyState.tumblr.com

Praise for David J. Unger's *The Emergency State*

The New York Times Book Review's **Editor's Choice**

"Unger should be commended for contributing to the debate. . . . Persuasive."
—*San Francisco Chronicle*

"Unger's broad indictment of defense policy—bipartisan if not nonpartisan—is sure to spark considerable and worthy debate." —*Publishers Weekly*

"An important perspective about opportunities missed and roads not taken."
—*Kirkus Reviews*

"Thoughtful work for your smart political readers." —*Library Journal*

"David Unger's informative, historical, and incisive narrative clearly illustrates that the challenge of upholding democratic principles is a constantly evolving challenge for even the most mature of democracies and makes clear that there is no trade-off between security and the respect for human rights and civil liberties."
—Kofi Annan, Secretary-General of the United Nations (1997–2006)

"Like a skilled surgeon, David Unger lays bare the pathologies that have disfigured U.S. national security policy over the course of many decades. The result is a thoughtful, judicious, immensely readable, and vitally important book." —Andrew J. Bacevich, author of *Washington Rules* and *The Limits of Power*

"The United States has grown into an overweening national security state, Unger argues in this provocative book. Agree with it or not, his biting analysis will make Americans think long and hard about how to balance the nation's role in the world with the imperatives of protecting liberty, accountability, and prosperity at home."
—Charles Kupchan, author of *No One's World*; professor of international relations, Georgetown University; senior fellow, Council on Foreign Relations

"In *The Emergency State*, David Unger documents with great passion as well as precision how the emergency state, started by Roosevelt and continued by other presidents since, has not only undermined our civil liberties but has failed to promote our security or, in recent times, improved our prosperity. His 10-point plan for restoring a constitutional democracy deserves serious debate."
—Morton H. Halperin, senior adviser at the Open Society Foundations

"I have read David Unger's excellent book on U.S. foreign policy with interest. Mr. Unger clearly has a keen grasp of the contradictions in America's relationship with the outside world. I hope that this book will find a wide audience; then perhaps we can have an honest debate about where the true balance of U.S. interests lies."
—Erik Jones, professor of European studies, and director, Bologna Institute for Policy Research

"*The Emergency State* is a wake-up call for all Americans. David C. Unger brilliantly traces the origins and relentless growth of the national security state and the expansion of presidential power at the cost of individual freedoms." —David Wise, author of *Tiger Trap* and coauthor of *The Invisible Government*

THE EMERGENCY STATE

AMERICA'S PURSUIT OF ABSOLUTE SECURITY AT ALL COSTS

DAVID C. UNGER

PENGUIN BOOKS

PENGUIN BOOKS
Published by the Penguin Group
Penguin Group (USA), 375 Hudson Street,
New York, New York 10014, USA

USA | Canada | UK | Ireland | Australia | New Zealand | India | South Africa | China
Penguin Books Ltd, Registered Offices: 80 Strand, London WC2R 0RL, England
For more information about the Penguin Group visit penguin.com

First published in the United States of America by The Penguin Press,
a member of Penguin Group (USA) Inc., 2012
Published in Penguin Books 2013

THE LIBRARY OF CONGRESS HAS CATALOGED THE HARDCOVER EDITION AS FOLLOWS:
Unger, David C.
The emergency state: America's pursuit of absolute security at all costs / David C. Unger
p. cm.
Includes bibliographical references and index.
ISBN 978-1-59420-324-4 (hc.)
ISBN 978-0-14-312297-5 (pbk.)
1. National security—United States. 2. Crisis management—United States. 3. National security—United States—Decision making. 4. Security sector—United States—History. 5. United States—Politics and government—20th century. 6. United States—Politics and government—21st century. I. Title.
II. Title: America's pursuit of absolute security at all costs.
UA23.U464 2012
355'.033073—dc23
2011040107

Printed in the United States of America
1 3 5 7 9 10 8 6 4 2

DESIGNED BY GRETCHEN ACHILLES

FOR KATHLEEN QUINN

CONTENTS

Introduction 1

CHAPTER 1 Losing Our Way 19

CHAPTER 2 The Godfather 27

CHAPTER 3 The Framing of the Permanent Emergency State 50

CHAPTER 4 Runaway Train 83

CHAPTER 5 Belated Realism 100

CHAPTER 6 Tunnel Vision 118

CHAPTER 7 Emergency Repairs 130

CHAPTER 8 Damage Control 147

CHAPTER 9 A Different Path 158

CHAPTER 10 The President We Wanted 185

CHAPTER 11 Soft Landing 203

CHAPTER 12 Bridge to Nowhere 224

CHAPTER 13 Come the Destroyer 252

CHAPTER 14 Hope Abandoned 267

CHAPTER 15 Beyond the Emergency State 281

Conclusion 296

Acknowledgments 309

Notes 313

Bibliography 331

Index 343

INTRODUCTION

We Americans have built the world's most powerful military. Yet now we live in greater fear of external and internal dangers than before World War II. We have reordered the world economy to American specifications. Yet globalization has fed our fears of outsourced jobs and unassimilable immigrants. We have filled our malls with more consumer products than previous generations could have imagined. Yet we enjoy less economic security than our parents, and we worry, with good reason, that global competition will mean fewer good jobs and relentless downward pressure on our children's living standards. We have fought repeated wars to preserve the world's freest democracy. Yet for seven decades we have been yielding our most basic liberties to a secretive, unaccountable emergency state—a vast but increasingly misdirected complex of national security institutions, reflexes, and beliefs that so define our present world that we forget that there was ever a different America. But there was, and we could have it again.

America's emergency state was originally designed to wage hot war against Nazi Germany and cold war against Soviet-led international Communism. Its institutions, and the outdated worldview they embody, are not good at protecting us against today's most dangerous international threats, as the events of 9/11 and the wrongly targeted and disastrously mismanaged wars that followed painfully demonstrate.

That should not surprise us. Using American military power wisely in an age of financial interdependence and keeping Americans safe from terrorist networks in an age of borderless globalization are very different challenges from waging another world war, hot or cold—the challenges our institutions and policies were originally designed to meet. The world has fundamentally changed, but those institutions and policies have not.

The signature institutions of the American emergency state include the Central Intelligence Agency, the Defense Department, and the White House National Security Council. All three were created in 1947. Over the years, their actions and policies have transformed the way we see ourselves and define our place in the world. The secure, prosperous, individualistic American democracy that won World War II has become a country anxious about the world, fearful of its economic future, and inattentive to the erosion of its constitutional principles. Life, liberty, and the pursuit of happiness have given way to permanent crisis management: to policing the planet and fighting preventive wars of ideological containment, usually on terrain chosen by, and favorable to, our enemies. Limited government and constitutional accountability have been shouldered aside by the kind of imperial presidency our constitutional system was explicitly designed to prevent.

Postwar presidents have assumed broad foreign policy and war-making powers never intended by the Constitution. The postwar Pentagon has woven a worldwide web of military bases, thereby entangling America in costly misalliances and creating artificial new security interests where none previously existed. Postwar Congresses, politically driven by emergency state demagogy, have diverted trillions of tax dollars from essential domestic needs toward expensive weapons and security alliances, leaving public services impoverished, taxpayers angry, and our fiscal and trade accounts chronically unbalanced.

These changes have been incremental—a gathering trend, not a single dramatic transformation. Yet over the span of seven decades, they have completely transformed the United States.

Without recognizing it, let alone debating it, America has slipped into a permanent, self-renewing state of emergency. We have set aside the traditional balanced structures of our constitutional democracy in favor of the secretive executive agencies of the permanent emergency state. As this book will show, this change has deformed our politics, diminished our liberties, distorted our relations with the rest of the world, and undermined America's inherent economic strengths. It has also not made us safer—quite the contrary. It has made us more vulnerable, more isolated, and less free. We have needlessly narrowed our political choices, colonized our own economic development, and diminished our understanding of what it means to be an American.

The emergency state did not begin with the serial abuses of George W. Bush's presidency—from the Patriot Act to the cooked intelligence on Iraq, from Guantánamo Bay to Abu Ghraib—and getting America back on the course of constitutional democracy requires more than just changing presidents. The record of Bush's two terms shows us just how much harm emergency governance has done to America's ideals, reputation, and security. But our costly detour from America's traditional democratic course began much earlier. The emergency state took on its present contours in the days of Franklin Roosevelt, Harry Truman, and Dwight Eisenhower.

The Bush administration's policies did not come out of nowhere; nor did the leading personalities who formulated them and ordered them carried out. Those policies, and those policy makers, came out of the experience, and the logic, of the emergency state.

George W. Bush did not invent presidential war making—Harry Truman did. He didn't invent extraordinary rendition—Bill Clinton did. He didn't invent the theory of a unitary, sovereign executive—Richard Nixon did. Nor did Bush invent the practice of selectively invoking, and distorting, classified intelligence data to rally public support for dubious foreign interventions. Dwight Eisenhower did just that to justify the 1954 CIA coup in Guatemala. Lyndon Johnson did it to win congressional passage of the 1964 Tonkin Gulf Resolution.

The Bush administration did not do many things that other administrations had not done before. It just did them more radically, more foolishly, and more unsuccessfully than any recent predecessor. It was the Bush administration's failures on the battlefield and in the marketplace, not its trampling of constitutional procedures and liberties, that eventually turned the American people and the Congress against it. Before Congress was outraged, it was complicit. Before the electorate rebelled, it approved. Before we threw those responsible for these constitutional abuses out, we voted them in for a second term.

And three years into the Obama administration, emergency state thinking and habits continue to damage our democracy, weaken our economy, and poison our international relationships. As a candidate, Barack Obama talked eloquently about the importance of presidents acting in accordance with the Constitution and the rule of law, and promised a new relationship with the world. But as president, Obama has addressed only a handful of Bush's most flagrant constitutional abuses while building his core foreign policies around the familiar emergency state model.

The assumptions and institutions of America's emergency state have been nurtured by thirteen successive presidential administrations, seven Democratic and six Republican. Its practices and values have been sustained, and continue to be sustained, by glib, overreaching formulas for national security that politicians and foreign policy experts have trained voters to demand from all candidates for national office.

The fifteen chapters that follow unpack the emergency state logic that guides the conduct of our politics and the actions of our government. They show the cumulative harm we have done to America's democratic heritage and future prospects by seven decades of heedless bipartisan expansion of national security institutions and thinking. They describe the damage we have done not just to our Constitution but to our national security and our international economic position. And they illuminate the overlooked connections between these wider consequences and the middle class's present discontents.

American history took a fateful turn after World War II. The emergency state that Franklin Roosevelt created to fight and win that war lived on past the defeat of Germany and Japan and became a defining feature of the postwar peace. America entered the era of the permanent emergency state, an era that has outlasted the cold war by a generation and that distorts American political and economic life to this day.

Since the 1940s the traditional tenets of American democracy—limited military intervention abroad, checks and balances at home, executive accountability to Congress and the electorate—have ceded place to something radically different, something Washington, Jefferson, and Madison would have abhorred—the steady expansion of an unaccountable, presidentially directed national security establishment.

As we shall see in the pages ahead, this self-perpetuating security establishment, created in the name of protecting American liberties from Fascist and Communist threats, has cultivated its own ideology of official secrecy to shroud its actions from appropriate scrutiny and democratic debate. It has won public acceptance of its expanding powers through selective intelligence disclosures calculated to manipulate our consent by stoking our fears.

Democracies do need to keep secrets. The Constitution's framers recognized that. *The Federalist Papers* cited the discreet conversations with foreign governments needed to negotiate treaties as one obvious example. We might add others, like military planning details, the identities of undercover agents, and advance information about changes in the Fed's exchange rate or interest policies. But most of the secrets guarded by our emergency state do not fall into these legitimate categories. They are classified not to protect American lives or interests but to shelter controversial policies from critical scrutiny and debate, to shield politicians from democratic accountability, and to protect bureaucrats from public embarrassment. Americans are often the last to know what their government does in their name abroad, and then they are genuinely mystified as to why foreigners seem so "anti-American."

The founding fathers could not have anticipated the shrunken world of the twentieth century, nor America's expanded economic and security stakes in distant corners of it. But the scheme they designed was admirably adaptable. If there would not always be time for a president to go to Congress before engaging in hostilities, there could still be time for review and remedies later on. If presidents pressed their inherent powers as commanders in chief too far in wartime (or peacetime), there could be, and was, judicial review. Congress retained the power of the purse to cut off the funding of military and intelligence operations it disapproved of. The people retained their First Amendment rights to speech, assembly, and dissent, their Fourth Amendment guarantee against unreasonable or unwarranted searches, and their constitutional right to petition the courts for writs of habeas corpus against improper detention.

It was a design of such prescience and adaptability that it survived virtually intact for 150 years, despite a civil war, huge increases in population, globally expanding American economic interests, and revolutionary changes in wartime technology that effectively shrank the planet and ended America's geographic isolation. And then we set it aside—first to fight World War II, and then the cold war, and then after the cold war ended, the vaguer menace of rogue states, and then after 9/11, international terrorism.

We make a costly mistake in treating the founding principles of American democracy as sacred but obsolete eighteenth-century relics. The Enlightenment hopes for human liberation that those principles embody have become more achievable, not less, through the scientific advances, expanding abundance, and growing educational opportunities of the intervening centuries. Today's materially richer and militarily stronger America is in a far better position to live the democratic dreams of Franklin, Jefferson, and Madison than the embattled and struggling generation of 1776.

From the beginning, American national security policies have been shaped and molded by the rough-and-tumble of democratic political life. The Constitution's role is to set the standards against which these policies must be measured, upheld, or if necessary, overturned.

The emergency state as we know it today—with its presidential encroachments on congressional and judicial powers, its institutionalization of government secrecy, and its politically lubricated links between military spending, export balances, and domestic employment—got its real start around 1940, almost two years before Congress declared war on Japan and Germany. From the vantage point of 2012, Franklin Roosevelt can be seen as a founding father of modern extraconstitutional presidential war making, the military-industrial complex, and covert federal surveillance of lawful domestic political activity. Of course, Roosevelt did not deliberately set out to break new constitutional ground in any of these areas. Constant improvisation, not deliberate prior design, was the Roosevelt style. Nor would Roosevelt's innovations have taken on such lasting significance if his postwar successors had followed the usual pattern and dismantled the wartime emergency state after 1945.

But they didn't.

Roosevelt's emergency state wasn't dismantled in 1945, after Japan's surrender ended World War II. It wasn't dismantled in 1953, when the big-government Democrats lost the White House to the (traditionally) small-government Republicans. It wasn't dismantled in the 1970s after Vietnam, Watergate, and a weakening dollar should have warned us that the postwar security state model was unsustainable. It wasn't dismantled in 1991 when the cold war ended.

Americans, having lived through the successive crises of the Great Depression, World War II, and the cold war, have become so used to living in a permanent state of emergency that the normal workings of American democracy have faded to a distant memory. Americans have thought about the world through a cold war frame for so long that many of us find it hard to imagine other approaches to foreign policy. Mainstream political leaders in both parties have offered little help. And if politicians had offered something different, they might well have been punished for it at the polls. Continued cold war formulations were politically safer, even if they ultimately left Americans less safe in a world of new and different threats.

Instead of initiating a return to America's founding democratic principles, the post-1989 era brought a desperate search for new foreign enemies that were scary enough to justify continued emergency state government at home. If real dangers were not sufficiently threatening, they could be hyped. That's what the first President Bush did, to an absurd degree, with Manuel Noriega in Panama. And it's also what he and his two successors did, less absurdly but still inaccurately (and knowingly so), with Saddam Hussein in Iraq. Demonizing Saddam served various ends—looking tough to American voters, increasing presidential power, and expanding American influence in the Middle East. Protecting America (as opposed to projecting American power) was neither the main goal nor the main result.

Insisting on absolute security has brought only absolute insecurity, as minor and manageable annoyances are redefined as potentially mortal threats that must be preventively eliminated. Generations of simplistic political sloganeering have confounded Americans' ability to make the most crucial distinctions among the potential threats confronting our country. Our future security demands a return to clearer thinking about which dangers are imminent and pose a serious threat to Americans and which do not.

In the real world, all threats are not equally serious and urgent, and military force is not always the trump card of American power. Our repeated failure to make such essential distinctions makes us more vulnerable internationally, not more secure—and it is eroding our democracy, and our economy, at home. Because we cannot preventively extinguish every potential threat, we need to develop a hierarchy of current threats, and to understand the criteria on which such a hierarchy should be based.

Instead, we have allowed ourselves to be seduced by sound-bite formulas that reflect neither our real security needs, nor our constitutional principles, nor our national purposes. In the two decades that America has stood alone as the world's sole superpower, these formulas have grown ever more ambitious and unrealistic. Americans have been sent off on quixotic preventive campaigns to suppress all present and potential dangers, and they have been warned of the dire consequences of settling for anything less. Perversely, if predictably, these campaigns have left Americans feeling less secure, not more, than in the cold war 1960s, 1970s, and 1980s, when a mismanaged superpower crisis might have brought instant national annihilation.

Candidates for office are now required to recite a kind of national security catechism that displaces goals with methods and replaces real security with the security state. We unthinkingly equate internationalism with the emergency state variant of it that we have grown used to since the 1940s. We have a tendency to tell ourselves that if the United States were to choose its military interventions more carefully, demand accountability from its secret agencies, and submit major foreign policy choices to congressional and public debate, it would be falling back into dangerous pre–Pearl Harbor isolationism.

We blind ourselves to the lessons of the irregular wars that have bloodied us in Vietnam, Iraq, and Afghanistan, imagining that they are somehow exceptions and that our military failures on these typical modern battlefields should not challenge our notions of unchallengeable American military power.

Inflating lesser dangers, conjuring up false analogies to Munich appeasement, and overstating superpower nuclear threats did not provide America with any added margin of preventive security in the 1990s. Instead, it left us inattentive to our real vulnerabilities. Keeping the CIA, the Pentagon, and the national security bureaucracy on a cold war footing during those years left us looking in all the wrong places and choosing all the wrong responses while a very different sort of enemy began targeting America in the years leading up to 9/11.

America has wasted hundreds of billions of dollars over the past twenty years on redundant nuclear weapons, ineffective missile defenses, and costly fleets of aerial combat fighters, as if our main security threat still came from a rival high-tech global superpower. Instead, we should have been urgently reassessing the dangers and opportunities created by the radically different international realities of globalized trade and travel, porous international borders, and Middle East conflicts that long ago ceased to be proxy battles between Washington and Moscow.

Al Qaeda has no intercontinental ballistic missiles, jet fighters, military alliances of satellite nations, or KGB-like international espionage networks. It has no fixed address against which traditional deterrence or retaliation can be targeted. But by 1995 the CIA already knew that bin Laden associates had plotted to fly passenger jets into symbolic targets in Washington and Paris. We built our military strategies and spending around yesterday's conflicts, failing to adjust our defenses to repel a very different kind of threat.

As we learned on 9/11, we now live in a world where loosely organized terrorist networks armed with box cutters can pose a more imminent threat than nuclear-armed states. We should have long ago redirected our security dollars away from faded cold war threats like Russian missiles and submarines and spent them instead on protecting our highly vulnerable domestic transportation infrastructure and chemical plants.

Al Qaeda's terrorists might still have penetrated strengthened homeland defenses. But at least they wouldn't have made their way through underprotected airports while we surrounded Russia and China with strategically irrelevant bases leased from unstable autocrats. Al Qaeda *can* be contained and weakened, but not with the same military tools that are most effective against rival superpowers or regional aggressor states.

Yet not even 9/11 shook the complacency of Washington's national security thinking. After Al Qaeda struck, using our own jetliners as weapons of mass destruction, the Bush administration simply shut its eyes to the new realities and proceeded with the preprogrammed responses of the national security establishment—an irrelevant high-tech Pentagon spending spree and an irrelevant regime-changing invasion of Iraq. It coupled this with the declaration of a vaguely defined global war on terror that had no clear objectives and was intended to go on for decades. That implied a future in which presidents could assume far-reaching war powers at the further expense of democracy without needing to invoke any specific and immediate dangers.

In pursuit of a guaranteed security that not even the richest and most militarily powerful country in human history can realistically hope to attain, we have been allowing our national institutions to be transformed for the purposes of endless war and empire, gravely endangering the future of our democracy. While civil libertarians and social critics have raised alarms for years, until very recently most Americans seemed to assume that we had traded in our fusty and impractical democratic traditions for a new and more profitable social contract: Our elected leaders would assume whatever expansive powers they deemed necessary to make us internationally secure while slashing taxes, shredding regulations, and shrinking government at home to leave us as free as possible to make money.

But like the derivatives-backed securities that we were repeatedly assured were AAA-reliable, that new social contract has plunged into default. America's position in the international economy turned out to be less solidly based than the bipartisan wisdom of recent Republican and Democratic administrations assured us. China's export surpluses and huge dollar reserve holdings were not just reassuring symbols of America's political stability and consumer appetites. They turned out to be mechanisms for increased Chinese economic power and leverage over Washington's financial policies.

Many of the most serious problems facing America's economy today result from a series of choices postwar administrations have made about international economic policy based primarily on America's foreign policy goals and ambitions and not necessarily on the domestic prosperity and needs of America's people.

In the early postwar years, Washington's international economic policies proved highly beneficial for the domestic economy as well. America's chief foreign policy goal in the late 1940s and 1950s was to blunt further Communist advances in Europe. The tools the Truman administration chose for achieving this goal were NATO and the Marshall Plan. Hundreds of thousands of American soldiers would help stiffen Western Europe's military spine, while billions of American dollars would help rebuild its war-shattered economies. Along with the public dollars of Marshall Plan aid came the private dollars of expanded American business investment and trade. Much of this American money flowed right back to American companies as payments for American exports or as repatriated corporate profits.

This phase of American international economic policy worked out very well for American companies, workers, and consumers. It helped ensure that postwar demobilization didn't lead to a postwar depression, as American policy makers had feared. Instead, the promise of expanding markets encouraged a sustained period of productive private investment that fueled a productivity-driven boom on both sides of the Atlantic. These were the golden postwar decades of upward mobility, low unemployment, rising living standards, and expanding government- and employer-paid benefits in the United States and Western Europe.

Then in the mid-1960s, transatlantic economic relations began to change. Europe was back on its feet economically. Its rising manufacturing output began to compete with America's for those still-expanding markets. It was scarcely a competition on equal terms, either for European companies or for American workers. Some of Europe's rising output was now produced by transplanted American corporate subsidiaries; some of what American companies had once exported from the United States, they now produced abroad and sold abroad. Some of the profits that these companies once reinvested in American factories they now invested in foreign factories.

Before long, more dollars were flowing out of America than were flowing in—not just to pay for goods and services imported by American consumers, but also to pay for the foreign wars, military bases, and security alliances required by American foreign policy. They also paid for expanding investments by American companies in foreign production facilities and for the cost of imported raw materials—especially after OPEC began sharply raising its oil prices in 1973.

With the dollar legally enshrined as the world's chief reserve currency, Washington could buffer itself against some of the usual policy consequences of chronic international deficits. The United States could still borrow money in international financial markets at favorable interest rates. Washington was not forced to adopt the kind of stop-go fiscal policies that hobbled growth in some European economies. And America's indispensable role as military defender and nuclear guarantor of Western Europe against potential Soviet aggression allowed Washington to muscle European governments into putting up with these inherently unequal terms of international economic competition.

Yet these geopolitical trump cards dealt by American foreign policy could only buy time and some political space. They could do nothing to reverse the growing economic imbalances; they only permitted American policy makers to ignore those imbalances as they grew more extreme. Successive administrations of both parties put off politically difficult corrective actions. Europe's eventual response was the European Union and the euro. With the Soviet threat gone and with China and other Asian surplus countries growing increasingly wary of holding their foreign exchange reserves in depreciating dollars, those terms are now likely to be bargained anew, with America holding a weakened hand.

The second major theme of postwar American foreign policy was to promote capitalist development in Europe's former colonies and neocolonies. One purpose was to create new opportunities for American business (again, often at the expense of the European companies that had enjoyed privileged positions in these countries during the colonial era). Another was to bind these newly independent countries to America's side in the cold war.

Under all American presidents from Truman to Reagan, promoting capitalist development and applying cold war loyalty tests to foreign governments led to providing military support and foreign aid to "friendly" leaders. That happened in Greece and Turkey in the 1940s, in the Philippines in the 1950s, and in Vietnam in the 1960s. It also led these American presidents to authorize CIA destabilization operations and other pressures against "unfriendly" leaders—e.g., in Guatemala and Iran in the 1950s, Indonesia in the 1960s, Chile in the 1970s, etc.

After 1960, with Western Europe (and Japan) economically stable and militarily secure, the third world became the main theater for U.S. foreign policy. But until the late 1980s, containing Communism remained Washington's principal foreign policy goal.

Postwar American foreign policy has been much less of a success story in the third world than it had been in Europe. And it helped prepare the way for the wholesale export of well-paying American and European jobs to pacified, cheap labor dictatorships where free labor markets could not operate because basic worker rights were denied at gunpoint.

This model of globalization has been a great boon to the shareholders of American-based multinational companies—but not to American workers, America's abandoned Rust Belt cities, or America's increasingly negative trade balance. The years after 1970 have seen a sustained and apparently irreversible falloff in genuinely productive investment in the United States and, as a result, chronic fiscal, trade, and dollar imbalances. A weakening dollar spurred OPEC to raise oil prices in 1973 and again in 2007. Lagging domestic investment has brought long-term stagnation in America's rate of productivity growth, accompanied by declining living standards for American workers.

Economists hotly debate the reasons for falling productive investment in the United States after the late 1960s. There is no single cause. But the growing stampede by American companies to move industrial production to third-world countries with governments friendly to cheap-labor, weak-safety-net, export-platform capitalism is one crucially important factor. In other words, to the extent that American foreign policy has succeeded in the third world, it has tended to undermine America's own prosperity, living standards, and trade balances at home.

Since the end of the 1980s, Europe has been economically unified, the cold war has been consigned to history, and once-underdeveloped countries like China and India have become economic heavyweights. But instead of a basic rethinking of American international economic policies, the last two decades have seen a redoubling of Washington's efforts to create a globalized economy based on offshore production and deficit-powered domestic consumption. Those efforts encouraged the growth of ever more intricate financial derivatives that, by seeming to define away risk, helped sustain the ever-larger international flows of foreign savings into American borrowing needed to lubricate an increasingly unbalanced international system.

We failed to draw the hard but salutary lessons we should have from experiences like the Vietnam War, our growing dependence on imported energy (and the military and foreign policy costs of protecting those who provide it), and our drastically deteriorating trade imbalances (as the world that Washington made safe for American capital investments lured jobs and factories overseas). Instead, Ronald Reagan declared it morning in America, and voters thrilled to his nostalgic vision of a great leap backward to the cold war glory days of the 1940s and 1950s.

We acted as if America's slide into ever-deeper fiscal and trade deficits had changed nothing important in the world and that therefore nothing important had to change in the way the United States related to it. But important things had changed. And the United States, which did more than any other country to bring about those changes, still refuses to acknowledge or adapt to them.

With no Communism left to contain, America redefined its strategic goal in the early 1990s as enlarging the arena for global capitalist development. Without ever acknowledging it, Washington replaced its defensive cold war narrative with a frankly offensive one. It was Woodrow Wilson's old utopian vision of making the world safe for American democracy, with no militarily threatening enemy in sight. But politicians and policy makers still told Americans that they were engaged in a struggle for economic and ideological survival that they could not afford to lose. As in the days of the Truman Doctrine and universal containment, political leaders from both parties continued to miscast peripheral interests as vital interests, citing them as proof that the world was still so dangerous that we dared not step back from the emergency state and reclaim our constitutional democracy.

Successive bubbles in Wall Street, Silicon Valley, and residential real estate during the Clinton and G. W. Bush years helped blind us to our underlying problems. We lulled ourselves into reprising our favorite heroic cold war role as the one indispensable nation on the global stage. We consumed ourselves into complacency. When the ever-growing inverse financial pyramid collapsed of its own weight in 2008, the incoming Obama administration set about to rebuild that pyramid using the same set of flawed blueprints.

• • •

America has been borrowing to consume in increasing doses for four decades. Were it not for the deference our creditors long paid to America's geopolitical power, the size of our consumer market, and the dollar's role as an international reserve currency, we would have been forced to adjust to changing international economic realities long ago. Now, with the global financial crisis energizing economic nationalism in Europe and Asia and with China and America's other creditors increasingly looking for more profitable ways to leverage their international surpluses, that long grace period may be coming to an end. The consequences for American borrowers and consumers could be extremely painful.

When America was the world's workshop during the post–World War II decades, its capital exports helped increase the global market for American-made goods. When America was in surplus with the rest of the world, it could easily afford ever-swelling military budgets and ever-expanding global security commitments. Today, with 14 million Americans unemployed and the Pentagon's deficit spending financed by borrowing from China, persisting in the obsolete emergency state model undermines America's national security and domestic prosperity as well as our constitutional democracy.

Beyond the current, fragile, jobless recovery, we face an alarming long-term prospect that almost no one foresaw as recently as five years ago—the possibility of a complete breakdown of the neoliberal model of globalization on which our national security strategies and our personal livelihoods now rest. On top of the legacy of increased reactive tribalism, anti-Americanism, and clash-of-civilizations ideology sown by the Bush administration, we must now reckon with the worldwide fragility of credit markets, the high volatility of international trade, and the growing social pressures created by prolonged unemployment and austerity budgets.

One-shot stimulus spending, publicly funded bank bailouts, diplomatic reengagement with the world, and shifting troops from Iraq to Afghanistan will not be enough to get us back on a sustainable course.

These cautious palliatives do not realistically address the underlying global economic imbalances that brought down the international financial system and that must be corrected to allow a sustainable economic recovery. Nor do they provide an effective counter to the decentralized networks of nonstate-sponsored terrorists and sleeper cells that brought down the World Trade Center's twin towers in 2001. At best, the Obama administration's current policies can bring us back to the moment before disaster struck, with no reassurance that it will not strike again, and again.

A more hopeful and sustainable solution will require a radically different foreign policy, national security, and economic paradigm better suited to today's world—one that reinforces rather than undermines America's greatest strengths. That cannot guarantee us absolute security or ever-rising prosperity. But it can increase the odds in our favor. And it can revitalize our democracy as well.

We might consider what our foreign policy would look like today were we to again ground its foundations in the context of our Constitution, which envisions an accountable government in the foreign as well as the domestic arena.

A revitalized American democracy would help us think more clearly about our place in the twenty-first-century world and about how to defend ourselves against twenty-first-century threats. That's more than we can expect from the ossified, unaccountable cold war national security bureaucracy we still rely on today.

Returning to our constitutional traditions would not require sacrificing our national security or our military might. Far from ignoring dangers from potentially hostile powers and threats to our liberty from abroad, the Constitution makes clear that providing for the common defense is one of the principal purposes of our national government. To that end, it gives Congress the power to declare war, to raise and support armies, and to maintain a permanent navy to defend our shores and protect our commerce from threats near and distant. Congress has shown itself quite capable of exercising those powers. It approved eight separate declarations of war over the first century and a half of American constitutional history, most recently in World War II. And it has repeatedly appropriated the money necessary to fight those declared wars to a successful conclusion.

The emergency state will not dismantle itself. It will have to be dismantled, and that will require persistent political effort. The emergency state is the only form of American government and foreign policy that most living Americans have ever known. Moving beyond it will require penetrating its closed logic and challenging its bureaucracy to serve America's real interests, not its own.

This book is written with those hopeful objectives in mind. It aims to inform and democratize our national security debate. To that end, it reexamines long-held assumptions about the kind of policies needed to keep Americans secure and prosperous. They need to be reexamined precisely because they are long held, born of different times and different threats, and not sufficiently reconsidered against the challenges of the twenty-first century.

CHAPTER ONE

LOSING OUR WAY

The United States began as a daring experiment in self-government, a bold challenge to Old World ways of absolute monarchy, restricted liberties, and endless dynastic and religious wars. The founders of American constitutional democracy, men like James Madison, Thomas Jefferson, and Benjamin Franklin, thought long and hard about why past experiments in liberty had lapsed into tyranny. They thought they understood one very important reason for these breakdowns—immersion in constant, habitual, and ultimately unnecessary wars (what we would today call wars of choice).

The founders initially tried to avert these dangers through the weak, decentralized government of the Articles of Confederation. It didn't work. We think of eighteenth-century America as pastoral and isolated. The real situation was less benign. The new American republic, occupying a narrow Atlantic coastal enclave, was an economically dynamic yet militarily vulnerable newcomer in a dangerous and fiercely competitive world. To survive and prosper, it needed to steer a safe course between clashing and covetous global military giants like Britain and France.

So America's founding leaders tried again. At the Constitutional Convention, they overcame their misgivings and created a stronger central government, warily granting the new federal Congress power to raise a national army and maintain a national navy. Deliberately separating the war-making powers they so feared, the framers designated the new federal president as commander in chief of those national armed forces.

Governors would control the state militias. Citizens would retain the right to bear arms. And to further offset the risks of an overcentralized government, an overpowerful executive, and an overmilitarized foreign policy, the framers established a careful system of checks and balances and divided powers meant to assure that every executive decision would ultimately be reviewed and, if necessary, reversed.

James Madison, the Constitution's principal author, believed that only by carefully separating and balancing governmental powers could the new American republic safeguard its liberties and ideals from the corruption and tyranny that had destroyed republican Rome and the city-state republics of the Italian Renaissance. Madison understood that the single gravest threat to that balance and those liberties would be a lapse into the endless cycle of wars and rivalries for global dominance that plagued eighteenth-century Europe. Wars brought crushing taxes and a swollen national debt. Wars threatened the constitutional balance by aggrandizing presidential power. And wars meant encroachments on civil liberties.[1]

To reassure the wary, the Constitution's framers agreed to add a Bill of Rights. Many of the rights enumerated in these first ten amendments—the guarantees of free speech (First Amendment), due process (Fifth), and trial by jury (Sixth), the prohibitions against unwarranted searches (Fourth) and cruel and unusual punishment (Eighth), and the Constitution's protection of the right of habeas corpus—have an eerily contemporary ring. They were meant to guard against the kind of emergency state we live under today.

These constitutional limits were reinforced by a series of doctrines associated with the founding generation and its immediate successors. These doctrines set safe parameters for America's foreign policies, military actions, and alliances that served to discourage frequent warfare, helping to maintain the constitutional balance and guard against the rise of a tyrannical leviathan state.

George Washington's Farewell Address (drafted by Hamilton) advised Americans to pursue commercial relations with the world but avoid political entanglements with European nations and their constant wars. Thomas Jefferson's first inaugural similarly called for "peace, commerce, and honest friendship with all nations, entangling alliances with none." The Monroe Doctrine not only enjoined the powers of the Old World from meddling in the affairs of the New, it also explicitly forswore American involvement in the affairs of Europe. Monroe's secretary of state, John Quincy Adams, spoke of an America that did not go abroad "in search of monsters to destroy."

Some of this advice was meant only to see America safely through its vulnerable early days. But over the course of the nineteenth century, these cautionary words coalesced into a popular American mind-set about foreign policy that became difficult for even the most internationally ambitious presidents to openly challenge. Intentionally or not, these time-hallowed strictures helped preserve the constitutional balance for the first century and a half of American independence. Wartime presidents, like Lincoln and Wilson, could briefly exercise expanded powers. But in times of peace, Congress jealously guarded its considerable authority over international as well as domestic affairs.

From the earliest days, presidents tried to stretch their executive authority. They assumed military and police powers not explicitly or even implicitly granted by the Constitution. During a war scare with France, John Adams used the Alien and Sedition Acts to jail political critics. Thomas Jefferson launched combat operations against the Barbary pirates without prior congressional approval. James Polk provoked an expansionist war with Mexico, fought in part so the slave South would not be territorially hemmed in by free states and nations. During the Civil War, Abraham Lincoln creatively reinterpreted the Constitution in his efforts to save the Union. His successors presided over a decade of military government in the defeated South. As the nineteenth century gave way to the twentieth, American troops used routine torture and overwhelming firepower to suppress the large numbers of Filipinos who resisted annexation of their islands by the United States.

Supporters and critics alike saw such episodes as temporary departures from normal constitutional procedure. Leading American politicians (exemplified by Lincoln) still measured and justified their actions in terms of the country's founding principles and documents. Even slavery advocates, Indian removers, and imperialists felt compelled to demonstrate that their actions and beliefs adhered to America's founding ideals and constitutional design. America's Manifest Destiny justified the conquest of a continent but provided no writ for overseas adventurism into areas unsuitable for future statehood.

The expanded emergency powers that nineteenth- and early-twentieth-century presidents assumed in wartime were not carried over into subsequent periods of peace. They were not institutionalized and perpetuated as happened later with the post–World War II emergency state. Powers ebbed and flowed between presidents and Congresses, between government and citizens. Supreme Court decisions leaned one way, then another. But throughout the nineteenth century and into the twentieth, the Constitution's underlying system of checks and balances remained the essential reference point for political debate and judicial review.

This long constitutional tradition began to yield ground at the start of the twentieth century. The closing of the western frontier, the rise of economic trusts, and growing competition from the imperial states of Europe and Japan in world markets quickened the appetite of leaders like Theodore Roosevelt and Woodrow Wilson for stronger presidential government and more activist foreign policies. The growth of sprawling and congested cities and the arrival of millions of non-English-speaking, often illiterate, immigrants challenged Jeffersonian ideals of limited government and provided fodder for foreign policy demagoguery. Progressive-era presidents like Theodore Roosevelt and Wilson glorified presidential authority and disparaged constitutional restraints as being hopelessly out of date.

All wartime presidents have expanded presidential power. The Constitution's language is open to such expansion, especially for constitutionally declared wars. That was the pattern followed by Wilson during World War I. On the road to America's entry, he resorted to systematic deceptions of Congress and the public. Once the war began, he presided over a greatly enlarged governmental role as purchaser in the private economy. A Trading with the Enemy Act granted Wilson, and all future presidents, far-reaching unilateral powers over international commerce, at home and abroad, whether future Congresses declared war or not.

During and immediately after the war, Wilson oversaw a constitutionally dubious expansion of unaccountable executive branch powers and a vast growth in governmental secrecy and surveillance, and he markedly increased the scope and ambitions of federal law enforcement at the expense of First Amendment rights. At Wilson's urging, Congress passed wartime Espionage and Sedition Acts that criminalized legitimate foreign policy debate over the rights and wrongs of the conflict. Magazines advocating peace or American neutrality were banned from the mails. Hundreds of Americans were jailed for criticizing the war or opposing military recruitment. Government spies infiltrated, raided, and ransacked the headquarters of antiwar and antimilitary organizations.[2]

America's neutrality at the start of both world wars was consistent with its traditional foreign policy doctrines. By keeping American troops over here, while American exports supplied the needs of a world at war over there, Wilson, and later Franklin Roosevelt, likely saved hundreds of thousands of American lives and certainly spurred America's economy (although economic mobilization for war, when it came, spurred it even more). But both presidents eventually concluded that the United States could not afford to remain neutral as to the wars' final outcomes. It needed to help decide those outcomes on the battlefield so that it could help shape the economics of the postwar peace.[3]

Unfortunately, Woodrow Wilson never saw fit, or never knew how, to explain these compelling economic realities to the American people. Wilson understood the economic arguments. That's why, after years of vacillation, he moved swiftly after Germany's January 1917 announcement of unrestricted submarine warfare to seek a congressional declaration of war. Wilson's war message to Congress frankly acknowledges this.

But then, like most of Wilson's war and postwar speeches, it veers off into a very different explanation of American motives and objectives. Wilson, the political science professor and son of a southern Presbyterian minister, felt himself on more comfortable moral and political ground when he was making uplifting speeches about waging a war to end all wars and to make the world safe for democracy.

Giving a more candid account of American interests would have been a tough political challenge. Wilson would have had to take on a century-old American tradition of avoiding and condemning European balance-of-power politics. But Theodore Roosevelt had already begun to challenge that tradition and had become even more popular for doing so. Had Wilson built on that promising start, he could have prepared the American people to understand and democratically debate the country's national security requirements in an age of global American commerce and global American interests.

The empty pieties he chose to peddle instead brought him little lasting political gain. While the sharp contrast between Wilson's professed idealism and the ugly world of imperial rivalries that he promised to transcend briefly made him a hero in Europe and the United States, the adulation proved fleeting. It lasted just a few months, not long enough to shape the peace at Versailles or win Senate support for his new League of Nations.

Wilson's refusal to recognize and engage with the economic and political realities of European power politics let the victorious Allies transform his proposals for a generous, idealistic peace into the disastrous, economically punitive Versailles peace treaty that helped push the world into a global depression and a second world war and disillusioned many of his early progressive supporters. Wilson's refusal to engage with domestic political realities and articulate American self-interest made it easier for the Republican-led Senate to reject American membership in the league, rendering it ineffective from the start.

Wilson's conduct of the war and its aftermath got America's initiation into global power politics off to a bad start. Constitutional liberties were trampled. Damaging precedents for abuses of presidential power were set. And instead of leading a democratic national debate over how to look after America's expanding international interests, this educator president conjured up absolutist moral fantasies of good and evil, nurturing a rhetorical habit that has made it much harder for Americans to think clearly about their real interests in a complex and changing world.

Wilson's proto–emergency state was not dismantled until after the Republicans returned to office in 1921. Some of its worst abuses came after the war was over, during the Palmer Raids of 1919–21. Following a series of terrorist bomb attacks by anarchists, Wilson's attorney general, A. Mitchell Palmer, warned of imminent Red revolution. He invoked the Espionage and Sedition Acts to round up thousands of immigrants and suspected radicals. Their names were culled from lists drawn up by the young J. Edgar Hoover, then head of the Justice Department's General Intelligence Division. Many were held and interrogated for months without proper warrants. Hundreds of immigrants were summarily deported.

Wilson's Sedition Act was repealed in 1921. (His Espionage Act remained on the books and was unsuccessfully invoked by the Nixon administration in 1971, when it tried to bar *The New York Times* from publishing the Pentagon Papers.) A full return to constitutional normality came only in 1924, when Calvin Coolidge chose a noted critic of the Palmer Raids, the former Columbia Law School dean Harlan Fiske Stone, as attorney general. Stone denounced the Wilson era's "lawless" and "tyrannical" practices and imposed strict new guidelines on government intelligence gathering.

Stone removed some of the worst abusers from the Justice Department. But as part of his housecleaning, he promoted J. Edgar Hoover to run the department's Bureau of Investigation (precursor of today's FBI). Hoover, a consummate bureaucratic politician, managed to persuade leading civil libertarians that he had only been Palmer's unwilling accomplice and that he deplored his former boss's tactics—tactics that Hoover later raised to an art form and made a key pillar of the permanent emergency state. To ensure against a return to Palmer's tactics, Stone imposed clear new guidelines. "The Bureau," he declared, "is not concerned with political or other opinions of individuals. It is concerned only with their conduct and then only such conduct as is forbidden by the laws of the United States."

Stone's constitutionally appropriate standard held for a little more than a decade. Then Franklin Roosevelt, alarmed at the popularity of Depression demagogues, worried by gathering war clouds in Europe, and spurred on by his own political hubris, picked up where Wilson had left off.[4]

CHAPTER TWO

THE GODFATHER

Franklin Delano Roosevelt believed in a strong presidency. In his first two terms, he vastly expanded the powers of the executive branch to wage war against the Depression, reconfiguring the founders' vision of checks and balances beyond anything they would have recognized as American constitutional government. Then, beginning in 1940, with German armies driving to the Atlantic and Britain fighting on alone for its survival, FDR went much further than he would have dared in a world still at peace. In doing so, Roosevelt built the foundations of today's emergency state.

America's Constitution expands presidential powers in wartime, and American political tradition encourages wartime presidents to stretch those powers even more. War presidents have amassed greater power with each successive American war.

But Roosevelt was not yet a war president in 1940, at least not in constitutional terms. He did not ask Congress to declare war. He would have had a politically tough fight on his hands if he had, since America had not been attacked. And 1940 was an election year, in which Roosevelt was seeking an unprecedented third presidential term. Most Americans still hoped and believed that Britain could hold out without military help from the United States. Franklin Roosevelt did not care to tell them otherwise.

Instead, he began to exercise some of the expanded military and political powers of a war president without first seeking the constitutional authority to do so.

Disguising and denying his real intentions, Roosevelt the politician stroked, tested, and reassured public opinion, while Roosevelt the chief executive used the diplomatic powers of the presidency and the military authority of the commander in chief to draw American forces steadily closer to armed protection of British cargoes and undeclared naval war against Germany in the open Atlantic.

His failure to consult with Congress or keep it accurately informed of his actions on the long road from statutory neutrality to active belligerency set a pernicious precedent for his postwar successors. Congress's constitutional authority to declare war becomes meaningless when presidents can commit American prestige and troops before the House and Senate have a chance for informed debate.

History vindicated Roosevelt's military judgment. Britain could not have held out on its own much longer without the substantial military and material support Roosevelt provided during those desperate months. But history has not vindicated Roosevelt's methods. In a constitutional democracy, the ends do not justify the means, especially when those means turn out to have long-lasting consequences. The Constitution-bending shortcuts Roosevelt pioneered in these months have been expanded upon by peacetime successors from both parties, with very costly results for America's constitutional democracy and national security.

While Roosevelt maneuvered the country toward undeclared war, he secretly connived with J. Edgar Hoover (behind the backs of his successive attorneys general) to monitor "subversives" of the left and right. He encouraged the growth of a secretive national police and intelligence apparatus—accountable only to the president. From Roosevelt's day onward, this apparatus acted as if it had not only the right but the duty to spy on law-abiding citizens, disrupt their First Amendment rights, and make democratic deliberation of national security issues impossible by overclassifying essential information.

On Roosevelt's authority, Hoover drew up lists of Americans to be rounded up and detained in the event of armed conflict. Roosevelt's covert collaboration with Hoover was soon expanded to authorize secret FBI spying on the president's political opponents, including anti-interventionist members of Congress. The FBI was not investigating crimes; it was providing the president with political intelligence about the plans and associations of his critics.[1]

That wasn't all. Once America was legally at war, Roosevelt authorized the military to round up tens of thousands of law-abiding Japanese Americans, citizens included, and force them into what he himself called concentration camps, overriding their constitutional rights and the advice of his own Justice Department.

Roosevelt's third main contribution to the emergency state was constitutionally scrupulous but cast a far-reaching shadow on future democratic decision making about national security issues. To achieve the fastest possible conversion of America's Depression-slowed economy into the industrial arsenal of a worldwide antifascist alliance, Roosevelt used his wartime executive authority to mobilize war production and reward participating companies, using methods that directly paved the way for what soon became a permanent, politically embedded military-industrial complex. Congress's power of the purse cannot serve its function of democratically allocating public resources among competing public needs, and continually adapting America's military capabilities to changing national security threats, if obsolescent weapons programs become entrenched as pork barrel jobs programs defended by well-funded corporate lobbyists.

Roosevelt's innovations, and his successors' elaborations, have given us a far more powerful peacetime presidency than our Constitution envisions—and than our democracy can safely accommodate. Postwar presidents have slipped the bonds of constitutional accountability in vast and vastly consequential areas of national security policy.

Roosevelt's ad hoc constitutional innovations led to transformative changes in the relationship between the American people and their government, and between American democracy and American foreign policy. The precedents he set, and his successors' decisions to continue down the same paths, make FDR the godfather of America's emergency state.

• • •

Roosevelt's actions of the early 1940s came in the midst of a fierce domestic debate over whether the United States could or should remain neutral in the widening European war. The broad outlines of that debate are still familiar to us. But the constitutional and democratic arguments that informed many of its participants have been all but erased from our national memory. These arguments cast the emergency state in a new and illuminating light—the light of a generation that did not already take its main features for granted.

The debate prior to Pearl Harbor was not simply between farsighted liberal interventionists and myopic right-wing isolationists, as many history books now portray it. The American anti-interventionist movement was too broad and politically diverse to be grouped under any simple ideological description. The positions people took depended not just on how they felt about Germany but also on how they felt about the British Empire and, not least, on whether they felt that Woodrow Wilson's World War I emergency state had posed a bigger threat to American constitutional democracy than Kaiser Wilhelm's armies.

The largest and best-known anti-interventionist organization of the early 1940s was the America First Committee. By the time of Pearl Harbor, America First had in fact become a right-wing isolationist fringe group, out of touch with mainstream American opinion and shamelessly apologizing for Hitler's crimes. It was abandoned by many of its far-left supporters after Nazi Germany invaded Soviet Russia in June 1941, an event that turned Communist Party members and their Popular Front followers into instant interventionists. Liberal and centrist supporters fell away a few months later, when Charles Lindbergh, by then the committee's best-known spokesman, began to lace his speeches with anti-Semitism and Nazi apologetics. America First finally disbanded after Pearl Harbor.

But for most of its brief existence, America First was part of a more broad-based movement, rooted in the cautionary lessons that a wide variety of Americans drew from the experience of World War I, and their fears about the disastrous effects another world war could have on American democracy.

The America First Committee was founded in September 1940 by Yale law students and undergraduates, many of whom later became noted internationalists, including a future president of the United States, Gerald Ford; a future Peace Corps director, Sargent Shriver; and a future president of Yale, Kingman Brewster. Robert Maynard Hutchins, then president of the University of Chicago, served on its board.

Other early supporters included Charles A. Beard, America's leading progressive historian; Sinclair Lewis, the first American Nobel laureate in literature, whose novels were known for scathing portrayals of midwestern parochialism; and Oswald Garrison Villard, a leading civil rights and civil liberties activist and longtime editor of *The Nation* magazine. Chester Bowles, the advertising executive who later became Roosevelt's wartime price administrator, then a UN official in the Truman era as well as ambassador to India under both Truman and John F. Kennedy, was also an early America First activist. So was Norman Thomas, the Socialist Party leader.

America First attracted veterans who felt their sacrifices had been exploited for selfish, imperial, and destructive ends by the victorious Allies at Versailles; socialists and pacifists who had been persecuted and jailed during Woodrow Wilson's wartime emergency state and the postwar Palmer Raids that followed; and economic victims of the Depression who seethed over recent congressional testimony about wartime profiteering and prowar lobbying by Wall Street in defense of its British loan arrangements. It also included idealistic college students who had not personally experienced the First World War but whose ongoing political education was enormously influenced by such disillusioning revelations about their parents' world war.

The anti-intervention movement's main congressional support came from western and midwestern senators who had long been associated with the Progressive movement and the insurgent presidential challenges of Theodore Roosevelt in 1912 and Robert La Follette, Sr., in 1924. These included Republicans like Gerald Nye, William Borah, Robert La

Follette, Jr., and Hiram Johnson and like-minded Democrats like Burton K. Wheeler. The "peace progressives" were originally more concerned with domestic reform than foreign policy. They favored grassroots democracy and distrusted the growing political power of corporations and Wall Street. They had rallied around Theodore Roosevelt's 1912 challenge to the increasingly conservative, business-dominated Republican Party organization. Johnson was TR's running mate that year, and Wheeler had run for vice president on the ticket headed by La Follette's father in 1924. Most of the peace progressives had gone on to support, at least initially, domestic elements of Franklin Roosevelt's New Deal.[2]

But unlike both Roosevelts, they came to strongly believe that the future of American democracy depended on preserving constitutional limits on presidential power. By 1940 they were convinced that Franklin Roosevelt was trying to subvert those limits, most dangerously in his weakening of the Neutrality Acts to provide American arms and aid to Britain.

America First opposed not only U.S. military involvement in the war but also economic support for the Allies (believing, accurately, that such economic support had helped draw America into the First World War). To counter news stories about Nazi atrocities, the committee called attention to the massacres, famines, and brutalities that accompanied British and French imperial rule in Africa and Asia.

For most of the committee's progressives, liberals, and socialists, opposition to American intervention stemmed not from a provincial indifference to foreign problems or from a naïve or malevolent neutrality between liberal democracy and fascism but from a determination not to repeat America's disillusioning experience of World War I. Their fears for American democracy were well founded. Their belief that America could stand aside from the new European conflict unharmed was not.

Roosevelt had a more farsighted view of American interests. Seeing revived international trade as the key to long-term economic revival, he also believed that American democracy would be more imminently threatened by Britain's defeat and a Nazi-controlled Atlantic. And obviously, he was far less concerned about the risks to democracy of strengthened presidential war powers.

Hitler posed no direct military threat to the United States, at least not in 1941. But his victory over Britain would have posed a very direct economic threat. From the earliest days of the American republic, the prosperity of the United States required open and expanding transatlantic trade. That reliance grew greater as America industrialized, urbanized, and modernized its transportation routes between inland farms and coastal ports.

America's transatlantic trade would have been gravely threatened if Germany drove the British navy from the seas and imposed a German-centered, closed continental economy on Europe, as Hitler clearly intended. Similar German intentions (and actions, in the form of unrestricted submarine warfare) had forced America's belated entry into World War I.

Without access to European markets, America's efficient farms and factories could produce far more than American domestic markets could absorb. Without European outlets for these exports, American farmers would go broke, factories would shut down, and workers would lose their jobs. Imports mattered, too. Raw materials needed for making steel and automobiles—like manganese and rubber—weren't available in sufficient quantities within the United States. They had to be imported, and the main sources were in areas controlled by the prewar British and French empires.

The collapse of transatlantic trade during the 1930s worsened America's Depression. Then the outbreak of European war in 1939 brought greatly increased demand for American goods, just as in 1914. But as with World War I, if World War II ended in German victory, those American exports would no longer be purchased. German nationalist and protectionist policies would favor German merchant ships over American in European ports and favor the output of German factories and farms in Europe's markets.

Even an Allied victory that America had had no hand in would carry economic risks. A victorious Britain and France would continue to grant trade preferences to their imperial dominions at American expense if they were free to do so.

But that was not the way Americans in 1940 remembered World War I. Woodrow Wilson had not summoned them to a crusade to keep Germany from shutting American goods out of European markets. He had summoned them to a crusade to make the world safe for democracy. And from the vantage point of 1940, that crusade looked like a tragic mistake.

Wilson's self-deceptions, failures, and unwillingness to engage in honest political debate at home on America's economic self-interest in an Allied victory had unleashed a powerful political disillusionment and anti-interventionist backlash.

Twenty years later Franklin Roosevelt was still reckoning with that backlash, in the form of the Neutrality Acts and the range of sentiments animating the America First Committee.

Roosevelt, who had served in Wilson's administration, had by then come to share Wilson's understanding of the economic imperatives that gave America a vital interest in Britain's survival. But learning all the wrong lessons from Wilson's political mistakes, he chose not to lead but to deceive.

Roosevelt falsely caricatured all opponents of his covert interventionist policies as isolationists. He deceptively promised to keep American boys out of combat. And he stealthily maneuvered to provide first economic, and then military aid to the British cause.

In an echo of Wilson, who ran for reelection in 1916 on the carefully worded past-tense slogan "He kept us out of war," Roosevelt promised in his 1940 reelection campaign that "your boys are not going to be sent into any foreign war," by which he really meant that he would seek a declaration of war against Germany only after American forces were attacked—a risk Roosevelt deliberately courted with his naval policies in the North Atlantic the following year. Roosevelt confided in Churchill, but not in Congress or the American people. He tap-danced around the Neutrality Acts. When he had to publicly acknowledge what he was doing, he justified his actions with homely but misleading analogies and recycled Wilsonian idealism.

Wilson's political skills had been limited. FDR's were not. He won the 1940 elections going away, with a 10 percent popular vote margin over the internationalist Republican, Wendell Willkie, and with 449 electoral votes to Willkie's 82. And as the man who had rescued America from the depths of the Depression, Roosevelt enjoyed broad credibility on the economic and employment issues he could have raised to make the interventionist case realistically and honestly. Instead, as Lyndon Johnson would do in 1964 and Richard Nixon in 1972, Roosevelt chose maximizing votes in an election he would have won anyway over following the honest and constitutional path.

Roosevelt's first problem was getting around the Neutrality Acts, which Congress enacted with the explicit intention of barring the kind of activities it believed had pulled the United States into the First World War. The first of these acts, in 1935, barred exporting American-made arms to any country at war. The 1936 act further banned American loans or credits to belligerents. The 1937 version, recalling how German U-boat attacks on British passenger ships like the *Lusitania* and American merchant vessels carrying cargo to Britain had greased the path to American entry into World War I, prohibited U.S. ships from carrying any passengers or goods to any country at war and barred American citizens from traveling on the ships of any such country.

But at Roosevelt's behest, the 1937 act introduced a temporary "cash-and-carry" waiver allowing belligerent nations to pick up nonmilitary goods from American ports as long as they paid in cash. Congress agreed, since its main concern had been the kind of loans and credits to Britain it believed had led America into war in 1917. But, distrusting Roosevelt, Congress refused to renew the cash-and-carry language when it expired in early 1939.

Until the outbreak of war in Europe in September 1939, these neutrality provisions were largely theoretical. That fall Roosevelt got Congress to approve new "cash-and-carry" language that allowed belligerents to pick up military as well as nonmilitary supplies from American ports. American ships were still barred from war zones, but it was left up to Roosevelt to define these zones. FDR's hope was that only Britain and France would have the cash and the ships to make use of the revised cash-and-carry waiver. But within a matter of months, France fell to the Nazis and Britain ran out of ready cash.

Roosevelt's first solution, acting on his own authority, was to give Britain fifty U.S. Navy destroyers in exchange for ninety-nine-year leases on British naval bases in the Western Hemisphere. The public rationale for this swap—approved in early September 1940, when the Battle of Britain was at its height—was that Washington could not allow the risk of those bases falling into German hands if Britain was overrun. Probably not. But since it undid a succession of congressionally passed neutrality laws, Congress should have been asked to authorize the swap.

Within a month Hitler put aside his plans for invading the British Isles. But Britain's military plight remained desperate. Until Germany invaded Russia in June 1941, Britain stood alone against the full might of the German war machine. Roosevelt, meanwhile, had been reelected in November 1940 on his misleading pledge not to send American boys into a foreign war. Honoring his partner's political fiction, Churchill asked in January for "the tools to finish the job," a job that both Roosevelt and Churchill knew by then could not be finished without those very American boys.

The answer to Churchill's pleas, after a two-month congressional battle, was the Lend-Lease Act of March 1941. Lend-Lease allowed Roosevelt to keep providing Britain with aircraft, tanks, and other war matériel with or without payment, on the theory that they were being used to fight an enemy that also endangered the United States.

By passing Lend-Lease, Congress effectively repealed the Neutrality Acts. But it didn't, and didn't intend to, declare war. Ignoring the line Congress had implicitly drawn, Roosevelt issued a succession of orders to the U.S. Navy that put America on a clear path to war with Germany weeks before the Japanese attack at Pearl Harbor.

Predictably, German submarines responded to Lend-Lease by stepping up their already lethal campaign against British and American merchant shipping. Roosevelt hit back by ordering the navy farther and farther out into the open Atlantic to protect these endangered cargoes.

In April 1941 the United States established a protectorate over Greenland, and Roosevelt unilaterally declared a new U.S. security zone stretching to the mid-Atlantic. In May Roosevelt declared an unlimited state of national emergency in the United States. In July he ordered American military forces to occupy Iceland. In early September a German submarine exchanged fire with a U.S. Navy destroyer. A week later Roosevelt authorized navy ships to shoot German and Italian vessels on sight. A few days after that, U.S. Navy destroyers and submarine hunters began escorting British and American merchant ships as far as Iceland, at which point the British navy took over.[3]

Roosevelt's successive orders had brought the United States into open, though undeclared, naval warfare with Germany. At the end of October, Germany sank a U.S. destroyer, the *Reuben James*. In mid-November Congress formally repealed what remained of the Neutrality Acts. American merchant vessels could now be armed and carry war supplies directly to Allied ports. Roosevelt waited for the Germans to take what seemed the inevitable next step toward open combat, allowing him to ask Congress for a declaration of war against Germany. But before that could happen, Japan attacked Pearl Harbor, and Congress quickly declared war on Japan.

Japan's attack did not necessarily guarantee American entry into the Atlantic war. In fact, popular pressure to fight back in the Pacific might even have delayed it. But four days after Pearl Harbor, Hitler declared war on the United States, leading Congress to declare war on Germany as well as Japan. Roosevelt's brief foray into presidential war making was finished. Constitutional procedures took over. They were good enough to fight and win the war.

By the time of Pearl Harbor, Roosevelt had pretty much won the domestic argument over intervention. And with Japan's attack and Germany's subsequent declaration of war against the United States, Roosevelt had no more need for constitutional shortcuts. Congress declared war as the Constitution envisioned.

Yet Roosevelt's short-circuiting of honest debate in those years—and the way mainstream historians came not only to accept this but to applaud it as farsighted and courageous—set some very damaging precedents. From Roosevelt's day forward, American presidents have found it easier to caricature honest critics of this or that proposed military intervention (or of the need for democracy to defer to the emergency state) as "isolationists" than to engage in democratic debate about the national security pros and cons. Today, to label a person or an argument "isolationist" usually stops a foreign policy discussion dead in its tracks. And invoking Munich or Hitler, even in arguments over tin-pot dictators with only local military capacities, has the same thought-freezing effects.

We can now see that the danger Hitler posed to America in 1941 was, in fact, grave and worsening. But the sound-bite version of the 1941 debate has been invoked repeatedly over the years to justify a wide range of interventionist policies under a wide variety of circumstances, most of them neither grave nor worsening, and many of which Franklin Roosevelt himself would presumably have rejected out of hand.

How different, in constitutional terms, was Roosevelt's course in the first eleven months of 1941 from the actions taken by Lyndon Johnson during the Tonkin Gulf incident—actions few historians of the Vietnam War consider wise or justified? Roosevelt was right to judge Hitler a real threat to America. Lyndon Johnson was wrong to put Ho Chi Minh in the same category. But in a nation ruled by laws, decisions on war and peace cannot safely be left to the fallible judgment of presidents alone.

Much more has been written about Roosevelt's devious path toward involving America in the Atlantic war than about the devastating inroads he authorized and encouraged against basic political and constitutional freedoms. These ranged from secret FBI monitoring of his political opponents to the internment behind barbed wire of tens of thousands of law-abiding Japanese American citizens.

Roosevelt's contributions to the domestic emergency state probably affected more Americans and did graver damage to the day-to-day fabric of constitutional democracy than his stretching of presidential war powers. And they are far harder to justify in terms of any legitimate national security threats. If you believe that the snooping, wiretapping, and habeas corpus provisions of the Patriot Act went too far, many of the same objections equally apply to the domestic intelligence operations authorized by Franklin D. Roosevelt.

Roosevelt and his top legal officials were fully aware of the disastrous civil liberties record of the Wilson administration during World War I. They were determined not to repeat those mistakes. "Twenty years ago," Attorney General Frank Murphy told *The New York Times* in 1939, "inhuman and cruel things were done in the name of justice; sometimes vigilantes and others took over the work. We do not want such things done today, for the work has now been localized in the F.B.I." The problem was that by "localizing the work in the F.B.I.," Roosevelt succeeded in centralizing and institutionalizing the repression.

Many of the worst abuses grew out of Franklin Roosevelt's direct dealings with J. Edgar Hoover. Long before the United States declared war in December 1941, Roosevelt had established a pattern of ignoring the Congress, his own attorneys general, and the spirit of the First Amendment by ordering Hoover to conduct FBI investigations of vaguely and ideologically defined "subversives." This pattern also led to the systematic skirting of the Fourth Amendment, which prohibits "unreasonable searches" and requires search warrants to be specific and based on sworn claims of "probable cause."

Roosevelt and Hoover's shared goal was not to investigate and prosecute actual crimes but to amass political intelligence and compile lists of "security risks" who could be rounded up and detained if America went to war. Political intelligence being political, and Roosevelt and Hoover being political men, their new inflow of information was also used for domestic political purposes that had no clear connection with national security—for example, against ordinary citizens who opposed Roosevelt's policies on supporting and supplying the British war effort.

In May 1940, for example, Roosevelt's secretary passed on to Hoover hundreds of telegrams that had been sent to the president, with the following note attached: "As the telegrams all were more or less in opposition to national defense, the president thought you might like to look them over, noting the names and addresses of the senders." The FBI did just that.[4]

Beginning in 1936, Roosevelt, relying solely on his executive authority and not on any congressional statute, directed Hoover to conduct domestic intelligence operations. These operations had no clear relationship to law enforcement, or to the FBI's counterespionage responsibilities. As Hoover understood it, Roosevelt wanted the bureau to supply "executive officials with information believed of value for making policy decisions" and also to collect information about "subversive activities," a term never precisely defined.[5]

Carrying out these instructions, and interpreting them as he saw fit, Hoover began with broad FBI fishing expeditions aimed at uncovering foreign meddling in American affairs. The FBI kept lists of people subscribing to German, Italian, and other foreign-language newspapers and began monitoring law-abiding groups and individuals on the basis of suspicions, or informer allegations, that these groups and individuals may have associated with Communist, Nazi, Fascist, or nationalist organizations.[6]

These lists were compiled not just for monitoring and surveillance purposes. By the end of the 1930s, the FBI was including many of the names it had gathered on a "Custodial Detention List" of people who might be preventively interned in wartime. A 1940 instruction from Hoover to FBI field offices defined the criteria for inclusion on this detention list as people with "Communistic, Fascist, Nazi, or other nationalistic background."[7]

Bending the letter and the spirit of the Fourth Amendment, Roosevelt also authorized covert "national security" wiretaps, mail openings, and telegram intercepts of American citizens, the same kind of practices later made notorious by the George W. Bush administration. The Fourth Amendment states:

The right of the people to be secure in their persons, houses, papers, and effects, against unreasonable searches and seizures, shall not be violated, and no Warrants shall issue, but upon probable cause, supported by Oath or affirmation, and particularly describing the place to be searched, and the persons or things to be seized.

Congressional legislation and Supreme Court rulings in the course of the 1930s made clear that these Fourth Amendment protections applied to telephone conversations. The Communications Act of 1934 made it a crime to "intercept and divulge" communications. In a 1937 case, the Court ruled that agents of the federal government were not exempt from this prohibition on intercepting and divulging.

FBI wiretaps continued, but in March 1940 Attorney General Robert Jackson ordered them ended. Three months later Roosevelt personally overturned Jackson's ban. Under FDR's strained interpretation of the Constitution and the law, unwarranted wiretaps and other forms of unwarranted search were still permitted so long as the evidence they uncovered was used for investigative purposes only and not introduced in court. In other words, the FBI was given license to intercept and use information gathered through unwarranted wiretaps, but not to publicly divulge it as evidence in court. Roosevelt also decided that neither the Communications Act prohibitions nor the Fourth Amendment applied at all in "grave matters involving the defense of the nation," or what we today would call national security cases. That exception was very broadly construed. In 1941 Attorney General Francis Biddle, following Roosevelt's new guidelines, approved FBI wiretapping of the Los Angeles Chamber of Commerce.[8]

There is a direct line connecting these early federal snooping programs to the FBI's later bugging of Martin Luther King, Jr.'s hotel rooms and civil rights strategy sessions during the 1964 Democratic Convention. That line leads on to the Nixon White House's bugging of its own national security aides, reporters, and political opponents—and more recently to the sweeping, unwarranted "national security" wiretaps of the George W. Bush administration.

Under Roosevelt's interpretations, the Fourth Amendment, explicitly written to protect citizens from snooping by agents of the federal executive without a court warrant, would now be interpreted to allow federal agents to covertly snoop on citizens whenever the president or the attorney general felt they had good cause to do so. These operations blurred the lines between legitimate surveillance and counterespionage against actual agents of hostile foreign powers, and more dubious actions that targeted American citizens whom Roosevelt or Hoover believed to be politically sympathetic to foreign ideologies, or just critics of Roosevelt and Hoover.

In 1938 Roosevelt, Attorney General Homer Cummings, and Hoover "explicitly decided not to seek legislative authorization for the expanding domestic intelligence program," to head off possible criticism or objections. The following year, after Roosevelt had proclaimed a limited national emergency, administration officials began telling Congress about some of what the FBI was doing under those emergency powers. Congress registered no objections, "although members did seek assurance that F.B.I. intelligence could be curtailed when the wartime emergency ended."[9]

With Hoover claiming authority directly delegated from the president, Roosevelt's four successive attorneys general sometimes had trouble tracking and controlling the bureau's activities. Homer Cummings and Frank Murphy approved the basic guidelines of domestic intelligence programs, leaving the details to Hoover. When Robert Jackson sought to impose tighter supervision over the Custodial Detention List, Hoover fought him off for five months. Two years later Francis Biddle ordered the list abolished as "impractical, unwise and dangerous." Hoover disobeyed, merely changing the name of the list to the "Security Index" and ordering references to it kept out of official FBI reports.[10]

Hoover never got his chance to preventively detain Communists during the war. By the time of Pearl Harbor, Russia had entered the war against Hitler and was fielding the most important Allied fighting force in Europe. The American Communist Party line abruptly swung around from militantly antiwar and prolabor to prowar, antistrike, and antidissent. Communists demanded that the government impose even tougher measures against war critics. That left only the leaders of the much-smaller Trotskyist groups to be arrested for their opinions and speech under the 1940 Smith Act. That un-American law originated in Congress. But Roosevelt was happy to sign it and approve the arrests and prosecutions.[11]

And in 1942 Roosevelt pushed Biddle to indict twenty-eight American Fascists, wartime isolationists, and outspoken Roosevelt haters under the 1917 Espionage Act and the 1940 Smith Act. They were charged with conspiring to overthrow the government and demoralize the armed forces by advocating Fascist and isolationist ideas.

Advocacy alone is enough for conviction under these laws. But the trial was never concluded. The death of the presiding judge resulted in a mistrial after the defendants had turned the court proceedings into a publicity bonanza for their cause and an embarrassment to the administration. Roosevelt may have hoped for a show trial. But the defendants put on a better show.[12]

Roosevelt also used the 1939 Hatch Act, which made it a crime for any federal employee to belong to "any political party or organization which advocates the overthrow of our constitutional form of government in the United States," to conduct extensive "loyalty" investigations, a practice that smoothed the way for the McCarthy-driven loyalty probes of the Truman and Eisenhower years.

The most sweeping wartime preventive detention program was the internment of some 110,000 Japanese Americans, most of them born in the United States and American citizens. It was personally authorized by Roosevelt in Executive Order 9066 of February 1942, urged on by Secretary of War Henry L. Stimson and California attorney general Earl Warren. Under the same executive order several thousand German American and several hundred Italian American resident aliens were also interned.

The shock of Pearl Harbor, like the shock of 9/11 sixty years later, unleashed panicky public fears that played on deeply rooted prior prejudices and required no supporting evidence. Roosevelt did nothing to resist those fears, even though Hoover and others assured him that the Japanese American population as a whole posed no real security threat.

A quickie official investigation into Pearl Harbor chaired by Supreme Court Justice Owen Roberts reported in January 1942, without factual support, that espionage by Japanese residents of Hawaii had been widespread. White farmers in California, who had long viewed their Japanese neighbors as unwanted competitors, immediately seized upon that claim to demand their removal.

A policy of interning Japanese American citizens explicitly on the basis of their race would have been unconstitutional. Roosevelt got around this constitutional problem by invoking his powers as commander in chief to authorize the War Department to designate military areas of whatever extent it saw fit anywhere in the United States and to exclude whatever people it chose to designate from those areas and relocate them in military-run camps elsewhere.

Under Roosevelt's executive order, Lieutenant General John DeWitt, head of the army's Western Defense Command, excluded all those with as little as one-eighth Japanese (or Korean) ancestry from mainland Pacific coastal areas and southern Arizona and confined them to inland internment camps. "It makes no difference whether he is an American citizen, he is still a Japanese" and hence a potential spy or saboteur, DeWitt told a House subcommittee in 1943. Interestingly, most of the 150,000 ethnic Japanese living in Hawaii were never interned, suggesting that real security concerns were little more than a pretext.[13]

J. Edgar Hoover disagreed with the Japanese internment policy, not because he held more enlightened racial views but because he believed the FBI was capable of identifying would-be saboteurs without rounding up all Japanese Americans. Attorney General Francis Biddle disagreed with it as well, calling the Japanese internment policy "ill-advised, unnecessary and unnecessarily cruel." But he still went along with it. Congress passed enforcement legislation the following month, which the Supreme Court upheld in 1944. Hugo Black, usually a firm supporter of civil liberties and the Bill of Rights, wrote the main opinion.

That 1944 decision has never been reversed. But in 1984 a federal court in California overturned the conviction of Fred Korematsu, the man who had taken the original case to the Supreme Court. It found, on the basis of wartime Justice Department documents, that the federal government had deliberately misled the Court on the military necessity of interning Japanese Americans.[14]

Roosevelt was also the first president since the Civil War era, and the last until George W. Bush, to hold trials by military commission in the United States. He did so in the summer of 1942, at the suggestion of Attorney General Biddle, to try eight German agents who had been captured on Long Island preparing to commit sabotage. No act of sabotage had actually been committed, and at least one of the Germans had tried to turn himself, and the others, in. But Roosevelt wanted guaranteed convictions, and death sentences, under loosened legal rules, which he got.

Biddle later recalled FDR saying to him: "I won't hand them over to any United States Marshal armed with a writ of habeas corpus."[15] All eight were convicted and sentenced to death. The Supreme Court upheld Roosevelt's use of a military commission, declaring that the eight Germans were "unlawful combatants." Roosevelt commuted the sentences of two men who had cooperated with investigators to long prison sentences. The other six were promptly executed.

Roosevelt's sweeping wartime mobilization of the economy repeated the pattern of past American wars and violated no basic constitutional principles. But the unprecedented scope of this mobilization swelled the size, reach, and power of the executive branch. Franklin Roosevelt created the military-industrial complex that Dwight Eisenhower pointed to less than two decades later as a potentially disastrous threat to America's liberties and democratic processes. Eisenhower's 1961 warning recognizably echoes Madison's 1795 concerns.

Roosevelt did not want to assume direct government control of the war economy. Nor did he want to create a single powerful War Industries

Board, as Woodrow Wilson had done during World War I, believing this would delegate too much presidential power to its chairman. Instead, Roosevelt created multiple planning and regulatory agencies with overlapping lines of authority and tried to induce voluntary business cooperation by guaranteeing high profits. As Secretary of War Henry Stimson put it in his diary in 1940: "If you are going to go to war, or prepare for war, in a capitalist country, you have got to let business make money out of the process or business won't work."[16]

American industry was finally emerging from the Depression. Traditional production lines like those to manufacture cars were again becoming profitable. Businesses were reluctant to switch over to war production without guarantees that the government would buy their output. After having experienced more than a decade of underutilized capacity and weak demand, manufacturers were reluctant to expand the specialized war-production lines the government wanted, fearing that there would be no buyers for these items once peace returned.

The steps the Roosevelt administration took to overcome that reluctance helped give birth to a military-industrial complex that outlived its wartime origins to become a potent economic and political force for the remainder of the twentieth century and into the twenty-first.

Washington created special tax breaks that let businesses write off the costs of expanding production lines at accelerated rates. It persuaded companies to bid on contracts for planes and tanks they had never produced before by guaranteeing repayment of all production costs plus an agreed level of profit—the so-called cost-plus contract that soon became standard practice for defense contractors. It eased antitrust rules to encourage cooperative arrangements that further reduced business risks. It provided direct government investment to build synthetic rubber plants that were then leased to the rubber companies to run on a cost-plus basis. Oil companies agreed to build new interstate pipelines, but only after the government guaranteed them against any losses.

To achieve the voluntary cooperation it wanted, the government structured a unique and enduring military-industrial marketplace, with private companies reaping guaranteed profits while the taxpaying public assumed some of the traditional market risks.

There were also compulsory elements to Roosevelt's economic mobilization arrangements. But they were made more palatable for business by the administration's policy of recruiting business executives like William Knudsen of General Motors, Charles Wilson of General Electric, Edward Stettinius of U.S. Steel, and Donald Nelson of Sears, Roebuck to serve in key mobilization agencies. The decisions made by these agencies affected the whole economy, not just war-production industries. They helped develop wage and price guidelines and consumer rationing policies and helped decide on the allocation of scarce supplies, like rubber and petroleum, usually after negotiations with the affected businesses.

Businesses often got a sympathetic hearing because top agency officials included thousands of "dollar-a-year men," top business executives who continued to draw their corporate salaries while collecting a symbolic payment of one dollar a year from the government agencies they worked for. Through these connections and for other reasons as well, the overwhelming majority of war contracts went to America's largest corporations.[17]

With these defense-contractor-friendly policies, Roosevelt was able to turn America into the Arsenal of Democracy that provided desperately needed Lend-Lease supplies to Britain and Russia and that equipped America's own troops for victory over Germany and Japan. But like so many of Roosevelt's successful improvisations, the military-industrial complex survived the special circumstances that justified its creation and began to have detrimental effects on postwar American military planning and spending.[18]

Cost-plus contracts tend to eliminate normal market pressures for cost efficiency and all but invite the huge overruns that now predictably drive up the program costs of virtually every plane, ship, submarine, and ground combat system the Pentagon buys. Such contracting practices have also created a group of militarily dependent contractors who cannot operate profitably under normal market conditions. As a result, the Pentagon sometimes ends up buying extra quantities of expensive and militarily unnecessary weapons systems, like nuclear attack submarines, mainly to keep defense contracting companies in business and their skilled designers and engineers on the payroll.

Roosevelt's approach to military-industrial mobilization also gave birth to new political alliances with long-lasting effects. The dollar-a-year system spawned new, and sometimes surprisingly warm, working and social relationships between idealistic New Deal reformers and wealthy business executives who now found themselves working side by side in the service of shared war-production goals. These two groups had often been on the opposite sides of bitter regulatory and distributional battles during the 1930s and, even when they weren't fighting, tended to live in separate sociological and ideological worlds. Wartime cooperation seemed to soften these attitudes and shift the postwar liberal Democratic agenda away from divisive issues of class toward a vision of labor-management cooperation based on expansive Keynesian economic policies.[19]

Leading Keynesian liberals, like Leon Keyserling, chairman of the Council of Economic Advisers in the Truman administration, came to view the rapid growth of cold war defense spending, and deficits, as a positive liberal tool for maintaining full employment and steady economic growth, a view that later came to be known as military Keynesianism.[20]

Increased military spending, whether justified or not, also promised electoral dividends for the Democratic Party during the early postwar years. Under Democratic presidents from Harry Truman through Lyndon Johnson, military buildups tended to center on equipping larger conventional forces, with many of the additional jobs going to traditional industrial regions like the Northeast and Midwest, which were Democratic Party electoral strongholds. Republican presidents, from Eisenhower onward, tended to direct more defense dollars toward newer high-technology weapons, which generated more jobs in the Sun Belt states. Until 1965, congressional liberals were generally more likely than conservatives to vote for military spending. After that conservatives, many of them no longer fiscal conservatives when it came to defense, provided most of the votes.[21]

But by then military contractors had begun perfecting the art of spreading jobs around to subcontractors in every electorally significant state and congressional district. The F-22 stealth fighter, an air-to-air combat plane whose diminished military value after the cold war ended no longer justified its ever-mounting costs, survived another two decades primarily because it generated subcontracting jobs in as many as forty-four states.[22]

The persistence of the military-industrial complex Roosevelt created in these years helps explain why America now spends so much building the wrong kinds of weapons for the wars we fight today, and why it gets so much less value than it should for virtually every procurement dollar it spends. It also explains why it seems politically impossible to cut big-ticket weapons spending even when international strategic conditions change, political majorities in Washington change, and more compelling claims on the federal dollar—like health care, climate change, and deficit reduction—seem to demand attention.

CHAPTER THREE

THE FRAMING OF THE PERMANENT EMERGENCY STATE

By the time Franklin Roosevelt died on April 12, 1945, eighty-two days into his fourth term, he had changed American constitutional democracy almost beyond recognition. The return of peace later that year barely interrupted the continuing transformation. FDR had built a big peacetime federal government to fight the Depression; Harry Truman built an even bigger one to shape the postwar world.

Roosevelt's New Deal had pushed presidential powers to their peacetime constitutional limits in the name of economic revival. Truman's policies pushed beyond those peacetime limits in the name of national security. V-J Day should have signaled a return to peacetime constitutional balance. Instead, it brought the extension and expansion of wartime presidential power into the postwar era.

Allied victory over Germany and Japan brought challenges that no peacetime American president had previously faced. History's most widely destructive war had transformed the international dimensions of American security. It had swept away the prewar world of rival industrial economies and multiple military powers, leaving only one intact and functioning industrial economy—America's—and only two military great powers—the United States and the Soviet Union.

America could not just pull back, as it had done after the First World War, and let the victorious European allies sort out Europe's future. That would have left an unequal match between Britain and Russia that could easily have ended with the United States denied the economic access to Europe that it had fought four years to regain. But American history provided no widely accepted model for continuing U.S. involvement in European affairs, let alone one consistent with America's traditions of constitutional democracy, distaste for entangling alliances, and aversion to peacetime standing armies.

Roosevelt had done little to prepare Truman, or America, for what lay ahead. The wartime emergency state Truman inherited was not of his own making. But because of the choices Truman then made as president, America was still in a state of warlike emergency when he left office nearly eight years later.

Breaking with American tradition, Truman flexed war-rooted presidential powers in the succeeding years of peace. He kept the unlimited state of national emergency Roosevelt had proclaimed in 1941 in full force until 1947. He kept most of its emergency provisions in effect throughout his term and bequeathed them to his successors. The emergency state never ended. Cold war presidents from both parties thought of themselves and acted as war presidents. And so have the four presidents who have held office since the cold war ended.

Harry Truman created something new in America, something we live with today, something that connects our wars in Iraq and Afghanistan with our trade and budget deficits, with the disproportionate growth of the financial sector over the past four decades, and with today's unsustainable foreign borrowing.

Truman's decisions in these years created the peacetime emergency state. Unlike the wartime emergency state, the peacetime variety has no logical termination, no moment when the emergency clearly ends and normal constitutional procedures come back into force. A new, security-based set of justifications for expanded presidential powers in peacetime was born.

Nowhere does the Constitution put the president in charge of America's foreign policy. Quite the contrary, it grants Congress the sole power to regulate foreign commerce, declare war, raise and support armies, maintain a navy, regulate these military forces, define and punish offenses against the law of nations, and make rules concerning captures on land or water. And it requires presidents to get the advice and consent of the Senate to all international treaties, ambassadorial appointments, and the choice of senior executive branch officials.

Truman's peacetime emergency state was a logical outgrowth of twentieth-century presidential history. America's global ambitions grew with its economic power, and so did presidential ambitions to assume a larger executive role at the expense of Congress and the Constitution, particularly in foreign policy and national security. Theodore Roosevelt, Woodrow Wilson, and Franklin Roosevelt had shown the way.

But Truman's creation of the peacetime emergency state was not the only possible sequel to that presidential history. The realities of postwar power and weaponry did not make Truman's course inevitable. A succession of specific foreign policy choices Truman made from the time he took office through the end of 1950 led America to the permanent emergency state. They foreclosed the possibility of a less universalized containment, a less militarized postwar America, and a government and society less inclined to impose loyalty tests and define past or present ideological nonconformity as a crime.

Truman's largely improvised responses to the unique international situation of the late 1940s created an enduring American political mindset that shaped the policies and constrained the choices of all his presidential successors. Truman could have made different choices with different consequences—consequences more in step with the traditions of American constitutional democracy. We owe it to ourselves to consider some of those alternatives. We would be living in a very different America today if Truman had made different decisions.

But we also should recognize that Truman wasn't making his decisions in an international vacuum. Events compelled him to address issues and regions that prewar American presidents had safely ignored. When Truman took office, the prewar world in which those presidents had made their foreign policy choices had been politically, economically, and physically destroyed by a half-decade of cataclysmic world war.

Across the Atlantic, America's most important European trading partners had been far more badly damaged than they had been after World War I. Britain, whose naval power had helped force open global markets and keep America's enemies at a distance, was gravely weakened. The British pound sterling, which had helped finance and lubricate world commerce, no longer had the strength to play that essential role.

Industrial Europe was devastated, unable to afford American imports or compete with American exports. The continent's premier economic and military power, Germany, was in ruins and about to be occupied and partitioned. To Germany's east, west, north, and south, countries crushed under the Nazi war machine were struggling to reclaim their lost sovereignty, solvency, and legitimacy.

The Soviet Union, having borne the Wehrmacht's destructive brunt almost alone after June 1941, pushed back after Stalingrad and over the next two years decisively broke through the cordon sanitaire of anti-Communist states that the West had erected around it after World War I. The longer Britain and the United States delayed opening the western front Roosevelt had first promised Stalin for 1942, the farther west Russia's army had advanced. By April 1945 Soviet power stretched into Central Europe, backed by what had become Europe's most powerful remaining army.

If Stalin meant to advance farther, America was the only military power that could conceivably stand in his way. Britain, France, and China were now great powers in name only. Europe's Asian colonies were in open revolt, its African colonies not far behind. Japan, prewar Asia's leading economic and military power, lay prostrate and pulverized.

America had not had to fight on its own soil after Pearl Harbor. It had suffered far fewer casualties in proportion to its population than the other major combatants. And it now possessed the world's only nuclear weapons. America was the master of the global ruins and the inevitable lead designer of the postwar international system. Britain looked to it for continued loans, Russia for reconstruction aid, France for protection against revived German militarism, and China for support against Mao's growing Communist insurgency.

Truman's challenge was to figure out what kind of international system best served American needs and how to go about building it. Roosevelt had bequeathed to him lofty postwar goals and expectations but few working mechanisms for fulfilling them.

At a minimum, Truman was determined to use America's victory and new commanding role in world affairs to prevent any repetition of the economic and military nightmares of the preceding sixteen years. No one wanted a return to the Depression economics that only wartime military spending had relieved. The value of American exports had increased more than sevenfold from 1932 to 1945. The postwar economic order would have to protect access to the transatlantic and transpacific markets that America would need to sustain domestic prosperity once war orders began to fall off. The postwar security system would have to be able to block the rise of a new Hitler or Axis alliance. Failure to design such a system after World War I had just drawn America into a costly Second World War.[1]

Returning to the internationally disengaged American foreign policy of the interwar era was thus not a realistic option. But that still left crucial questions about where and how American engagement should be directed and what were the most important lessons to draw from those prewar policy failures.

One set of questions concerned defining America's postwar security perimeter. Were America's most vital interests limited to Western Europe and Asia's Pacific Rim, the two regions that had drawn the United States into World War II? Should postwar foreign policy pivot around America's interest in maintaining security and stability in those two regions and keeping them open to American trade and investment?

Would such a restricted application of American power in a politically and economically shattered postwar world invite revolutionary chaos or

Soviet adventurism elsewhere, which could then imperil these two core regions? Or to the contrary, would unnecessarily universalizing U.S.-Soviet competition turn America into a militarized global police force permanently engaged in a succession of wars that diverted resources from domestic needs, expanded presidential powers, and undermined American democracy?

Truman was to combine elements of both these approaches—the Western Europe–centered Marshall Plan and the universalized Truman Doctrine and NSC-68—the passive containment that said there would be no American military challenge to Soviet power in Eastern Europe and the active containment that approved sending American military forces across the partition line in Korea and up to the Chinese border.

A second set of questions concerned closely related issues of collective security. Had the weaknesses of interwar collective security arrangements—from America's failure to join and strengthen the League of Nations to British and French appeasement at Munich—emboldened the dictators and tempted them to launch a war they might not otherwise have fought? If so, did the remedy lie in the design Roosevelt had left behind for a new, stronger international organization, built on the foundations of the wartime Big Three alliance (plus a nominally great power China) and stiffened by a Security Council designed to let America, Britain, and Russia jointly police the world?

Or was the right lesson from the interwar years to see Stalin as a potential new Hitler, to call a halt to Roosevelt's policy of trading concessions to Soviet force majeure in Red Army–occupied Eastern Europe for Stalin's cooperation on the United Nations, and to move instead to build a new, purely Western system of collective security backed by America's military power and nuclear monopoly?

Truman's almost instant decision to start pushing back against Stalin doomed the Security Council to paralysis from the start, and with it Roosevelt's "four policemen" vision of preventive collective security. In its place, Truman ended up promoting a very different form of collective security and deterrence, through American-dominated anti-Soviet military alliances like NATO. Truman's approach was a sharp break with America's long tradition of shunning peacetime entangling alliances. It also broke with the Wilson and Roosevelt versions of collective security through a single world organization, reverting instead to the older European model of rival alliances that Wilson believed had contributed to the outbreak of World War I.[2]

A third major set of questions concerned the looming issue of postwar decolonization. Here the interwar years offered no useful guidance. In the early days of World War II, Japan had grabbed the resource-rich Southeast Asian colonies of the Netherlands, France, and Britain. With Japan nearing defeat, these European powers meant to forcibly reclaim their old colonies, and they expected American support. Europeanists in the State Department and the Office of Strategic Services argued that supporting the European colonial powers in these efforts would strengthen anti-Communist forces in Western Europe. State's Asian specialists instead advocated honoring America's own anticolonial heritage, open-door trading interests, and the language of the 1941 Atlantic Charter by siding with thc lcftist nationalist movements fighting for independence.[3]

Truman mostly equivocated, refusing to support Asian Communists like Ho Chi Minh but also resisting European pleas for direct American military help.

During the first months of his term, Truman played for time, deferring foreign policy decisions when he thought he could, feeling his way often erratically and inconsistently when he felt he had to act. Still operating in Roosevelt's enormous shadow, he was not eager to challenge his predecessor's vision of the postwar world. But Truman shared neither Roosevelt's deeply rooted disdain for European colonialism nor his strongly held belief that Washington could and should engage in pragmatic cooperation with Stalin.

By 1945 Roosevelt had spent years at the center of the international stage. Truman had not. Yet Truman was an intelligent, well-read man, a shrewd politician, and a World War I combat veteran. He was an unelected president in 1945, though as well qualified for the job as many of his elected predecessors. But his prepresidential career had done little to prepare him for the kind of complex foreign policy calculations that confronted him from the day he took office.

Truman's main interests and goals had been domestic. But he felt that his Fair Deal domestic agenda would be lost if he did not show the American people that he could stand up to Stalin.

Disappointments were growing with the results of Yalta, but at the time these focused on Stalin's supposed bad faith in implementing the agreements, not on the loophole-ridden commitments that Roosevelt had reluctantly accepted. Roosevelt, hailed, and now mourned, by the public as architect of wartime victory, was seen as having more than held his own with Stalin and Churchill. Truman, lacking Roosevelt's wartime record and political charisma, could afford nothing less. What Roosevelt had done with artful diplomacy, Truman would now try to do with blunt words and reminders of American military and economic power.

As it turned out, many of Truman's most important domestic goals, including national health insurance, were sacrificed to pay for the military buildup required by his new global containment policies. His desire to demonstrate that he would not let Stalin put anything past him led, step-by-step, to the construction of the postwar emergency state and its dominant national security paradigm.[4]

Truman first became a national figure in 1941, when Senate Democrats chose him to chair a special committee probing waste and profiteering in federal military contracts. The experience taught Truman much about the domestic world of military contracting and the business executives and generals who ran it, but brought him no significant exposure to wider international issues. His early thoughts about the war in Europe were uninformed and simplistic. Days after Germany invaded Russia in June 1941, he advised: "If we see that Germany is winning we ought to help Russia and if Russia is winning we ought to help Germany, and that way let them kill as many as possible, although I don't want to see Hitler victorious under any circumstances. Neither of them thinks anything of their pledged word."[5]

Truman's eighty-two days as vice president did little to further his education in world affairs or postwar planning, since Roosevelt kept him uninformed and uninvolved. FDR was gravely ill by the time he was inaugurated for the fourth time in January 1945, as those close to him clearly saw. But he couldn't or wouldn't acknowledge the likelihood that he would not live out his full term and made no serious effort to plan for an orderly, or even an informed, transition.

Urgent foreign policy choices pressed in on Truman from the start. Should he authorize American forces (and their British allies) to race the Red Army to Berlin as Churchill urged, or remain within the Yalta-designated Anglo-American occupation zones as Eisenhower recommended? How much slack should he cut Stalin over Poland to preserve the Big Three wartime alliance and fulfill Roosevelt's goal of a postwar world policed by the victorious Allied military powers working together through the new United Nations Security Council? At Yalta, American military leaders had believed that Russian entry into the war against Japan might save as many as 2 million American casualties. In return, Stalin had been promised an occupation zone in northern Korea, restored Russian influence in Manchuria, and the return of islands Russia lost to Japan in their 1905 war. Then, in mid-July 1945, America successfully tested its new atomic bomb. Should Truman wait for Stalin to honor his Yalta commitment to join the Pacific war within three months of the German surrender? Or should America press on to defeat Japan on its own, at the likely cost of higher American casualties but denying Moscow any further Asian gains, including a possible say in postwar occupation policies?[6]

Looming behind these questions was the all-important issue of what kind of global power relationship Washington would seek between the war's two main victors and surviving powers—the United States and the Soviet Union (and, in a much weaker second tier, Great Britain).

Truman took Eisenhower's advice on Berlin. He challenged Stalin from the start over Poland, even before the San Francisco founding conference of the United Nations convened on April 25, 1945. He played for time on the endgame with Japan, hoping a successful test of the atomic bomb would make his choice easier.

Truman's advisers could only guess about how Roosevelt might have intended to resolve the important remaining differences between American and Soviet objectives in Europe. The publicly announced Yalta decisions left obvious gaps, and Roosevelt left no clear record of his own intentions.

Roosevelt had left behind some postwar blueprints—Yalta on the basic political and territorial settlement, Bretton Woods on economic institutions, and preliminary discussions on United Nations mechanisms for collective security and decolonization—but they were ambiguous and incomplete. When the Big Three bargained over the fate of postwar Europe and Asia at Yalta in January–February 1945, Germany had not yet been defeated and Stalin had not yet entered the war against Japan. Truman would have to fill in the final details of a European and Asian settlement, define America's postwar relations with the Soviet Union, and most important of all, explain an unfamiliarly internationalist foreign policy to Congress and the American people.

With no strong foreign policy views of his own and no personal electoral mandate, Truman valued continuity. He kept most of FDR's foreign policy officials. But neither he nor they had any way of knowing exactly how Roosevelt had intended to handle many of the issues now facing them. FDR, a master of ambiguity and postponement, may not have known himself.

Roosevelt had usually made his own foreign policy decisions, on the spot, with minimal consultation with his secretary of state or other cabinet officials. He had relied on his political instincts, his personal interactions with Churchill and Stalin, and the reports he received from a shifting cast of informal emissaries, like Harry Hopkins and Joseph Davies, whom he sent on sensitive international missions.

Stalin's immediate intentions were clearer, and he was still around to pursue them. Stalin wanted to push Russia's security frontiers westward at least to where they stood on the eve of the German invasion in June

1941, allowing him to keep what he had taken during the period of the Stalin-Hitler pact, or, more ambitiously, to restore some of the old czarist frontiers of 1914. Roosevelt had been willing to accommodate Soviet security concerns but was also committed to restoring the independence of Poland and other Central European states. Roosevelt never accepted Stalin's power play on Poland and kept coming back to the issue, but he also kept avoiding a showdown over Poland that could have imperiled the successful launching of the United Nations at San Francisco. The nature and composition of Poland's postwar government were still contested issues when Roosevelt died.

What Truman and most other Americans did not fully comprehend that April were the underlying realities of Yalta, now made painfully clear through the subsequent opening of the American, British, and Soviet diplomatic archives. By the time the Yalta conference convened, Soviet armies fully controlled Poland; no Western military force was in any position to challenge that, and Stalin was unyielding in his insistence on a compliant, handpicked Polish government. That was a bitter political pill for Britain, which had entered the war over Poland, and for the United States, with 6 million Polish American voters, almost all anti-Communist.[7]

Neither Roosevelt nor Churchill resigned himself to Stalin's plans. But both recognized there was little they could do beyond fighting for deliberately vague and ambiguous language keeping open the theoretical possibility of free elections and a more representative Polish government. Instead, they decided to trade off Stalin's fait accompli on Poland for diplomatic concessions on other issues—Roosevelt for Stalin's agreement to join the United Nations on American terms and to enter the war against Japan; Churchill for the free hand in Greece and Italy that Stalin had earlier conceded to Britain.[8]

Both hoped that Stalin, having gotten his way, would allow them to preserve at least the appearance of a face-saving diplomatic compromise. Stalin wasn't much interested in playing this game. His power play on Poland was mainly about Poland, claiming the spoils of victory and restoring a historic Russian sphere of influence and security zone. That embarrassed and infuriated Roosevelt and Churchill and complicated the prospects for postwar Big Three cooperation. But while Roosevelt lived, it never brought a rupture.[9]

Stalin wanted to rebuild Russia into an impregnable socialist industrial power, and he counted on using massive German reparations shipments, enforced favorable trade relations with Central Europe, and continued access to American Lend-Lease aid to achieve this goal. Roosevelt had had no problems with Russian rebuilding or continuing Lend-Lease. But he had insisted that all of Europe be open to American trade and investment on equal terms.

Roosevelt saw a functional Big Three within a workable United Nations as the indispensable element of a successful postwar settlement, an arena where difficult issues like Poland could be smoothed out in the months and years to come.

Some of the State, War and Navy Department officials to whom Truman turned for foreign policy advice had been outside Roosevelt's innermost policy-making circle. Most of them were aware of the general direction of Roosevelt's thinking, but some, like George F. Kennan, then number two in the Moscow embassy, disagreed with it. Others, like Averell Harriman, the U.S. ambassador in Moscow, and Admiral William Leahy, the White House chief of staff and principal liaison to the military high command, had supported Roosevelt's conciliatory diplomacy at Yalta but had grown increasingly frustrated with Stalin's hard-line behavior on Poland, POWs, and other issues in the weeks that followed.

The desire of Harriman and others to see a correspondingly tougher tone from Washington might not have mattered much had FDR remained alive. It mattered much more after Truman suddenly became president.

Truman, the man who had declared Russian promises worthless in 1941, saw Stalin's power plays in Poland as a clear violation of Yalta and an unmistakable portent of future Communist aggression. He failed to grasp the essential connection between his preferred 1941 policy of letting Russia grind out a costly victory over Germany in the east and the unpalatable 1945 result of triumphant Russian armies occupying Eastern Europe.

From his very first days in office, Truman began fighting to force Stalin to live up to supposed Yalta commitments on Poland to which Stalin had never actually committed himself. This was the issue Truman used to dress down Soviet foreign minister Molotov on the eve of the San Francisco founding conference of the United Nations in April 1945. And it was one of the main reasons Truman abruptly cut off Lend-Lease shipments to Russia the following month, just days after Germany's surrender.[10]

Stalin felt he had a strong hand. The Red Army was in possession of Poland and eastern Germany. A new and untested American president had just assumed office. Stalin wasn't looking for a rupture with Washington. He wanted American Lend-Lease aid for reconstruction and expected, as during the war, that Washington might sometimes play a useful diplomatic balancing role between Russia and Britain.

But Stalin also sensed an opportunity to fill in the gaps left at Yalta to maximum Russian advantage. Stalin pressed for his agenda on Poland and Germany. Truman advisers like former senator James Byrnes, whom Truman named secretary of state that July, Assistant Secretary Dean Acheson, and Ambassador Harriman in Moscow (counseled by his deputy, Kennan) urged the new American president to push back, firmly and promptly, which he did.

Other advisers, like Navy Secretary James Forrestal and his longtime associate Paul Nitze, offered a more alarming reading of the situation. They suspected, based more on analogies to Hitler and Munich than on hard evidence, that Stalin was not just consolidating a buffer zone in Central Europe but preparing to challenge America for global supremacy in a third world war that could start at almost any time. They told Truman he needed to decide right away whether he would follow the appeasing path of Chamberlain at Munich, or the preparedness path of Roosevelt after Lend-Lease.

Were Forrestal and Nitze right about Stalin's ultimate ambitions? Probably not, judging from subsequent Russian international behavior and documentary evidence from this period. What we can never know is how Stalin might have behaved if Truman had taken a less confrontational line. All we know for sure is what did happen. And what did happen is that America assumed the worst about Russian intentions and acted accordingly, and by doing so probably made some of its own dire prophecies self-fulfilling.

For Truman, with tough-minded ideas about how to conduct foreign policy and no nuanced understanding of Central European history and politics, the policy advice from both camps of advisers seemed to converge. He quickly became convinced that the only hope for peace was to keep America on a war-preparedness footing and start drawing firm lines right away. Stalin might or might not be the next Hitler, but Truman was determined not to be the next Chamberlain.

For Roosevelt in 1940, preparedness had meant accelerating prewar economic and military mobilization. For Truman in 1945, it meant slowing the pace of postwar demobilization.

At the war's end America, with a total population of just under 140 million, had roughly 12 million men under arms—about 40 percent of the male population between the ages of 18 and 45. Many of those not in uniform were working in war industries.

Maintaining America's wartime level of full mobilization indefinitely was neither politically possible nor economically realistic. American draftees in World War II had been called up for the duration of the conflict plus six months, and most were discharged by early 1946. The total in all services fell to 3 million that year and by 1947 it was 1.6 million. But 1.6 million was still five times the size of America's peacetime military in 1938.

Millions of Soviet soldiers were also discharged in the immediate postwar years but at a less rapid rate. By 1947 Soviet military forces outnumbered America's by more than two to one. The United States could not hope to match Soviet military manpower in Europe. Moscow enjoyed the advantages of a slightly higher population, significantly higher draft calls, and a totalitarian regime that felt free to mobilize military and civilian manpower with minimal political constraint.

But Washington alone had atomic bombs. From the first successful bomb test near Alamogordo, New Mexico, in July 1945, America's nuclear monopoly became a crucial factor in Truman's strategic calculations. Without it, he probably would have actively courted Russian military cooperation against Japan, as Roosevelt had at Yalta, and would have placed more value on holding together the Big Three alliance to jointly police the postwar world.

Developing the atomic bomb had seemed a military necessity. Germany, with the help of some of the world's leading nuclear physicists, was racing to build its own fission weapon. Had the Nazis won this first nuclear weapons race, it might have changed the course of the war. As it turned out, they never came close.

By the time of the Alamogordo test, Germany had surrendered, and a defeated Japan was seeking surrender on terms virtually identical to those Washington later accepted after having dropped atomic bombs on Hiroshima and Nagasaki.[11]

At Yalta in January, Roosevelt had pressed Stalin to agree to enter the war against Japan within three months of Germany's surrender in the hope that by tying down Japanese forces in Manchuria, Russia could help minimize what his commanders feared would be a heavy American death toll in the final amphibious assault on Japan's home islands. By August the collapse of Japanese air and sea defenses and America's bomb had partially eased those fears and completely reversed America's policy goals. Now Truman saw the bomb as a way to hasten Japan's surrender, minimize Russia's contribution to victory in the Pacific, and thereby deny Moscow any claim to share in the occupation of postwar Japan.

Truman's decision to use the bomb was meant to deliver a long-term message to Moscow as well as a short-term message to Tokyo. That decision, and Truman's idea of using America's atomic monopoly as a diplomatic trump card against Russia, helped set the tone of the forty-year cold war nuclear arms race.[12]

There was no way Truman could have stopped Russia from developing its own atomic bomb. That effort was already under way before he assumed office. But as Secretary of War Henry Stimson and others tried to warn Truman, swaggering atomic diplomacy poorly served longer-term American interests.

As early as June 1945 Truman called on Congress to enact Universal Military Training, which would have required a year of military training for every physically able male at age eighteen. That would have harked back toward constitutional tradition by providing for a relatively small peacetime standing army that could be rapidly expanded to a fully mobilized, at least partially trained force.

Congress repeatedly refused to go along. It renewed selective service in 1946 but let it lapse a year later, when the War Department estimated it could fill its personnel needs without conscription. In June 1948, after a further fall in force strength to just under 1.5 million and with cold war tensions rapidly rising, Congress temporarily reinstated peacetime selective service for two years. Then came Korea, then Vietnam, then the all-volunteer army. Through it all, U.S. force strength remained above 2 million from 1951 through 1991.[13]

Federal military spending followed a roughly similar U-shaped trajectory. After an even sharper immediate postwar decline—a fall of roughly 90 percent from 1945 to 1948—it rebounded even more robustly than force strength. By the time Truman left office, the Korean War and the spending increases called for under NSC-68 brought military spending back to more than half the 1945 level.[14]

Military preparedness was one element of Truman's postwar foreign policy; drawing diplomatic and ideological lines was another. Even before Germany surrendered on May 7, 1945, Truman started treating Moscow more like a potential enemy than a wartime ally. In April, to prove he was no Chamberlain, Truman lectured Soviet foreign minister Molotov over Poland and Yalta. In May, just five days after Germany's surrender, he sharply cut back Lend-Lease shipments to Russia.

Truman seemed not to have fully appreciated that some issues had been deferred at Yalta and that many of Stalin's spring 1945 positions on Germany and Poland were self-interested attempts to fill in the blanks, not clear violations of solemn agreements. If he had understood this better, he might have chosen to oppose Stalin on selected issues, like German reparations and four-power access to Berlin, but not across the board.

Such a more nuanced approach could have included continuing American Lend-Lease shipments to Russia as part of an effort to see whether FDR's attempt to shape the United Nations as a more realistic collective security organization than the failed League of Nations could be made workable.

That is the course Roosevelt likely would have attempted had he lived. Truman never seriously considered it. Instead, he walked away from Roosevelt's vision of collective security and led the United States into newly expansive visions of national security and the permanent emergency state.

When the Big Three leaders met at Potsdam that July to follow up on Yalta and finalize a European peace settlement, Truman resisted compromise on most disputed issues, having learned in the course of the summit that American scientists had successfully tested an atomic bomb. Stalin wasn't prepared to yield ground either, so the conference fell far short of its goals, leading, over time, to a divided Europe and Germany and deferring a European peace settlement for more than four decades.

Potsdam effectively ended any realistic possibility of the kind of postwar Big Three cooperation for which Roosevelt had long hoped. What had changed so decisively in those four months was not the international situation but the identity of the American president. Truman may have wanted continuity, but within four months of taking office, his own decisions had helped create a postwar world far different from any Roosevelt had anticipated. Well before Churchill's "Iron Curtain" speech (1946), the Truman Doctrine and the Marshall Plan (1947), the Communist coup in Czechoslovakia and the Berlin blockade (1948), the Soviet atomic bomb and Mao's victory in China (1949), and the North Korean invasion of the South (1950), the cold war era had effectively begun.[15]

It began because by the summer of 1945 Truman had decided that American and Soviet objectives in Europe and Asia could not be safely reconciled without jeopardizing American security and prosperity. He quickly moved on to a set of policy positions that logically flowed from that decision—that consolidating western Germany was preferable to neutralizing and disarming all of Germany, that Roosevelt's vision for the United Nations was undesirable and unworkable, and that the United States needed to retain its monopoly of nuclear weapons for as long as possible. Stalin responded in kind.

Stalin might have obstructed the workings of the UN Security Council anyway, making Roosevelt's four policemen plan unworkable. He might have divided Germany to assure himself a totally free hand in the east (though that seems unlikely since most of the German industrial machinery and output he wanted to get his hands on was in the west—in the British-occupied Ruhr). He almost certainly would not have loosened his political and military grip on Soviet-occupied Eastern Europe. And he would have continued racing to develop his own atomic bomb as a strategic equalizer at the earliest possible date.

Stalin's choices were an essential element in starting, shaping, and continuing the cold war. But this book is primarily about America's choices, and whether different American decisions could have produced better outcomes for American democracy and American interests at home and abroad. Just as Truman's policies did not operate in a vacuum, Stalin's didn't either. If the postwar breakdown of American-Soviet cooperation was inevitable, the all-encompassing, globalized nature of the cold war as we came to know it for the next four decades was not inevitable.

And neither was the emergency state.

Harry Truman melded a sequence of serious but essentially separate U.S.-Soviet disputes over postwar political settlements, spheres of influence, and security perimeters in Europe and Asia into a narrative evoking a single, unified global conflict analogous to war, an undeclared war that was now cold but that could, and later sometimes did, turn hot. From the beginning, Truman's cold war narrative was used to justify wartime presidential powers and wartime constraints on the exercise of constitutional democracy.

Having portrayed these multiple confrontations as part of a single, global conflict, Truman went on to define the stakes of that conflict in universalized terms that blinded the American people to distinctions between wars of ideological choice and wars of national necessity. He deliberately hyped limited and localized threats to win legislative authorization and financing for his cold war policies. To carry out those policies, he reorganized the military, international affairs, and intelligence branches of the U.S. government along the lines of a permanent wartime national security state.

Truman thereby locked in the policies and politics of the emergency state for decades to come.

Although Truman had served ten years in the U.S. Senate, he developed politically unrealistic and constitutionally dubious notions of almost unlimited presidential power. And although (or perhaps because) his political background was largely domestic and insular, he developed similarly unrealistic notions of almost unlimited American global power.

Truman correctly perceived that the United States would emerge from the Second World War as the world's most powerful nation by far, especially after the successful atomic bomb test of July 1945. What he did not understand, as FDR had always understood, was that not even the world's most powerful nation had the limitless material and military resources needed to unilaterally enforce American preferences in every corner of the postwar world.

Roosevelt sought to husband American power by setting priorities. And he sought to multiply that power by keeping the wartime Big Three alliance together in the collective security harness of the United Nations. Truman hurried to free American power from that Big Three harness. And he indiscriminately took on new security commitments, often without the means to see them through successfully.

Truman never appreciated that a foreign policy that failed to match means to ends could not be sustained militarily, economically, or politically over the long haul—or at least not within the framework of traditional American constitutional democracy. The Truman Doctrine of limitless, universal containment, which misguided American foreign policy until it led to the disaster of Vietnam, would never have persisted so long had it not been so well insulated from public scrutiny and debate by the psychology and institutions of the peacetime emergency state created during these same years.

The realistic alternative to Truman's overextended foreign policies was not the get-along-with-Russia-at-any-price utopianism of former vice president Henry Wallace, whom Truman fired as commerce secretary in 1946. Wallace's overly benign view of Stalin provided a perfect foil for Truman's equally naïve threat inflation.

The true alternative was the more targeted version of the containment approach favored at different times and in different ways by hardheaded realists like the State Department Soviet specialist George Kennan and the widely read newspaper columnist Walter Lippmann.

Kennan had never believed that Roosevelt's pursuit of a cooperative relationship with Stalin could work. He felt that Russian history and Bolshevik rule had created a system that was inherently expansionist and always had to define a mortally threatening external enemy to justify the internal repression it needed to survive. Once Germany and Japan were defeated, Kennan was certain, Moscow would cast the United States as its new enemy no matter what Washington did.[16]

But Kennan understood, as Truman did not, that American military and economic power was finite and that an unlimited worldwide contest with Moscow would exhaust the United States and undermine its liberal democracy. Instead, he proposed containment—a strategy that focused American power on deflecting Soviet pressures against core areas truly vital to American national security and relying on tactical balance-of-power alliances elsewhere.[17]

That was Kennan's own view of containment as he developed it in the late 1940s and especially after he left the State Department in 1949. But his most widely read writings on the subject—the Long Telegram he sent from the U.S. embassy in Moscow in 1946, and the "Mr. X" article he wrote for *Foreign Affairs* magazine the following year—could also be used to justify a more universal and militarized view of containment, and they regularly were by Truman administration diplomats like Secretary of State Dean Acheson. That was also the way Lippmann read the "Mr. X" article, which inspired him to write a lengthy series of critiques of the foreign policy mistakes to which universal containment could easily lead. Within a few years, however, it became clear that Lippmann and Kennan, both balance-of-power realists, were not so very far apart.[18]

The version of containment Truman finally propounded in his Truman Doctrine speech of March 12, 1947, was thoroughly universalist and provided its listeners with very little guidance about which areas mattered most to America's national security and what kind of limits might or might not be placed on future American military and economic commitments.

The immediate problem facing Truman in March 1947 was how to respond to Britain's announcement the previous month that it could no longer afford to provide economic support for the anti-Communist governments of Greece and Turkey. Britain had long treated these two strategically located countries as vital to its commerce and imperial defense. Greece guarded British naval access to the Suez Canal and thus to India. Turkey sat astride the straits separating Soviet Black Sea naval ports from the Mediterranean.

Churchill had fiercely defended Britain's interests in both countries before and after Yalta, even securing Stalin's assent to stand aside and let British troops reinstall an unpopular Greek royalist government at gunpoint in 1944. But by early 1947 Britain's war-weakened economy could no longer sustain a Churchillian policy in the eastern Mediterranean. With Britain's allies in Athens and Ankara both under heavy external pressure—civil war was raging between Yugoslav-backed Greek Communists and British-backed royalists, and Moscow was pressuring Turkey over control of the straits—London asked Washington to take over.

Greece and Turkey had not previously been areas of great American foreign policy concern, but that was in large part because they had been under British protection. In the world of 1947, defending the borders of Mediterranean Europe from further Communist advances fit even the most minimal definition of containment. Greece and Turkey were defensible pressure points in a region of vital American interests where the United States held most of the strategic advantages. American support for both seemed reasonable even to prudent foreign policy realists like Lippmann. What they objected to mightily (and as it turned out, presciently) was how Truman went about portraying and selling his new policy to Congress and the American people.[19]

Truman knew he would face considerable public skepticism. After an initial six-month honeymoon, trust in his presidential leadership, as measured by Gallup, had rapidly eroded. In November 1946 the Republicans had won majority control of the House and the Senate for the first time since 1932. By early 1947 Truman was rebounding in the polls. But a war-weary American public remained reluctant to take on new security commitments. Midwestern Republicans and southern Democrats in particular questioned the need for extending American protection to areas that had never before been considered vital American interests. Others wondered whether the United Nations might be a more appropriate, less internationally divisive vehicle for supporting Greece and Turkey.[20]

Senator Arthur Vandenberg of Michigan, the new Republican chairman of the Senate Foreign Relations Committee, allegedly advised Truman that the only way he would get approval for the aid to Greece and Turkey was to make a speech and "scare hell out of the American people." Whether it was Vandenberg's idea or not, that is exactly what Truman did. In a speech to a joint session of Congress on March 12, 1947, he proclaimed his new doctrine.[21]

Parts of that speech could have provided the rationale for a realist policy of limited containment, specific to Greece and Turkey. Truman offered an overheated but recognizable description of the Greek civil war and its stakes:

> *The very existence of the Greek State is today threatened by the terrorist activities of several thousand armed men, led by Communists, who defy the Government's authority at a number of points, particularly along the northern boundaries.*

He pointed to Greece's strategic geopolitical location:

> *It is necessary only to glance at a map to realize that the survival and integrity of the Greek nation are of grave importance in a much wider situation. If Greece should fall under the control of an armed minority, the effect upon its neighbor, Turkey, would be immediate and serious. Confusion and disorder might well spread throughout the entire Middle East. . . . Should we fail to aid Greece and Turkey in this fateful hour, the effect will be far reaching to the West as well as to the East.*

But the far-reaching policy Truman then proposed rooted itself not in geopolitics, pressure points, or specific national interests but in sweeping Wilsonian assertions about American security requiring a world made safe for American democracy by the extension of Washington's protective power:

> *We shall not realize our objectives . . . unless we are willing to help free peoples maintain their free institutions and their national integrity against aggressive movements that seek to impose upon them totalitarian regimes. . . . Totalitarian regimes imposed on free peoples, by direct or indirect aggression, undermine the foundations of international peace and hence the security of the United States.*

Truman then summoned the nation to an unlimited global struggle against a monolithic ideological enemy:

> *Every nation must choose between alternative ways of life. . . .*
>
> *One . . . is based upon the will of the majority, and is distin-*

guished by free institutions, representative government, free elections, guarantees of individual liberty, freedom of speech and religion, and freedom from political oppression.

The second . . . is based upon the will of a minority forcibly imposed upon the majority. It relies upon terror and oppression, a controlled press and radio, fixed elections, and the suppression of personal freedoms.

I believe that it must be the policy of the United States to support free peoples who are resisting attempted subjugation by armed minorities or by outside pressures.

That support, Truman explained, should be mainly economic. But Washington was stepping in to replace Britain in Greece, and Britain had coupled its financial aid with direct injections of military force.

Finally, Truman spelled out the scary alternative to the policy he proposed:

If we falter in our leadership, we may endanger the peace of the world—and we shall surely endanger the welfare of our own Nation.[22]

Truman had constructed a simple, global narrative frame that would be used to justify, or even require, American support for any armed resistance to leftist, anticolonialist, or nationalist forces anywhere. It did not matter if the rightist forces that America was backing had democratic legitimacy. It did not matter if the leftist forces America was fighting had local roots. It did not matter if the area being contested was vitally important to American security. It did not matter how much the struggle cost in dollars, lives, or America's global reputation.

Truman's exaggerated rhetoric launched the overreaching doctrine of global containment, from which Democratic successors like John Kennedy and Lyndon Johnson found it almost impossible to step back, even when faced with disproportionate losses in a marginal cause like Vietnam. Echoes of Truman ring through later speeches of John F. Kennedy on the cold war, Lyndon Johnson on Vietnam, and George W. Bush on Iraq.

This kind of overheated rhetoric, with its globalizing of every local struggle and failure to define priorities and limits, has become the standard way the American emergency state evades necessary democratic debate about national security issues, leading to unwise policy choices followed by crippling public backlashes when the rhetorical exaggerations wear off and the overlooked reality forces itself painfully into view.

The Truman Doctrine became the point of no return for universal containment. Truman's verbal hyperbole in support of more narrowly calibrated actions was the opposite of Roosevelt's stealthy path to intervention in 1941. But it was just as deliberately deceptive and had even more damaging long-term consequences.

Truman's ideological markers radically expanded Washington's sense of the international security frontiers it had to defend, supplanting more traditional strategic doctrines based on more limited definitions of America's specific geographic and commercial interests.

New perimeters required new institutions. Truman oversaw the institutionalization of the peacetime emergency state through the 1947 National Security Act. This formally created the emergency state's main agencies—the Department of Defense, the Joint Chiefs of Staff, the Central Intelligence Agency, and the National Security Council.

The idea, at first, was to incorporate some of the hard lessons America had learned in the course of World War II. Intelligence analysis needed to be centralized and streamlined to prevent another Pearl Harbor. The War and Navy departments needed to be merged to minimize interservice rivalries for resources and wasteful duplication.

Foreign policy and military policy needed to be as closely coordinated in peacetime as they were during war, since America's expanded international responsibilities added a military dimension to foreign policy decision making. That eroded the State Department's autonomy, as traditional concepts of foreign policy gave way to the newer concept of national security policy.[23]

With more than one cabinet department involved in national security policy, ultimate decision making gravitated toward the White House, requiring the growth of a newly specialized White House national security staff.

Truman favored permanent institutions, and after long bureaucratic turf battles, repeated congressional wrestling matches between interested committee chairmen, and a series of statutory amendments extending over several years, these began to take shape.

The Central Intelligence Agency, originally created as a central clearinghouse for intelligence analysis, relied on one vaguely worded clause of the National Security Act to engage in covert operations, including meddling in foreign elections and overthrowing foreign governments. The much-larger National Security Agency has no statutory basis in the act but was created by Truman through a classified executive order. Subject to minimal congressional oversight, it was used by Richard Nixon and George W. Bush to spy on Americans, in apparent violation of the Fourth Amendment.[24]

As the wartime emergency state evolved into the permanent emergency state, these institutions became its natural bulwarks and sometimes the independent power centers Roosevelt had been so eager to avoid. National security is inherently harder to democratically debate than foreign policy, especially when much of the information essential for informed debate is kept classified. Senior White House national security officials, unlike senior State Department foreign policy officials, do not require Senate confirmation and can be sheltered from direct congressional oversight through claims of "executive privilege." The CIA, and other branches of the sprawling intelligence community, operate in secret and largely beyond the reach and rule of American law.

These agencies are also essential ingredients for constitutionally unaccountable presidential foreign policy making, lying ready at hand for any postwar president who has cared to use them. Not surprisingly, every postwar president has succumbed to the almost irresistible temptation they offer. Congress rarely complains. The public only objects when presidential wars go sour or secret intelligence abuses turn into public scandals.

The Truman Doctrine had preached universal containment but initially practiced it mainly in Europe. Two weeks after Congress approved aid for Greece and Turkey, Secretary of State George Marshall proposed the European economic recovery plan that came to bear his name.

Wartime devastation of European industry had left the United States the principal remaining producer of industrial and consumer goods. The Bretton Woods financial system had established the dollar as the postwar world's main reserve currency, enabling the United States to extend worldwide credit without squeezing its domestic economy.

But Europe still lacked the financial resources to buy American imports and lift its living standards high enough to ensure political and social stability. That threatened both Washington's European containment strategy and America's own postwar prosperity.

Marshall's plan helped solve both problems by providing American taxpayer dollars to help rebuild Europe's economies, which would necessarily require increased purchases of American goods. More than $13 billion in Marshall Plan aid was transferred to Europe between 1948 and 1951, the equivalent of more than $100 billion in 2011 dollars.

The unprecedented American commitment to Europe mattered even more than the money. Right-wing parties in France and Italy were tainted by wartime collaboration with Hitler and Mussolini. Communist parties allied with Moscow were buoyed by their experiences as armed resistance fighters. Postwar governments, based on broad, politically incoherent antifascist coalitions, struggled for stability and legitimacy. In these years, American commitment and credibility were crucial to the self-confidence of the center-left and center-right parties that would soon emerge as the political mainstream of capitalist Western Europe.

America rose to the occasion. But American policy makers clung to their romantic memories of this period long after the occasion passed.

• • •

In the Truman era, the Marshall Plan worked as intended, delivering increased prosperity and political stability on both sides of the Atlantic. Western Europe's economies and living standards rebounded. Large Communist parties in France and Italy were politically marginalized.

American factory owners finally put aside their fears of a postwar depression and ratcheted up investment and output to meet rapidly expanding international and domestic demand. Rising investment brought rising productivity. American companies shared some of the gains with their workers, forging a new, more cooperative social contract that held for almost twenty years. It was a tripartite contract—this was the era of big business, big labor, and big government. As long as America's position as the primary producer of high-value industrial goods remained unchallenged by cheap labor competitors abroad, Washington could pursue stimulative Keynesian demand-management policies at home without serious risk of stagflation. The demand Washington stimulated created productive American jobs.

The Marshall Plan didn't just expand European markets for U.S.-made consumer goods. American companies also sold Europe the capital goods with which it rebuilt its own consumer industries. U.S. companies also built or bought factories in Western Europe, attracted by lower European labor costs and the special tax incentives Washington put in place to encourage such capital exports.

These were the golden decades of Western Europe's "economic miracle," with rapidly rising output, wages, and social benefits and unemployment rates so low that European economies recruited "guest workers" from Turkey, North Africa, and poorer European regions like southern Italy to keep their factories running.

And while Europe's labor costs were lower than America's in the early postwar years, European economic recovery and full employment soon narrowed the gap. By the late 1960s European recovery, built in part on American investments and capital goods exports, put new competitive pressures on American companies and workers. But it was a competition between high-wage first-world economies, quite different from the intense pressures that America would begin to feel once its international economic policies facilitated the wholesale transfer of manufacturing and service industries to low-wage third-world countries starting in the 1970s.

Containment's European side received a further boost when, in 1949, Truman led the United States into its first ever peacetime military alliance—the North Atlantic Treaty Organization. American generals were not happy about this permanent extension of U.S. military commitments. Realists like Lippmann would also have preferred a more geographically limited alliance—with American and Soviet troops withdrawn from a disarmed, neutral Germany—in the hope of avoiding a permanent East-West division of the European continent.

But by 1949 that hope already seemed unrealistic. The year before, Moscow and its local Czechoslovak Communist allies had toppled the last genuine popular front government in Soviet-occupied Central Europe and replaced it with a puppet satellite regime. And in response to American-sponsored moves to economically and politically unify western Germany, Stalin had imposed a land blockade on West Berlin.

To Truman and much of the national security leadership empowered by the new National Security Act, the cold war was becoming ever more menacing and more global. The Soviet Union tested its first atomic bomb in August 1949. The same year Mao Zedong's Communists entered Beijing, forcing Nationalist leader Chiang Kai-shek (Jiang Jieshi), one of Roosevelt's original four policemen, to flee ignominiously to Taiwan.

In April 1950 the NSC proposed a new global strategy (in a document designated NSC-68) that became, in effect, the (un)constitutional charter of the emerging security state. It declared, as a matter of national policy, that the ends of thwarting the Communist threat justified any American means, peaceful or violent, overt or covert, and thus, by implication, constitutional or unconstitutional:

> *The assault on free institutions is world-wide now, and in the context of the present polarization of power a defeat of free institutions anywhere is a defeat everywhere. . . . Thus unwillingly our free society finds itself mortally challenged by the Soviet system. No other value system is so wholly irreconcilable with ours, so implacable in its purpose to destroy ours, so capable of turning to its own uses the most dangerous and divisive trends in our own society, no other so skillfully and powerfully evokes the elements of irrationality in human nature everywhere, and no other has the support of a great and growing center of military power.*[25]

Later that year Truman usurped congressional war-making authority to wage the Korean War as a presidential "police action," authorized by the United Nations but not by the U.S. Congress. As Dean Acheson later explained it, "the thing to do was to get on and do what had to be done as quickly and effectively as you could, and if you stopped to analyze what you were doing . . . [a]ll you did was to weaken and confuse your will and not get anywhere."[26]

The Korean War was initially popular. In fact, one reason the Truman administration bypassed a congressional declaration of war was to avoid fanning popular expectations of a World War III fought till the unconditional surrender of Moscow and Beijing. But hopes for a decisive military victory rose when Truman chose to ignore clear warnings from Beijing and let his top war commander, General Douglas MacArthur, drive American troops deep into North Korea, close to the Chinese border. Instead of merely containing further Communist advances, a policy under attack from Republicans as cowardly and a betrayal of those already under Communist rule, Truman was now following the harder line of NSC-68 and seeking to roll back Communism in North Korea with American military force.

Those hopes of a military rollback of Communism were soon dashed when Beijing poured hundreds of thousands of its own troops across the border, inflicting heavy casualties on American forces, pushing the front line back toward South Korea, and turning the conflict into a lengthy, deadly stalemate. Americans quickly became disenchanted with what had become an unwinnable land war on the Asian continent in an area of marginal American interests. The only real American interest became Washington's "credibility," which was only on the line because the Truman administration had unwisely put it there.[27]

But the Truman administration was now stuck with an unpopular containment policy, an unwinnable Asian war, and no politically tenable exit strategy. Republican critics of Truman's foreign policies and foreign policy makers found a powerful champion in a freshman Republican senator, Joseph McCarthy of Wisconsin. McCarthy had no respect for the emergency state's institutions. But his smear campaigns against foreign service officers and private citizens he accused of being "soft on Communism" chilled all realistic prospect of democratic debate about America's conduct of the cold war and the damage that conduct was causing to our constitutional tradition.

Joseph McCarthy grabbed national attention in February 1950 by waving around a list he said contained the names of more than two hundred Communist Party members working for the State Department. But the phenomenon now known as McCarthyism started much earlier, in the anti–New Deal backlash that began shortly after Roosevelt's landslide 1936 reelection.

The House Un-American Activities Committee, established before the war and chaired by Texas Democrat Martin Dies, Jr., held hearings to investigate alleged ties between New Dealers and Communists. HUAC subpoenaed witnesses and threatened them with contempt citations unless they provided the names of personal and political associates.

After the Republicans won the 1946 congressional elections, the new GOP majority used the same techniques to investigate Communist influence in Hollywood. In 1948 the State Department became a target when HUAC investigated espionage allegations against Alger Hiss, a former senior State official who had been part of Roosevelt's delegation at Yalta. Congressman Richard Nixon's pursuit of Hiss made him a national figure, helping him win election to the Senate two years later, and two years after that to the vice presidency as Eisenhower's running mate.

The State Department as a whole came under steady McCarthyite fire after the 1949 Communist victory in China's civil war. Republicans charged that Truman, and Secretary of State Dean Acheson, had "lost" China by coddling supposed Communists in the State Department—hence McCarthy's list. Such accusations took on an added political sting when Chinese Communist "volunteers" poured across the North Korean border to hurl American troops southward in late 1950.

As foreign policy analysis, these charges missed the point. It was Chiang Kai-shek, not Dean Acheson or State Department Asia specialists, who had lost China to the Communists.

But as a domestic political strategy, they hit the mark, sending the Truman administration into near panic. Loyalty boards scoured government personnel files, with minimal regard for due process, looking for any signs of ideological unreliability. As a result, some of the State Department's top Asia specialists lost their jobs, and nuanced analysis of Chinese developments fell out of favor.

The McCarthyite impulse to blame every setback abroad on the secret infiltration of the U.S. government had many roots, including the existence of some real Communists in government ranks. The abrupt shift of American foreign policy from Roosevelt's wartime alliance with Stalin to Truman's exhortation less than two years later that every nation must choose between two diametrically opposed ways of life made such arguments more plausible. The rise of the permanent emergency state seemed to provide further validation of the need for wartime vigilance at the expense of constitutional liberties. McCarthyism also found congenial soil in traditional midwestern Republican reaction to the newly internationalist and interventionist postwar policies of both political parties and resentment of the northeastern elites who espoused those policies.

McCarthyism stifled debate about American policies and purposes at a time when such debate was badly needed. But unlike most other features of the emergency state, it was not a new assertion of presidential power but a reassertion of congressional power. Congress was acting within its constitutional rights when it challenged State Department witnesses and demanded access to documents and personnel files the

Truman administration preferred to keep secret. Though the Constitution's procedures were honored, its purposes were poorly served. The constitutional system cannot function when policy debate becomes treason and taboo.

Checks and balances are designed to restrain excesses of the legislative branch as well as the executive. Presidents swear to "preserve, protect and defend the Constitution of the United States," including the Bill of Rights. Truman, and his attorney general, J. Howard McGrath, did not mount a very vigorous defense. Instead they attempted to preempt Congress with an increasingly proscriptive loyalty program designed to weed out federal employees based on their opinions, their associations, or the political prejudices of FBI reviewers, and to close such "loopholes" as Fifth Amendment protections.[28]

The Truman administration's response to McCarthyism is an early emergency state example of the Democratic Party's characteristic defensiveness in the face of conservative efforts to equate liberalism with Communism. Decades of such defensiveness have shaped the party's policies and discourse and still constrain the thinking of its foreign policy specialists today.

CHAPTER FOUR

RUNAWAY TRAIN

When Warren Harding orchestrated a Republican comeback after World War I, his winning slogan in 1920 had been a "return to normalcy"—in other words, an end to the wartime emergency state and Wilsonian foreign policy adventurism, and a return to the traditional business-friendly small-government Republicanism of William McKinley and William Howard Taft.

That would not have been a plausible platform for Dwight Eisenhower, who won the White House for the Republicans in 1952. He had been Roosevelt's supreme allied commander in Europe during the war and the first military commander of Truman's new NATO alliance. Ike symbolized America's new outward-looking security policies, and the bureaucratic changes at home and entangling alliances abroad that went with them. He stood for more efficient and economical business-military management, not for fundamentally different policies.

Eisenhower was no traditional Republican. He joined the party in 1952, the same year he became its presidential candidate. Both parties had wooed him, recognizing that his almost-unchallengeable military credibility and prestige would be a formidable electoral asset atop either ticket. He entered the Republican race only after leaders of the party's eastern internationalist wing convinced him that he alone could deny the nomination to Senator Robert Taft of Ohio. Taft, the internationalists feared, would turn the party away from the European issues that mattered most to them. Eisenhower, by contrast, had been closely involved with European issues since the war years.

Robert Taft was a traditional Republican. He called for restoring a constitutionally restrained executive and a limited international agenda. On issues of presidential power and the Constitution, Taft's views coincided with those of his father—the former president and chief justice William Howard Taft. But on foreign policy questions, he was more often allied with the rival wing of the old Republican Party—old Bull Moosers and western and midwestern peace progressives like Senators Borah, Johnson, Nye, and Wheeler. Senator Taft saw the emergency state created by Franklin Roosevelt and Harry Truman as a dangerous threat to the constitutional balance that he (and his father) believed to be an essential element of American democracy. Taft had opposed the peacetime draft before World War II, challenged Roosevelt's wartime internment of Japanese Americans as an affront to constitutional liberties, and refused to vote for the NATO treaty in 1949, criticizing it as too provocative, too expensive, and too entangling.[1]

Republican internationalists like Governor Thomas E. Dewey of New York, Senator Henry Cabot Lodge, Jr., of Massachusetts, and John Foster Dulles, a prominent Wall Street lawyer and diplomat, dismissed Taft's approach as too cautious and old-fashioned to protect American interests in the postwar world. They accepted the emergency state but believed it needed to be made more cost-effective and business-friendly. As Republicans, they were uneasy with Truman's globalized foreign policy commitments and the expanding military budgets these required. As hard-line anti-Communists, they saw containment as a morally compromised acceptance of an unacceptable status quo. As fiscal conservatives, they saw it as ruinously expensive. The cold war, they argued, could be won more cheaply, decisively, and righteously by brandishing American nuclear weapons.

Their candidate, Eisenhower, had worked comfortably with Roosevelt and Truman. But he was shaped by a very different professional background. Both the patrician Roosevelt and the middle-class Truman were career politicians and convinced believers in big, interventionist government. Eisenhower was a career military officer in an era when most officers believed they had a professional duty to steer clear of party politics and voting.

After graduating from West Point in 1915, Eisenhower spent the next twenty-five years in the economically sheltered environment of the peacetime army. With a secure job, a government paycheck, and most of his material needs provided for by the War Department, Ike managed to preserve a strong attachment to traditional American values and small government.

Such paradoxes were typical of Eisenhower. He was America's first bureaucratic war hero—the seemingly uncomplicated Middle American who managed the complex multinational military enterprise that defeated Hitler. He was a convinced anti-Communist but could cooperate pragmatically with Red Army marshals in the closing phases of World War II. He believed America needed to limit its international security commitments but let his secretary of state, John Foster Dulles, ring the world with anti-Communist military alliances. After extricating America from the Korean War, Eisenhower was determined to avoid another American land war in Asia, but he knowingly stepped further into the Indochina quagmire.

John Foster Dulles not only represented bipartisan continuity in American foreign policy, he embodied it. He had been an official delegate to the UN's founding conference and chief negotiator of the U.S.-Japan peace treaty under Truman, as well as chief foreign policy adviser to Republican presidential candidates Dewey and Eisenhower. His foreign policy beliefs seemed to incorporate the secular messianism of NSC-68 and the moralistic Presbyterianism of his minister father and missionary grandfather.

Similar establishment influences shaped the secretary of state's younger brother, Allen, whom Eisenhower chose to run the CIA. Allen Dulles began his intelligence career in the wartime OSS, spent five postwar years as head of the Council on Foreign Relations, and then became deputy director of central intelligence late in the Truman administration, before Eisenhower promoted him to run the agency. Allen

Dulles remained director of central intelligence into the Kennedy administration, losing that position only in the aftermath of the Bay of Pigs disaster.

Eisenhower's two terms became so associated with iconic cold war images—Soviet tanks in Budapest, Sputnik, Moscow's downing of an American U-2 spy plane—that the idea that the cold war might not have continued on an uninterrupted trajectory from Truman to Eisenhower now seems almost unthinkable. Maybe so—by the start of 1953, the United States and the Soviet Union were such bitter, irreconcilable, mutually fearful rivals that it is hard to imagine Eisenhower changing course no matter what happened in Moscow.

But something very important did happen in Moscow just forty-four days after Eisenhower took office, and a more imaginative American response might well have changed subsequent history. On March 5, 1953, Stalin died.

Stalin had personally molded the Soviet system, and Soviet foreign policy, since the late 1920s. It was essentially a one-man show. Truman had taken a tough line with Moscow because he personally distrusted Stalin. American policy makers saw or imagined Stalin's hand behind every confrontation of the 1940s and behind North Korea's invasion of South Korea in 1950. In the eyes of many Americans, Stalin was following in Hitler's footsteps.

But now Stalin was dead. Russia was still Communist, nuclear-armed, and Godless. Its troops still occupied Eastern Europe. But Stalin's unprepared successors, distracted by their own Kremlin rivalries and hoping to build support by improving living standards at home and smoothing some of the dangerous raw edges of Red Army–backed Communist rule in Eastern and Central Europe, seemed to some Western leaders (Churchill, for example) to be probing for some kind of cold war détente. Eisenhower's own ambassador in Moscow, Charles Bohlen, later regretted that he had not pressed the new administration much harder to take greater advantage of this potential opportunity for better relations. He observed that "there might have been opportunities for an adjustment of some of the outstanding questions, particularly regarding Germany," and he referred to the new prime minister, Georgy Malenkov, as more moderate, "with a more Western-oriented mind than other Soviet leaders."[2]

On public occasions, the new Soviet leaders started speaking in milder, more flexible tones, emphasizing their desire for peaceful relations, especially with the United States. Behind the scenes, they urged Communist Chinese and North Korean leaders to negotiate more constructively with Washington on a Korean War armistice.

As pressure grew for some kind of American response, the Eisenhower administration was torn. Some, like John Foster Dulles, urged making the most of what looked like a period of Soviet weakness and disarray to press for advantage on long-standing issues like consolidating a Western European military and economic bloc (including western Germany). Others, including Eisenhower himself, wanted to give Moscow a chance to demonstrate that behind its less belligerent rhetoric lay genuine good intentions.

The initial result was Eisenhower's "Chance for Peace" speech, delivered before the American Society of Newspaper Editors on April 16, 1953. While putting all the blame for existing cold war tensions on Moscow, the speech went on to suggest that if the new Soviet leaders now chose to follow a more accommodating path, including free elections across Eastern Europe and an end to all ongoing and future Communist insurgencies in Asia, America would respond with its own positive gestures.

It was classic Eisenhower. He sincerely wanted an end to the cold war. He also insisted on achieving 100 percent of the American cold war agenda. And he seemed to honestly believe that if Soviet leaders were men of goodwill, they would have no problem accepting America's agenda.[3]

This first chance for peace, if that was what it was, proved fleeting. Two days after Eisenhower's hopeful-sounding speech, Dulles told the same gathering of newspaper editors that it would be unwise to put any faith in the new Soviet tone and that only building up America's strength could bring real peace. Eisenhower and Dulles did not usually disagree.

They just spoke in very different tones. And Russian listeners, like Americans, did not always know what to make of those tonal differences.

The main interest of the Kremlin's new leaders was consolidating and protecting their own power. They worried that Stalin had overextended Soviet power. Easing international tensions might win them some breathing room. But if Eisenhower wasn't interested, there were other methods of consolidation, the brutal ones they had learned from Stalin over the years. Before the year was out, the new Soviet leadership arrested and killed one of their own, Stalin's former secret police chief, Lavrenty Beria, and used tens of thousands of Soviet troops to crush an anti-Communist workers' revolt in East Germany.

Yet the underlying fluidities and ambiguities of the post-Stalin era soon reasserted themselves. Nikita Khrushchev, who emerged as the new Soviet leader over the course of Eisenhower's first term, introduced market-inspired economic reforms and a limited cultural "thaw," an early inspiration for the more far-reaching reforms undertaken by Mikhail Gorbachev thirty years later. A more agile American diplomatic response in this period might have significantly reduced cold war tensions or reaped the kind of mellowing of the Soviet system that Kennan's containment theory had predicted and sought.

We will never know. Neither political party in Washington had positioned itself, or prepared public opinion, for that kind of agility.

The cold war had begun over a set of clearly identifiable European issues—pushing back against Stalin's bullying over Poland and Germany, mellowing Soviet power by containing its further expansion, and defending and revitalizing non-Communist Europe.

But by the early 1950s, it been transformed into a worldwide ideological struggle—a "defense of free peoples everywhere" (even if some of those free peoples regrettably had to be defended through the agency of repressive, right-wing pro-American dictatorships). American blood had been shed fighting Communists in Korea. And by 1952 both parties had built their foreign policy platforms around the assumption of a long-term, all-encompassing global cold war.

While the Kremlin's new leaders spoke in less belligerent tones, they were still Communists. Most had been closely associated with Stalin's policies and crimes. As foreign minister, V. M. Molotov had personified Stalin's belligerence over postwar German and Eastern European issues. As head of the security police, Lavrenty Beria had helped design and carry out Stalin's domestic reign of terror.

Reaching out to this group to test its intentions would have been politically problematic for Dwight Eisenhower. It held even less appeal for Dulles. Had they explored the possibility of detente, leading Democrats would surely have accused them of naïveté, weakness, isolationism, and worse.

Pursuing the cold war as if nothing important had changed was easier and carried far less political risk. The new national security ideology carried the day. But that may have forfeited an early chance to actually make America more secure. Had Eisenhower and Dulles been more willing to acknowledge that all Communists were not necessarily alike—that Stalin's heirs might pursue different policies than Stalin and that Chinese Communists might pursue different policies than Soviet Communists—it might have been possible to contain the nuclear arms race at a much earlier phase, to get a twenty-year head start on reducing East-West military confrontations in Germany and Berlin and on normalizing American relations with Communist China.

Apart from continuing Truman's already-established policy of providing behind-the-scenes American support for Tito's Yugoslavia, Eisenhower and Dulles showed little interest in acknowledging or exploiting the competitive nationalisms that were already eating away at the supposed world Communist monolith, especially in Asia. In China, Mao Zedong was beginning to question Russian models and motives. In Vietnam, Ho Chi Minh sought not just to win Vietnamese independence from France but also to preserve it from future encroachments by the traditional national foe—China. In North Korea, Kim Il Sung looked for ways to maximize his own freedom of action by playing off his two neighboring Communist patrons and protectors.

Recognizing, and exploiting, these divisions would have meant acknowledging that the planet could not be neatly divided into a Washington-led free world and a Moscow-led Communist bloc. It would have meant recognizing that nationalism could be a powerful force of its own, particularly in the underdeveloped countries and former colonies of the emerging third world.

There was no place for neutralist, non-Communist nationalism in the bipolar worldview of Eisenhower and Dulles, as their clumsy and generally chilly relations with Nasser, Nehru, and Sukarno—and the American-backed overthrow of Mohammad Mossadegh in Iran—amply demonstrated. In Dulles's view neutralism was "an immoral and short-sighted conception."[4]

Though Eisenhower and Dulles agreed on virtually all of these policies, their public statements reflected a division of labor between the affable, well-liked president and the stern, scolding secretary of state. Eisenhower, in keeping with his wartime reputation for apolitical pragmatism, tried to appear above the fray. He fulfilled his campaign promise to end the war in Korea and expressed his desire to cap his successful military career by further service as a soldier of peace. He appealed to American hopes for freedom from the threat of Soviet nuclear attack. But his signature peace proposals were designed to win over optimistic American voters, not suspicious Kremlin politicians.

Consider his "Atoms for Peace" plan of December 1953, inviting all nuclear weapons states to turn over some of their stockpiles to a UN International Atomic Energy Agency for use in building nuclear power plants around the world.

It sounded like swords into plowshares, but it wasn't. Just two months earlier Eisenhower had signed off on the new administration's National Security Policy, which declared the absolute necessity for Washington to develop a "massive atomic capability" to deter Soviet aggression.[5]

Eisenhower meant to increase, not reduce, America's nuclear stockpile, and he knew well enough that the Soviets, still behind but believed to be rapidly catching up, were not about to give up their nuclear equalizer or freeze current stockpiles to their own clear disadvantage. His real aim was to promote a new imagery of the peaceful atom that the United States was prepared to share with developing countries, and to head off fears that Moscow might score propaganda points by making such an offer on its own. The ultimate result was the contradictory dual mission of today's IAEA, promoting the proliferation of nuclear power plants while trying to slow the proliferation of nuclear-enrichment technologies for weapons purposes.[6]

Then there was Eisenhower's "Open Skies" proposal of 1955, which would have allowed the United States and Russia to conduct open aerial surveillance of each other's military installations. Arms control agreements require some form of verification. But Eisenhower's main goal was not arms control but surveillance, of the kind that would soon be provided, without Soviet consent, by high-flying U-2 spy planes and later by space satellites. Since the days of Stalin, Soviet leaders had been obsessively secretive, even when they had nothing to hide but the embarrassingly low living standards of their people. In the mutually suspicious atmosphere of 1955, they were clearly not about to allow American military overflights if they could help it.

Neither Atoms for Peace nor Open Skies could be a plausible first step toward a less hostile relationship between the United States and the Soviet Union. Perhaps a period of détente and trust building might have eventually softened Soviet opposition—that kind of patient, coordinated American diplomacy did lead to arms control breakthroughs in the later eras of Nixon-Kissinger and Bush-Baker. But no such attempt was made under Eisenhower. Instead, Dulles pursued a policy of unremitting rhetorical confrontation punctuated with thinly veiled nuclear threats against the Soviets and the Chinese. And he did so with Eisenhower's full, and usually fully informed, backing.[7]

Eisenhower continued traveling the high road by holding the first summit meetings between an American president and top Soviet leaders since Potsdam. But unlike Roosevelt's earlier meetings with Stalin, there was no common wartime purpose to lubricate the inevitable frictions, just day-to-day cold war hostilities.

Whatever goodwill came out of the July 1955 Geneva summit was obliterated by the Soviet tanks that crushed Hungary the following year. Similarly, the hopeful "Spirit of Camp David" that followed Eisenhower's September 1959 meeting with Khrushchev was snuffed out by the Soviet downing of an American U-2 spy plane in May 1960. Khrushchev also exploited that incident to deliberately wreck the third scheduled Eisenhower-Khrushchev summit in Paris later that month.

At the very end of his term, Eisenhower famously alerted the country to the growing danger of an emerging "military-industrial complex." Never before in peacetime had America maintained a large standing army and a permanent arms industry. This unprecedented combination, he warned, had grave implications for the structure of American government and society that could endanger "our liberties or democratic processes." But Eisenhower did far less than he might have during his eight years in office to prune back that military-industrial complex and defend America's liberties and democratic processes from its growing threat.

The military-industrial complex was more entrenched, and its threat to American liberties more pervasive, on the day he gave that warning speech—January 17, 1961—than it had been when Eisenhower first took office eight years earlier.

On assuming office, Eisenhower set out to contain the explosive growth in military spending that had marked Truman's second term. America's military spending increased fivefold between 1948 and 1953, rising from 3.5 percent of GDP to 14.2 percent, with most of that rise coming after 1950 under the impact of the Korean War and the global containment strategy of NSC-68.[8]

Eisenhower and his fiscally conservative advisers believed that continued military spending at those high levels was economically unwise, politically un-Republican, and militarily unnecessary. Experience had taught Eisenhower to distrust the inflated budgetary estimates submitted by the military services. He knew firsthand the world of service rivalries and Pentagon empire building.[9]

The challenge was to square budgetary restraint with the Eisenhower-Dulles rhetoric of standing stronger against Communism than their Democratic predecessors. The answer was Eisenhower's "New Look" approach to national security budgeting. By relying more on America's nuclear weapons advantage and less on conventional forces, the New Look promised to contain spending as well as roll back Soviet power.

This would require a change in America's overall containment strategy, and a corresponding change in the kind of military pressure backing up American diplomacy. Instead of Truman's universal containment, which committed America to react anywhere the Communists tried to advance, Eisenhower would choose to selectively engage the enemy at times and places of America's own choosing. And instead of trying to match the Soviet Union and its Warsaw Pact allies in the number of ground forces—an expensive and perhaps impossible challenge—the United States and NATO would rely on America's advantage in nuclear weapons.

As Dulles put it in 1954:

> *If an enemy could pick his time and place and method of warfare—and if our policy was to remain the traditional one of meeting aggression by direct and local opposition—then we needed to be ready to fight in the Arctic and in the Tropics; in Asia, the Near East, and in Europe; by sea, by land, and by air: with old weapons and with new weapons. . . .*
>
> *The basic decision was to depend primarily on a great capacity to retaliate, instantly, by means and at places of our own choosing. Now the Department of Defense and the Joint Chiefs of Staff can shape our military establishment to fit what is our policy, instead of having to try to be ready to meet the enemy's many choices. That permits a selection of military means instead of a multiplication of means. As*

a result, it is now possible to get, and share, more basic security at less cost.[10]

Nuclear weapons could play that kind of role, however, only if Western allies and Eastern foes alike believed that Washington would actually use them. To that end, Dulles advertised his willingness to go to the brink of nuclear war. In a 1956 interview in *Life* magazine, he cited three occasions in the preceding three years in which he claimed that the administration had averted war by threatening massive nuclear bombardment—preventing the Korean armistice talks from breakdown in 1953; preserving non-Communist governments in South Vietnam, Laos, and Cambodia after the French defeat at Dien Bien Phu in 1954; and deterring a Chinese Communist invasion of the tiny Chinese Nationalist–held islands of Quemoy and Matsu in the winter of 1954–55.[11]

Perhaps war could also have been averted and American diplomatic goals achieved without Dulles's nuclear brinkmanship. By threatening American nuclear attack, Eisenhower and Dulles certainly got Communist China's attention and helped convince Beijing that it too needed nuclear weapons. And since Moscow—still presumed by Washington to be Beijing's master and protector—already had nuclear weapons, Dulles's nuclear brinkmanship also helped convince the American public that the cold war had turned into an existential war for survival that the slightest diplomatic miscalculation in Asia could turn not only hot but nuclear.

In Europe, the Eisenhower administration showed much greater restraint. When anti-Soviet revolts in East Germany, Poland, and Hungary put to the test the Republican promise to replace a morally compromised long-term containment strategy with swift and satisfying rollback, the Eisenhower administration wisely chose not to risk nuclear war to redeem its extravagant Wilsonian rhetoric. Under the Republicans as under the Democrats, the cold war had settled in for a long haul.

Another way Eisenhower and Dulles tried to get more military punch out of lower military spending was by stringing a set of new regional military alliances like SEATO and CENTO around Soviet and Chinese borders. But unlike their militarily credible namesake, NATO, these turned out to be largely paper pacts. Their main effect was perverse—to extend explicit or implicit American commitments to far-flung, and expensive-to-defend, corners of the world where America had no important economic or security stake. In later years, America's supposed SEATO commitment became a major justification for military escalation in Vietnam. Dulles had opened a back door to the universal containment (and land war in Asia) that Eisenhower had wanted to slam shut.

The New Look stretched America's national security dollars. But it didn't make Americans feel any more secure.

In purely budgetary terms, the New Look was at least a partial success. After inheriting a 1953 military budget of $484 billion (constant 2011 dollars), Eisenhower left his successor a 1961 budget of only $390 billion (constant 2011 dollars). Much of that savings came from the end of the Korean War, which allowed the Pentagon to reduce the size of America's armed forces from more than 3.5 million in 1953 to less than 2.5 million in 1961. Meanwhile, thanks to economic growth, military spending as a share of gross domestic product fell over Eisenhower's two terms from 14.2 percent to 9.4 percent.[12]

New Look budgetary restraints heightened the appeal of covert CIA operations like those that overthrew elected governments in Iran (1953) and Guatemala (1954). These seemed to offer a low-cost way of achieving spectacular foreign policy results. No nuclear weapons had to be brandished. No formal American responsibility had to be acknowledged. All that was needed was a secret executive branch agency ignoring constitutional checks and balances and international law.

The CIA, nominally designed as a presidential clearinghouse for intelligence information, now moved decisively into the new arena of covert operations, drawing authority from vague language in the 1947 National Security Act that authorized it "to perform such other functions and duties related to intelligence affecting the national security as the National

Security Council may from time to time direct." This provided presidents with an important new tool of secret foreign policy making, shielded from public scrutiny and congressional oversight.[13]

Allen Dulles was already known as an enthusiastic supporter of these kinds of covert operations when Eisenhower chose him to lead the CIA—far more so than his predecessor, Walter Bedell Smith. And Dulles enjoyed something of an inside track for getting covert operations approved since Eisenhower had delegated so much of the management of his administration's foreign policy to Allen Dulles's brother, the secretary of state. In 1956 Eisenhower headed off a proposal from the Second Hoover Commission to provide some congressional oversight of foreign intelligence.[14]

Create a capacity in the American government, and it will be used. Create a secret, presidentially controlled capacity, and it will be used to short-circuit congressional scrutiny and public debate. Truman used the CIA's early covert operations to secretly aid anti-Communist parties in the 1948 Italian elections. That seemed almost quaint after Eisenhower and Dulles, who used the agency to violently overthrow governments, whether they were Communist or not.

The first known target was Iran's democratically elected prime minister, the secular nationalist Mohammad Mossadegh. Mossadegh's nationalism was directed mainly against Britain, which had meddled in Iranian politics for decades and whose Anglo-Iranian Oil Company (now known as BP) collected most of the revenue from Iranian oil fields. When Mossadegh nationalized Anglo-Iranian, Eisenhower saw a chance both to elbow aside the Iranian nationalists and to grab a share of those revenues for American oil companies.

In an operation led by Kermit Roosevelt, TR's grandson, the CIA collaborated with British intelligence to overthrow Mossadegh. The shah of Iran, whose father Britain and Russia had forced to abdicate as a German sympathizer in 1941, was restored to power. Anglo-Iranian had to yield some of its previous monopoly to American oil companies. Secular nationalism never recovered, and Iranian opposition leadership later passed to the Shiite clergy and its leader, Ayatollah Khomeini.

Eisenhower and Allen Dulles next moved against the elected left-wing nationalist government of Guatemala. The land reform programs sponsored by President Jacobo Árbenz challenged the power of Guatemala's largest landlord, American-owned United Fruit. As in Iran, the coup was a quick success, the sequel a long disaster. The thirty years of civil war that followed killed a quarter million Guatemalans.

The final Eisenhower-Dulles CIA covert operation was the invasion of Cuba by CIA-trained exiles landing at the Bay of Pigs, planned in the Eisenhower years but not launched until the first months of the Kennedy administration. After the CIA's cover was blown, Kennedy then called off planned CIA air strikes that were meant to destroy Cuba's air force. Going ahead without CIA cover would have constituted open U.S. aggression, and Kennedy wasn't prepared to go that far. Fidel Castro survived to dominate Cuba for another half century.

More constitutionally scrupulous foreign policy ventures might have fared just as disastrously as the three CIA covert operations described above. But at least they would have been acknowledged and debated before and after the fact. The American people would have understood what was being done in their name, and the otherwise inexplicable anti-Americanism these policies provoked in other countries might have been better comprehended.

Given the sometimes less-than-brilliant outcomes, alternative policies might have been considered. As it was, Americans grew accustomed to living in a dangerous bubble of innocence and ignorance. American voters often knew less about their country's actual foreign policy than people living in the countries it played out in.

If the New Look was an attempt to rein in military budgets and save American democracy from becoming a garrison state, it ended up giving birth to what David Wise and Thomas Ross called the Invisible Government.[15]

• • •

It was under Eisenhower that Americans began to accept the new emergency state system of government as a bipartisan fixture of national life, an inseparable part of America's destined passage from interwar isolationism to postwar global leadership.

For all of Eisenhower's basic decency and firm belief in American constitutional principles, he never blinked at covertly ordering the illicit overthrow of leftist or neutralist third-world governments. His eight years in office helped institutionalize the emergency state through covert intelligence actions and a global web of entangling alliances. The alternative of democratically debated, constitutionally conducted American global leadership was never seriously considered.

It scarcely could have been, given the chilling political climate created by government loyalty oaths and blacklists, Senator Joe McCarthy's demagogic "investigations," and J. Edgar Hoover's expanding blackmail files.

All of these were carryovers from the Truman administration. But Eisenhower, for all his distrust of big government, did nothing to rein in aggressive congressional witch hunts or restrain the unconstitutional snooping of J. Edgar Hoover's FBI. To the contrary: Attorney General Herbert Brownell granted the FBI significantly expanded authority to bug rooms, including bedrooms, with hidden microphones to collect intelligence information.[16]

Two years after Eisenhower's landslide reelection in 1956, the Democrats came back strongly in the 1958 midterm congressional elections. The Soviet Union's successful launch of the first man-made space satellite in October 1957 had dented American pride and Eisenhower's image as a strong leader. If Moscow could launch a satellite into Earth orbit, it could likely launch intercontinental ballistic missiles as well. (In fact, it had already tested one two months earlier.) Eisenhower, the hero of Normandy and World War II, was now painted by Democrats as a man dangerously behind the times, overtaken by new and threatening technologies and too fiscally cautious for national security.

A new Senate subcommittee headed by Henry Jackson proposed administrative reforms in national security management. Jackson's committee charged, wrongly as it turned out, that Eisenhower had allowed the Soviets to open a dangerous "missile gap" over a lagging United States. John F. Kennedy made this charge a central feature of his 1960 presidential campaign. Eisenhower knew from U-2 reconnaissance photos that the charge was false, but in order to maintain the secrecy of those flights, he never offered a vigorous rebuttal.

Eisenhower had hoped his legacy would be more affordable military budgets and an easing of cold war tensions through successful summitry. Instead, it turned out to be the embarrassing Russian capture of a U-2 spy plane pilot, a wrecked summit, a phony missile gap, and the Bay of Pigs fiasco. By clinging to outdated cold war assumptions about monolithic Communism, dangerous neutralism, and America's global credibility being everywhere on the line, Eisenhower defeated his own ambition of limiting universal containment and restraining the military-industrial complex.

The foreign policy paradigm that fed all that military-industrial spending—universal containment—was one that Eisenhower had run against but once in office could never bring himself to fully renounce.

CHAPTER FIVE

BELATED REALISM

John F. Kennedy brought new energy and imagery to the emergency state. He had promised voters he would pursue universal containment with new vigor, and he proceeded to do so, financed by the deficit-spending, money-multiplying magic of Keynesian economics. Kennedy expanded the ambitions of American globalism, promoted new doctrines of third-world counterinsurgency and flexible response, went to the brink of nuclear war over Soviet missiles in Cuba, and deepened America's ill-fated military commitment to South Vietnam. He also struggled to reimpose presidential authority over CIA operations and to reassert civilian control over the Joint Chiefs, and he negotiated the cold war's first nuclear arms control agreement.

Kennedy's term began with his closest supporters vowing to reinvigorate the cold war after what they portrayed as the doddering late Eisenhower era. It abruptly ended, less than three years later, with many of those same supporters voicing fears that Lyndon Johnson would move the country back to unreconstructed cold war policies after the hopeful, peace-seeking late Kennedy years.

It was a complicated, contradictory time, almost as elusive of clear definition today as it was fifty years ago. The legend of Camelot—that one brief shining moment that stood apart from all that came before and all that came after—was skillfully woven by the Kennedy family and the legion of sympathetic and sentimental journalists and biographers it attracted.

One version of the Camelot story portrays Kennedy, angered by the CIA's incompetence and lack of candor in the Bay of Pigs fiasco and then shocked at the Joint Chiefs' reflexive nuclear saber rattling in the Cuban missile crisis, moving to free himself from the national security bureaucracy and chart out a new and less dangerous American foreign policy in the last year of his presidency.[1]

Did Kennedy's American University speech of June 1963—calling for a more humane understanding of the Russian people and more focused efforts to contain the nuclear arms race—signal this new direction? Had Kennedy lived, would he have refused to Americanize the war in Vietnam as Lyndon Johnson went on to do? JFK's assassination, never explained to the satisfaction of the American public, further complicates the mystery.[2]

It may be emotionally satisfying to fill in the blank spaces of Kennedy's unfinished presidency in wishful ways that seek to preserve the shining legend of Camelot and distance it from the decade of disappointments that followed. But history invites a different and much more constructive exercise—revisiting the alternative trajectories that were available to American foreign policy in 1963 and that, at least in some cases, remain available to us today.

"The torch has been passed," Kennedy proclaimed in his inaugural address, "to a new generation of Americans. . . ."

That new generation included the forty-three-year-old JFK, the first American president born in the twentieth century, forty-four-year-old Robert McNamara as secretary of defense, forty-one-year-old McGeorge Bundy as national security adviser, and thirty-five-year-old Bobby Kennedy as attorney general. Most of the memorable speeches were written by Theodore Sorensen, then thirty-two.

These were men who came of age during the emergency state and accepted the cold war as a given. Dean Rusk, half a generation older than the others, had been an assistant secretary of state under Truman, closely involved in decision making on the Korean War. As secretary of state under Kennedy and Johnson, he brought the same early cold war thinking, with its exaggerated Achesonian visions of monolithic Communism and neighboring states falling like dominoes, to the war in Vietnam.

Kennedy's team shared none of Eisenhower's misgivings about the expanding military-industrial complex. McNamara, a registered Republican recruited from the presidency of Ford Motor Company to bring modern business management principles to the Pentagon, was a product of that complex.

"Let every nation know," Kennedy boldly proclaimed in his inaugural address, "that . . . we shall pay any price, bear any burden, . . . oppose any foe to assure the survival and the success of liberty."

It was the Truman Doctrine of universal containment with pizzazz, a commitment to unlimited engagement anywhere and everywhere without regard to the presence or absence of vital American interests or limits of American military and financial resources.

The New Frontiersmen's faith in America's unlimited global power drew on the experience of World War II; their belief in universal containment harked back to Truman. Their economic views were shaped by the wartime success of military Keynesianism, which seemed to demonstrate that the stimulative power of military spending would painlessly absorb temporary deficits through faster economic growth.

Kennedy embraced this open-ended commitment enthusiastically and urged his fellow Americans to do the same: "I do not shrink from this responsibility—I welcome it. . . . The energy, the faith, the devotion which we bring to this endeavor will light our country and all who serve it—and the glow from that fire can truly light the world."[3]

Kennedy was not a stickler for cabinet government and preferred working through informal groups of trusted advisers. He did not want to delegate operational decisions to Rusk the way Eisenhower had done with Dulles. Kennedy wanted to be able to make day-to-day foreign policy decisions directly from the White House.

That required an important structural innovation in the emergency state, the transformation of the job of the special presidential assistant for national security affairs into the modern position of national security adviser. Kennedy moved his special assistant, McGeorge Bundy, into the west wing of the White House, expanded his authority and staff, and had him channel important diplomatic, military, and intelligence reporting directly into the new White House situation room.

Part of Bundy's job was managing this vastly expanded information flow so that Kennedy could stay adequately informed, without being overwhelmed. An even more critical part was to draft decision memos so that Kennedy could choose among the often-conflicting views of senior policy makers at State, the Pentagon, and other agencies.[4]

Some of Bundy's successors, like Brent Scowcroft, have followed his example of not undercutting the secretary of state's role as the public face of American foreign policy. Others, like Henry Kissinger, Zbigniew Brzezinski, and Condoleezza Rice, have advertised their closer access to the president and greater influence. But all have been crucial policy makers and advisers, and none, unlike the secretary of state and other top officials, has been subject to congressional confirmation and oversight.

Presidents need candid advice from advisers they trust. But this exercise of unaccountable powers over the gravest decisions of war and peace undermines the intent of the founding fathers and the logic of the Constitution. Making the national security adviser a congressionally confirmable position would not automatically reestablish constitutional balance in foreign policy. But it is a necessary step in that direction.

Kennedy's first direct presidential experience of the emergency state came with the Bay of Pigs fiasco in April 1961. He inherited plans for a CIA-backed invasion of Cuba by anti-Castro exiles that had been developed by Allen Dulles with the backing of Eisenhower (and Vice President Richard Nixon).

This was scarcely a case of Kennedy being stuck with a policy he disagreed with. During the 1960 presidential campaign, the Kennedy camp had issued a statement pointing to the exiles as offering the hope of overthrowing Castro, then (inaccurately) complaining that "thus far these fighters for freedom have had virtually no support from our government."[5]

Fourteen years after the Truman Doctrine, universal containment had become unquestioned dogma for both parties. Although Cuba posed no security or economic threat to the United States, no president, from either party, dared consider the idea of coexisting with an increasingly Communist regime ninety miles off Key West—especially not a Democrat who had just won a close election and whose party the Republicans never missed a chance to blame for "losing" China.

What Kennedy was stuck with, however, was an invasion plan whose success depended on covert American air support. Allen Dulles's plan followed the usual pattern of CIA covert operations under Eisenhower—like those in Iran and Guatemala—with local partners operating in the foreground and the U.S. logistical and financial support on which their success depended kept largely hidden from public view.

When the CIA's original cover story about defecting Cuban air force pilots was prematurely blown, Kennedy was left with the choice of overt American intervention or leaving the exiles to their fate. He chose the latter course, vowing to never let the CIA put him in such an impossible spot again.

It was an important lesson for Kennedy about the capacity of emergency state agencies like the CIA to put even presidents in uncomfortable situations with unacceptable choices. He was also unhappy with the advice and options he had been given by the Joint Chiefs.

What bothered Kennedy about the Bay of Pigs was not the existence of the emergency state, its use in casually overthrowing foreign governments, or the underlying theory of universal containment that justified such overthrows whether or not vital American interests were directly at stake. What truly bothered him was the way emergency state agencies had tried to marginalize presidential authority, by withholding crucial information and then defining his remaining options too narrowly.

And that was the problem Kennedy set out to fix.

Within a year Allen Dulles, and his deputy for special operations, Richard Bissell, had been replaced by John McCone and Richard Helms, new CIA leaders who owed their rise, and presumably their loyalties, to Kennedy.

Kennedy turned to a military man he trusted, retired general Maxwell Taylor, asking him to study U.S. covert and paramilitary operations and make recommendations. Taylor soon returned to active service as Kennedy's personal military adviser, then in 1962 as chairman of the Joint Chiefs. Kennedy also sought advice from General Edward Lansdale, who had helped design counterinsurgency programs in the Philippines under Truman and in Vietnam under Eisenhower.

In 1962 Kennedy was ready to launch new operations against Cuba. His program, Operation Mongoose, involved the State and Defense departments as well as the CIA. Kennedy picked Lansdale to direct these efforts, with Robert Kennedy playing an informal coordinating role. Mongoose also tried to enlist American mob figures in plots to kill Castro.[6]

Kennedy's changes aimed at imposing a greater degree of accountability and oversight on the emergency state. But it was accountability only to the president and a few of his trusted friends and relatives, not to Congress or the Constitution.

Tighter political control from the White House can also work against American constitutional democracy, as Lyndon Johnson and Richard Nixon would soon demonstrate. Kennedy's efforts generated a great deal of ill will and mutual suspicion between Kennedy's inner circle and some newly reined-in members of the intelligence community. But they did little to roll back the emergency state.

Kennedy's own obsessive plotting against Castro was as reckless and extraconstitutional as the Bay of Pigs. But before anything came of it, in the fall of 1962 Khrushchev blindsided Washington with a far more dangerous form of nuclear adventurism—secretly deploying Soviet intermediate- and medium-range nuclear-capable missiles to Cuba. Unlike the Bay of Pigs and Mongoose, Khrushchev's ploy challenged the entire cold war strategic relationship between Moscow and Washington, all the more so because it was carried out amid official Soviet assurances that no offensive missiles would be deployed.

Khrushchev's deception infuriated Kennedy and politically embarrassed him. It came during a midterm election year, and the first public charge of Soviet missile activity in Cuba was made by Republican senator Kenneth Keating of New York in late August. Kennedy denied those claims, based in part on Moscow's assurances. But then in mid-October U-2 surveillance photos clearly revealed Soviet missiles in various stages of assembly.

Kennedy responded to the October U-2 photos by assembling an informal group of fifteen of his top foreign policy and military advisers. Their meetings over the next thirteen days were recorded on Kennedy's secret White House taping system and have since been transcribed and published as *The Kennedy Tapes*.[7]

Kennedy was puzzled as well as angry. The Soviets had never before based nuclear weapons outside the Soviet Union. Moscow's own ICBMs could hit targets virtually anywhere in the United States. As Kennedy recognized from the start, adding Soviet missiles in Cuba would mean shorter warning times in the event of nuclear attack. But whether a missile attack came from the Soviet Union or Cuba, the warning times would be much too short to evacuate American cities, but long enough to launch a devastating nuclear counterattack. Why, Kennedy wondered, would Khrushchev take such cosmic risks for such a marginal tactical gain?[8]

The answer Kennedy and his advisers came up with was Berlin. West Berlin was a vulnerable geographic outpost for the West, just as Cuba was for the East. Moscow had shown that with the 1948–49 Berlin blockade. And holding on to Berlin, the symbol of victory in World War II, was much more central to Western Europe's sense of security than holding on to the accidental gain of Cuba was to Moscow's.[9]

Kennedy recalled Khrushchev's aggressive bullying over Berlin at their Vienna summit sixteen months earlier, when Khrushchev, calling Berlin a bone in his throat that must be removed, had threatened to sign a separate peace treaty with East Germany, forcing the West to recognize and negotiate with the client East German regime over access to West

Berlin. Khrushchev had overplayed his hand at Vienna, trying to take advantage of a president he viewed as weak, inexperienced, and reeling from the Bay of Pigs embarrassment. It recalled the way Khrushchev had tried to exploit the U-2 incident with Eisenhower, wrecking the 1960 Paris summit.[10]

Khrushchev had not stormed out of the Vienna meeting as he had in Paris. But any chance for mutual understanding was destroyed. Khrushchev backed off on the threat of a separate peace treaty but gave East Germany the go-ahead to build the Berlin wall. Kennedy felt obliged to erase any impression of weakness. By October, U.S. and Soviet tanks confronted each other at Berlin's Checkpoint Charlie. Each side had orders to fire back if fired upon. Both sides stepped back, but tensions over Berlin continued through the first half of 1962.

In the summer of that year, Khrushchev secretly sent Soviet medium- and intermediate-range missiles to Cuba. When U-2 surveillance photos late that summer picked up the presence of Soviet surface-to-air missile sites, and Senator Keating charged that Soviet "rocket installations" were being constructed, Moscow assured Washington that no offensive missiles would be supplied. Kennedy then publicly warned that if the Soviets did provide offensive missiles or other similarly threatening arms to Cuba, "the gravest issues would arise."[11]

Given the Bay of Pigs and Operation Mongoose, Khrushchev's cover story about nonnuclear antiaircraft missiles seemed plausible to Kennedy and most of his senior advisers. Moscow had no history of stationing strategic nuclear missiles abroad, the strategic advantages of doing so seemed not worth the risks, and no U-2 photos of the new longer-range missile sites had yet appeared.

John McCone, Kennedy's new director of central intelligence, still worried about offensive missiles. But few inside the administration shared his doubts. Then a new set of U-2 photos taken on October 14 showed launch sites being built for medium-range and intermediate-range ballistic missiles, the former with a range of 1,000 miles and the latter 2,200 miles. The medium-range missiles could target Washington, D.C.; the intermediate-range missiles could reach San Francisco. (Both cities, of course, were already vulnerable to Soviet-based ICBMs.)

Technically, Khrushchev was doing just what Eisenhower and Kennedy had recently done when they sent medium-range (1,500-mile) Jupiter nuclear missiles to Italy and Turkey. But Khrushchev was doing so in an international and U.S. political context where Kennedy felt compelled to react.[12]

Keating's continued pressure guaranteed that. So did Khrushchev's false assurances and Kennedy's own warning of "the gravest issues" arising. All that came after Khrushchev had already committed his own prestige by sending strategic missiles to Cuba.

But even without all that, Kennedy could not have failed to react strongly. Before coming to office, Kennedy and other Democrats had (wrongly) accused Eisenhower of letting the Soviets create a "missile gap" in their favor. Sending the Jupiters had been approved, in part, to refute that charge.

By 1962 Kennedy knew that there was no missile gap and no military advantage to the Jupiter deployment. But in the aftermath of the Vienna summit and the Berlin crisis, he felt he had to go ahead with the Jupiter deployment anyway to demonstrate his resolve. In fact, by then the United States had roughly 7,200 nuclear warheads strategically deployed worldwide and the Soviet Union around 500.[13]

More fundamentally, Kennedy's choices were shaped by Truman's doctrine of universal containment and Eisenhower's defense strategy of massive nuclear retaliation. Universal containment elevated any perceived change in the global balance into a matter of U.S. credibility. Massive nuclear retaliation linked that credibility to Washington's willingness to counter such perceived changes with the threat of nuclear war.

Universal containment plus nuclear deterrence theory thus set a deadly trap that could lead to incinerating the planet over relatively inconsequential miscalculations on the Soviet-American global chessboard.

• • •

It didn't seem to matter that much to Kennedy and his advisers that Soviet missiles in Cuba did not greatly change the overall nuclear balance. What mattered more to them was the fear that Washington's failure to respond sufficiently forcefully to offensive missiles in Cuba, especially after Kennedy's warning about "the gravest issues," would cause America's strategic credibility to crumble, its European allies to panic and seek terms from Moscow, and Latin America to be swept by an unstoppable wave of Castroite revolutions. And responding forcefully enough meant being willing to risk all-out nuclear war.[14]

As Kennedy explained to his advisers on October 16: "Last month I said we weren't going to [allow it]. Last month I should have said that we don't care. But when we said we're *not* going to, and then they go ahead and do it, and then we do nothing, then I would think that our risks increase."[15]

As if this were not surreal enough, Kennedy's people fully realized that the very Europeans and Latin Americans they were trying to reassure were not very eager for a forceful American response over Cuba. Europeans, in particular, feared that an American embargo on Cuba, which mattered little to them, would provoke a Soviet blockade of Berlin, which mattered a great deal to them. Kennedy recognized this fear and worried that such an outcome would fracture rather than reassure the Atlantic alliance. Rusk thought the U.S. air strikes he advocated could spur local Communists to overthrow the pro-Washington governments of "Venezuela, for example, or Guatemala, Bolivia, Chile, possibly even Mexico."[16]

Still, most of Kennedy's advisers initially favored military action, and the Joint Chiefs began planning for waves of air strikes against the missile bases, to be quickly followed by a full-scale invasion to remove the Castro government and any hidden missile sites the air strikes might have missed. Robert Kennedy opposed any surprise air strikes as Pearl Harbor–like and un-American. Robert McNamara favored air strikes as a first step. Maxwell Taylor thought air strikes might do the job without an invasion, which he opposed. Deputy Defense Secretary Roswell Gilpatric and former ambassador to Moscow Llewellyn Thompson pushed the alternative idea of a naval "quarantine." (They didn't want to evoke any parallels to Berlin by calling it a blockade.)[17]

Air force chief of staff Curtis LeMay argued strongly for immediate full-scale military action, raising political as well as military arguments that Kennedy likely considered impertinent if not insubordinate: "I think that a blockade, and political talk, would be considered by a lot of our friends, and neutrals as being a pretty weak response to this. And I'm sure a lot of our own citizens would feel the same way, too. You're in a pretty bad fix, Mr. President."[18]

Kennedy resisted the Joint Chiefs' pressure for immediate military action and ordered a naval blockade, while continuing military preparations for possible air and ground action later if needed. He understood that Soviet ships might challenge the blockade, leading to war, or that Khrushchev might order a counterblockade against Berlin. But Kennedy thought there was at least a chance that Khrushchev might back off instead, if Washington could offer him a face-saving diplomatic way out of the impasse that wouldn't jeopardize his own grip on power at home.

That couldn't be a swap of Cuba for West Berlin, which would destroy the Western alliance. Nor could it be an open swap of Soviet missiles in Cuba for American Jupiters in Italy and Turkey. But a covert swap of those strategically marginal missiles, along with a public American pledge not to invade Cuba, ultimately proved the key to a peaceful, mutually face-saving solution, though not before the world had been brought to the edge of nuclear devastation.

Had it fallen over that edge—which Kennedy and his advisers considered a realistic possibility—that surely would have been the ultimate abrogation of the constitutional scheme—annihilation without representation, without public debate or congressional deliberation. But it didn't.

Though the naval blockade was technically an act of war, no war ensued. Kennedy invoked his authority as commander in chief to move the navy into position and issue the orders to stop and search incoming ships. His actions were not that different from what Roosevelt had done in the North Atlantic in the months before Pearl Harbor. But while Roosevelt wanted to get into a naval war with Germany, Kennedy wanted to avoid any kind of war with the Soviet Union.

Kennedy's top advisers kept their deliberations secret during the thirteen-day crisis, but once they decided on the embargo, they discussed it with twenty congressional leaders of both parties. Kennedy then informed the public in a relatively candid speech on national television that stressed some of the nuances of American policy and avoided Trumanesque hype. There was no need to "scare hell" out of the American people. The possibility of direct military confrontation with a nuclear-armed Soviet Union was scary enough.

Some features of the final deal, like the quid pro quo on the Jupiters, were not publicly disclosed at the time. But these arguably fall within the framers' understanding, acknowledged in *Federalist* 64, of the need for secrecy in international diplomatic negotiations.

Historians rightly consider the Cuban missile crisis a showcase of John F. Kennedy's best leadership qualities. Kennedy hagiographers portray it as an example of his firmly but calmly standing up to Khrushchev's adventurism and thereby forcing Khrushchev to back down.

Not quite. Kennedy kept his cool, didn't let his more hawkish advisers stampede him, and dodged the deadly synergy of universal containment and massive nuclear retaliation. But in the end it was also good luck, and Khrushchev's own sense of proportion, that allowed the world to escape nuclear incineration during October 1962.

That close call with Armageddon seems to have driven home to Kennedy the fatal logic of linking a foreign policy of universal containment to a military strategy based on massive nuclear retaliation. After the Bay of Pigs he had extricated presidential freedom of action from emergency state agencies that sometimes seemed to be on autopilot. But he found himself still constrained by the perverse logic of America's global doctrines—he had felt obliged to knowingly take the world to the brink of nuclear war over what he knew to be only a second-order increment to an existing nuclear threat.

From his first days in office, Kennedy had sought to escape the "nukes or nothing" dilemma he had been left by Eisenhower's cost-conscious defense budgets, Dulles's brink-of-nuclear-war diplomacy, and that era's Republican notions of limited, asymmetrical containment, of not responding to every perceived Soviet advance but acting only selectively at times and places of Washington's choosing.

Two weeks before Kennedy's inauguration, Khrushchev had publicly pledged to support wars of national liberation. Kennedy believed that Washington could not afford the luxury of responding only selectively at times and places of its own choosing and with no other credible counterweapon than the threat of devastating nuclear attack.

In his inaugural address, Kennedy had proclaimed a Truman-style willingness to "pay any price, bear any burden . . . to assure the survival and the success of liberty." Six months later, in a televised address to the nation during the Berlin crisis of July 1961, he declared, "We intend to have a wider choice than humiliation or all-out nuclear action."

Kennedy brought back Truman's vision of universal containment as well as Truman-era national security hands like Dean Rusk and Paul Nitze, and harsh critics of Eisenhower defense policies like General Maxwell Taylor. And he turned to Keynesian economic advisers like Paul Samuelson and Walter Heller who assured him that larger defense budgets would help pay for themselves by stimulating faster economic growth.[19]

Perhaps. Keynesian formulas still worked smoothly in the less-open world economy of 1961. But the original military rationale for increased spending, the supposed Soviet superiority in ICBMs and ground forces that Kennedy had made so much of during his presidential campaign, quickly crumbled.

Shortly after taking office, Kennedy learned from U-2 surveillance photos and other intelligence that there was no missile gap, at least not in Moscow's favor. The United States still had a very healthy lead in operational ICBMs. A more careful reading of intelligence also showed that Washington had been seriously overestimating the size of Soviet army divisions for years. Using more realistic numbers, McNamara's Pentagon concluded that NATO actually had more troops than the Warsaw Pact.[20]

Kennedy publicly acknowledged this far-more-favorable strategic balance but went ahead with his military buildup anyway. He had become personally wary of Khrushchev, especially after the Vienna summit and the Berlin crisis, and he began to worry that a Kremlin leader aware of his own side's weakness might prove more reckless than a leader who thought that the strategic balance, and time, favored Moscow.[21]

Besides, Kennedy still wanted to widen the range of military responses available to him to permit a more activist version of global containment. To flex American conventional military muscle in Berlin, Kennedy had called up 148,000 reservists. To prepare for the next such confrontation, he increased draft calls, expanded the size of the active duty forces by more than 200,000, and pressed European NATO allies to add to their conventional forces.[22]

These additional American troops made it possible for Kennedy to mobilize a credible potential invasion force during the Cuban missile crisis without hollowing out American military strength in Europe and increasing Berlin's vulnerability to Soviet countermoves.[23]

Kennedy intended this larger American military mainly for cold war confrontations in Europe. He realized that U.S. troops would be less effective, and less welcome, if used to counter wars of national liberation in the former colonial world. Truman's experience of Korea cautioned against further U.S. land wars in Asia. The French experience in Indochina cautioned against Western conventional armies fighting locally rooted Asian irregulars.

But Kennedy did not want to let Khrushchev's embrace of national liberation wars go unanswered. To meet this challenge, Kennedy expanded and developed the military's special forces and assigned them a new counterinsurgency role. American special forces commando units had operated behind enemy lines in World War II. During the Eisenhower years they were trained with similar offensive operations in mind.

With their commando training, their psychological warfare and intelligence orientation, and their foreign language skills, the special forces were also well suited to bolster pro-American regimes in the former colonial world facing national liberation wars.

Using them this way clearly appealed to Kennedy, not just as an answer to national liberation wars, but as an expansion of the emergency state, and as a potential way around the Joint Chiefs, whom he distrusted until he installed Maxwell Taylor as chairman in October 1962. Operating outside the normal military chain of command, and engaging in covert undeclared wars, special forces missions sometimes resembled paramilitary versions of CIA covert operations.

The historical precedent Kennedy looked to was Edward Lansdale's successful mission to the Philippines in the early 1950s, which had helped turn back the tide of the Communist-supported Hukbalahap insurgency.

Lansdale was an OSS veteran and air force officer assigned as an adviser to the Joint U.S. Military Assistance Group in the Philippines. He felt that the key to successful counterinsurgency was to identify, build up, and then closely advise indigenous military and political figures who could provide counterinsurgency operations with local leadership and credibility. Washington's role was to provide money, intelligence, and military advisers, while the local partners would provide the troops and win the political struggle for hearts and minds.[24]

Ramón Magsaysay had proved an ideal local partner for Lansdale's strategy in the Philippines. Then in 1953, with French power in Indochina crumbling, Eisenhower sent Lansdale to Vietnam, hoping he could export his successful Philippine formula. Lansdale spent the next four years there, giving similar advice and support to Ngo Dinh Diem. But Vietnam was not the Philippines, Diem was not Magsaysay, and Lansdale enjoyed less success.

Lansdale returned to Washington, becoming deputy assistant secretary of defense for special operations under Eisenhower, then moving up to assistant secretary under Kennedy. Kennedy eagerly sought out Lansdale's advice on covert offensive operations in Cuba and counterinsurgency programs in Southeast Asia and elsewhere.

Kennedy's new emphasis on counterinsurgency, like his expansion of America's conventional forces, gave him and his successors new options for pursuing universal containment with less reliance on nuclear brinkmanship.

But as Vietnam was to show, these new tools had their own limits. American counterinsurgency efforts can succeed when the circumstances are right, as they were in the Philippines, or fail when they are not, as in Vietnam. The most that outside counterinsurgency assistance can hope to achieve is to help an otherwise politically and militarily viable local partner defeat an insurgent challenge. If no such partner exists, counterinsurgency is not a viable tactic. At that point Washington's only real choices are massive American military force or a negotiated retreat.

Because he did not want another Korea or Dien Bien Phu, Kennedy resisted Americanizing the Vietnam War for as long as he was president, hoping, against mounting evidence, that South Vietnamese political and military leaders would rise to the occasion.

That hopeful hedge did not remain available to his successor for very long. By late 1964 the CIA and American military commanders in Vietnam pronounced the South Vietnamese government and army essentially defeated. With counterinsurgency no longer an option, and unwilling to accept a negotiated retreat, Lyndon Johnson decided to fight the American land war in Asia that he knew he could not win and that so many American strategists had warned against since Korea. More than 58,000 Americans died in a country where the United States had no vital interests beyond upholding the credibility of universal containment and blocking the fall of a series of imaginary dominoes.[25]

Kennedy meant his buildup of America's conventional military forces and his expansion of counterinsurgency capabilities to supplement, not replace, American nuclear weapons superiority. His underlying goal was to develop a range of flexible military responses that would let the United States respond to any challenge anywhere at an appropriate level and gradually escalate that response as needed.

In the course of his term, Kennedy more than doubled the number of American nuclear weapons, tripling their destructive power. He doubled the number of land-based ICBMs and increased the fleet of Polaris missile submarines by more than 50 percent.[26]

Yet Kennedy also worried about the nuclear arms race. In his inaugural address he warned that neither Washington nor Moscow could be comfortable with a situation that left "both sides overburdened by the cost of modern weapons, both rightly alarmed by the steady spread of the deadly atom, yet both racing to alter that uncertain balance of terror that stays the hand of mankind's final war." In September 1961 he created the independent Arms Control and Disarmament Agency, following through on a proposal he had made while a senator.

The missile crisis probably quickened Kennedy's efforts to reduce nuclear tensions. His June 1963 commencement address at American University was notable for its frank acknowledgment of Soviet suffering in World War II and its recognition of both sides' shared danger of nuclear devastation. It was in that speech that Kennedy announced the opening of three-way talks with the Soviet Union and Britain on a nuclear test ban agreement.

But what made that agreement possible was an abrupt change in Moscow's negotiating position, announced three weeks later by Khrushchev.

American nuclear arms control proposals had long been thwarted by Moscow's refusal to accept intrusive inspections of its territory. Without such inspections, no American president was willing to trust Soviet compliance with a test ban or other arms control agreement.

By the early 1960s Washington was confident it could monitor atmospheric and underwater nuclear tests from afar, but not underground tests, which could be indistinguishable from earthquakes. But Moscow said it was only interested in a total test ban, without the intrusive inspections on which the West insisted. Then on July 2, Khrushchev announced he would agree to a limited test ban, excluding underground tests. Negotiations began on July 15 and were successfully concluded ten days later.

The Limited Test Ban Treaty spared the world from further contamination with radioactive fallout from U.S., Soviet, and British atmospheric tests. It began a long, and often interrupted, process of arms control negotiations that eventually led to actual reductions in both sides' nuclear stockpiles. But it did nothing to diminish U.S.-Soviet competition for strategic nuclear supremacy. Kennedy himself had fed that drive with his missile gap charges in the 1960 campaign and by persisting with his strategic nuclear buildup even after discovering that the United States had a comfortable lead in nuclear weaponry.

Campaign charges of American nuclear vulnerability, often as factually off base as Kennedy's, would become an American political tradition through the end of the cold war and even beyond.

Each side's anxieties fed the other's. Moscow's long-term response to Khrushchev's humiliating climbdown in the Cuban missile crisis was an accelerated, and eventually successful, drive for strategic nuclear parity.

In 1962, the year of the Cuban missile crisis, the United States had 7,211 strategic nuclear warheads and the Soviet Union had 522, already enough to deter, or alternatively to destroy, each other. In 1989, after both sides had diverted trillions of dollars from potentially more productive uses, Washington had 13,967 and Moscow had 12,117. The balance of terror remained unchanged.[27]

CHAPTER SIX

TUNNEL VISION

Like Harry Truman two decades earlier, Lyndon Johnson vowed to continue the policies of his fallen predecessor. But Johnson's presidency, like Truman's, ended up profoundly changing the direction and temper of the country. It ushered in a dark new phase of the emergency state, characterized by a massively escalated presidential war, vastly expanded White House political spying, and a steadily widening "credibility gap" between Johnson's statements about the Vietnam War and the perceptions and suspicions of the American people.

John Kennedy had scarcely been a paragon of constitutional democracy—far from it. His path to the White House had been lubricated by family money and backroom political deals. As president, he had been a buccaneering cold warrior, an avid consolidator of executive and family power, largely indifferent to civil liberties, and at best, an opportunistic and wavering supporter of civil rights.

Yet almost despite himself, Kennedy's youthful looks and inspirational rhetoric had helped stir a remarkable outpouring of democratic idealism, especially among college students.

For Kennedy, the Peace Corps was primarily a tool for winning hearts and minds in the cold war. But for thousands of young Americans, it was a way to put their education to work for the world's poor. For Kennedy, whose Senate civil rights record had been less than stellar, placing an October 1960 phone call to the jailed Martin Luther King, Jr., sent a timely signal to black and liberal voters shortly before election day. For many of those voters, and others still too young to vote, it identified Kennedy with the civil rights cause.

Johnson's presidency generated a different set of feelings in America—frustration, violence, and national division. Johnson's growing political isolation, coupled with his headlong expansion of the emergency state, eventually spurred an estranged Congress to begin reclaiming some of its long-abdicated constitutional powers, a tendency that grew stronger under Richard Nixon. But with the democratic idealism of the early 1960s having long since yielded to disenchantment and cynicism among the broader population, Congress's fitful and belated stirrings never quite struck the kind of connections with popular feeling that might have fueled a true grassroots democratic revival.

Kennedy's assassination suddenly thrust Johnson into the job he had always wanted, the single most powerful job in the world. Unlike Truman, Johnson never doubted that he was up to it, and he fiercely distrusted those Kennedy hands he suspected of thinking otherwise. He would not be a Kennedy-style president. He would be a Johnson-style president. He would shape up the Democratic majorities in Congress and get things done.

Johnson's main policy interests, like Truman's, were largely domestic. Both men tended to be overly wary of looking weak on foreign policy issues and thereby losing political support for their domestic agendas.

FDR and JFK had had the self-confidence to be selective in choosing their foreign policy fights. Roosevelt had recognized military realities in Eastern Europe. Kennedy had withdrawn the Jupiters from Turkey and accepted a coalition including neutralists in Laos.

Truman and Johnson had no taste for playing that kind of long-term diplomatic chess. Johnson believed that the Republicans had destroyed Truman by blaming him for "losing China." No one was going to be able to blame Lyndon Johnson for "losing Vietnam."

The Vietnam War did not dominate Johnson's presidency from day one. Passing Kennedy's civil rights bill and winning election in his own right in 1964 came first. But by mid-1964 the military and intelligence reports Johnson was seeing convinced him that American military advisers alone could not save South Vietnam from military defeat.

Fearing the political backlash that might follow a negotiated retreat and fearing the political costs of acknowledging that he was rapidly Americanizing a dubious Asian war, Johnson moved ahead by misrepresentation, incremental escalation, and stealth. Even after winning a decisive electoral victory that November, Johnson continued on this politically deceptive, militarily unpromising, and ever more costly course—losing sight of more vital national security issues like arms control, undermining the federal budget and price stability, and finally consuming his own presidency.

By the time Johnson became president, the Saigon government had been in continuous crisis for the past six months. Three weeks earlier South Vietnamese army generals, with the implicit approval of Washington and the U.S. embassy, had ousted Ngo Dinh Diem (and, to Kennedy's horror, also murdered Diem and his unpopular brother, Ngo Dinh Nhu). Right up to the time he was assassinated, Kennedy still hoped, against mounting evidence, that a less corrupt, more effective government might come to power in Saigon and revitalize the war effort.[1]

That never happened. Diem's ouster was followed by a succession of further coups and juntas, none able to restore much political stability or military effectiveness. By early 1964 the Joint Chiefs were advising Johnson that to ensure victory in Vietnam, he would need to lift the restrictions Kennedy had put on the U.S. military role. Specifically, they recommended U.S. air strikes against the North and the introduction of U.S. combat troops into the South to defend against Hanoi's expected retaliation. Otherwise, they warned, South Vietnam might fall. In May the CIA added its own assessment that Saigon's authority was steadily eroding and its position could become "untenable" by the end of 1964.[2]

That was a loss Kennedy had seemed willing to contemplate, at least hypothetically. But Johnson never seriously considered accepting Saigon's defeat. Kennedy took a dynamic view of the global contest with Moscow that made him willing to consider cutting American losses in one arena to strengthen Washington's hand in another. Johnson, a master of that kind of tactical maneuvering in domestic politics, never saw room for such nuance in foreign policy. He remained a true believer in Truman's universal containment doctrine as formulated in NSC-68.[3]

To Johnson, accepting defeat anywhere meant losing credibility everywhere. He believed in the domino theory that Eisenhower had first applied to Indochina in 1954. Johnson felt that the fall of Saigon would almost inevitably lead to the fall of Southeast Asia and eventually to the collapse of the West. He was equally sure that "losing Vietnam" would defeat the Democrats at home and end his own political career.[4]

But Johnson also knew that Truman's war in Korea had cost the Democrats votes, and he was determined to win the 1964 presidential election by the largest possible margin. He tried, for as long as possible, to avoid any public indication that he was even considering Americanizing the war. But by the spring of 1964, that was clearly the direction in which Johnson was headed, while hoping he could delay any public commitment until after the November elections.[5]

Johnson kept his real intentions from Congress. But he also wanted the cover of a congressional resolution in case things turned sour—as, for example, they had in Korea after the Chinese counterattacked in late 1950. Going to Congress for a resolution required an incident, ideally a North Vietnamese attack on an American position.

On August 2 three North Vietnamese patrol boats fired on the U.S. Navy destroyer *Maddox* while it conducted electronic surveillance in the international waters of the Tonkin Gulf.

The North Vietnamese attack was not unprovoked. The *Maddox*'s surveillance mission was designed to support South Vietnamese patrol boat raids against the North Vietnamese coastline. Unable to catch up with the fast, U.S.-supplied South Vietnamese patrol boats inside their own territorial waters, the North Vietnamese patrol boats fired torpedoes and machine guns against the slower, unsuspecting U.S. destroyer. The *Maddox* suffered no significant damage. But Johnson now had his incident. In fact, he thought he had two when naval officials erroneously reported a second attack against the *Maddox* and another destroyer two days later.[6]

When Johnson reported the events to the American people on August 4, he omitted any mention of the American intelligence mission and described the attack as "open aggression on the high seas against the United States of America." He promised a "limited and fitting" response.[7]

The next day Johnson sent a message to Congress requesting a resolution endorsing not only that initial response but also unspecified future American military responses to future North Vietnamese actions.

He invoked supposed American military obligations under the Eisenhower-era treaty establishing SEATO (although this in fact required only consultation). He echoed the Truman Doctrine, stating, "This is not just a jungle war, but a struggle for freedom on every front of human activity." And he called on Congress to join him "in affirming the national determination that all such attacks will be met, and that the United States will continue in its basic policy of assisting the free nations of the area to defend their freedom."[8]

This was a broad blank check. The actual text of the joint resolution that Congress overwhelmingly approved the next day was even broader, approving and supporting "the determination of the President, as Commander in Chief, to take all measures to repel any armed attack against the forces of the United States *and to prevent further aggression*" and "to take all necessary steps, including the use of armed force, to assist any member or protocol state of the Southeast Asia Collective Defense Treaty requesting assistance in defense of its freedom" (emphasis added).[9]

At thc timc, Amcrica had only 16,000 military advisers in Vietnam and no combat troops. To rack up a convincing congressional majority, Johnson gave no public hint of the escalatory steps he was already considering. The House approved the Tonkin Gulf Resolution by a vote of 416-0. The Senate vote was 88-2, with Democrats Wayne Morse of Oregon and Ernest Gruening of Alaska casting the only dissenting votes.

It wasn't a constitutional declaration of war, but Johnson, and later Nixon, used it to justify years of undeclared ground, air, and naval warfare.

Unlike FDR's relatively brief undeclared North Atlantic naval war in 1941, this was an extended evasion of the Constitution. Once the American phase of the war got under way in early 1965, it continued under emergency state presidential authority for eight years, costing the lives of more than 55,000 Americans and more than 1 million Vietnamese.

By this time LBJ had all but decided on Americanizing the war. But he also wanted to position himself as a peace candidate against his 1964 Republican challenger, Barry Goldwater. In a sense, he was; Goldwater supported using nuclear weapons to defoliate Vietnamese rain forests in order to make it easier to find and attack Communist infiltration routes.

But Lyndon Johnson already had in mind an Americanized war. And he deliberately withheld that information from the voters. He attacked Goldwater for advocating the bombing of North Vietnam and the use of American combat troops when Johnson was himself weighing the same steps. Just days after the Tonkin Gulf Resolution, Johnson condemned "others" who were "eager to enlarge the conflict" and "call upon us to supply American boys to do the job Asian boys should do."[10]

Considering the postelection sequel, this was mendacity on a level with FDR's 1940 campaign pledge that "your boys are not going to be sent into any foreign war."

Johnson won, gaining 61 percent of the popular vote and carrying the electoral vote by a margin of 486-52.

Then he escalated. He ordered sustained bombing raids against North Vietnam beginning in early March 1965. A week later he sent 3,500 Marines to protect American air bases—the first dispatch of American combat forces to an Asian war zone since Korea. In July he doubled draft calls and ordered in forty-four more combat battalions, bringing the total American force to 125,000. By the end of 1965 it was nearly 185,000. Johnson knew by then that the course he had chosen would require sending many more American troops to Vietnam over the next few years. (The number more than doubled in 1966, to more than

385,000, and passed the 500,000 mark in 1968.) But he did not tell that to the American public.[11]

Although Johnson was determined to escalate as much as necessary to deny Hanoi victory, he understood that his South Vietnamese allies could not win either. And remembering what happened when Truman let MacArthur drive to the Yalu in 1950, he did not want to escalate beyond the point that might bring Soviet or Chinese forces into the war. (China had tested its first nuclear bomb in October 1964.) That was the real meaning of Johnson's repeated assurance that "we seek no wider war," although the American people wrongly took it to mean that he planned no further escalation in Vietnam itself.

That left American policy in an impossible bind. Washington had ruled out defeat or a negotiated compromise. South Vietnam's political incapacities ruled out eventual victory or a South Vietnam that could be left to stand on its own. And international circumstances ruled out the possibility of the United States tapping into its global military strength to shorten the war or force a negotiated settlement on terms it would accept. Washington could, and did, quantitatively escalate, with more troops and more bombs. But it could not qualitatively escalate.

Under these circumstances, holding to a policy of universal containment was impossible. But it would take Richard Nixon to see that. Lyndon Johnson retreated into denial instead.

Johnson also delayed raising taxes to pay for the war, although his economists recommended it, with war costs mounting and the domestic economy spurred to full employment by government spending and mounting draft calls. Johnson feared tipping the public off to his plans for future escalation and thereby losing political support and fiscal space for pursuing his Great Society programs.[12]

As he explained to Doris Kearns Goodwin in 1970:

I knew from the start that I was bound to be crucified either way I moved. If I left the woman I really loved—the Great Society—in order to get involved in that bitch of a war on the other side of the world, then I would lose everything at home. All my programs . . . But if I left that war and let the Communists take over South Vietnam, then I would be seen as a coward and my nation would be seen as an appeaser and we would both find it impossible to accomplish anything for anybody anywhere on the entire globe.[13]

Then came the Tet offensive of January–February 1968. At tremendous cost and sacrifice to themselves, North Vietnamese and Vietcong fighters attacked highly visible targets previously thought almost invulnerable, from the imperial citadel in Hue to the U.S. embassy in Saigon. Communist losses were staggering. Lyndon Johnson's loss of credibility was politically fatal.

When Johnson talked about the Communist losses, Americans weren't impressed. They had been hearing about enemy body counts for years, and the enemy kept getting bolder. Johnson had claimed to see the light at the end of the tunnel too many times. What Americans saw was Tet.

Johnson was a shrewd enough politician to understand that he could not run again in 1968. He promised to seek "an honorable peace." But shackled to the universal containment assumptions of the emergency state, he seemed not to know how. To him, an honorable peace could only mean attaining his basic war aim—proving to Hanoi that it could not win. And that aim was as unattainable in 1968 as it had been in 1964.

General William Westmoreland's March 1968 request for 200,000 more American troops was rejected. Congress never would have approved it. But the American bombing of North Vietnam continued. The Paris peace talks that began that May went nowhere. Hubert Humphrey's Democratic presidential candidacy twisted in the wind, caught between loyalty to Johnson and an electorate fed up with Johnson's war. Five days before election day, Johnson finally announced a bombing halt. But it was too late. Humphrey's Republican opponent, Richard Nixon, had hinted at a plan to end the war. Independent candidate George Wallace drew off the votes of white Democrats angered by Johnson's strong civil rights record and anxious over rising crime and violence in the increasingly black inner cities.

Johnson's years of deceptions to maximize voter support took their toll. Nixon won a clear Electoral College majority but only 43.4 percent of the popular vote. Humphrey trailed with 42.7 percent while another 13.5 percent went to Wallace.

Johnson knew he had become a polarizing figure. But he was quicker to understand criticism from the right than from the left. As a southern politician himself, Johnson was not surprised to see white southern voters turn against the Democrats over civil rights. He knew that he had enacted more far-reaching civil rights legislation than any other president since Reconstruction, and he was proud of it.

But he could not grasp or accept the anger his Vietnam policies and his chronic dissembling about them had stirred among liberal Democrats and young people. He knew that he had insisted on a middle military course, rejecting advice from military advisers and Republican critics that might have shortened the war but might also have widened it. He knew that he had followed the dictates of universal containment, regularly espoused by his three presidential predecessors.

He had not changed the fundamental American cold war policy of resisting Communist advances, and yet he faced unprecedented antiwar opposition. Johnson therefore concluded that his critics at home were being directed by Communist powers abroad and asked J. Edgar Hoover to have the FBI prove it. Johnson reached similar conclusions about militant black critics at home, especially after repeated outbreaks of inner-city rioting.

But Johnson's misuse of the FBI for domestic political spying actually began much earlier, not to gain intelligence on urban riots or antiwar demonstrations, but to outmaneuver other Democrats at the August 1964 party convention in Atlantic City, New Jersey. According to a former top bureau official, William Sullivan, Johnson was concerned about a challenge to the all-white Mississippi delegation by civil rights advocates. He also feared that Robert Kennedy's supporters might try to derail his own presidential nomination in favor of their candidate.[14]

Sullivan later testified that at Johnson's request, Hoover had sent a special FBI squad under Deke DeLoach to the convention. There they bugged Martin Luther King, Jr.'s hotel room, posed as television journalists, and monitored delegates and civil rights activists, feeding what they learned to Johnson's own political operatives.[15]

Two months later, at the height of the 1964 presidential campaign, Washington, D.C., police caught one of those Johnson operatives, Walter Jenkins, in a sexually compromising position with another man. According to Bill Moyers, then also a top Johnson aide, LBJ suspected that members of Barry Goldwater's political team had set up Jenkins, and he demanded that the FBI find out who it had been. Moyers reported that Johnson told him: "You call DeLoach and tell him if he wants to keep that nice house in Virginia, and that soft job he's got here, his boys better find those bastards."[16]

Sullivan also reported that Johnson would use the FBI to dig up derogatory information on Democratic Party senators who opposed him, and then leak the information to the Senate Republican leader, Everett Dirksen.[17]

In all of this, Johnson was following closely in the footsteps of his political mentor and presidential model, Franklin Roosevelt. Other presidents, including Truman and Kennedy, made use of the FBI for purely political spying. But Johnson did so more systematically than any other president since Roosevelt.[18]

The emergency state came naturally to Lyndon Johnson. It had shaped his entire political life.

Lyndon Johnson left office in January 1969 with a nearly balanced federal budget and an international trade surplus. The unemployment rate was 3.4 percent, the lowest in fifteen years. Only the inflation rate, at 4.4 percent, was troubling. Although inflation would soar much higher in the next decade, it had remained below 2 percent throughout the early 1960s. Its rise after 1966 was largely attributable to Johnson's early refusal to raise taxes to pay for the Vietnam War, despite advice from his Keynesian economists that the overheating full-employment economy needed cooling down.

But other factors were at work that would soon make it almost impossible for Johnson's successors to successfully employ the Keynesian economic management tools that had worked so well during most of the 1960s. The terms of international economic competition had changed. And postwar American foreign policies had helped change them.

Washington's efforts to revive the war-wounded economies of Western Europe and Japan in order to fend off internal and external Communist threats had succeeded spectacularly—perhaps too spectacularly for the competitive fortunes of the American domestic economy.

In the early postwar decades, rising foreign demand had helped spur productivity, boosting investments in American industry, stimulating strong economic growth, and making possible a remarkable sustained rise in the real earnings of American workers. Washington reinforced that virtuous cycle by pressing for liberalized international trade and investment rules and more freely convertible currencies.

But as the European and Japanese economies got back on their feet, they became more competitive producers. Paradoxically, wartime damage to their industrial infrastructure turned into a competitive advantage as newer, more efficient infrastructure took its place. The historically lower wage levels of these countries also lured increasingly mobile international capital to their shores.

As European and Japanese wage levels began to catch up to American levels, the wage and price calculations of America's high-mass-consumption economy began to change. Expanding consumer markets in Europe and Japan made American companies less dependent on domestic consumer demand and therefore less inclined to follow Henry Ford's old dictum about needing to pay their workers enough to be able to buy their products. With American companies less tied to the U.S. national economy, economic policy managers in Washington found themselves with correspondingly less influence over business decisions and national economic outcomes.

Finally, the dollar's status as an international reserve currency encouraged the accumulation of large "Eurodollar" reserves—dollars that remained offshore and largely beyond the Federal Reserve's regulations. This reduced the U.S. government's power to manage the money supply and credit creation, two key Keynesian economic management tools.

These Keynesian demand-management tools (which American policy makers had relied on during the 1940s, 1950s, and 1960s) worked best in largely self-contained markets where companies could pass on increased tax, regulatory, and labor expenses to consumers without worrying about being undersold by business competitors. With the revival of international economic competition, American companies became much more sensitive to such costs and more inclined to consider moving production facilities to lower-cost, more business-friendly locations overseas. That in turn made Washington more reluctant to employ tax and regulatory tools that might further discourage domestic business investment.

These changes in the international economic environment did not directly affect the evolution of the emergency state, at least not right away. But the divide they began to open between the economic interests of growing numbers of working Americans and those of the economic elites who design American foreign policies led successive administrations to become increasingly deceptive about their international economic policies and trade negotiations.

CHAPTER SEVEN

EMERGENCY REPAIRS

By the time Richard Nixon was sworn in as president, the emergency state was in crisis.

Truman's universal containment had marched America into the quagmire of Vietnam. Roosevelt's broad electoral coalition had been shattered by the McCarthy, Kennedy, and Wallace insurgencies. Swelling peacetime draft calls had radicalized domestic foreign policy debate and sparked angry protests on campuses and in the streets. An economically revived Japan and Europe challenged America's easy postwar dominance of international markets.

Nixon recognized the severity of the crisis, correctly analyzed its fundamental causes, and spent most of his presidency trying to rescue and rebuild the emergency state.

He nearly succeeded. Daring policies like the switch to an all-volunteer army, "Vietnamization" of the Indochina war, the surprise opening to China, détente, and newly nationalist trade and currency policies kept foreign and domestic enemies off balance. But in the end, Nixon's compulsive secrecy and paranoia and his penchant for using emergency state institutions to pursue personal political ends fatally enmeshed him in the Watergate cover-up, cutting short his presidency and leaving the emergency state more exposed to its critics than ever before or since.

Nixon's bid to rescue the emergency state necessarily began with the challenge of extricating the United States from the disaster Johnson had left behind in Vietnam. Johnson's catastrophic mishandling of Vietnam, which had helped make Nixon president, had gravely weakened America's global leadership.

Johnson's repeated escalations had been meant to demonstrate American resolve and credibility. They had instead demonstrated America's inability to impose its will on a poor, technologically backward enemy. In the process Washington had isolated itself from its European allies, alarmed its more vulnerable third-world clients, and unraveled the cold war consensus at home.

With more than 500,000 U.S. troops in South Vietnam, Hanoi could not win a decisive military victory—but neither could Washington, and that was what really counted. Johnson had recklessly staked America's global credibility on forcing Hanoi to pull back. He had always believed that there was some level of military pain that would force Ho Chi Minh to the table on American terms. But that level was never found, even after a substantial portion of America's full conventional might was engaged.

When Hanoi chose to press on, American power looked hollow. Washington could bomb North Vietnam, but it could not preserve an independent, non-Communist South Vietnam. Once America withdrew its troops, Saigon would crumble. All Nixon could hope to control was the timing and the appearances of the inevitable American withdrawal and South Vietnamese collapse.

Nixon understood that withdrawal could not be avoided, just stretched out. He could not begin to repair domestic consensus, rebuild the military, and respond credibly to crises elsewhere with more than 500,000 American troops bogged down indefinitely in Vietnam. He had assured voters during the presidential campaign that he had a plan for peace, though he did not offer details.

Nixon's vagueness served his purposes. As a Republican heir to Eisenhower and Dulles, he well understood that the pursuit of universal containment had dangerously overextended America's military and economic commitments. He wanted to cauterize the steady bleeding of American power and prestige in Vietnam. But he wanted to do so carefully and deliberately, which meant slowly. Precipitate withdrawal could signal geopolitical weakness to Moscow and invite Soviet adventurism elsewhere. The whole point of withdrawal for Nixon was to rebuild American strength.

Nixon bought the time he needed by phasing out the draft and "Vietnamizing" the war. Eisenhower had taken only six months to reach a ceasefire agreement in Korea. Nixon spent four years creating the preconditions for what he called "peace with honor" in Vietnam. Those preconditions were not intended to salvage South Vietnam's independence. (They couldn't and they didn't.) They were designed to rebuild America's global geopolitical position.

Within two months of taking office, Nixon had appointed a commission to study the creation of an all-volunteer military. That could not be done right away because the army needed too many new enlistees—250,000 men were drafted in 1969. But Nixon started withdrawing U.S. combat troops from Vietnam that July. In November he signed legislation creating a draft lottery, which freed hundreds of thousands of draft-age young men from any realistic risk of conscription.

By the end of 1969 Nixon had reduced U.S. troop strength in Vietnam by 115,000. The next year he announced a two-year transition to an all-volunteer army and brought home almost 150,000 more troops. By the end of 1971 another 125,000 had been withdrawn, and the last U.S. combat troops left in August 1972. By then draft calls had already fallen 80 percent from Nixon's first year. The transition to an all-volunteer military was completed on July 1, 1973, by which time the last remaining American troops in Vietnam had been withdrawn under the terms of the Paris Peace Accords.

Moving to an all-volunteer military had other attractions for Nixon besides defusing student protests. Laissez-faire economists like Milton Friedman had long promoted the idea. Nixon himself had favored it in his 1960 presidential campaign.

It had other consequences as well. Peacetime conscription had not been part of the constitutional scheme because the framers never wanted a peacetime standing army. Instead, they envisioned a world where ordinary citizens, exercising their Second Amendment right to keep and bear arms—and knowing how to use them—could be readily assembled into state-commanded militias. In case of foreign war, these citizen soldiers, along with merchant sailors, could be quickly called on to swell the ranks of the small professional army and navy.

That eighteenth-century arrangement would have left America unprepared for the rapid mobilization it needed after Pearl Harbor. Roosevelt had persuaded a reluctant Congress to enact America's first peacetime draft in 1940. Truman's abortive postwar plan for universal military training, with all able-bodied men between the ages of eighteen and twenty required to undergo twelve months of military training and then remain on call for the next six years, would have resembled a modernized version of the framers' vision. But it never won congressional support.

So for the first quarter-century of the cold war, America maintained a large, peacetime standing army, based on conscription, and much of it was deployed overseas—in Europe, Japan, South Korea, the Philippines, and then Vietnam. This avoided one of the founders' nightmares—an overly powerful military force at home—but at the cost of triggering a different one: permanent military commitments overseas. The draft was not much of a political issue between Korea and Vietnam. It worked smoothly enough when most U.S. military interventions were brief and had broad popular support, although selective service distorted labor markets and treated (generally well-off) college students better than (generally less well-off) high school graduates and dropouts.

Johnson's rapid U.S. troop escalations in Vietnam put the system under heavy stress. By late 1966 monthly draft calls had risen to between 30,000 and 40,000. At those levels selective service was going to be a lot less selective, making students and other young men even more receptive to an antiwar movement that was already gathering strength. In the 1950s, being apolitical had seemed a smart career move to many students. In the late 1960s that seemed almost dangerous.

It would be overly simplistic to see the student antiwar movement as wholly or even mainly a function of the draft. But some connection is clear, and the framers probably would have wanted it that way, as yet another check on the waging of unwarranted, undeclared wars. Phasing out the draft bought Nixon time and political space to end the war his way.

The all-volunteer force has not provided the same kind of political check on presidential military adventurism but has instead encouraged the growth of a distinctive military culture, which is not particularly healthy for American constitutional democracy.

In the wake of Vietnam, army leaders like Creighton Abrams and Colin Powell wanted to ensure some kind of check on presidential war making. To that end, they designed the post-Vietnam military force structure to require reserve call-ups for major military operations. The theory was that disrupting the family lives and careers of adult reservists would have political costs that no president would want to incur lightly. Unfortunately, it has not worked out that way. The George W. Bush administration's overuse of reserves in Iraq and Afghanistan resulted in great hardships to the affected reservists but did not seem to seriously inhibit presidential war making.

Nixon used the time and political space he had bought to pursue his idea of "Vietnamization"—shifting military responsibility for the war back to the South Vietnamese forces whose ineffectiveness and weak morale had led to the introduction of American combat troops in the first place. By now no American military or political leader believed that South Vietnamese troops could be trained to take over. At most there was a wishful hope that President Nguyen Van Thieu could put together a government that might last a "decent interval" after a U.S. withdrawal.

There was no effective South Vietnamese military. If there had been, Johnson could have won the war. This was only about buying time: time to put the sequencing of Johnson's escalation into reverse. South Vietnam's military failed to perform. The United States went back to relying on airpower, which it knew from the Johnson years would not break

Hanoi's will. It wasn't meant to. It was meant to show that the United States had impressively destructive firepower that it could use without incurring the domestic political costs of using American ground troops.

Even Congress's careless delegation of its war powers went back through the time machine. In January 1971, after half the U.S. troops in Vietnam had been withdrawn, Congress repealed the Tonkin Gulf Resolution. In November 1973, after the Paris Peace Accords had been signed and all U.S. troops were gone, it passed the War Powers Act—limiting presidential authority to send troops into combat or imminent danger without congressional approval to ninety days. Although the War Powers Act left presidents far freer to wage undeclared wars than the Constitution's framers ever intended, neither Nixon nor any of his successors accepted the act's provisions as binding.

When Nixon spoke about having achieved "peace with honor" in Vietnam, he was not talking about honoring Washington's commitment to preserve an independent non-Communist South Vietnam. He was talking about preserving America's own global power and prestige. Vietnam could not be portrayed as an American victory, or even a draw, as Eisenhower had achieved in Korea. After the "decent interval" Nixon and Kissinger felt they had bought in Paris, Saigon would fall (as it finally did in April 1975, by which time Nixon himself had been brought down by Watergate). And in the zero-sum game of universal containment, defeat with honor did not exist.

So if there could be no escaping defeat, Nixon needed to escape universal containment instead. His diplomatic opening to China provided the perfect escape route, and Nixon was particularly well situated to pull it off. His long career as a zealous anti-Communist, reaching back to his scathing denunciations of Truman for having "lost" China in 1949, helped insulate him from attack when he wrote, in a 1967 *Foreign Affairs* article, "We simply cannot afford to leave China forever outside the family of nations." Instead, Nixon proposed a Kennan-style policy of containment and regional alliances aimed at moderating Chinese foreign and domestic policies so that China could be brought back into the international family.[1]

By 1967 there was a strong case to be made for reconsidering America's increasingly unrealistic policy of recognizing only Chiang Kai-shek's Nationalist government based in Taiwan, and Richard Nixon wasn't the only one making it. Some of Lyndon Johnson's advisers were also suggesting a more nuanced approach to Beijing. Johnson himself had privately mused about it as early as 1964. The Communist regime on the mainland was firmly established and not going to go away. So, by then, was the Sino-Soviet split. Furthermore, Communist China was now a nuclear power, having successfully exploded a nuclear bomb in 1964. Britain had recognized Beijing in 1950, France in 1964.[2]

But Johnson, still traumatized by the "losing China" argument used against Truman in 1949, took no action. He worried about what the Richard Nixons of the world might say about a new American opening. Richard Nixon never had to worry about that. And Johnson had gotten himself so tangled up in a version of the domino theory that cast Hanoi as China's proxy that he would have had a hard time explaining any China opening, even to himself.

Richard Nixon did not have that problem. He faced the opposite challenge of overturning the zero-sum logic of universal containment and collapsing dominoes so that he could execute a strategic retreat from Vietnam while still projecting global geopolitical strength.

Nor did Nixon have enough time for the lengthy process of containment and moderation he had alluded to in the 1967 article. Nixon's opening did not come in response to any moderation of Chinese Communism domestically or internationally. When Nixon took office in 1969, Mao's chaotic purge of party moderates known as the Cultural Revolution was in high gear. Internationally, Beijing was assailing Moscow for abandoning the cause of Marxist-Leninist world revolution. Yet barely two weeks after Nixon's inauguration, he began secretly exploring the idea of a bold new rapprochement with Beijing.

That rapprochement came about over the next three years primarily because Nixon needed to cover his retreat in Vietnam and because Beijing genuinely feared a preemptive nuclear attack by Moscow, perhaps with behind-the-scenes American approval and collaboration.[3]

Nixon and Kissinger prepared the China opening in secrecy, negotiating behind the backs of the State Department, Congress, and the American people. The first public hint of thawing relations came in April 1971, when China's national Ping-Pong team invited its American counterpart to visit the mainland, accompanied by five American journalists. Nothing like this had happened since the Communist takeover in 1949, and it was followed by a series of promising words and gestures. Then in early July, in a deal brokered by the military government of Pakistan, Kissinger himself secretly flew to Beijing and met with Zhou Enlai.

A few days later, on July 15, Nixon revealed that trip and announced that he had himself accepted an invitation to visit China early the following year "to seek the normalization of relations between the two countries and also to exchange views on questions of concern to the two sides."[4]

Nixon went to China the next February, meeting with Mao Zedong as well as Zhou. China was not prepared to normalize relations until Washington broke diplomatic ties and phased out military shipments to Chiang Kai-shek's Nationalist government on Taiwan. This was further than Nixon was prepared to go in 1972, although he didn't rule out the possibility of doing so later. Both sides settled for an ambiguous compromise formula, incorporated in points 11 and 12 of the lengthy Shanghai Communiqué at the end of Nixon's visit. Each side separately stated its own, somewhat different, view on the Taiwan question. The American version declared:

> *The United States acknowledges that all Chinese on either side of the Taiwan Strait maintain there is but one China and that Taiwan is a part of China. The United States Government does not challenge that position. It reaffirms its interest in a peaceful settlement of the Taiwan question by the Chinese themselves. With this prospect in*

mind, it affirms the ultimate objective of the withdrawal of all U.S. forces and military installations from Taiwan. In the meantime, it will progressively reduce its forces and military installations on Taiwan as the tension in the area diminishes.

Formal recognition was deferred (for another seven years, as it turned out). But Nixon and the Chinese had established the basis for an effective geopolitical partnership.

On other international issues, China made no verbal concessions to American sensibilities or Nixon's political needs. In point 6, for example, China stated:

Wherever there is oppression, there is resistance. Countries want independence, nations want liberation and the people want revolution—this has become the irresistible trend of history. . . . The Chinese side stated that it firmly supports the struggles of all the oppressed people and nations for freedom and liberation. . . . All foreign troops should be withdrawn to their own countries. The Chinese side expressed its firm support to the peoples of Viet Nam, Laos and Cambodia.

But this revolutionary posturing was largely for public show, as transcripts of closed-door meetings between the two sides in this era amply demonstrate.[5]

Secret contacts and closed-door understandings can be a useful tool of American diplomacy, a way of securing private commitments from foreign leaders that they dare not make in public. But when America's own leaders make binding commitments in the name of the American people, the norms of American constitutional democracy must be respected. Nixon and Kissinger did not respect those norms and played by their own emergency state rules. They deliberately bypassed State Department expertise in international law and in the history of U.S.-China relations. They made secret deals that bound the United States without anyone outside the Nixon White House knowing about it or having any policy input. They shared information and accountability only with each other.

The Shanghai Communiqué was neither lawyered in the executive branch nor debated and ratified in the legislative branch. Yet the United States has considered itself solemnly and irrevocably bound by the one-China formula of point 12 of that communiqué for the past forty years—worse, bound by China's particular interpretation of the communiqué's deliberately ambiguous formula. What has become America's most important bilateral relationship has also become essentially a presidential, rather than an institutional, constitutional relationship.

Nixon's opening did not directly lead to today's deeply entwined economic relationship between the United States and China. In 1972 the relationship, for both sides, was primarily about geopolitics and triangulating each side's previously one-to-one relationship with the Soviet Union.

For the United States, and for Nixon, it was primarily about redefining containment. By triangulating with China, Nixon could create the appearance of an American strategic outmaneuvering of Moscow that could provide cover for the otherwise embarrassing spectacle of defeat in and retreat from Vietnam.

By recognizing that Beijing and Moscow were great power rivals and not, as Johnson had continued to claim, a single Sino-Soviet Communist monolith, Washington could finally free itself from the unattainable requirement of universal containment. If a gain for Beijing could mean a loss for Moscow (or vice versa), the United States would no longer automatically stand to lose global credibility any time a Beijing-friendly or Moscow-friendly regime came to power. It was no longer a zero-sum world, and the United States had regained the freedom to fight back at times and places of its own choosing.

This post-Shanghai world Nixon had ushered in was a stage for ultra-realist contests for national advantage, not the kind of ideological struggles to which Truman, Eisenhower, Kennedy, and Johnson had summoned the nation. In some ways it harked back to FDR's calculating triangulations between Churchill and Stalin during the Second World War. At times it recalled Orwell's cynical world of *1984*, when war was permanent and only the name of the current enemy changed—"We have always been at war with Eastasia," the people of Orwell's Oceania are told, when, in fact, they have always been allied with Eastasia and at war with Eurasia.

That is surely what it looked like when the Carter administration gave America's covert blessing to China's 1979 invasion of Vietnam, less than a decade after Washington had finally extricated itself from years of costly warfare undertaken to keep Vietnam from falling to an advancing Chinese Communism.[6]

Nixon was seeking more than just an anti-Soviet partnership with Beijing. To maximize American geopolitical leverage, he wanted a real U.S.-Soviet-Chinese triangle. That required pursuing détente with Moscow—a process Eisenhower had begun, Kennedy had resumed, and Johnson had largely neglected in his obsession with Vietnam.

Nixon's new geopolitical triangle did not have to be equilateral. That would have tended to give equal standing to all three powers, which was not what Nixon had in mind. Nixon and Kissinger saw China as their more favored partner. It was weaker, poorer, and deeply frightened of Moscow, and therefore, they believed, it was less dangerous.

But Moscow was too dangerous a rival to ignore. And unless the nuclear arms race could be better managed, it threatened to weigh down the deficit-plagued American economy. Nixon's overall goal was restoring economic and military solvency to American power by more realistically matching policy goals to available resources.

That would require serious arms control negotiations with Moscow, conducted in ways that did not drive a renewed wedge of distrust between Washington and Beijing. Nixon and Brezhnev met three times between 1972 and 1974. The first of these meetings was less than three months after Nixon's trip to Beijing. The third was barely five weeks before Nixon resigned the presidency.

Arms control and expanded trade were the main themes of all three meetings. Under the Nixon-Kissinger theory of "linkage," granting Moscow better access to Western trade and investment would give Washington added leverage over Soviet behavior on a wide range of other issues.[7]

Détente served American and Soviet purposes in the 1970s. For the United States, it made it easier for Nixon and his immediate successors to escape the interventionist logic of universal containment during a period in which the American public refused to approve new military interventions (or even covert CIA operations, as in Angola in 1976). For the Soviet Union, it provided a way to safely manage relations with the United States and guard against a Chinese-American offensive military alliance directed against Moscow.

It was a formula for managed rivalry, not an end to the cold war. It applied most clearly to nuclear arms control and reducing tensions in Europe, least clearly to proxy battles in the third world, where nationalist mass movements and tottering dictatorships added to the volatile and combustible mix.

But in the hyperbolic habit of emergency state foreign policy discourse, Nixon and Kissinger oversold détente to the American people, deliberately leaving the impression that it would mean no more Soviet adventurism or support for leftist movements anywhere. Doing a Harry Truman in reverse, they "un-scared hell out of the American people." Their deceptive rhetoric, like Truman's, exacted a heavy price in years to come.

At Yalta, FDR had accepted the unpleasant reality that Stalin had already occupied Eastern Europe and would not give it up. He made a realist's bargain and traded what he could not change in Poland for Soviet cooperation on Japan and the United Nations. Similarly, Nixon recognized that he had no power to end the cold war, only to make its burdens more manageable for an America weakened by Vietnam.

By playing the China card and pursuing détente with Moscow, Nixon helped extricate Washington from the unsustainable burden of universal containment and better manage the costs and dangers of the nuclear arms race. These were substantial accomplishments. But Nixon, like FDR, oversold his accomplishments and concealed the messy realism of his diplomatic bargaining from the American people.

As Moscow opportunistically played out its own understanding of the newly managed rivalry in places like Africa and Afghanistan, much of the American public felt betrayed and angry and wanted to fight back. Much as in the 1940s, when Americans took offense at supposed Russian violations of Yalta provisions that they were sure existed but to which Stalin was equally sure he had never agreed, Americans were angered by Brezhnev's supposed violations of détente.

Just one month after announcing the China opening, Nixon announced a set of new and almost equally shocking departures in American economic policies. Dollars would no longer be automatically convertible to gold at the fixed rate specified under Bretton Woods. A 10 percent tax surcharge would be applied to all imports entering the United States. Domestic wages and prices would be frozen for ninety days.

The United States had earlier run balance-of-payments deficits, due in large part to the cost of maintaining international military bases and waging the Vietnam War. Recurring payment deficits put ever more paper dollars in foreign hands, but the positive U.S. trade balance and strong U.S. economy had kept the problem within manageable bounds.

By the early 1970s that was changing. In 1970 the U.S. annual inflation rate had climbed to 5.7 percent, the highest since the Korean War. In 1971 U.S. international trade accounts went into deficit for the first time in the twentieth century. That put still more paper dollars into foreign hands and weakened international confidence in American economic strength.

The foreign dollar holdings were not necessarily a problem, since the dollar was an international reserve currency. But the weakened international confidence was.

Rising U.S. inflation shrank the dollar's real value and made foreign dollar holders more eager to convert their depreciating paper money into gold, whose market value rose as the dollar fell. Increasing gold redemptions further bled U.S. dollar reserves, making paper dollar holders still more nervous about the currency's value.

Nixon felt he had to act. By closing the gold window, he halted the outflow of gold. Foreigners could no longer exchange their dollars for gold but could still use them as international reserves. Nixon had at least achieved a form of symptomatic relief, although U.S. trade deficits continued to grow, the dollar's floating market exchange rate against gold continued to sink, and once Washington lifted the wage and price controls that succeeded the initial freeze, U.S. inflation accelerated to higher levels than before.

The main architect of Nixon's new economic policy had been Paul Volcker, then serving as undersecretary of the treasury for monetary affairs. Its economic nationalism appealed to Volcker's boss, Treasury Secretary John Connally, who bluntly told European finance ministers that year that it was "our currency, but your problem."[8]

The new economic policy was also of a piece with Nixon's own foreign policy realism. Nixon never had much interest in or understanding of economics. But he believed he had grasped the underlying reality. Just as America's international geopolitical political leadership could no longer be based on the unrealistic pretensions of universal containment, its international monetary hegemony could no longer be based on the automatic trade surpluses America had effortlessly enjoyed during the early postwar years, when Europe and Japan were weakened competitors.

Much of Nixon's new economic policy—the wage and price controls, the import surcharge—was constructed on Keynesian-era assumptions about Washington's ability to steer the economy by managing domestic demand. Those assumptions had been undercut by the increasingly internationalized economic world of the 1970s, a world American foreign policy makers had worked hard to bring about. Europe and Japan had become increasingly tough competitors, multinational corporations used international transfer pricing and tax-avoidance strategies to stage end runs around government policies, and huge pools of offshore dollars now lay beyond direct U.S. regulatory control.

The most important lasting effect of Nixon's actions was the elimination of dollar-gold convertibility from the continuing dollar-reserve-based international monetary system. This freed the United States from the last visible constraints on its ability to run expanding trade, payments, and fiscal deficits.

That freedom was not much help to Gerald Ford or Jimmy Carter in their losing battles against stagflation. Globalization had progressed far enough to thwart traditional Keynesian demand-management tools but not yet far enough to bring its own new market-disciplining mechanisms into play. But starting about a decade later, with deregulation, declining union power, and the increasing availability of cheap consumer imports from newly transplanted factories in Asia, Nixon's jettisoning of dollar-gold convertibility helped make possible the credit-driven, low-inflation, stagnant-wage, high-consumption economy of the Reagan, G. H. W. Bush, Clinton, and G. W. Bush era.

On June 13 of that same eventful summer of 1971, *The New York Times* published the first installment of what came to be known as the Pentagon Papers. These were extensive excerpts from the Pentagon's forty-seven-volume secret internal history of America's involvement in Vietnam between 1945 and 1967. These classified studies were leaked to the *Times* by Daniel Ellsberg, a former State and Defense Department analyst who had helped compile the internal history.

Nixon's initial reaction to the publication was mild. He realized that the documents covered a period before his presidency, cast Kennedy and Johnson administration policies in an unflattering light, and made his own record of Vietnamizing the war and reducing American casualties look better, if only by comparison. And his instincts steered him away from prosecuting the *Times*, which could politically backfire on him, and toward identifying and prosecuting the actual leaker.[9]

But a series of conversations over the next few days with Alexander

Haig, Henry Kissinger, Attorney General John Mitchell, and others changed Nixon's mind. These subordinates initially seemed more upset at seeing the Pentagon Papers published than Nixon himself was. Kissinger worried about North Vietnam taking heart from American disarray and demoralization, about South Vietnam being embarrassed, and about other governments not being willing to share secrets with Washington. Mitchell was worried about losing a chance to stop the *Times* by not taking swift legal action.[10]

Nixon still had doubts, but on June 14 he authorized Mitchell to seek an injunction against the *Times*. The initiative came from Mitchell and represented a significant new assertion of emergency state power. Never before had an American court ordered prior restraint against a newspaper based on government claims of a national security threat.

The very next day a federal judge issued a temporary restraining order halting the *Times* from publishing further excerpts. Ellsberg then handed copies of the documents to *The Washington Post*, which began publishing them on June 18. Mitchell got a court order against the *Post*. But other newspapers began publishing excerpts, and finally, on June 30, the Supreme Court freed the *Times* and the *Post* to resume publication as well. That same day Daniel Ellsberg was indicted for espionage and theft.[11]

On July 24 Nixon authorized a special undercover unit that would later be known as the White House Plumbers. Its members came to include a former CIA agent, E. Howard Hunt, and a former FBI agent, G. Gordon Liddy. The Plumbers' first known operation was an illegal burglary at the office of Ellsberg's psychiatrist that September 3, seeking potentially damaging information on Ellsberg. Soon afterward Hunt and Liddy went to work gathering intelligence for Nixon's reelection campaign, and both played prominent roles in the June 17, 1972, illegal break-in at the Democratic National Committee's offices in the Watergate complex.

Nixon's initial reaction to the Pentagon Papers had been mild, perhaps because they did not disclose information about his own administration. But leaks that did reveal the workings of his administration could drive him to self-destructive excess. To him, such leaks justified the White House Plumbers, the Watergate cover-up, and the sweeping claims of executive privilege that the Supreme Court eventually struck down in *United States v. Nixon*. As Nixon revealingly explained his thinking to David Frost in 1977, "when the president does it that means that it is not illegal."[12]

That kind of thinking has little in common with American constitutional democracy. But it underlies many of the extraconstitutional practices of the emergency state.

Richard Nixon was a clear-sighted champion of the emergency state. He understood its needs almost intuitively and often responded to them with boldness and imagination. But his close personal identification with the emergency state also made him obsessively secretive, paranoid about enemies, and unusually prone to confuse his own political survival with national security.

In his first term, Nixon's fluent grasp of geopolitics allowed him to rescue the emergency state from grave crisis and lead it forward to new glories. But Nixon had no comparable fluency or interest in American constitutional democracy. His clumsy mishandling of the Watergate cover-up drew in and discredited three crucial pillars of the emergency state—the White House, the CIA, and the FBI. By the time of his forced resignation in August 1974, the emergency state stood exposed and discredited before the American people.

CHAPTER EIGHT

DAMAGE CONTROL

The final blow to Richard Nixon's presidency had been the so-called smoking gun tape, one of sixty-four tapes the Supreme Court ordered him to release after striking down his claim of absolute executive privilege in *United States v. Nixon* in late July 1974. The tape recorded Nixon signing off on a plan to enlist top CIA officials in the Watergate cover-up. Once it became public, Nixon's remaining supporters deserted him. Three days later Nixon announced his resignation.

The "smoking gun" conversation took place between Nixon and his chief of staff, H. R. Haldeman, on June 23, 1972, less than a week after the Watergate break-in. Haldeman tells Nixon that acting FBI director L. Patrick Gray (Hoover had died the previous month) had lost control of the criminal investigation. FBI agents were now beginning to trace some of the money paid to the Watergate burglars, which would have connected the break-in to Nixon's reelection campaign.

Nixon agrees to a plan suggested by Haldeman to help Gray shut down the FBI investigation. They agree to have the CIA director, Richard Helms, or his deputy, Vernon Walters, falsely tell Gray that the FBI was coming dangerously close to national security secrets relating to the Bay of Pigs invasion and that it now needed to back off. (Haldeman thought that that cover story would be persuasive to the FBI investigators because four of the five men arrested in the burglary were involved in anti-Castro politics in Miami.)

In legal terms, Haldeman's plan involved a criminal conspiracy to obstruct justice. Once Nixon had been heard agreeing to it, impeachment and conviction seemed certain, had he tried to remain in office.

The plan also involved crossing a dangerous domestic political threshold for the emergency state. The main purpose of the CIA was to give presidents the ability to operate abroad outside U.S. and foreign law. The agency's only real accountability was to the presidents it served. And direct presidential responsibility for CIA actions was shielded by the doctrine of "plausible deniability."

There were no traceable paper trails, no published budgets, no effective congressional or judicial oversight mechanisms. Granting a president such unchecked powers abroad ran counter to American constitutional democracy. Letting a president use those powers at home, as Nixon had done, for partisan political purposes and to conceal criminal acts, raised the chilling specter of presidential dictatorship.

Franklin Roosevelt and Lyndon Johnson had also abused emergency state powers for domestic political ends when they used the FBI to spy on law-abiding critics at home. Both had been insulated from any danger of impeachment by loyal Democratic Party congressional majorities. Richard Nixon was not.

Even before the "smoking gun" tape was revealed, the Democrats felt that Nixon, with his enemies lists and punitive tax investigations by the IRS, was using the expanded presidential powers of the emergency state for partisan political purposes. The "smoking gun" tape proved they were right and strengthened the legal case for impeachment. Once that tape was released, Nixon's last Republican defenders had to choose between saving the emergency state and trying to save Richard Nixon's already-doomed presidency. Not surprisingly, they chose the emergency state.

Gerald Ford became president. In emergency state terms, he was a somewhat ambiguous figure. He did not share Nixon's obsessive drive to expand presidential power, though as House minority leader he had helped enable Nixon's actions. Ford hoped to undo some of the harm Nixon had done in that regard. In his inaugural address he promised a presidency of "openness and candor," declaring, "our long national nightmare is over."

But Ford did not feel a sense of constitutional discomfort, as Eisenhower had, with the presidentially directed national security institutions built up since the Second World War. As a member of Congress from 1948, and part of the Republican leadership from the early 1960s, Ford had been a reliable supporter of those institutions. He had left his Yale Law School days as an America First, constitutionalist objector to presidential interventionism far behind.

Ford had been a consistent hawk on the presidentially waged Vietnam War and was one of the few members of Congress in whom Nixon had confided during the secret 1970 bombing of Cambodia. Later, Nixon had enlisted Ford's help in trying, unsuccessfully, to sustain his veto of the 1973 War Powers Act.[1]

That was one of Ford's last congressional battles as minority leader before Congress confirmed him as vice president in December 1973.

For the next nine months Ford continued to loyally support Nixon's foreign policies. But it wasn't just loyalty. After Ford became president, he kept most of those policies in place, as well as Nixon's partner in designing them, Henry Kissinger, whom he kept on as secretary of state and national security adviser.

Ford also kept on James Schlesinger, whom Nixon had moved from the CIA to the Pentagon in the last month of his presidency. To fill the vacancy this created at the CIA, Ford chose William Colby, an agency veteran, who had been in overall charge of pacification programs in Vietnam. That included the notorious Phoenix program, allegedly responsible for torture and the murders of more than 20,000 Vietnamese suspected of being Vietcong members or sympathizers. But once in the top job, Colby emerged as a reformer, pressing on with the investigation Schlesinger had already begun into past CIA activities that appeared to violate the agency's legislative charter. To replace Al Haig as White House chief of staff, Ford chose Donald Rumsfeld, a close political ally from the days both had served in the House, before Rumsfeld left Congress to work in the Nixon administration.[2]

The first part of Ford's presidency coincided with the "decent interval" Nixon and Kissinger had tried to establish between the Paris Peace Accords and the likely collapse of South Vietnam. The idea was to create enough distance between American withdrawal and South Vietnamese defeat to make these appear as almost separate events. In that way, they hoped to minimize the damage to America's international image and credibility.

The endgame turned out to be far more abrupt and messy than Nixon, Kissinger, and Ford had hoped. Khmer Rouge forces overran Phnom Penh on April 18, 1975, and took control of Cambodia. Less than two weeks later, on April 30, Saigon fell to the North Vietnamese army, amid frantic scenes of desperate Vietnamese trying to climb aboard the American helicopters evacuating the U.S. embassy and other strategic locations.

For months Ford and Kissinger had tried to direct blame for South Vietnam's deteriorating military position toward the Democratic-led Congress, which, after Watergate, had cut back American military aid more than 40 percent. That cut helped accelerate the timing of the final North Vietnamese offensive but did not affect its inevitable outcome. Not even half a million American troops had any realistic hope of preserving a non-Communist South Vietnam, as Nixon himself had clearly recognized more than six years earlier.[3]

Ford and Kissinger's protests over congressional aid cuts were sincerely felt and well served the purposes of the original "decent interval" strategy. The Ford administration could claim that America's South Vietnamese proxy had been defeated not by Communist arms abroad but by Democratic votes in Congress.

Similar motives led Ford to send American combat forces into action against the Khmer Rouge that May to rescue the crew of a U.S. merchant ship, the *Mayaguez,* that had been seized by armed Cambodian patrol boats in international waters. Ford and Kissinger believed that the capture of the *Mayaguez,* coming less than a month after the fall of the two Indochinese capitals, would send a dangerous message of American powerlessness and international vulnerability that could be effectively countered only by a display of Ford's willingness to use military force.

Carrier-based aircraft bombed Cambodia's main port and an air base while 175 Marines assaulted the offshore island where the *Mayaguez*'s crew was thought to be held. Eighteen Americans were killed and fifty wounded. By then the crew of the *Mayaguez* had already been released and set adrift. An American destroyer picked them up later in the day. Ford notified Congress of the military action following the formal notification procedures of the War Powers Act. He was the only president ever to do so. But by the time Ford notified Congress, the brief military action was over.

Ford had acted well within the historical tradition of presidents using their authority as commander in chief to order military action dating back to Thomas Jefferson and the Barbary pirates. Whether he acted wisely is a harder question, given the American fatalities and the safe release of the *Mayaguez*'s crew. What seems beyond dispute is that his main motive was not rescue but the international military reputation of the emergency state.

But after the Vietnam debacle, and even more after Watergate, the ground rules of presidential war making and related questions of military assistance changed significantly—though, as it turned out, only temporarily. The presidential powers of the emergency state were seriously and effectively challenged by the constitutional powers of an energized and critical Congress. Much of that new energy came from an electorate aroused by growing opposition to the Vietnam War and later by the public revelations of Constitution-threatening abuses of presidential power during Watergate.

In 1970 Democratic senator George McGovern and Republican Mark Hatfield introduced an amendment that would have cut off funds for U.S. military operations in Vietnam at the end of that year. The Senate voted it down in September by 55-39, a closer margin than anyone would have thought possible before Tet.

That December both houses invoked Congress's power of the purse to limit presidential war making by passing the bipartisan Cooper-Church amendment. Cooper-Church cut off further funding for U.S. military operations on the ground in Cambodia and Laos. (The stronger Senate version would also have cut off funds for U.S. air strikes in Cambodia unless specifically authorized by Congress.) It was enacted into law on January 5, 1971. Less than two weeks later Congress repealed the 1964 Gulf of Tonkin Resolution that Lyndon Johnson had used as congressional cover for the undeclared war.

In a separate congressional challenge to emergency state presidential overreach that year, in late June Democratic senator Mike Gravel entered 4,100 pages of the Pentagon Papers into the record of his Senate Subcommittee on Public Buildings and Grounds, where they could be publicly read aloud with constitutional immunity from prosecution.

In 1973, after the announcement of the Paris Peace Accords, Congress passed the bipartisan Case-Church amendment, which barred further U.S. military action in Cambodia, Laos, and Vietnam after August 15 of that year. That fall Congress passed the War Powers Act over Nixon's veto.

The midterm elections of 1974 strongly reinforced the ranks of insurgent senators and representatives determined to reassert the constitutional powers of legislative oversight that had fallen out of use during decades of emergency state presidencies. Nixon's abuses of unchecked presidential powers were still fresh in voters' minds—kept alive by Ford's decision that September to grant Nixon a full and unconditional pardon for "all offenses against the United States which he . . . has committed or may have committed or taken part in during his presidency."[4]

Ford's stated motive was to avoid a divisive trial. But by prematurely cutting off further judicial investigation of Nixon's possible criminal offenses, he divided the nation anew, raised suspicions of a possible preresignation deal, and helped the Democrats win an even larger congressional victory. The Democrats gained four Senate seats to extend their majority to 61-38, and added forty-nine in the House to give them a margin there of 291-144.[5]

Those results set the stage for what became known as "the year of intelligence"—1975. The new Congress got to work investigating past intelligence abuses, creating mechanisms for legislative oversight, and thereby, it hoped, restoring the lost constitutional balance. By the end of 1974 there was strong public demand for such efforts, thanks in considerable part to the investigative journalism of *New York Times* reporter Seymour Hersh (who five years earlier had been the first reporter to break the story of the My Lai massacre by American troops in Vietnam).[6]

On December 22, 1974, under the headline "Huge C.I.A. Operation Reported in U.S. Against Antiwar Forces, Other Dissidents in Nixon Years," a *Times* story by Hersh disclosed "a massive, illegal intelligence operation" against protesters during the Nixon years that reported directly to then–central intelligence director Richard Helms and maintained intelligence files "on at least 10,000 American citizens." It also described a long list of other illegal CIA activities inside the United States dating back to the 1950s, "including break-ins, wiretappings and the surreptitious inspection of mail." These latter activities had been uncovered, Hersh reported, when Helms's successor at the CIA, James Schlesinger, had ordered a search of the agency's domestic files.

Hersh's story caused shock waves in the country, in the Congress, and in the Ford White House, which quickly asked Schlesinger's successor, William Colby, what other dark revelations might still be lurking in the CIA files. As it turned out, there were plenty. While the White House quickly shifted into damage control mode, Congress pressed onward. On the last day of 1974, the outgoing Congress passed the Hughes-Ryan Act, which required presidents to report all future CIA covert operations to appropriate congressional oversight committees within a fixed time limit.[7]

On January 4, 1975, Ford appointed a blue-ribbon commission chaired by Vice President Nelson Rockefeller to investigate the illegal CIA domestic activities reported in Hersh's story. As Ford himself explained to an astonished group of *New York Times* editors at a January 16 White House lunch, he had carefully chosen a commission of responsible establishment types and limited their inquiry to domestic spying because, as he had learned in the CIA briefings he received after the Hersh article, still-secret CIA files pointed to a decades-long history of presidentially authorized assassination plots against foreign leaders.[8]

Ford was not looking for a cover-up and could not have gotten away with one in the public climate of 1975. The Rockefeller Commission uncovered useful information that the soon-to-be-formed congressional investigating committees put to good use. Ford's hope, rather, was to keep overall control of the investigation, and the definition of which CIA activities would remain off-limits to investigators, within the executive branch. That too was something that the climate of the times and the temper of Congress would not allow. The *Times* editors honored their understanding that Ford had been speaking off the record and did not report his new disclosure. But the word inevitably got around, and by the end of February Daniel Schorr reported it on the *CBS Evening News*.[9]

By then the Senate and House had already set up their own investigating committees on intelligence abuses. The Senate investigation, chaired by Frank Church, established constructive relations with Director of Central Intelligence William Colby (to Kissinger's fury) and over the next two years produced fourteen reports on a variety of abuses by domestic agencies like the IRS and the FBI as well as on CIA covert operations and National Security Agency violations of the Fourth Amendment. These reports provide an essential guide to the practices and mentality of the emergency state even today, since many of the abusive practices discovered and condemned in these reports have been revived since 9/11.

The House inquiry, originally chaired by Lucien Nedzi of Michigan but then shifted in July to Otis Pike of New York, took a more assertive approach, relying on Congress's power of the purse and its authority to subpoena witnesses and information. The Pike Committee resisted CIA attempts to shape its investigative agenda and restrict access to agency information. It sought to go beyond investigating illegal activities and abuses and aimed to establish real legislative oversight by vetting budgets and evaluating the effectiveness of agency programs.[10]

The CIA, backed by the Ford administration, resisted. The agency wanted to restore its public reputation after the sensational disclosures of 1974 and 1975, but not at the price of subjecting a key branch of the emergency state to the full range of congressional oversight envisioned by the Constitution. The Ford White House wanted an intelligence agency that remained an instrument of presidential foreign policy, with just enough oversight to spread political responsibility for any future abuses.[11]

The CIA felt, probably accurately, that at least some Pike Committee members and staff viewed much of what the agency had been doing with skepticism and suspicion. It viewed the committee and staff members with similar skepticism and therefore concluded that the people's representatives could not be trusted with the nation's security secrets. Chairman Pike insisted otherwise. But by the end of the year he had lost the argument. The December 23, 1975, assassination of the CIA's Athens station chief by a left-wing Greek terrorist group pointed to the potential human costs of poorly protected secrets. Although the Pike Committee had nothing to do with the Athens case, the Ford administration made effective use of it.[12]

On January 29, 1976, the House voted to withhold release of the Pike Committee report until the White House certified that doing so would have no adverse effects on CIA intelligence activities. That certification never came. But excerpts of the report were soon leaked to *The New York Times* and the full text to *The Village Voice*.

By this time the Ford administration had taken on a harder-line complexion after a series of late-1975 personnel changes that press commentators labeled the "Halloween Massacre." Trying to court conservative Republican support for the 1976 presidential election, Ford had moved to marginalize those the Republican right saw as too liberal (like Vice President Nelson Rockefeller), too cooperative with congressional investigating committees (like Director of Central Intelligence William Colby), too identified with détente (like Henry Kissinger), and too insubordinate to presidential authority (like Defense Secretary James Schlesinger).

Rockefeller announced he would not run for vice president in 1976. Ford recalled George H. W. Bush from Beijing to succeed Colby at the CIA. Kissinger remained secretary of state but was replaced as national security adviser by his deputy, Lieutenant General Brent Scowcroft. Donald Rumsfeld took over from Schlesinger at the Pentagon, and Rumsfeld's deputy, Dick Cheney, became White House chief of staff.

The analogy to Nixon's Constitution-straining "Saturday Night Massacre" during Watergate was overblown. But taken together, the personnel shifts represented a step back from Ford's earlier promises of transparency and healing toward the Nixon tradition of defending the expanded presidential powers of the emergency state.

That seemed particularly true of Rumsfeld and Cheney, who grew increasingly unhappy and even alarmed at the pruning back of aggrandized presidential powers by Congress and the courts. With the Ford administration not politically strong enough to halt this pruning process, which still enjoyed strong public support, the forty-four-year-old Rumsfeld and the thirty-five-year-old Cheney began their lengthy transformation into the grumpy not-so-old men of the emergency state. A quarter-century later they would return to power older and grumpier and determined to rebuild an even more powerful "unitary executive" than the one that had self-destructed during Vietnam and Watergate.

The memory of those constitutionally assertive Democratic Congresses of the mid-1970s is the nightmare that truly haunts today's big-government, strong-presidency conservatives and neoconservatives: not the doomed McGovern presidential campaign of 1972, not the politically inept and often flailing Carter presidency, but the successive Congresses that came remarkably close to reestablishing American constitutional democracy in the 1970s.

In 1976 the public was still behind an activist Congress. In November the Democrats retained their 61-38 Senate majority and picked up an additional House seat to give them a 292-143 margin there. And Jimmy Carter, a Georgia Democrat with no prior Washington experience, was elected president.

CHAPTER NINE

A DIFFERENT PATH

The late 1970s were unsettling for Americans—an era of stagnating real wages, accelerating inflation, and unaccustomed humiliations abroad, like the 444 days that American diplomats were held hostage by Iranian students in Tehran. President Jimmy Carter's responses to these challenges were generally ineffective and often inept.

Few would argue that Lyndon Johnson had responded effectively or skillfully to the challenge of Vietnam, or Richard Nixon to the declining dollar, rising trade deficits, and Watergate. But Johnson and Nixon (and later Reagan) knew how to look in command even when their decisions were disastrous. Americans had come to expect that commanding image from their presidents at least since the days of FDR and Truman.

Carter was different. Americans voted for him in 1976 as much for who he wasn't as for who he was. After a demoralizing series of failed presidencies and scandals, voters gravitated to a candidate who did not seem to be a bully and an arm-twister like Johnson, a schemer and a deceiver like Nixon, or a Washington insider like Ford. Carter also demonstrated that he could win the votes of white southern Democrats without being racially divisive like George Wallace. Americans wanted to feel good about themselves and their role in the world again. They wanted a government that did not conceal war plans, plant wiretaps, and commission political black bag jobs. Carter promised that he "would never lie" to them.

But what kind of leader would Carter be? Not since Calvin Coolidge had anyone with so little experience on the national stage become president.

His inaugural address signaled a clear change in direction. In place of the martial exhortations and global pretensions of his recent predecessors, Carter invoked the democratic dreams of the founding fathers. "I have no new dream to set forth today," he declared, "but rather urge a fresh faith in the old dream."

He hoped, by the end of his term, to have "enabled our people to be proud of their own government once again." To earn that pride, he would end the bankrupting overstretch of universal containment and the alien amorality of cold war realpolitik. "We have learned that 'more' is not necessarily 'better,' that even our great nation has its recognized limits, and that we can neither answer all questions nor solve all problems." And "to be true to ourselves, we must be true to others. We will not behave in foreign places so as to violate our rules and standards here at home."

This was an ambitious agenda, however modestly stated. New dreams are standard inaugural fare. To summon "fresh faith in the old dream" required reversing the habits and expectations built up over the past four decades of American history. It required dismantling the emergency state and reinforcing constitutional democracy. To rebuild America's shattered self-confidence and lead it in a significantly different direction required leadership qualities, and an understanding of Washington, that Carter turned out not to have. In the end, it was not enough to just not be Johnson, Nixon, or Ford.

Carter's presidential candidacy had been shaped by the same national experiences and political currents that had led legislators from both parties to reassert Congress's constitutional war-making and oversight powers—that is, by Johnson's escalations and failures in Vietnam, by Nixon's abuses of executive privilege and emergency state agencies in Watergate, and by press revelations about CIA complicity in domestic spying and foreign assassination plots.

Yet Carter and the congressional constitutionalists had very different ideas about how to right these emergency state wrongs. Carter wanted to go back to the democratic dreams of Jefferson's Declaration of Independence. Congress wanted to go back to the democratic structures of Madison's Constitution.

Carter blamed the cynical and militarized foreign policies of Johnson and Nixon for betraying America's founding dreams and believed that his own policies promoting democracy and human rights would renew them. Carter's ideas about democracy owed more to Hollywood's *Mr. Smith Goes to Washington* than to the structural blueprint of the American Constitution.

The constitutionalists in Congress took a more structural approach. They believed that the pattern of constitutional abuses and foreign policy failures revealed by the Pentagon Papers, Watergate, and the Church and Pike investigations pointed to a breakdown of the system of checks and balances that the founders had carefully erected to preserve democratic government. They wanted to monitor and prevent future presidential abuses by restoring the balance between the legislative and executive branches. That required effective new oversight mechanisms and tightened legislative charters for emergency state agencies like the CIA, the FBI, and the National Security Agency, which secretly monitored the electronic communications of American citizens in defiance of the privacy guarantees and warrant requirements of the Fourth Amendment.

Different ideas about the role of Congress and an almost complete lack of personal trust divided Carter's inner circle of Washington outsiders from Senate constitutionalists in both parties like Frank Church, Charles Mathias, Birch Bayh, Mark Hatfield, and Ted Kennedy and their House counterparts like Leo Ryan, Pete McCloskey, Ron Dellums, and Otis Pike.

Carter long suspected Kennedy of plotting behind his back to restore Camelot. Relations between House Speaker Tip O'Neill and Carter's chief political aide Hamilton Jordan were notoriously icy.[1]

These legislators had rallied their colleagues to defend the Constitution against emergency state power grabs under Nixon and Ford. They were prepared to cooperate with Carter in creating new arrangements more consistent with American constitutional democracy. And in some cases they and Carter reached compromises that put in place workable mechanisms for congressional and judicial oversight of executive branch powers.

Responding to the abuses uncovered by the Church and Pike committees, Congress passed the Foreign Intelligence Surveillance Act (FISA) of 1978, which reinstituted warrant requirements for intelligence wiretaps of domestic phone conversations. Carter willingly signed FISA. And he honored the spirit of the Freedom of Information Act by banning the classification of documents that were clearly unrelated to national security. For the first time in the emergency state era, U.S. government officials were asked to consider the public's right to know when classifying information.

But Carter took few initiatives of his own to harness congressional support for a constitutionally based presidency and foreign policy, and by the end of his term, he had reversed direction, in pursuit of greater secrecy and less presidential accountability, seeking and obtaining the repeal of the 1974 Hughes-Ryan Act, which had expanded congressional oversight of covert action.

In its place, Congress passed the Intelligence Oversight Act of 1980, which set detailed rules for reporting covert intelligence operations to the responsible oversight committees in each house. But the 1980 act also allowed the president to defer notification of covert action if he felt it was necessary to do so—a huge loophole that the Reagan administration would use to authorize the secret arms deals with Iran that helped finance the criminal follies of the Iran-Contra affair.

Carter's failure to work more effectively with Congresses in which his party held clear majorities was not simply a result of personality conflicts and Carter's lack of Washington experience. Similar problems later plagued Bill Clinton and Barack Obama. One underlying cause was that for the past forty years, successful Democratic Party presidential candidates have had to assemble their nationwide majorities around a much broader mix of electoral constituencies than those that typically vote for Democratic senators and representatives in the party's main legislative bases.

In the 1970s congressional Democrats still generally looked to the party's traditional voting base of blue-collar and public-sector union members and minority groups in urban industrial areas of the Northeast, Midwest, and Pacific coast. That gave them a strong interest in pushing for union-friendly laws and regulations, a strengthened social safety net, and steady flows of federal dollars to local contractors and municipal governments.

But successful Democratic presidential candidates could not afford to write off the South's 166 electoral votes. Nor could they disregard the growing demographic weight of the suburbs—where more than 40 percent of Americans now lived. This helps explain why southern governors won the Democratic presidential nomination four times between 1976 and 1996. It also helps explain why so much of Jimmy Carter's legislative agenda failed to spark much enthusiasm among congressional Democrats.[2]

As a Washington outsider, Carter imagined that he and his pollsters could directly commune with the voters over the heads of Congress. That formula had succeeded on the campaign trail. But it left Carter without the firm political base and the Washington allies he needed to survive the relentless succession of crises and partisan attacks that every president faces, let alone the political space to engineer fundamental changes in the nation's outlook and policies.

When U.S. diplomats were taken hostage in Iran in November 1979, when Russian troops poured into Afghanistan that December, and when inflation neared 15 percent in the spring of 1980, Americans looked to Carter for the kind of stirring words and stirring actions (if not necessarily stirring results) that four decades of emergency state presidencies had accustomed them to expect. Instead, Carter offered introspection, an unsteady hand, and erratic policies. His reputation, and his presidency, never recovered.

That failure to meet public expectations of presidential leadership had enormous and lasting significance, because in its clumsy way Carter's vision of a renewed American democracy and a less ideological, less militarized, liberal internationalism represented a realistic alternative to the emergency state. And he offered it at a time when the dangers of continuing down the emergency state path were conspicuously evident—Vietnam, Watergate, fiscal problems at home, and dollar problems abroad. The moment was ripe, the alternative was realistic, Carter's commitment was genuine, and the tremendous power of the American presidency stood behind him.

Jimmy Carter was an ambitious politician, but he was neither a cynical nor a particularly worldly man. He believed in his family, in his born-again Christian faith, and in America. When he promised a government as good as the American people, he sincerely meant it. His vision of governmental virtue harked back to what he believed were the unpretentious simplicities of the early American republic.

After delivering his inaugural address, Carter forswore the ceremonial ride to the White House in the presidential limousine and instead took a forty-minute walk down Pennsylvania Avenue to his new home. He cut the size of the White House staff by a third and went through the first two years of his term without a chief of staff. He installed solar panels on the White House roof and a wood-burning stove in the living quarters.

His actions set a good presidential example for a country that needed to restrict wasteful energy consumption and a government that needed to cut back on unnecessary hiring. But they had no real relation to rolling back the emergency state and returning to the constitutional democracy of America's earlier days.

In a May 1977 commencement speech at Notre Dame, Carter presented his new foreign policy vision, one he described as connecting "our actions overseas with our essential character as a nation." He proposed "a foreign policy that is democratic, that is based on fundamental values, and that uses power and influence, which we have, for humane purposes." That last idea owed more to Woodrow Wilson than to the founding fathers. But it was a striking departure from the emergency state vision of NSC-68, of a democracy forced to act like its totalitarian enemies in order to defeat them. Carter explicitly repudiated that view and cataloged some of its baleful consequences.

"For too many years," he acknowledged, "we've been willing to adopt the flawed and erroneous principles and tactics of our adversaries, sometimes abandoning our own values for theirs. We fought fire with fire, never thinking that fire is better quenched with water. This approach failed," Carter concluded, "with Vietnam the best example of its intellectual and moral poverty. But through failure we have now found our way back to our own principles and values, and we have regained our lost confidence."

In words he would later repudiate, Carter boldly declared that "being confident of our own future, we are now free of that inordinate fear of communism which once led us to embrace any dictator who joined us in that fear." And in a call for transparency that was at once an indictment of his predecessors' secretiveness and an exoneration of the American people—who were innocent, because they had been kept ignorant, of what was being done in their name—he promised "a foreign policy that the American people both support, and, for a change, know about and understand."

Carter's new foreign policy agenda would be defined by a worldwide commitment to free speech and individual human rights, détente with Russia and China, nuclear and conventional arms control, aid for the developing world, peace negotiations between Israelis and Arabs, and support for black majority rule in white-ruled southern Africa. In place of military confrontation between the Communist East and capitalist West, there would be a partnership for development between the rich North and the poor South.

Carter understood that in the circumstances of 1977 there would be little public support for sending American soldiers into combat abroad again unless the nation's security was directly and obviously threatened. His ambitious policy goals would therefore rely on what we now call soft power, the power of America's economy and example, rather than the use or threat of American military force. Or as he explained it, "We can no longer expect that the other 150 nations will follow the dictates of the powerful, but we must continue—confidently—our efforts to inspire, to persuade, and to lead."[3]

Carter was turning his back on more than a quarter-century of assertive American leadership, of universal containment, of scaring the hell out of an American people that six previous presidents had assumed would otherwise revert to an instinctive isolationism. And he was premising this enormous change on a new national self-confidence in the world barely two years after American confidence had been shattered by the sight of desperate Vietnamese clinging to helicopters evacuating the last Americans from Saigon.

Perhaps an FDR or a Ronald Reagan could have rallied Americans at such a moment to head off in entirely new policy directions. Jimmy Carter certainly wanted to. But he lacked the instinctive political touch and the solid political base, in Washington and in the country at large, to pull it off. From the beginning, the Carter administration was hobbled by an unbridgeable contradiction—a president who wanted to shed the imperial optics of his recent predecessors but still expansively use the presidential powers of the emergency state at home and abroad.

A more fundamental problem came from the internal inconsistencies of Carter's foreign policy vision and its disconnectedness from American historical traditions. Carter's human rights policy was supposed to be universal, applicable to right-wing dictators aligned with the United States as well as left-wing dictators aligned with the Soviets. But the single standard Carter had proclaimed was hard to apply and harder to explain to many Americans while the cold war still raged.

Criticizing Moscow and Havana for imprisoning dissidents and restricting immigration might tarnish the international reputation of America's enemies. Criticizing the shah of Iran for systematic torture and ordering his army to fire on civilian protest marchers could undermine a strategic ally's hold on power. America would be safer and better liked if its allies were more respectful of their people's human rights. But Carter had inherited a lot of allies who didn't see it that way, and getting from here to there could be perilous.

Shifting the spotlight from East-West to North-South concerns was also a problematic idea, especially with armed East-West conflicts still playing out in Africa. The North-South phraseology of those days was always more of a European intellectual fashion than an American one. Much of the global South had only recently emerged from European colonialism, its development stunted by its enforced subordination to a European-imposed international division of labor.

For the European center-left, *North-South* was a euphemism for economic reparations. The United States, as the richest nation of the global North, could have contributed to this process and earned political goodwill. But it all sounded naïvely altruistic to many American ears. A more politically promising course for Carter would have been to return to the earlier rhetoric of Franklin Roosevelt and Kennedy, which had cast the United States as a longtime foe of European colonialism with a special commitment to third-world development.

Many of the inherent tensions in Carter's new foreign policy paradigm played out within the administration itself. The State Department, under Cyrus Vance, pressed détente, North-South issues, and human rights, while the National Security Council, under Zbigniew Brzezinski, pushed back with more traditional realpolitik positions grounded in the cold war.

At home, Carter repeatedly sought to bypass Congress and reach out to public opinion through television. He never learned how or why to work with Congress, although he had strong Democratic majorities in both houses throughout his term. Abroad, Carter wanted to be the opposite of Richard Nixon. But his most influential foreign policy adviser, Zbigniew Brzezinski, wanted to outdo Henry Kissinger in grandiose geopolitical theorizing and running foreign policy out of the White House.

Carter talked about returning to America's founding principles, but he never seemed to grasp the essence of the founding constitutional design. His commitment to honesty and transparency in government and a less militarized foreign policy would surely have pleased the framers of our constitutional system. But for them, the more fundamental point was preserving liberty and preventing tyranny by ensuring that presidential powers would never push beyond the limits of congressional oversight and the restraining power of the purse.

Carter himself was not an overreaching president, although some of the policies he pursued in his last year in office—on Afghanistan, Iran, and credit controls, for example—had no firm constitutional basis. Repairing American constitutional democracy after three decades of the emergency state required an experienced veteran of national politics, a Mr. Madison, not a Mr. Smith.

Carter's signature domestic initiative was energy independence. It concerned foreign policy as well. Americans had been surprised and angered by the temporary oil embargo that Arab exporters had imposed in retaliation for American support of Israel in the October 1973 Midcast war. The sharply higher gasoline prices and long gas station lines that that embargo briefly produced were a rare post-1945 instance of visible economic pain at home as a direct result of American foreign policy choices abroad.

Cheap oil had long been considered an American birthright, guaranteed by America's military victory in World War II and essential to the mobile, high-consumption American lifestyle. Price rises dictated by third-world oil producers, like defeat by third-world Communist armies, were not supposed to happen in a world shaped by the American emergency state. By the time Carter came to office, the immediate crisis of the Arab oil embargo had passed. But as Carter recognized, the underlying dynamics of supply and demand were making America ever more vulnerable to foreign pressure.

Carter strongly believed that rebuilding self-confidence at home and regaining the freedom to make wise foreign policy choices abroad depended on reducing America's foreign oil dependence through an aggressive government-led program of increasing energy efficiency and developing alternative energy sources from coal and nuclear to solar power and synthetic fuels.

Not only would this program blunt the effect of any future Arab embargoes, Carter argued, but it would protect the environment at home and would challenge and strengthen American democracy. Carter called it, in a phrase originally coined by the early-twentieth-century American philosopher William James, "the moral equivalent of war." His critics soon reduced this to "MEOW."

Some of Carter's energy predictions proved too pessimistic. He claimed, for example, that world energy demand would exceed world supplies by the late 1980s. That underestimated the extent to which rising real prices would lead to new exploration and would make reserves that were more costly to extract economically viable.

But on the most important fundamentals, Carter was exactly right. Artificially low prices had made Americans the world's most wasteful energy consumers. Until 1970 America had produced more oil than it consumed. But excessive consumption was now making the United States increasingly, and needlessly, import dependent.

Carter understood that greater American dependence on imported oil would increasingly draw the United States into Persian Gulf quarrels that it could otherwise stand aloof from or help mediate. He also understood that conservation through increased energy efficiency was the cheapest way to narrow the gap between American demand and domestic supply. And more efficient energy consumption could help protect America's environment. A national program of energy conservation, improved efficiency, and development of alternative fuels could create hundreds of thousands of new jobs in the United States.

Carter's televised energy addresses to the nation were remarkable in tone. They addressed Americans as adults, without sugarcoating or condescension. In the first such speech, in April 1977, Carter's very first words were: "Tonight I want to have an unpleasant talk with you about a problem unprecedented in our history."

Instead of falsely reassuring Americans that they were more virtuous than others elsewhere, Carter accurately reported that "ours is the most wasteful nation on earth. We waste more energy than we import. With about the same standard of living, we use twice as much energy per person as do other countries like Germany, Japan and Sweden."

Instead of telling Americans how much better off they were now than in the days of his Republican predecessors, Carter correctly warned that things were getting worse: "I know that some of you doubt that we face real energy shortages. The 1973 gasoline lines are gone, and our homes are warm again. But our energy problem is worse tonight than it was in 1973 or a few weeks ago in the dead of winter. It is worse because more waste has occurred, and more time has passed without our planning for the future. And it will get worse every day until we act."

If America did not act, Carter warned, "we will live in fear of embargoes. We could endanger our freedom as a sovereign nation to act in foreign affairs. . . . Inflation will soar, production will go down, people will lose their jobs."[4]

To avoid these consequences, Carter proposed a variety of measures, including a national energy strategy, the creation of a strategic petroleum reserve, and incentives for home insulation and for solar and other alternative energy projects.

Carter's program supplemented the automobile fuel economy standards Congress had enacted in 1975. These required year-by-year step-ups in the average miles-per-gallon performance of new cars. From a starting point of 13 miles per gallon in 1975, performance requirements more than doubled to 27.5 by 1985. That helped reduce American oil imports by more than 40 percent, to 1.85 billion barrels in 1985—roughly one-third of what Americans consumed that year. Had the year-by-year step-ups continued, America could have further substantially reduced its dependence on foreign oil, with positive consequences ranging from lower trade deficits to greater freedom of action in our foreign and military policies.

Instead, regulation, like adult presidential speechmaking, fell out of favor. Candor and calls for sacrifice had helped make Carter a one-term president, and none of his successors wanted to repeat that experience.

Fuel economy requirements for cars remained stuck at 27.5 miles per gallon for the next twenty years. Meanwhile actual fuel efficiency declined, as low gas prices and laissez-faire energy policies encouraged millions of Americans to switch to oil-guzzling SUVs, which did not count against the passenger car standards because they were classified as light trucks. By 2006 oil imports had risen to nearly 5 billion barrels—more than two-thirds of annual consumption.[5]

Jimmy Carter's hopes for a new direction in foreign policy began unraveling almost from the start. The first portent of trouble came in the unexpectedly strong Senate opposition to treaties Carter negotiated in 1977 to transfer control of the Panama Canal to Panama. The negotiating effort had originally been bipartisan—begun under Lyndon Johnson, nearly concluded under Richard Nixon, and finalized under Carter. All had seen it as a way to phase out an anachronistic colonial vestige dating to Theodore Roosevelt and remove a chronic irritant in U.S.–Latin American relations.

But by the time Carter submitted the two treaties to the Senate, Ronald Reagan and other critics had stirred up a petulant, nationalist reaction, falsely claiming that ratification would endanger America's military security and access to the canal. After a long and bruising fight, which saw John Wayne weighing in on Carter's side, the treaties were ratified, with just one vote to spare.

The message seemed to be that the American people wanted an end to Vietnam-style military interventions but were not willing to scale down their geopolitical expectations of controlling events abroad. They wanted a respite from the excesses of the emergency state but weren't interested in a new and different foreign policy paradigm. They would object to anything that looked like an American retreat, even a relatively costless one with offsetting benefits in foreign goodwill. And they expected Carter to stand by even the most unattractive American clients from the old paradigm, like the Nicaraguan dictator, Anastasio Somoza, and the shah of Iran, when their power was threatened.

Complicating Carter's problems, the Soviet Union wasn't interested in a new paradigm either. Moscow was even having second thoughts about détente. The liberalized access to the American economy that Nixon and Kissinger had promised the Kremlin fell through after congressional neoconservatives attached the Jackson-Vanik amendment to the 1974 trade act. That linked Soviet trade benefits to free emigration rights for Soviet Jews and others who wished to leave.

Jackson-Vanik was a higher domestic price than Brezhnev was prepared to pay. For Moscow, Vietnam had been neither a defeat nor a lesson in imperial overstretch. It had been an energizing victory for their client and ally, North Vietnam. Soviet leaders feared China as a threat and a rival. But that mainly spurred them to increase their support for third-world revolutionary movements to keep these from moving into Beijing's camp.

By the time the Panama Canal treaties were ratified in the spring of 1978, both Somoza and the shah were in deep political trouble. Carter did not move reflexively to save them, as earlier presidents probably would have done, and as many Americans now expected and urged him to do. Nor did he move boldly to distance Washington from the increasingly violent and repressive efforts of these traditional American clients to remain in power, as the new foreign policy vision of his Notre Dame speech had suggested he would.

Instead, Carter hesitated, probably the worst possible course of action under the circumstances. Washington did not recognize the severity of either crisis until it was too late. Carter's belated policy responses were consistently out of phase with rapidly moving events. What might have helped earlier had become futile or even counterproductive by the time it was tried.

Granted, there were no easy or obvious answers to either crisis. The rot in both regimes had been building for years. So had the elemental anger of the regimes' opponents. It was Carter's bad luck that the explosions happened on his watch. They also happened at a time when no American president could have credibly threatened to use military force to back up Washington's diplomatic pressures.

• • •

Nicaragua did not have much real geopolitical importance to the United States in 1978. But after more than a century and a half of the Monroe Doctrine and almost twenty years of Fidel Castro, many Americans felt that it did. Besides, Nicaragua was just a few hundred miles from the Panama Canal and had a long history of American military and political interference. U.S. Marines had occupied the country from 1912 to 1933. When the Marines departed, they left behind a U.S.-trained and -organized military force, the Nicaraguan National Guard, whose leader had been handpicked by the American ambassador.

That National Guard leader was Anastasio Somoza García, whose son, Anastasio Somoza Debayle, was Nicaragua's president in 1978. It was in reference to the senior Somoza that FDR reportedly said, "Somoza may be a son of a bitch, but he's our son of a bitch." Whether or not Roosevelt actually uttered those words, they suggestively convey the early relationship between Washington and the Somozas. Somoza still had powerful supporters in the U.S. Congress, and Carter was reluctant to offend them, particularly while the Panama Canal treaties and other administration legislation hung in the balance.[6]

By 1978 the opposition to Somoza was being led by a far-left guerrilla movement, the Sandinista Front for National Liberation. The front took its name from Augusto Sandino, who had led a revolt against the earlier U.S. Marine occupation and had been murdered by the elder Somoza in 1934. This conflict, and its pro- and anti-American elements, had deep historical roots.

But Carter's foreign policy makers had other historical parallels in mind. Robert Pastor, the director of Latin American affairs at the National Security Council, recalled Washington's complicity in the overthrow and death of Salvador Allende in Chile five years earlier, and argued against any U.S. attempt to remove Somoza from power. Anthony Lake, the director of policy planning at the State Department, had lived through the unhappy consequences of Washington's support for the 1963 coup in South Vietnam that overthrew and killed Ngo Dinh Diem. Those prior experiences led both men to oppose any early U.S. effort to hasten Somoza's removal—at a time when moderate forces still might have been able to take over and hold off the Sandinista challenge, or at least prevent the complete Sandinista takeover that occurred in July 1979. In the end Somoza fared no better than Diem or Allende. He was gunned down by a Sandinista hit squad in Paraguay in September 1980.[7]

The Nicaraguan crisis only began to get serious attention in Washington in January 1978, when the murder of a leading anti-Somoza newspaper editor, Pedro Joaquín Chamorro, enraged and polarized public opinion. Venezuela's center-left president, Carlo Andrés Pérez, urged Carter to ease Somoza out of power and help Nicaragua's non-Communist opposition take over. Instead, Carter sent a particularly ill-timed letter to Somoza, praising him for the alleged progress he was making on human rights issues and national reconciliation. But by then it may already have been too late to promote a moderate third force, particularly with Chamorro no longer around to lead it.[8]

Pérez, a friend of Chamorro's and close to Carter, feared that a far-left revolution in Nicaragua could set off shock waves in democratic Venezuela, where social divides were widening between a narrow and affluent bipartisan elite and a poor and frustrated majority. Once the Sandinistas were in power, Pérez favored trying to work with the movement's more moderate elements. Carter took a similar view, maintaining diplomatic relations with the new Sandinista government and continuing American aid to Nicaragua until the day he left office.

Iran, unlike Nicaragua, had enormous geopolitical significance. It was OPEC's second-largest oil producer, it bordered on the Soviet Union, and it had purchased billions of dollars in sophisticated weaponry from the United States—more than $5 billion worth in 1977 alone. The shah, who owed his throne to the CIA, had been designated as America's regional guarantor of Persian Gulf security under the Nixon Doctrine. "Protect me," Nixon had said to the shah in 1972. Carter himself had toasted the shah in Tehran in December 1977 for making Iran "an island of stability in one of the more troubled areas of the world," even though by then the angry demonstrations that would drive the shah from power thirteen months later had already begun.[9]

Carter was flattering an important ally, not offering a dispassionate analysis. But considering Iran's importance to American policy and the CIA's long involvement in Iranian affairs—the United States had helped organize and train SAVAK, the shah's notorious secret police agency—it was telling that Washington did not seem to understand until very late in the Iranian crisis that the shah might actually be overthrown.

Here was a country where the full panoply of the emergency state had long been deployed in what Washington clearly considered a strategic relationship. But the close military, intelligence, and diplomatic relations between Washington and Tehran served to blind American policy makers rather than give them any special insight or leverage. Because American policy was wedded to the shah, American diplomats and intelligence agents made very little effort to find out about or contact his critics. The CIA relied too much on its sources in SAVAK. The White House, State Department, and U.S. embassy lived by the assumptions of the Nixon Doctrine. One unhappy consequence was that during the decisive year of 1978, American policy frequently seemed paralyzed and at least one step behind the rush of revolutionary events.[10]

Conditioned by years of cold war rivalry, Carter administration officials theorized about the intentions of the pro-Moscow Tudeh party and overlooked the rising strength of the revolutionary Islamic followers of Ayatollah Ruhollah Khomeini. In August 1978 the CIA reported that the shah's grip on power was not threatened. The next month the Defense Intelligence Agency said that he was "expected to remain actively in power over the next ten years." Four months later he was gone.[11]

The wisest policy for Washington in 1978, had it understood what was really going on, would have been to seek out and work with moderate elements both inside and outside the shah's regime in the hope of preserving constructive relations whether or not the shah remained in power. But even by then, it may well have been too late. The forces that toppled the shah were so elemental, so much a product of twentieth-century Iranian history, and so many years in the making that there probably was not much Carter could have done to deflect them. And the well-known (to Iranians) history of the CIA's leading role in the 1953 coup was a trump card in the hands of the revolution's most radical and anti-American element—the followers of Ayatollah Khomeini.

Still, America's intelligence failures and clumsy and inconsistent policy responses contributed to the growing feeling among Americans that Carter did not know what he was doing on important foreign policy issues and that America's prestige and security in the world, already damaged by Vietnam, were being further damaged by his mistakes. Selling Americans on a new foreign policy paradigm required a sure and steady hand, and Carter did not have one.

The most damaging blow of all was the radical student takeover of the American embassy in Tehran on November 4, 1979, in which sixty-three American diplomats were taken hostage, along with three more seized at the Iranian foreign ministry. Some of the hostages were released later that month, but fifty-two were held captive for the 444 remaining days of the Carter administration.

Carter's decision the previous month to let the exiled shah come to the United States for cancer treatment was a serious mistake. The shah could easily have received appropriate medical treatment elsewhere, and the United States was having a hard enough time looking out for its basic security and economic interests in a turbulent revolutionary Iran without handing the perfect symbol of continued U.S. loyalty to the shah to America's worst Iranian enemies. The U.S. embassy in Tehran had counseled strongly against it, but Brzezinski had convinced Carter to go ahead, urged on by Henry Kissinger, David Rockefeller, and other American friends of the shah.[12]

Admitting the shah provided the immediate pretext for the embassy takeover. But the real cause was the power struggle between the radical followers of Ayatollah Khomeini and other elements of Iran's original broad revolutionary coalition. The U.S. embassy served as a powerful symbol for the radical mullahs because it evoked the toxic legacy of the CIA's role in the overthrow of Mossadegh in 1953.

Further, the Islamic radicals suspected that with access to the embassy files, they could show that some of their more moderate rivals in the provisional revolutionary government had maintained contacts with U.S. diplomats. That would not have been very surprising, since members of that government openly favored maintaining correct relations with the United States. These considerations help explain the radical students' references to the embassy as a spy nest and their efforts to piece together shredded embassy documents to implicate their Iranian political rivals.

Carter, the hostages, and the United States became helpless pawns in the bloody internal power struggle for control of the Iranian revolutionary state. Carter's efforts to negotiate the hostages' release through Iranian president Bani-Sadr's government were exploited by the radical clerics to humiliate Carter and discredit Bani-Sadr, whom they eventually forced out of office in 1981.

America's humiliation was compounded when Carter, despairing of diplomacy, ordered a secret and poorly prepared rescue raid that ended with no rescue but a fiery crash between two of the mission's aircraft, killing eight American soldiers.

Conservatives saw the failed rescue mission as further evidence that Carter did not understand how to use military force to protect American interests. Liberals wondered what had happened to Carter's new foreign policy paradigm. Secretary of State Cyrus Vance resigned in protest over the episode.

In late December 1979, just over two months after the American hostages were seized in Tehran, the Soviet Union sent what soon amounted to more than 100,000 troops into Afghanistan.

Neoconservatives and cold warriors in Washington, already alarmed over what they viewed as a pattern of Soviet pressures and American retreats since Vietnam, saw the invasion as a primal challenge to American global interests. It was the first time since 1945, they pointed out, that Soviet forces had crossed a national frontier outside Europe. A newly confident Kremlin, they argued, was now pursuing the old czarist dream of creating a warm-water port, and the old Communist dream of moving the Red Army into the oil-rich Persian Gulf region.

In response, Jimmy Carter announced a grain embargo against the Soviet Union, reinstated draft registration, and ordered a U.S. boycott of the 1980 Moscow Olympics. And he told the nation he had earlier been wrong to characterize cold war fears of Communism as "inordinate." Détente was officially dead. The cold war had resumed.

The real story, it turned out, was more complicated. Moscow's main motive was not expansion but preventing an embarrassing Communist defeat in Afghanistan. And five months *before* the Soviet invasion, Carter had approved sending U.S. aid to Afghan Islamic guerrillas, actually hoping that it might draw in Soviet troops.

For months Moscow had been resisting requests for Soviet troops from the radical leftist regime that had seized power in Kabul in 1978. The local leftists' reckless and brutal campaign to force a rapid transformation of Afghanistan's traditional society had helped spark tribal and religious revolts. The leftist authorities in Kabul understood that they could not defeat these revolts without military help from Moscow. But when Soviet troops finally did arrive in December 1979, one of their first missions was to kill Afghanistan's pro-Soviet president, Hafizullah Amin, whom Moscow did not trust and considered an obstacle to restoring peace.

Afghanistan had long been a buffer state between East and West, going back to the nineteenth-century Great Game that played out in the frontier regions dividing British India and the expanding czarist dominions in Central Asia. Later, in the 1960s, independent Afghanistan's royalist government tried to play off Moscow and Washington and managed to attract development aid from both.

That balancing act began to break down in 1973, after a royal cousin, Mohammad Daoud, overthrew the monarchy and proclaimed a republic. Daoud's Pashtun nationalist politics set off an armed tribal rebellion in the north and drew Pakistan, worried about the loyalties of its own large Pashtun population, deep into Afghan exile politics. Five years later, after local Afghan Communists overthrew and killed Daoud and embarked on their own radical reforms, most of the country rose in armed revolt.

Some American cold warriors were alarmed by the Communist takeover in Kabul. One, however, sensed opportunity. He saw the potential for luring the Soviet Union into a Vietnam-style counterinsurgency war that would drain its global power. In July 1979, before any Soviet troops had entered Afghanistan, Brzezinski convinced Carter to approve secret U.S. support of the Afghan Islamic mujahedeen. This was the true start of what later came to be known as the Reagan Doctrine—U.S. support for armed rebels fighting Communist or pro-Communist regimes. After the Soviet invasion, millions of American dollars poured in to support the Islamic guerrillas, most of it funneled through the CIA. But money also flowed in through the Saudis and from Islamic charities in the Arab world that took up the Afghan struggle against godless Communism as a special cause. Pakistan's military intelligence agency, the ISI, chose most of the aid recipients. At a later stage Osama bin Laden became a key fund-raising figure for Arab recruits to the Afghan fighting.

Ultimately, Brzezinski's plan did contribute to the demise of the Soviet empire. Unfortunately, it also contributed to the rise of Al Qaeda.

Brzezinski himself weighed the trade-offs in a January 1998 interview with the French magazine *Nouvel Observateur*. The 9/11 attacks were still more than three years ahead, but Al Qaeda had already begun striking at American targets abroad. Asked if he had any regrets, Brzezinski replied:

"Regret what? That secret operation was an excellent idea. It had the effect of drawing the Russians into the Afghan trap and you want me to regret it? The day after the Soviets officially crossed the border, I wrote to President Carter, we now have the opportunity of giving to the U.S.S.R. its Vietnam war. Indeed, for almost 10 years, Moscow had to carry on a war unsupportable by the government, a conflict that brought about the demoralization and finally the breakup of the Soviet empire."

The interviewer then asked, "And neither do you regret having supported the Islamic fundamentalism, having given arms and advice to future terrorists?"

Brzezinski didn't regret that either: "What is most important to the history of the world? The Taliban or the collapse of the Soviet empire? Some stirred-up Moslems or the liberation of Central Europe and the end of the cold war?"

The interviewer tried again, "'Some stirred-up Moslems'? But it has been said and repeated [that] Islamic fundamentalism represents a world menace today."

"Nonsense!" Brzezinski replied, invoking the diversity of the Muslim world to distance his actions in Afghanistan from any wider connections or threats.[13]

Brzezinski's cold-war-rooted emergency state thinking effectively blinded him, and most of Washington, to the deadly new dangers posed by the jihadist forces they aided and encouraged. The Carter administration's classic emergency state response to Afghanistan may well have sped the Soviet Union's demise, but the test of foreign policy success is not winning a superpower chess game. It is making America safer and more secure. By that measure, Carter's Afghanistan policy was not a success.

What should Carter have done about Afghanistan in July 1979? Definitely not provoke a Soviet invasion. The Soviet system did not need Afghanistan to bring it down. And Afghanistan would have been much better off then and now without the Soviet invasion.

If Moscow had invaded anyway, without U.S. provocation, Washington should have aided the Afghan resistance. But it should have vetted the aid recipients itself, not handed the job off to a Pakistani military intelligence agency with its own Afghan agenda. And while more radical Afghan mujahedeen groups would have developed their own ties with Pakistan and Saudi Arabia, it badly served American interests to thrust the United States into the middle of that equation. Britain learned the hard way, through three costly Afghan wars, that the best thing an outside power could do about Afghanistan was to leave it alone.

In July 1979, as the Sandinistas were taking power in Managua, American diplomats were taking the measure of Iran's revolutionary government, and Islamic fundamentalist guerrillas were using American dollars to battle government troops and each other in Afghanistan, Jimmy Carter addressed the nation about "a fundamental threat to American democracy." His subject was not any of these challenges abroad but "a crisis of confidence" among the American people at home.

A new survey taken by Patrick Caddell, Carter's poll taker and sometime political adviser, reported that Americans no longer expected the future to be brighter than the past or present. It also showed that the country's confidence in Carter's leadership had fallen to 25 percent. One reason was a fresh round of gasoline price increases and lines at the pump. But instead of proceeding with his plans for another televised address on energy policy, Carter, urged on by Caddell, decided to address the crisis-of-confidence issue directly. The president retreated to Camp David for a week and invited politicians, business and labor leaders, clerics, and private citizens to tell him what they thought had gone wrong with his presidency. Then he addressed the nation.

Responding to Caddell's finding, Carter declared, "The erosion of confidence in our future is threatening to destroy the social and political fabric of America." That confidence, he went on, "is the idea which founded our nation and has guided our development as a people. Confidence in the future has supported everything else—public institutions and private enterprise, our own families, and the very Constitution of the United States. Confidence has defined our course and served as a link between generations. We've always believed in something called progress. We've always had a faith that the days of our children would be better than our own. Our people are losing that faith, not only in government itself but in the ability of citizens to serve as the ultimate rulers and shapers of our democracy."

Most of those pessimistic responders to Caddell's poll had likely been thinking about the future in material terms. The long postwar boom had sputtered out in the early 1970s. Productivity growth had slowed. Real incomes were stagnating. Factories were closing. Jobs were moving abroad. Economic prospects for the next generation looked grim. But Carter's concerns transcended the material. "We've discovered," he said, "that owning and consuming things does not satisfy our longing for meaning. We've learned that piling up material goods cannot fill the emptiness of lives which have no confidence or purpose."

Carter called for a renewal of faith and confidence, and then dramatically declared, "We are at a turning point in our history," with two possible paths before us. One "leads to fragmentation and self-interest. . . . It is a certain route to failure."

The other path, he continued, was the one pointed to by "all the traditions of our past, all the lessons of our heritage, all the promises of our future." That was "the path of common purpose and the restoration of American values. That path leads to true freedom for our nation and ourselves."

And then . . . Carter abruptly changed his theme and proceeded to outline the energy program he had originally meant to talk about, before briefly returning to the crisis-of-confidence idea at the end. Promising to do his best, but warning that he could not do it alone, he asked his listeners, "Whenever you have a chance, say something good about our country."[14]

Americans did not know quite what to make of this speech. This was not what they were used to hearing from their presidents. Its honesty and sincerity seemed refreshing. Early polls showed Carter's popularity rebounding. But to many it seemed like an attempt to exonerate a fumbling administration by blaming the people, an impression Carter reinforced by firing much of his cabinet two days after the speech. He didn't seem to be in command of the situation or even of his own administration. The polls soon turned negative.[15]

The fault wasn't all Carter's. Presidents who are obliged to always look decisive will frequently find themselves pressed into bad decisions, with lasting consequences.

The economy seemed to be slipping beyond Carter's control, too. By July 1979 inflation had climbed past 11 percent. Unemployment was at 5.7 percent and would reach 7.8 percent a year later. Those unemployment numbers do not seem so high by today's standards, but they were alarmingly high for a Democratic administration about to seek reelection. Carter's chief economic adviser, Charles Schultze, a distinguished Keynesian economist and former budget director under LBJ, tried all the demand-management techniques that had succeeded so well in the early and mid-1960s. But by the late 1970s they seemed only capable of feeding stagflation, as that decade's unusual combination of high inflation and high unemployment came to be called.

Domestic demand management is most effective when the government can exercise effective control over the money supply and international capital flows. Washington no longer exercised that kind of control.

When Nixon ended the dollar's convertibility to gold in 1971, he stopped a potential run on U.S. gold reserves from foreign dollar holders. Instead, those dollars piled up in the London Eurodollar market. That created a parallel money supply, unregulated by the Federal Reserve, that America's international banks and corporations could use for borrowing and investment purposes at home or (thanks to the dollar's status as an international reserve currency) abroad.

Those unregulated offshore dollars made it increasingly difficult for Carter's economists to measure and manage demand. The parallel financial system they formed part of would later help pave the way for a new system of low-cost globalized production that would tame U.S. price inflation by exporting high-wage jobs and importing low-cost goods.

But that was still in the future. China had not yet opened its economy. Neither had Mexico. The Iron Curtain had not yet fallen. America's main competitors were still the high-wage economies of Western Europe and Japan. Some of Carter's ideas for increasing America's energy efficiency might, given enough time to absorb the transitional costs, have improved America's export competitiveness and preserved more high-wage industrial jobs.

But time is just what Carter did not have, in the increasingly open and globalized economy that American foreign policy had been busily promoting for the past thirty years. With capital now free to flee abroad from every upward tick in American wage costs, benefit levels, tax rates, or environmental standards, Carter's efforts to apply Keynesian stimulus tended to produce stagflation instead of macroeconomic stability and full employment.

Nor could Carter subdue the resulting inflation without squeezing the economy and the Democratic Party voting base even harder than it was already being squeezed. But under the pressure of rising inflation and interest rates, that was what Carter ended up doing, perhaps unintentionally, when he chose Paul Volcker as the new chairman of the Federal Reserve during the summer of 1979.

By the time of the 1980 presidential election, inflation was nearly 13 percent, unemployment was 7.5 percent, and the American embassy hostages in Tehran were nearing their four hundredth day of captivity. Jimmy Carter won only 41 percent of the popular vote and lost even more decisively in the Electoral College, 489-49. He became the first elected president to be defeated for a second term since Herbert Hoover in 1932.

Despite the confluence of an opportune moment, a well-meaning leader, and a realistic vision, Carter had not managed to change the course of American history in the late 1970s. The cost of Carter's failure, as we shall see, has been three bipartisan decades of trying to match the politically appealing, but increasingly outdated, catechisms of the emergency state to the new dynamic and globalized world that American policies have done so much to create.

After a brief period in which the American people seemed receptive to a less imperial presidency, a less ideological foreign policy, and a more complex national narrative, the electorate changed its mind and reached back for the more familiar, reassuring, and heroic story line of the earlier cold war. Ronald Reagan was a master teller of that story. But if he had not been there to tell it, someone else probably would have. The Carter presidency, like the Ford presidency, was a temporary reaction to Vietnam and Watergate. And like all temporary reactions, it wore off with time.

That changing public mood also cut short congressional efforts to establish effective legislative oversight of the emergency state. By the end of the 1970s the aroused public that had fueled the political courage of congressional constitutionalists earlier in the decade had melted away. Vietnam and Watergate were no longer burning issues. Many Americans, reared on the heroic, crusading foreign policy imagery of the pre-Vietnam emergency state, were confused, concerned, and frightened by the murky new world of the 1970s and 1980s—a world where détente did not keep Cuban troops from being sent to Africa or Soviet troops from invading Afghanistan; a world where American clients could be toppled, American diplomats could be held hostage, and the almighty American dollar could come under global financial assault.

CHAPTER TEN

THE PRESIDENT WE WANTED

The United States went through a crisis of confidence in the second half of the 1970s, but not the one Jimmy Carter thought he had identified. Americans hadn't lost faith in themselves, or their belief that the United States should be strong and respected, or their conviction that the fate of freedom everywhere depended on American leadership. They had lost faith in Jimmy Carter's ability to lead them where they wanted to go. They still wanted no more Vietnams or Watergates. But they wanted a more confident and decisive president, one who demanded less from Americans and more from the rest of the world. Ronald Reagan knew how to be that kind of president.

Ronald Reagan put on a show that projected personal confidence and national destiny. He cut taxes, increased military spending, and announced that America would now take the offensive with Moscow by supporting armed anti-Communist guerrillas. He seized the geopolitical high ground—not by insisting on a single worldwide standard for human rights but by denouncing the Soviet Union as an "evil empire" and calling on Mikhail Gorbachev to "tear down that wall." In place of trying to manage the real-world nuclear arms race, he promoted his vision of a space-based shield that would make Americans feel as invulnerable as their nineteenth-century forebears had, with two vast oceans separating them from potential foreign foes.

Reagan's rhetoric seemed to vault America over the divisive, unsatisfying foreign policy arguments of the previous thirty-five years. He offered the old Republican rejection of containment without Dulles's decline-of-the-West gloom and nuclear brinkmanship. He revived the early cold war dream of rolling back Communism, but this time without exposing America to nuclear or even Korea-style conventional war. He proposed a solution to nuclear anxieties that did not require accepting strategic parity with Moscow or living with threats of mutually assured nuclear annihilation.

Reagan also ushered in a new economic era, making traditional battles over dividing the economic pie seem irrelevant. He forced labor unions onto the defensive, melted away inflation, cut taxes, and rolled up record fiscal and trade deficits without visible consequences. When Reagan ran for reelection in 1984, his commercials proclaimed that it was "morning again in America," with "interest rates and inflation down," America "prouder, stronger, and better," and families more confident in the future. That November 58.8 percent of the voters agreed.

Like Eisenhower and Nixon before him, Reagan had soothed the strains of a nation exhausted by the overreaching policies of a Democratic predecessor. Truman had pursued an unattainable military victory in Korea, and Johnson, driven by similar delusions of universal containment, had made the same mistake in Vietnam. Carter had avoided war but demanded wrenching changes in America's worldview and patterns of energy consumption that he lacked the leadership skills and political mandate to see through. Also, like Eisenhower and Nixon, Reagan made retrenchment look like advance. In foreign policy he resumed the offensive while carefully steering clear of war. In economic policy he vanquished inflation and eliminated gas lines without raising taxes or requiring energy conservation.

Reagan came to office promising to restore American pride, revitalize containment, and rebuild America's military. His chosen method was a substantial increase in military spending, meant to convince Moscow of Washington's determination to prevail, whatever it cost. Much of the additional money went into expensive new weapons systems—MX missiles, B-1 bombers, Trident II missile-launching submarines, two new nuclear-powered aircraft carriers, and hundreds of new attack fighters for the navy and air force.

In his first term Reagan increased military spending by nearly 30 percent in real, postinflation dollars. This was a complete departure from postwar Republican precedent. Eisenhower and Nixon each had significantly decreased real military spending. Eisenhower was a fiscal conservative who distrusted budget deficits as much as he distrusted the military-industrial complex. Nixon worried about growing international pressure on the dollar and overextended American military commitments.

Reagan's break with recent Republican precedent was all the greater since he coupled the huge military spending increases of his first term with large income tax cuts. Sharp reductions in discretionary domestic spending closed only a small fraction of the resulting fiscal gap.

Reagan was not overly concerned about deficits. He had cast aside traditional Republican fiscal conservatism for the new theories of supply-side economics, which taught that tax cuts eventually paid for themselves in added growth, and that budget deficits along the way did not much matter. And thanks to Nixon's closing of the gold window and move to floating exchange rates, Reagan could run up much larger fiscal and trade deficits than his predecessors without any immediate unpleasant international financial consequences.

By the end of Reagan's first term, the federal budget deficit had more than doubled, even after adjusting for inflation. Without Reagan's added military spending, that four-year deficit increase would have been cut in half. The nonmilitary portion of the budget remained consistently in surplus—military spending exceeded the total deficit for every year of Reagan's two terms.

Reagan did not buy all this expensive military hardware to fight major wars. That would not have been popular. And Reagan did not think it was necessary either. Reflecting a view of the world shaped by his earlier Hollywood and television career, Reagan believed that by putting on a show of spending that Moscow knew it could not afford to match, he could rebuild America's shattered military confidence and demoralize and domesticate the Soviet foe. That was why so much of the Reagan buildup went into expensive strategic weapons systems, capable of delivering nuclear weapons to Soviet targets.

Reagan's nuclear muscle-flexing made Moscow uneasy. But it initially made millions of Americans uneasy as well, swelling public support for the nuclear freeze movement that reached its peak in 1982–83.[1]

Reagan's show of strategic spending would be supplemented by flashes of Hollywood tall-in-the-saddle imagery and a legion of third-world extras harassing Soviet allies from Afghanistan to Nicaragua.

According to the doctrine proclaimed by Reagan's defense secretary, Caspar Weinberger, in 1984, America's own military forces would be sent into combat only under strictly defined conditions. They should be used only as a last resort, only when the vital interests of the United States and its allies were at stake, and only with clearly defined political and military objectives, in sufficient force to meet those objectives and with full assurance of public and congressional support.[2]

It's a sensible list. But the real point of the exercise, as Weinberger understood, was to rule out not just another Vietnam but almost any conceivable extended commitment of U.S. military forces to combat abroad. That was also the view of Weinberger's military assistant, Colin Powell, who as a young officer had lived through the army's harrowing Vietnam experience. When Powell went on to serve as chairman of the Joint Chiefs of Staff (1989–93), he embraced Weinberger's cautionary doctrine as his own.

Reagan's military buildup emphasized weapons that were designed to fight, deter, or impress a rival superpower. The Weinberger-Powell Doctrine reserved America's own military forces for wars of national security necessity, not third-world wars of choice. Yet it was in third-world military struggles—from Afghanistan to Africa to Central America—that Moscow and Washington had been sparring for advantage since Vietnam.

To retake the initiative in these contests, Reagan needed to recruit, fund, supply, and encourage third-world irregulars willing to challenge vulnerable Communist regimes. Washington could not afford to be too picky about which fighters it funded and how closely their political agendas coincided with Washington's. The CIA-funded Afghan mujahedeen included jihadist recruits from the Arab world who hated godless America as much as they hated godless Russia. Jonas Savimbi's American-backed UNITA guerrillas joined forces with apartheid South Africa in Angola. And the Nicaraguan Contras, whom Reagan lauded as freedom fighters, were trained by the freedom-crushing armed forces of Argentina's dirty war junta.

Unlike Eisenhower in Guatemala, Kennedy at the Bay of Pigs, or Carter and Brzezinski during the early stages of the Afghan war, Reagan very much wanted the fact of American support for these anti-Communist armies to be publicly known, if not all the messy details of whom the American money went to and exactly what they used it for. This public support for anti-Communist insurgencies was the essence of the Reagan Doctrine.

Inevitably, however, carrying out the doctrine meant delegating broad power to emergency state agencies like the CIA. Reagan put his former campaign manager, William Casey, in charge of the agency. Casey had run secret intelligence operations out of London for the OSS during World War II. He had gone on to serve as associate general counsel for the Marshall Plan, and then made a fortune on Wall Street. Turning his attention to Republican politics and fund-raising, he served in economic posts during the Nixon administration and then gravitated toward Reagan.

As director of central intelligence, Casey was a throwback to the freewheeling pre-Watergate days of the emergency state. He and his operational deputies operated with little White House restraint. Reagan's first four national security advisers—Richard Allen, William Clark, Robert "Bud" McFarlane, and John Poindexter—were weak managers and marginal policy players.

Congress had also begun to step back from the oversight role it had insisted on during the 1970s. The Intelligence Reform Act of 1980 had diluted the prior notification requirements of the 1974 Hughes-Ryan Act, licensing the CIA to begin covert operations before congressional oversight committees had been notified. Grants of additional autonomy to the emergency state rarely go unused, and Casey needed little further encouragement.

Under the Reagan Doctrine, funding for third-world anti-Communist fighters could be overt, as for example when Congress approved annual appropriations in the early 1980s for the Nicaraguan Contras. Later the Democratic majority in Congress, including many veterans of the 1970s battles over Indochina, began to have second thoughts about Reagan's Central America policies.

Democrats had little appetite for challenging Reagan on domestic issues, given the dismal Carter economic record and the post-1982 Reagan boom. But public opinion was less comfortable with Reagan's foreign policies. Standing tall was predictably popular. But Americans were uneasy about the growing nuclear chill with Moscow, and millions worried about getting sucked into a new jungle war in Central America.

Between 1982 and 1984 Congress passed a series of increasingly restrictive laws, known as the Boland amendments, prohibiting the use of Pentagon or CIA funds for military purposes in Nicaragua. Reagan's support for the Contras remained overt, but his legal channels for funding them were steadily cut off. To keep the Contra war going, administration officials like Oliver North and Elliott Abrams solicited funds from third countries like Saudi Arabia, Taiwan, and Brunei and from private citizens.

Eventually North, deputy director of political-military affairs for the NSC, came up with the idea of secretly selling American arms to Iran at inflated prices and diverting the profits to arm the Contras. Iran, then at war with Iraq, and having provoked both superpowers to refuse to sell it arms, was interested in buying the American TOW antitank missiles and Hawk surface-to-air missile spare parts North was offering.

But arms sales to Iran contravened American law and core Reagan administration policies. They violated the U.S. arms embargo against Iran, which had been in effect since the 1979 Tehran hostage crisis. Diverting the funds to arm the Contras violated the congressional Boland amendments banning the U.S. government from providing such arms.

The deal also violated Ronald Reagan's repeated promises never to bargain with terrorists. In return for the arms, the Iranian recipients had purportedly agreed to help arrange the release of seven American hostages then being held by Iran's Lebanese client, Hezbollah. During the period of the arms transfers, Hezbollah did in fact release three of the original hostages, but additional American hostages were taken to replace them.

Here was an emergency state trifecta. The Reagan White House had not just ignored Congress, it had defied a properly enacted law. The National Security Council had not just taken over policy making from congressionally accountable cabinet secretaries—both Secretary of State George Shultz and Defense Secretary Caspar Weinberger opposed the arms-for-hostages deal—the NSC had also carried out the illegal policy on its own.

President Reagan, required by article 2, section 3, of the Constitution to "take care that the laws be faithfully executed," had not only failed to follow the law and the constitutional separation of powers, he had repeatedly and falsely assured the American people that his administration had not traded arms for hostages when incontrovertible evidence showed that it had.

These were potentially impeachable offenses, as threatening to the constitutional balance as Watergate. And like Watergate, they were rooted in the institutions and mentality of the postwar emergency state.

In Watergate, the "smoking gun" had been Nixon's attempt to use the CIA to obstruct an FBI criminal investigation. In Iran-Contra, it was the use of the NSC staff to outflank congressional legislation and oversight. In Watergate, Nixon was covering up a domestic political break-in by hired burglars. In Iran-Contra, Reagan was carrying out an illegal American foreign policy involving real missiles, real hostages, a real Central American civil war, and a revolutionary Iran.

• • •

But Americans were in no mood to impeach Reagan, as congressional Democrats soon discovered. Instead he was indulgently presumed not to have truly understood the actions that his administration had engaged in and that he had personally approved. The revived constitutional spirit of the 1970s had evaporated, along with the sense of a foreign policy in crisis that gave rise to it.

Fourteen years after the ranking Republican on the Senate Watergate committee had famously asked of Richard Nixon, "What did the President know, and when did he know it," no Republican had the appetite to ask similar questions of Ronald Reagan. Oliver North, who, like Nixon, had concealed (and, in North's case, destroyed) White House documents to protect himself and others from prosecution, became a martyr and a hero to many Reagan supporters.

Eleven years after American public opinion, aroused by newspaper reports of domestic spying and foreign assassinations by U.S. intelligence agencies, had supported searching congressional inquiries and tighter oversight, a newly complacent public opinion preferred not to know the details of the sordid doings of presidential agencies that violated America's values and its laws.

Reagan's approval rating did drop more than 20 percent (from 67 to 46 percent, according to a *New York Times*/CBS News poll) in the month after the scandal became public. But he completed his term, with Frank Carlucci taking over as national security adviser and after him Colin Powell, when Carlucci replaced Weinberger at Defense in late 1987. By the time Reagan left office in January 1989, his poll ratings had rebounded almost to where they had been before the scandal broke.[3]

Vice President Bush, publicly insisting that he had somehow been "out of the loop" on the operational details (although he later acknowledged to the independent counsel's office investigators that he had been regularly informed about the arms shipments to Iran), was nominated and then elected president in 1988. Reagan's enduring popularity helped overcome Bush's own lack of political charisma. Fourteen administration officials were eventually indicted—and eleven were convicted—on Iran-Contra charges, most of which concerned withholding evidence, making false statements, or obstructing government inquiries. Five of those convictions were successfully appealed. President George H. W. Bush pardoned the remaining six, including Caspar Weinberger, in December 1992.[4]

The immediate lesson of Iran-Contra was the need for tighter management and clearer lines of authority within the NSC. That was a principal conclusion of the investigating commission that Reagan appointed, headed by Republican senator John Tower. It was also one of the main themes of Reagan's own televised explanation to the American people in March 1987.

But there is also a deeper, even more important lesson that seemed to get lost in the televised melodrama of the congressional investigations and the technical legal arguments that some of the accused individuals used to thwart prosecution by the Iran-Contra independent counsel, Lawrence Walsh.

The embarrassing foreign policy errors of Iran-Contra grew directly out of the extraconstitutional processes of the emergency state.

Running the operation through the NSC staff deprived the executive branch of the kind of professional expert vetting that was available in the State and Defense departments. Political appointees and other true believers like to dismiss this expertise as bureaucracy, but those experienced professionals might well have sniffed out some of the obvious scams and fabricators who led American policy and credibility over a cliff with their tales of "Iranian moderates"—just as twenty years later they might have avoided a lot of unnecessary grief in Iraq.[5]

Making and carrying out the nation's foreign policy behind the backs of Congress and the public may seem to be a good way to bypass critics, but it also bypasses the kind of hard debate that can refine overly simplistic policies into practical ones. It also opens a gulf between the nation's foreign policies and the people in whose name they are being carried out.

Operational secrecy and streamlined decision making are sometimes necessary—one thinks, for example, of ExComm, the ad hoc group of top advisers Kennedy assembled to discuss policy options during the Cuban missile crisis. But extraordinary procedures like these must be reserved for such true national emergencies, not used simply because an administration loses a funding vote in Congress. Once secret, unaccountable government becomes routine, constitutional democracy is undermined, and grave mistakes become almost inevitable.

Those were conclusions that the leading House Republican on the investigating committee, Dick Cheney, did not wish to reach. As Ford's chief of staff, Cheney had been chagrined to see congressional Democrats, emboldened by the presidential debacles of Vietnam and Watergate, challenge the emergency state powers that successive postwar administrations had amassed in the name of national security. Elected to Congress himself in 1978, Cheney had been pleased to see the Reagan administration begin reclaiming those powers.

If the Democratic majority now intended to use this latest example of White House overreach and lawlessness to again assert its constitutional role in foreign policy, Cheney was determined not to go along. He declared, as the hearings began in May 1987, that they "should seek above all" to find ways to strengthen, not restrict, the capacity of future presidents to act in times of crisis. He suggested that Congress had contributed to the crisis by its amendments restricting the government's ability to continue funding the Contras in ways that Congress had previously authorized.

When a bipartisan majority issued its final report that November, Cheney was a principal author of the minority dissent, which claimed that the majority had based its findings "upon an aggrandizing theory of Congress's foreign policy powers that is itself part of the problem."

Alleging that Congress, not President Reagan, had overreached its constitutional powers, the minority report argued that "unconstitutional statutes violate the rule of law every bit as much as do willful violations of constitutional statutes."

As for the actions of NSC staff, including violating the congressional restrictions on aid to the Contras and the American arms embargo against Iran, the minority report's authors declared their belief that "virtually all" of these activities "were legal, with the possible exception of the diversion of Iran arms sale proceeds to the resistance." Cheney and his coauthors claimed that the congressional restrictions applied only to the Pentagon and the CIA, not to the NSC staff.[6]

Unlike his three most recent predecessors, Reagan made no serious attempt to negotiate strategic arms control agreements during his first term. He showed little initial interest in arranging the summit meetings with Soviet leaders to which Americans had grown accustomed. Nor were nuclear anxieties calmed by Reagan's comments like his implication in a 1982 news conference that nuclear missiles deployed on submarines could be called back after they had been launched, his 1983 characterization of the Soviet Union as "an evil empire," or his 1984 quip during a microphone check: "My fellow Americans, I'm pleased to announce that I've signed legislation outlawing the Soviet Union. We begin bombing in five minutes."

But after Republican pollster Richard Wirthlin reported in 1983 that Reagan's nuclear weapons policies were one of the few losing issues in his 1984 reelection bid, Reagan's tone, if not his substance, began to change. Summits and strategic arms control returned to the presidential agenda, particularly after Mikhail Gorbachev became the new Soviet leader in March 1985 and began actively seeking sharp arms reductions as part of his program for cutting costs and reviving the Soviet economy.[7]

And the "Star Wars" missile defense shield that Reagan had begun talking about in 1983 became an increasingly important factor in negotiations with Moscow and public opinion in the United States. To American arms controllers and Soviet leaders, the Strategic Defense Initiative

(SDI) looked like a reckless quest for a destabilizing American nuclear first-strike capacity. From the 1960s onward the United States and the Soviet Union had deployed more than enough nuclear-armed ICBMs to destroy each other many times over.

What supposedly kept them from doing so was a carefully negotiated mutual balance of terror. That balance was called, appropriately enough, MAD, for mutually assured destruction. All the SALT (Strategic Arms Limitation Talks) negotiations that the Nixon, Ford, and Carter administrations had conducted with Moscow aimed at maintaining nuclear peace through the strategic stalemate of MAD.

The Reagan administration rejected further SALT talks. It rejected MAD. It rejected the idea of peace through deterrence. It rejected the status quo of rough nuclear parity between Washington and Moscow. It didn't want to wage nuclear war. Instead it sought "peace through strength." It wanted to restore the clear American nuclear predominance of the early cold war years.

Once again it was back to the future, back to the glory days of Truman and Eisenhower, back to the years before Vietnam and the international complexities of the 1970s, back to the era when a war-shattered Europe still looked gratefully to America as the leader of the free world.

Reagan's SDI promised to restore that lost nuclear predominance. To the public, and perhaps to Reagan himself, it offered the promise of an end to decades of living under the shadow of a civilization-destroying nuclear attack. To American military strategists, it offered a vision of restored nuclear supremacy. Leaders in Moscow grew concerned that with a space-based defensive shield in place, Washington might feel free to launch a preemptive nuclear attack on Soviet targets without fear of Soviet nuclear retaliation.

Such total invulnerability was a scientific impossibility, although the Reagan administration encouraged the public to think otherwise. Thirty years and more than $150 billion later, the Pentagon has not yet managed to develop a reliable ground-based missile defense capable of preventing even a modest North Korean attack. But even a partially effective shield would have forced Moscow to build many more offensive missiles to restore strategic parity. That would help bolster Ronald Reagan's appeal as a leader sincerely trying to rid the world of nuclear weapons. He would argue for a population-protecting shield. Moscow would predictably say no and refuse to negotiate cuts in offensive nuclear missiles while Star Wars was on the table.[8]

That was largely the way it played out during most of Reagan's second term, now with the added factor of Mikhail Gorbachev, who desperately wanted to cut Soviet military spending to liberate resources for the political and economic restructuring that he hoped could still revive a rapidly decaying Soviet Communism.

Reagan's military buildup and SDI did not create Gorbachev; the Soviet crisis did. But Reagan's policies and political appeal did much to create the constricting international parameters within which Gorbachev was compelled to operate.

Gorbachev had his own political appeal, especially to Americans and Europeans who had known nothing but hostility and immobility from a dreary succession of postwar Soviet leaders. Emergency state stalwarts like Casey and Robert Gates, who became deputy director of central intelligence in 1986, suspected that Gorbachev represented no more than the old Soviet menace in a new and seductively appealing guise. Reagan, encouraged by Secretary of State George Shultz, suspected otherwise and instinctively knew how to use the hopes Gorbachev had generated to his own diplomatic and political advantage, even when he stumbled over the details.

At the October 1986 Reykjavik summit meeting, just before the Iran-Contra scandal became public, a poorly briefed Reagan nearly traded away the American nuclear umbrella that held NATO together. All that stopped him was Gorbachev's refusal to finalize the deal in the absence of firm limits on SDI. Yet in the weeks that followed, White House spinners managed to convince much of the American public that Reagan and SDI were bringing the world tangibly closer to the dream of ending mutually assured nuclear destruction.[9]

• • •

Reagan came to office promising to rebuild America's economic strength to provide firm foundations (and revenues) for renewing its military power. This would be done, he explained, through supply-side economics—a program of personal and corporate tax cuts intended to create incentives to work and invest so powerful that they would bring in enough new revenues to pay for the tax cuts.

It didn't work out that way. Reagan's across-the-board income tax cuts were, as expected, enormously popular, almost addictively so, as far as the American political system was concerned. But they neither paid for themselves nor significantly boosted investment in American industry. One important reason they didn't was because three decades of American foreign policy had leveled the playing field for global investment in ways that often made it more attractive to invest abroad than at home. American corporations benefited. American workers didn't.

Everything else being equal, a lower tax rate makes investment more attractive. But everything else wasn't equal. Major American industrial companies now operated in an increasingly globalized market, with stiff competition from European and Japanese rivals pushing them to drive down costs by shifting production abroad where labor was cheaper. China, India, and Eastern Europe were still mostly outside the globalized production game. But Mexico, Singapore, Malaysia, Hong Kong, Taiwan, South Korea, and Saipan (in the American-ruled Northern Marianas) were not.

While Reagan's tax cuts succeeded in putting more money into the hands of high-bracket federal taxpayers, that money was unlikely to be invested in domestic American industry when offshore production offered much higher returns. Much of the tax cut windfall also went into luxury consumption, which seemed a better deal to wealthy Americans than investing in uncompetitive domestic industries.

Reagan's tax cuts thus failed to slow the deindustrialization of America that had already begun. Perhaps they even accelerated it. So did other Reagan policies, like increasing government-backed insurance coverage for investment abroad under the Overseas Private Investment Corporation while reducing funding for the Export-Import Bank, which helped subsidize the export of goods made in America. Reagan's international economic policies aimed, like those of earlier administrations, at lowering barriers to American investment abroad. But coupled with tight monetary policies and the budgetary havoc wrought by Reagan's military spending increases and tax cuts, they spread industrial devastation at home.[10]

With industry fleeing, military spending increasing, and federal taxes declining, rapidly rising fiscal and trade deficits were sure to follow. They did. The need to finance these rising deficits helped fatten Wall Street at the expense of Main Street. So did the loosening of international capital controls that followed Nixon's ending of the Bretton Woods monetary order.

Much of the tax cut money that did stay home went to expand America's financial sector, not to revitalize domestic industry. It created new jobs on Wall Street, but not jobs that many newly unemployed American textile, steel, or auto workers were qualified for.

Reagan's advocacy of a strong military, tough anti-Communist rhetoric, weak civil rights enforcement, and lower taxes played better politically among blue-collar "Reagan Democrats" in Rust Belt states like Michigan, Ohio, and Indiana than they did in New York. But their biggest economic benefits flowed to Wall Street.

When displaced blue-collar workers did begin to find work, it was often in the lower ranks of the service sector, as contract, temporary, or part-time employees in retail malls, fast-food chains, and expanding public and private medical services that paid a fraction of their former salaries and offered few paid benefits and no job security. It is not surprising that this growing group of downwardly mobile Americans grew increasingly disenchanted with Washington and with post-cold-war foreign policy paradigms built around an expanding network of free trade agreements.

Reagan's term began with a sharp recession, brought on by the tight money policies that the Federal Reserve began applying late in the Carter administration. That economic squeeze put an end to the stagflation of the 1970s. Threatened by runaway shops and frightened by Reagan's tough antilabor stance—symbolized by his firing of striking air-traffic controllers in 1981—labor unions turned docile.

For most of the population, real wages stagnated or declined. But consumption did not correspondingly decline. Working people, like the federal government, became increasingly dependent on credit—that is, on recycling the savings of some of the same countries to which America was exporting its industrial jobs or from which it was importing its oil. Washington's tight money policies through the first half of the 1980s kept the dollar strong, further undermining America's industrial exports but helping to attract the foreign funds needed to sustain increasing public and private borrowing.

By the mid-1980s, with unemployment sharply declining, consumption booming, the stock market soaring, and no apparent ill consequences flowing from federal deficits and private borrowing, Reagan had created the illusion of real prosperity. The underlying reality, however, was a hollowed-out economy with steadily increasing fiscal and trade deficits and accelerating industrial disinvestment.

Ronald Reagan, like Dwight Eisenhower and Richard Nixon before him, rescued the reputation and revived the spirits of the emergency state after a Democratic president who overreached his mandate and left the country in a sour mood. But where Eisenhower and Nixon had prescribed traditionalist Republican cures built around strategic and fiscal retrenchment and a scaled-down version of universal containment, Reagan offered something radically different.

Instead of lowering Washington's strategic sights, he raised them. Instead of worrying about widening deficits, he ignored them. Instead of narrowing the gap between America's international ambitions and its economic means, he widened them. And instead of translating the country's reluctance to commit American military force abroad into a more conciliatory diplomacy, he offset it with confrontational rhetoric and uncompromising demands.

And thanks to Reagan's political gifts—in conjunction with the accelerating Soviet collapse and America's own passage from Keynesian stagflation in the 1970s to the new low-inflation, widening-inequality, deficits-don't-seem-to-matter economic world of the 1980s—it all appeared to work out rather well, at least for a while.

Reagan had an actor's faith that reality was almost infinitely malleable. He saw nothing wrong with shutting out unpleasant or unwelcome facts in order to remain upbeat and optimistic. He could deny that he had traded arms for hostages, deny that no existing or immediately foreseeable technology could shield America's civilian population from incoming missiles, deny that missiles could not be turned back once launched, even deny that he really had cancer as he prepared for cancer surgery.

And he had a talent for persuading Americans that they too could live in a world they wanted to believe in, that they could return to the glory days when America was strong, respected, and economically and militarily unrivaled. Reagan's lasting legacy was to teach Americans that they could believe what made them feel good and cancel out interfering messages from outside reality.

Reagan wasn't a constitutional innovator. He was one of the most successful political salesmen ever to occupy the White House. And he sold Americans on an image of themselves and their place in the world—a permanent return to the glory days of the 1950s. That made it extremely difficult for his successors to tackle the increasingly serious problems of the next quarter-century, problems like arresting the postindustrial decline of the middle class, paying for vital public services including schools and health care, and protecting the security of Americans at home from the risks of nonstate terrorism in an increasingly borderless world.

Reagan is remembered for lowering taxes and inflation, restoring American pride, and winning the cold war—not for bypassing the Constitution and exporting American jobs. He left office having tamed the evil empire and the nuclear arms race. He had also tamed stagflation, even if he had done it with the help of smoke and mirrors and the dollar's international reserve currency role, and paying a high but largely hidden price in cumulative deindustrialization and deficits.

The fondly remembered image (not the mixed real record) of Reagan's eight years in office set the new parameters for what a successful American presidency should look like. Reagan's winning public personality gave him the most politically successful eight-year record of any American president since Franklin Roosevelt.

His lasting legacy was the Reagan presidential template, a set of models and formulas that every president has borrowed from ever since. It has always been a sure winner at the polls. But as the years have gone by, it has locked American politics into a worldview and a set of orthodoxies about taxes, the role of government, the uses of military power, and the nature of America's role in the world that were already backward-looking and nostalgic during Reagan's presidency and that are counterproductive and dangerous today.

Reagan's politically successful presidency seemed to be just what America needed after the five successive foreshortened presidencies of the 1960s and 1970s. But ultimately it proved too politically successful for America's long-term good. It enshrined a mythically heroic worldview and an increasingly out-of-date set of economic and foreign policies as a fixed and unchanging ideal in a world that was being radically transformed.

CHAPTER ELEVEN

SOFT LANDING

George H. W. Bush was Ronald Reagan's vice president and immediate political heir, but he was no Ronald Reagan.

Where Reagan's political touch was almost always sure, Bush's was frequently clumsy. Where Reagan projected confidence and optimism, Bush projected a blue blood's discomfort with hands-on politics and an unsettlingly displaced nervous energy. And where Reagan sometimes ignored reality to knit together a consistent narrative of individualism and anti-Communism, Bush sometimes tripped over cherished Republican and American narratives in pursuit of his own notions of foreign policy realism.

Bush and his secretary of state, James Baker, carefully counted votes in Congress and warheads in Moscow. But they were less careful about, or capable of, explaining where they were leading America. Bush lacked, as he acknowledged himself, "the vision thing."[1]

It fell to Bush to manage the endgame of the cold war. Much of the credit for making that possible belongs to the courageous people of Central and Eastern Europe who dared to confront their Communist masters with no advance guarantee that those police state regimes would peacefully give way. Mikhail Gorbachev played a crucial role by refusing to underwrite local Communist hard-liners with Soviet military force, as his Kremlin predecessors had done in Hungary in 1956 and in Czechoslovakia in 1968.

But the practiced, realist statecraft of George H. W. Bush was probably the single most important factor in ensuring that the resulting epochal power shifts in the heart of Europe unfolded peacefully and democratically. In Europe's recent past, a disintegrating empire usually spawned bloody wars, as rival powers, or previously captive nations, fought over the spoils.

That didn't happen when the post–World War II Soviet empire disintegrated. Skillful American diplomacy, both with Moscow and with Washington's Western European allies, was a major reason why. The only fighting in Europe during the Bush years was in the former Yugoslavia, which had left the Soviet orbit decades before.

The place where things could most easily have gone badly was Germany, whose relations with its European neighbors had generated tensions and wars for the past century. The idea of a reunified Germany still made France and Britain uncomfortable in 1989–90; Mikhail Gorbachev did not feel he could accept a reunified Germany in NATO and still survive as Soviet leader.[2]

But that was just what West Germany's political leaders wanted, and by 1990 most East Germans favored merging with the West. The idea of Moscow, Paris, or London standing in the way of that seemed ludicrous. But a new diplomatic framework had to be constructed that satisfied each country's minimum requirements.

Only the United States, with its own larger set of interests—including a united Germany, a transformed NATO, and a newly cooperative relationship with Moscow—could design and build that new framework. Doing so was Bush's great achievement, although James Baker did most of the diplomatic hard work.[3]

Successfully concluding the cold war and resolving its defining issue, Germany, in line with America's broadest international interests could have set the stage for an even greater American victory—dismantling an emergency state that had now outlived its original justification. This never seemed to occur to Bush. He was himself a creature of the emergency state, shaped by its institutions and its values. He found it hard to imagine an America without it. So did most Americans in 1989–90.

Fifty years of wartime presidential powers, compromised civil liberties, and policing the world had grown addictive. Bush dedicated the rest of his presidency to guiding the emergency state into the post-cold-war era.

When Bush first took office in January 1989, the cold war was not quite over. In Central America he inherited Reagan's ideologically driven campaigns to overthrow the leftist Sandinista government of Nicaragua and to support the antiguerrilla campaigns of the right-wing Salvadoran military, despite horrific human rights abuses. Aid to the Contras was still a controversial issue, and the Democratic majorities in Congress opposed it.

Bush wanted to defuse these Central American issues and move on, as Eisenhower had done with Korea and Nixon with Vietnam. Congress had already cut off military aid to the Contras, and the Sandinistas agreed to hold free presidential elections in early 1990.

In March 1989 Baker cut a deal with Democratic leaders in Congress that provided the Contras with another year of economic aid to sustain them until the election, but no military support. In return, Bush let Baker promise the Democrats the kind of oversight and continuing control over the purse strings that previous emergency state presidents had fiercely resisted. For the aid to keep flowing past November, four separate congressional committees would have to issue letters of approval.

That arrangement for continuing congressional supervision went far beyond what the Constitution required. Justice Department officials—who were not consulted—and conservative legal scholars opposed it, arguing, correctly, that it ignored Supreme Court decisions rejecting such legislative vetoes. But Bush wasn't interested in the constitutional theory. He believed he could gain congressional goodwill and increased freedom of action in other foreign policy areas he thought more important by shedding a losing quarrel on what he considered a secondary issue. Even on the narrow issue of Nicaragua, Bush's new approach was vindicated when the anti-Sandinista candidate, Violeta Chamorro, was elected president of Nicaragua the following year.

• • •

Bush squandered much of that goodwill a few months later by his obtuse attempts to conduct diplomatic business as usual with Beijing after the Chinese leadership had sent armed troops to gun down democracy demonstrators in Tiananmen Square. For weeks millions of Americans had seen television news reports of appealing, unarmed, and vulnerable-looking Chinese university students calling for American-style political rights. The students had erected a papier-mâché and foam statue vaguely resembling the Statue of Liberty that they called the Goddess of Democracy and made it a symbol of their protests. And then on the night of June 3–4, 1989, television viewers around the world watched army tanks roll into Tiananmen Square and saw soldiers firing on unarmed protesters with machine guns.

Many Americans, and many members of Congress, reacted angrily. Not George Bush, who issued a carefully drafted written statement that sought to strike a balance between registering American outrage and leaving open the possibility of a quick resumption of business-as-usual diplomacy. He failed miserably on both counts. Beijing saw Bush's statement as a signal that Washington sought to minimize the crisis, while millions of Americans concluded that Bush lived in an artificial foreign policy bubble that blinded him to the televised slaughter in Tiananmen Square. Instead of keeping open his diplomatic options, as Bush had intended, his out-of-touch response narrowed those options, as Congress became the vehicle for an aroused public opinion.[4]

Bush was misled by his belief that he had a special understanding of China policy, based on his experience as Washington's unofficial ambassador in Beijing during 1974–75. He had, but fifteen years later Bush's understanding was badly out of date. China had changed, and more important, the world had changed.

For years Americans had gone along with the idea, promoted by a succession of presidents, that China was moving away from Communism and repression. That was a convenient emergency state fiction, worthy of Orwell, during the cold war, when China was conspicuously allying itself with Washington against the Soviet Union and its proxies. But by the late 1980s Mikhail Gorbachev was winding down the cold war and freeing Soviet dissidents while Beijing was reining in reformist leaders and arresting democracy advocates.[5]

The Tiananmen Square movement had begun as an unofficial tribute to the ousted reform Communist leader Hu Yao Bang, who died on April 15, 1989. It had held together in part to take advantage of the worldwide media coverage of Mikhail Gorbachev's May 15–18 visit to Beijing, the first time top Soviet and Chinese leaders had met in twenty years. The narrowing of the Sino-Soviet rift and the end of the cold war undercut the logic of the American China policy Bush thought he understood so well.

Bush's strength was also his weakness. He believed in a foreign policy built around personal understandings between top leaders, and he ignored the hundreds of millions of Chinese and Americans who sometimes had very different ideas, as they did in June 1989.

James Baker, with a surer grasp of domestic politics, convinced Bush later that month to order a suspension of meetings between high-level American and Chinese officials. But less than two weeks after announcing the ban, Bush secretly sent his national security adviser, Brent Scowcroft, and Baker's deputy, Lawrence Eagleburger, to Beijing, where they met with Deng Xiaoping. If Bush's suspension of high-level exchanges did not apply to that meeting, what could it possibly apply to?

The same two administration officials paid a repeat visit to Beijing that December. Scowcroft was photographed raising a glass to toast a smiling group of high Chinese officials. Even more chilling to China's hunted and jailed democrats and their American supporters were Scowcroft's words. "In both our societies," Bush's national security adviser declared, "there are voices of those who seek to redirect or frustrate our cooperation. We both must take bold measures to overcome these negative forces." Later that month CNN broke the story of Scowcroft's earlier, secret trip.[6]

The two visits seemed to cast Bush as a cold war thinker out of step with a new era. The public reaction energized Democrats in Congress, like Senate Majority Leader George Mitchell and Congresswoman Nancy Pelosi, whose district included San Francisco's Chinatown. Along with others in Congress, they tried to reshape American policy toward China, a field that had been largely a presidential preserve since the original Nixon-Kissinger opening twenty years earlier.

By ignoring public opinion and trying to operate within the familiar, inherited structures of the emergency state, Bush weakened those structures and gave Congress a chance to reassert itself on foreign policy. Bush's congressional critics picked up the same tool that earlier Congresses had used against Henry Kissinger's realpolitik engagement with Moscow fifteen years before—linking low-tariff access to U.S. markets to human rights conditions. This was still a plausible domestic political strategy in 1989, before the surge of U.S. corporate investment in China began just a few years later. Chinese exports to the United States amounted to roughly $12 billion in 1989. Twenty years later they were nearly $300 billion a year.[7]

Between Scowcroft's two 1989 trips to Beijing, Soviet power in the former satellite states of Central and Eastern Europe had crumbled. Pro-Soviet regimes had been forcibly imposed on these countries by the Red Army after World War II, and forcibly reimposed on Hungary in 1956 and Czechoslovakia in 1968. Once Gorbachev made clear that Moscow would not send in troops again, these imposed and unpopular governments were doomed.

In May, Hungary began to dismantle its border fence with Austria, opening the way for East Germans and other east bloc nationals to freely cross to the West. In June, Poland held partially free elections, producing a new government led by the anti-Communist labor movement, Solidarity. In October, hundreds of thousands of East Germans took to the streets—by early November the Berlin wall had fallen. Later that month a "Velvet Revolution" swept away Communist rule in Czechoslovakia. Communist power also began to crumble in Bulgaria and, in the only violent Eastern European revolution that year, in Romania.

The absorption of these countries into Stalin's orbit had triggered the cold war, amid the mutual recriminations following Yalta and Potsdam. Their fate, and the possibility of further extensions of Soviet power into Western Europe, Greece, and Turkey, had been Truman's justification for the peacetime emergency state. Now they had reclaimed their independence.

George Bush found it easier to deal with the aftermath of successful democratic revolutions in Europe than with the crushing of the Chinese democracy movement by the Communist government in Beijing. The endgame in Europe, which played out over the issues of German unification, NATO, and U.S. and Soviet force reductions over the next three years, involved working the phones and the diplomatic circuit with other national leaders, which Bush enjoyed and did well. Managing American public opinion presented him with no problems, because the images that Americans were seeing on TV inclined them to support the policies Bush wanted to follow.

The European revolutions of 1989, as seen on television, seemed a fitting culmination to America's long cold war narrative. They reinforced a self-affirming story of wise American leadership and wise American strategy. Kennan's strategy of containing Soviet power until it mellowed from within had been vindicated. The free world had triumphed, with America at its head. Eastern Europe had played only a late, bit part in its own liberation, supplying the extras for the crowd scenes. Western Europe had been an unsteady and wavering partner. The visionary Ronald Reagan had stared down the evil empire and brought down the Berlin wall. Now America would send in the technician George Bush to organize the new world order.

Bush and Gorbachev met on a ship off Malta in December 1989 and acknowledged that the cold war was effectively over—although some in Bush's inner circle, like Scowcroft and his deputy, Robert Gates, and Defense Secretary Dick Cheney, still had their doubts. But no one in the Bush administration, and no major congressional Democrat, talked about ending the emergency state. Some did suggest that defense spending could be modestly reduced. Others suggested that Washington and Moscow could deepen their new diplomatic cooperation. These were apt suggestions, but much more fundamental questions went unasked.

For the first time since 1940, the United States no longer faced a global totalitarian threat. All the cumulative departures from America's constitutional design—from presidential war making to the classification of essential foreign policy information—could now be reconsidered.

Americans could safely debate the foreign policy they wanted to follow, the kind of military forces they wanted to maintain, and what it would take to ensure American security and prosperity in a post-cold-war world. Americans could decide what role they wanted to play in the international economy and the internal political disputes of other countries, and the purposes for which nuclear weapons should and should not be used.

These would be unfamiliar discussions. It had been a very long time since Americans had seriously debated any of these things. But the process could at least begin. Congress could hold hearings. Presidential commissions could investigate. Universities and civic groups could organize discussions. News organizations could report on the issues at stake.

Little of that happened. While Americans celebrated the end of the cold war, the institutions of the emergency state worked behind closed doors inventing new rationales for themselves while making minimal adjustments to the size and configuration of America's military forces.

Barely two weeks after the Malta summit, Bush ordered American military forces to invade Panama. It was the first time U.S. military forces had been used offensively since 1945 outside of a cold war context.

Panama's military dictator, Manuel Noriega, had been a cold war ally of the United States. He had helped keep the Contras in the field during the Boland amendment years and had been on and off the CIA's payroll since the early 1970s. Bush had even had a working lunch with him in 1976, when both headed their country's intelligence agencies.[8]

So why did Bush order in the troops? A White House statement on the morning of the invasion cited four purposes: "to protect American lives, restore the democratic process, preserve the integrity of the Panama Canal treaties and apprehend Manuel Noriega."[9]

That was not a very persuasive list. Noriega had been part of the Panamanian government that negotiated the canal treaties and had never challenged U.S. access to the waterway or the stationing of U.S. troops in the Canal Zone.

He had rigged Panama's 1989 presidential election, just as he had rigged the previous presidential election in 1984. That had not been grounds for a U.S. invasion of Panama, nor of any of the many other Latin American countries that used force and fraud to manipulate electoral outcomes during those years.

American prosecutors had wanted to indict Noriega for years for drug trafficking and other crimes but had been discouraged from doing so before 1988 by previous administrations grateful to him for national security favors. With the end of the cold war and Bush's change in Nicaragua policy, Noriega's favors were no longer needed.[10]

Nor had any American lives been endangered in Panama until Bush had ordered a deliberately provocative series of military exercises meant to push Noriega into a reaction that could be used to justify a U.S. military response.[11]

Noriega was a useful thug who had outlived his usefulness, not an urgent threat to America's security. Yet Bush had ordered American troops to invade his country, change his regime, and deliver him to the United States for trial with no cold war rationale and no congressional declaration of war.

Whatever else might have been on Bush's mind, invading Panama gave him an issue that would appeal to the Republican right, where he was politically weak. From the days of Reagan's opposition to the Panama Canal treaties, conservative Republicans had complained about giving away what Teddy Roosevelt had "stolen fair and square" and raised fears about Panamanian nationalists cutting off a vital commercial and naval waterway. Now Bush had shown a willingness to use American military force, knocked the nationalist Noriega off his pedestal, and hauled him away in chains.

Bush's 1989 invasion of Panama, like Reagan's 1983 invasion of the Caribbean microstate of Grenada on equally flimsy pretexts after pro-Cuban leftists had seized power there, was in the grand Teddy Roosevelt–era tradition of "splendid little wars"—easy victories over weak foes to demonstrate American macho.

Noriega became the prototype for America's new post-cold-war enemy, and its new rationale for military preparedness—the "rogue state."

By early 1990 the two leading military specialists among congressional Democrats, Senator Sam Nunn and Representative Les Aspin, were asking pointed questions about what kind of threats American forces would need to deal with after the cold war, and how large those forces, and overall military spending, needed to be. Bush and the Pentagon understood that they would have to come up with persuasive answers to get future budgets approved.

Defense Secretary Cheney and Colin Powell, now chairman of the Joint Chiefs, spent the next several months fashioning a plan for what came to be called the "Base Force." With 1.6 million troops, it would be about 25 percent smaller than the cold war military. But it would otherwise resemble the old force structure in almost every particular and would cost at least 90 percent as much.

Maintaining the force structure had been deliberate. Powell recognized that it would be much simpler to sell the military services on equally apportioned cutbacks than to radically reallocate resources among them to respond to what was, in fact, a radically changed security environment.

So the accompanying new national defense strategy managed to describe the new threat environment in such a way that it required many of the same war-fighting plans and new weapons system that would have been needed had the cold war continued.[12]

The military was ordered to prepare for a possible reconstitution of the Soviet threat, or one from a comparable globally deployed, high-tech military. It was ordered to be ready to fight and decisively win two simultaneous regional wars against second-tier military powers like North Korea and Iraq—both with armed forces and doctrines closely resembling those of the cold war Warsaw Pact. And it was configured to be able to fight these two regional wars on the basis of the Weinberger-Powell Doctrine requiring overwhelming force advantages.

Bureaucratically, this was a brilliant maneuver. It kept peace among the rival services. It pleased defense contractors, who made their biggest markups on high-tech cold-war-style weapons systems. And it left congressional Democrats to argue over how many major regional wars to prepare for, and whether they needed to be won consecutively or simultaneously.

Equal sacrifice was bureaucratically easier to sell than a military reconfigured for a changed world in which strategic nuclear forces, aerial combat fighters, and attack subs were likely to count for less, and boots on the ground, night vision goggles, and infantry armor were likely to count for more. But Powell and Cheney's Base Force plan has wasted trillions of borrowed budget dollars and has made American troops more vulnerable and America less secure ever since.

The projected budget savings would be only 10 percent—roughly $30 billion a year at the end of the five years, not nearly enough to move the federal budget away from deep deficits without new taxes. And such a large and expensive military would have to justify these burdens by lowering the national security threshold for U.S. military interventions.

In a speech at Aspen on August 2, 1990, Bush signed on to the Pentagon's plan, although his words seemed to point in a very different direction. Bush called for "restructuring," not mere reductions. "If we simply pro-rate our reductions," he warned, "cut equally across the board, we could easily end up with more than we need for contingencies that are no longer likely, and less than we must have to meet emerging challenges." But by accepting the Pentagon's artful definition of those new contingencies, Bush guaranteed that very little restructuring would take place.

"Even in a world where democracy and freedom have made great gains, threats remain. Terrorism. Hostage-taking. Renegade regimes and unpredictable rulers—new sources of instability—all require a strong and engaged America," Bush declared. But did they require the seventy-five B-2 nuclear bombers, eighteen Trident-missile-launching submarines, Midgetman ICBMs, rail-based Peacekeeper missiles, and SDI missile defense shield that Bush endorsed that day? These were weapons for cold war deterrence, not for dealing with hostage-taking renegades. Bush wedded a force structure for fighting the armies of traditional great powers to a rationale that emphasized terrorists, failed states, and rogues.[13]

The world had changed, but the weapons systems would not. Not all of the new and old threats invoked to keep military spending at 90 percent of cold war levels were implausible. But instead of setting rational new security and budget priorities, Bush let the Pentagon buy almost everything on the military-industrial complex's wish list—and this at a time when he was already feeling so pressured on deficits that he had felt compelled to abandon, at considerable political cost, his 1988 campaign pledge of "no new taxes."

When the cold war ended, the Bush administration punted on setting new strategic priorities. Instead, it let the Pentagon configure American military forces to fight the kind of wars it preferred rather than prepare for the more likely asymmetrical challenges against the sole remaining superpower—wars like the ones the American military has had to remake itself to fight in Iraq and Afghanistan. This failure of political leadership and strategic vision has had heavy long-term costs for America's security.

Converting America's cold war force of the early 1990s into the proportionately reduced Base Force was supposed to take five years. But Washington's full-strength cold war military was about to get one last workout. Just hours before Bush spoke at Aspen, Saddam Hussein had invaded Kuwait, claiming it as Iraq's twenty-ninth province. After a few days' hesitation, Bush decided to evict him by military force.

It would be just the kind of warfare for which the cold war American military was already configured and had been training for decades—

relocated from the north German plain to the Arabian desert, and waged against a weaker, less competent foe. It yielded a splendid victory and a seemingly unassailable argument for the new Base Force concept. It used the old force structure and it defeated a post-cold-war rogue.

The threat that Saddam's invasion posed to the control of world oil reserves was real, although the immediate threat was more to European and Japanese supplies than to those of the United States. America imported only 12 percent of its oil from the Persian Gulf region in 1990. But Iraq and Kuwait together accounted for 20 percent of known global reserves. If Saddam went on to grab Saudi Arabia's poorly defended oil fields, he would control 45 percent of those reserves. (And if that emboldened him to challenge Iran, a further 10 percent would be in play.)[14]

This was not a messy postcolonial war like Vietnam. It was an intervention Bush could, and did, frame in the resonant liberal internationalist traditions of Woodrow Wilson and FDR. Saddam had committed unambiguous aggression—the equivalent of Kaiser Wilhelm's violation of Belgian neutrality in 1914 and Hitler's invasion of Poland in 1939. Bush had rallied the UN Security Council, the modern version of FDR's four policemen. After the Iraqis had been thrown out of Kuwait, Bush opted for a modest Wilsonian peace without annexations, declining to divide the victorious allies by marching on to Baghdad.

But the historical parallels to America's role in World Wars I and II failed at two crucial points. First, there were no direct American security interests at stake in the gulf. Wilson had not sought a declaration of war when the kaiser's troops crossed the Belgian border; he sought one two and a half years later, when Germany ordered unrestricted submarine warfare against American shipping. FDR had not asked Congress to declare war when the Wehrmacht entered Poland; he did so two and a half years later, when Japan attacked Pearl Harbor.

By the time America entered both world wars, its own national interests were directly on the line. And in both cases Wilson and FDR had followed the Constitution and asked Congress to declare war. In the Persian Gulf, Bush had come up with a convincing simulation rather than a true parallel.

The issue at stake in Kuwait was not America's security but a particular model of American global leadership, as it had been defined during the emergency state years. And while Bush sought, and got, a congressional resolution approving military action, he claimed that he had sufficient authority to act without one. The resolution was better than nothing. But sending more than 300,000 American troops into battle requires the exercise of presidential war powers that only a formal declaration of war can constitutionally trigger.

Operation Desert Storm did not mark a return to earlier American internationalist traditions. It marked the post-cold-war revival of the American emergency state, with flights of hyperbolic rhetoric worthy of Truman and Acheson, such as Bush's suggestion during the run-up to the war that Saddam Hussein's actions were in some respects worse than Hitler's.[15]

The hundred-hour land battle for Kuwait—begun after thirty-eight days of devastating American air strikes knocked out Iraq's air defenses and crippled its military and industrial infrastructure—provided an awesome display of America's advanced information age weaponry, resourceful field commanders, and raw military power. The whole operation showcased the post-Vietnam Weinberger-Powell Doctrine of overwhelming numbers, clear military objectives, and a fast-track exit strategy.

The open desert terrain, the overcentralized Iraqi command structure, and Washington's decision not to carry the fight into Iraq, where it might have encountered unconventional forms of resistance, all contributed to producing the impression of an invincible American military that could win easy victories while suffering minimal casualties. The total number of American combat deaths was 147.

Bush proudly boasted that the "Vietnam syndrome" had been buried in the sands of Kuwait—by which he meant that American presidents no longer needed to fear the domestic political consequences of sending U.S. troops into battle even when the national security stakes were marginal or indirect. The emergency state was back in business. Nixon's all-volunteer military, Reagan's Weinberger-Powell Doctrine, and Bush's instinct for picking relatively soft targets and avoiding unconventional warfare had all contributed to the emergency state's post-Vietnam revival.

Bush had to overcome one other post-Vietnam obstacle—the American government's deepening international insolvency. It was here that Bush and Baker's perspicacious coalition building paid its biggest dividends. Since the war was fought to restore Kuwait, protect Saudi Arabia, and secure Europe's and Japan's oil, these beneficiaries were asked to pay most of its $61 billion cost. Their combined contributions amounted to $54 billion—two-thirds of it from the Saudi and Kuwaiti ruling families, most of the rest from Germany and Japan.[16]

The appearance of easy military victory had its costs. Bush's decision not to cross the Iraqi border and remove Saddam Hussein from power left important American objectives less than fully achieved. Despite continued sanctions and the low-intensity war conducted in the American-declared no-fly zones, Washington could never be confident that Saddam would not again threaten Kuwait or resume work on nuclear, biological, and chemical weapons. And when Iraq's Shiite majority and Kurdish minority took Bush's suggestion and rose up against Saddam, they were ruthlessly slaughtered. Washington belatedly carved out an autonomous sanctuary for the Kurds. But the Shiites found that they only had Iran to turn to, a consequence of the 1991 war that plagues American policy in Iraq to this day.

In 1991, however, the war seemed like an indisputable triumph. The quick victory of American arms, at a minimal cost in American lives and dollars, uncorked a flood of patriotic, martial pride in America unknown since before Vietnam.

The Pentagon portrayed the Gulf War as the prototype for an American military future based on remarkably accurate laser-guided weapons that steered clear of civilian targets and made it possible to keep American troops largely out of harm's way. Pentagon videos showcased clean hits by these futuristic "smart bombs," while in fact more than 90 percent of the American bombs dropped during Operation Desert Storm were old-fashioned dumb bombs, thousands of Iraqi civilians were killed, and the deliberate targeting of power grids, sewage treatment plants, oil refineries, and bridges inflicted significant damage on the civilian economy.[17]

Victory in Kuwait appeared to vindicate the Pentagon's plans to retain most of its cold war forces and configurations and simply switch its military mission from containing the Soviet superpower to containing regional rogues. After forty years and $11 trillion of emergency mobilization against the Soviet nuclear and ideological threat, America's reward would not be a peace dividend, releasing fiscal resources and democratic energies at home. It would be continued emergency and continued mobilization, not because a remotely comparable global threat remained, but on the dubious theory that the only way Americans could stay secure was through permanent global military dominance as a single superpower preemptively policing the world.

The new threat, in the eyes of Bush's Pentagon, was not a rival great power but a potential power vacuum. The new rationale for American military deployments would not be defending endangered allies or containing the Soviet threat but maintaining stability and the international status quo. The old mission, though ambitious, was finite and achievable. The new mission was infinite, permanent, and impossible.

Capitalizing on the war's popularity, the Pentagon spent much of the last two years of Bush's presidency fashioning ambitious new strategic doctrines, resisting further force reductions or spending cuts, and identifying new global threats that could justify its spending plans.

One possible contingency was the potential reconstitution of aggressive Soviet power. But that danger seemed increasingly remote as the Warsaw Pact dissolved, the Soviet Union collapsed, and Russian president Boris Yeltsin proved even more conciliatory and pro-Western than Mikhail Gorbachev. In July 1991 Bush and Gorbachev had signed the START I agreement, agreeing to reduce each side's nuclear warheads by roughly 30 percent and limiting the number of land-based missiles carrying multiple warheads. Two months later both followed up these negotiated cuts with unilaterally announced reductions of large categories of land- and sea-based short-range "tactical" nuclear weapons. A follow-up START II agreement, signed by Bush and Yeltsin in January 1993, provided for a further 50 percent reduction in long-range (strategic) warheads and elimination of the remaining land-based ICBMs carrying multiple warheads (MIRVs).

But a rival high-tech superpower was the only plausible military threat that could justify some of the biggest-ticket military spending items—like fighter aircraft designed for air-to-air combat or midocean fighting ships. At the end of Bush's term, the United States still had more than 18,000 nuclear warheads and a Pentagon mentality that viewed them as an essential tool for asserting offensive military dominance in regional conflicts around the world, not simply as a defensive deterrent against a potential nuclear attack against the United States. As Washington should have foreseen, but didn't, that kind of thinking provided rising or threatened regional powers with incentives to redress the local military balance by developing their own nuclear weapons.[18]

Another much-discussed threat was future regional "rogues," on the model of Manuel Noriega, the North Korean Communist dictator Kim Il Sung, and especially Saddam Hussein. Bush had just demonstrated America's ability to challenge and defeat such rogues without getting bogged down in a Vietnam-like quagmire.

Whether this was the wisest use of American power and resources after the long cold war was another matter. But it is politically hard to argue with success, and Desert Storm had been a popular success. Besides, from Truman's day onward, Americans had readily embraced the idea that a rogue ignored anywhere was a potential new Hitler enabled.

Only the United States, a succession of cold war presidents had declared, had the will and the power to crush these threats while they could still be easily crushed. No matter that Hitler had threatened the United States only because he had Germany's power and resources behind him. Evil was evil and America was America, and this was our self-appointed mission after World War II.

It was a flattering and heroic view of ourselves, until the costs of unilaterally policing the world began to seem too high. Vietnam had deeply discredited this oversimplified Munich analogy. But Bush's smashing triumph in Kuwait banished the Vietnam syndrome of self-doubt and revived that analogy's seductive appeal.

Bush himself applied the rogue doctrine selectively, deliberately overlooking the aggression and genocidal atrocities carried out, starting in 1992, by Serbia's leader, Slobodan Milosevic, and his Bosnian Serb proxies against defenseless Bosnian Muslims. Sarajevo is less than 450 miles from Munich, and what unfolded there was, in fact, Europe's worst genocide since Hitler. But Bosnia, unlike Kuwait, had no oil; a U.S. military intervention there would have found few allies; and military commanders from Colin Powell downward thought it would draw American troops into a messy and protracted conflict. Besides, Bush, having tried in vain to keep the Soviet Union from disintegrating, was not eager to involve the United States in the bloody breakup of Yugoslavia.

Paired with the threat from "rogues" was the threat from terrorists. In 1991 this word didn't refer to the nonstate networks like the later Al Qaeda; nor did it necessarily refer to groups that targeted civilians. It was then a more generalized epithet used by Reagan- and Bush-era officials against leftist guerrilla armies in Central America or elsewhere in the third world.

This linguistic blurring may be one explanation for why some of these same officials, returned to power under George W. Bush after 2000, were so determined to see connections between "rogues" like Saddam and the Al Qaeda terrorists who struck on 9/11. It may also help explain their predisposition for seeing America's armed forces as ideally suited to waging a global war against terrorism.

One year after Desert Storm, Americans got their first clear look at the Pentagon's newly emerging strategic narrative. A nearly final draft of a forty-six-page planning document was leaked to *The New York Times* by an official who believed the "post-cold-war strategy debate should be carried out in the public domain." The draft had been put together under the supervision of Paul Wolfowitz, then undersecretary of defense for policy. Those working on it included I. Lewis "Scooter" Libby, then principal deputy undersecretary of defense for strategy and resources, and Zalmay Khalilzad, then deputy undersecretary of defense for policy planning. All would go on to be major figures in the George W. Bush administration.[19]

News stories on the leaked document sparked an uproar among congressional Democrats. Senator Robert Byrd noted, "The basic thrust of the document seems to be this: We love being the sole remaining superpower in the world and we want so much to remain that way that we are willing to put at risk the basic health of our economy and well-being of our people to do so." Senator Joe Biden criticized the Pentagon's vision of a "Pax Americana, a global security system where threats to stability are suppressed or destroyed by U.S. military power," noting that setting up the United States as "the world's policeman" would, "not incidentally," "preserve a large defense budget."[20]

Others noted a parallel coincidence: the size and configuration of American forces required by the new planning document closely matched the outline Powell and the Pentagon had proposed two years earlier in the Base Force proposals. That had been before the Soviet Union collapsed and the Warsaw Pact dissolved. How could two such transformative strategic events not affect the Pentagon's force requirements? Bush and Cheney publicly distanced themselves from some of the leaked document's most controversial points and sent it back for revision.

While paying lip service to multilateralism, U.S. alliances, and the United Nations, the draft *Defense Planning Guidance* emphasized unilateral U.S. policies and power, acting through ad hoc "coalitions of the willing"—temporary groupings assembled by Washington for specific purposes and then discarded so as not to become a diplomatic or political brake on unilateral U.S. objectives. This was quite different from the kind of UN-based multilateralism that had guided Bush in the war for Kuwait.

And in contrast to the clearly defined and limited aims that Bush had pursued in Kuwait, the draft *Defense Planning Guidance* set ambitious goals in almost every corner of the globe. It made U.S. military forces responsible for defending Eastern Europe from Russian attack, fostering "regional stability" in the Middle East and the Persian Gulf, and preventing the emergence of a military power "vacuum" in the Pacific.

Instead of looking toward greater strategic and fiscal burden-sharing with U.S. allies, it set the opposite goal of preventing even friendly democratic states from expanding their own military capacities. It specifically discouraged European democracies from taking responsibility for their own security now that the cold war was over, calling instead for them to remain dependent on a U.S.-dominated NATO.

While acknowledging that Germany, Japan, and other rich and technologically advanced countries had legitimate interests of their own, the Pentagon document insisted that the United States must show the necessary leadership and "retain the preeminent responsibility" for protecting the interests of its allies and "friends" so that "they need not aspire to a greater role or pursue a more aggressive posture to protect their legitimate interests."[21]

The real problem was not so much the specific points of this global agenda but, with its absence of strategic choices, its insistence that even after the cold war was over, the United States needed to and could afford to pursue, and would be made more secure by pursuing, policies akin to universal containment. Its authors saw American security as requiring global American hegemony without seeming to recognize that such a domineering unipolar course might turn others against us and actually make us less secure—as in fact happened a decade later when some of the people behind the 1992 draft *Defense Planning Guidance* became leading policy makers in the George W. Bush administration.

After fifty years of world war, cold war, and the emergency state, the American people had arrived at a hard-earned moment of extraordinary international security. Unfortunately, in the name of consolidating that security, successive administrations spent much of the next sixteen years undermining it.

Bush, unlike Reagan, left no defining political legacy, no presidential template. His successors, not just Bill Clinton but his own son as well, looked hard for ways to demonstrate that they were not George H. W. Bush.

Bush's role in the evolution of the emergency state was a crucial one nonetheless. Just as Harry Truman, four decades earlier, had perpetuated and institutionalized FDR's wartime emergency state to create the peacetime, cold war emergency state, Bush preserved it intact into the post-cold-war world.

Freed from any specific emergency or mission, it would henceforth search for a suitably ambitious permanent mission, looking, under Clinton, to replace the containment of very real Soviet ambitions with the diffuse "enlargement" of America's global mission, and under George W. Bush to replace the cold war against a real and specific superpower rival with a permanent "global war on terrorism."

CHAPTER TWELVE

BRIDGE TO NOWHERE

Nobody had really expected George H. W. Bush to dismantle the emergency state. Bush had been a loyal servant of the emergency state and its institutions from World War II to the CIA to the White House. Bill Clinton, by contrast, had identified himself from the beginning of his political career with opposition to emergency state policies and institutions and evocations of America's broader democratic traditions. He had marched against the Vietnam War. He had helped manage George McGovern's antiwar "come home America" presidential campaign in Texas. He had run for president on a platform of "putting people first" that called for redirecting the nation's attention and resources from distant foreign policy adventures into repairing a domestic economy damaged by Republican policies of excessive military spending and spiraling deficits.

Clinton's politics, like America's, had moved to the right since the 1960s. But when a potentially embarrassing December 1969 letter he had written to an army colonel who had helped him secure a Vietnam-era draft deferment turned up in the middle of the 1992 New Hampshire Democratic primary campaign, Clinton, on the advice of his campaign aide, James Carville, decided to make the best of it, correctly guessing that many voters of his generation would understand and even sympathize.[1]

Political philosophy wasn't the only thing that had been on the twenty-three-year-old Clinton's mind when he wrote the letter. He had agreed to join the Reserve Officer Training Corps (ROTC) earlier that year to avoid having to report for induction. Now, with a high number in Nixon's draft lottery removing any risk of conscription, he wanted out of the ROTC commitment.

But the letter also conveys Clinton's earlier views on some of the demands the emergency state makes on American democracy. From a law seminar he had taken at Georgetown University, Clinton wrote, he "came to believe that the draft system itself is illegitimate. No government really rooted in limited parliamentary democracy should have the power to make its citizens fight and kill and die in a war they may oppose, a war which even possibly may be wrong, a war which, in any case, does not involve immediately the peace and freedom of the nation."

Clinton acknowledged that in a war for vital interests, like World War II, the draft was justified: "The draft was justified in World War II because the life of the people collectively was at stake. Individuals had to fight if the nation was to survive, for the lives of their countrymen and their way of life. Vietnam is no such case. Nor was Korea, an example where in my opinion, certain military action was justified but the draft was not, for the reasons stated above."[2]

Clinton had not yet attended Yale Law School. If he had, he might have been able to come up with a more workable principle—namely, that the draft was justified in constitutionally declared wars like World War II, but less obviously so in presidentially ordered police actions like Korea and Vietnam.

After Clinton's election as president in November 1992, the way at last seemed clear to achieve much deeper military spending cuts than Bush and Cheney's Pentagon had been willing to contemplate, along with a major reconfiguration of forces away from the cold war template Colin Powell had preserved in his Base Force model.

Leading congressional Democrats, including House Budget Committee chairman Leon Panetta and House Armed Services Committee chairman Les Aspin, had spent much of the past three years calling for deep cuts and cancellations of expensive cold war weapons systems like the F-22 tactical fighter and strategic ballistic missile defenses and costly boondoggles like the C-17 transport plane and the vertical takeoff Osprey. Clinton had picked up on these themes during his successful presidential campaign.

Now Clinton was in the White House, Panetta was budget director, Aspin was defense secretary, and the Democrats were firmly in control of both houses of Congress. Yet at a time when the global strategic environment allowed deep military spending cuts, when the voters expected them, and when the deficit-ridden U.S. economy required them, the new Clinton administration proposed only cautious trims that realized only very modest fiscal savings.

Aspin, taking over as defense secretary, promised a "Bottom-Up Review" that would jettison cold war assumptions and force requirements. But when Aspin's review came out in October 1993, its assumptions about the need to be able to fight and win two simultaneous Desert Storm–size regional wars closely tracked those left behind by Cheney's Pentagon. Its war-gaming models assumed that enemy armies would be built around tank forces, like those of the old Warsaw Pact or Saddam Hussein's Iraq. It envisioned multilateral coalitions but insisted that "our forces must be sized and structured to preserve the capability to act unilaterally, should we choose to do so." The force requirements that followed from those assumptions largely kept Powell's Base Force model intact. The Base Force, which Powell had planned for 1.6 million troops, fell only to 1,450,000 in Clinton's last year.[3]

During the presidential campaign Clinton had promised to cut military spending by as much as $100 billion (which he later scaled down to $60 billion) over the next five years from the levels the Bush administration had projected. That sounded like a big number on the campaign trail. But the promised $60 billion cut should be measured against the more than $1.35 trillion the Clinton Pentagon ended up spending over those five years. And by Clinton's second term, real defense spending was once again trending upward.[4]

From the beginning Aspin had trouble coming up with budget projections that could deliver on Clinton's relatively modest $60 billion target. He found it hard to set clear priorities and make hard choices. Aspin had entered Congress in 1971 as a liberal Democratic critic of Pentagon policies and budgets. But in his eight years as chairman of the House Armed Services Committee, he had become a Washington insider, familiar and increasingly comfortable with Pentagon habits of thinking and planning.

That never won him much respect with the services. Men accustomed to military precision reacted poorly to Aspin's disorganized managerial style. Aspin, instead of bringing new post-cold-war thinking to the Pentagon, was led by the Pentagon's own entrenched ways of seeing things to yield ever more ground, until he gave up on even the modest force realignments and scaling back of war scenarios he had advocated in Congress.

Aspin embraced almost the full range of hypothetical threat contingencies the Bush Pentagon had left behind, the supersized and misallocated cold war force structure that those contingencies had been used to justify, and the long list of expensive weapons systems that had lost their military rationale with the end of the cold war but continued to be funded. That did not leave much scope for significant additional budget savings.

Aspin's Bottom-Up Review even added some new and surprising Pentagon missions. Under "Objectives of Our Armed Forces," it included:

- "Use military-to-military contacts to help foster democratic values in other countries."
- "Protect fledgling democracies from subversion and external threats."
- "Redirect resources to investments that improve both our defense posture and our competitive position economically."[5]

Aspin put himself in an even tighter budgetary box by yielding to pressure from the armed services to stipulate that U.S. forces must be able to fight and win two simultaneous regional wars, perhaps unilaterally (a requirement he had rightly challenged as unrealistically rigid during his congressional days).[6]

He further inflated force requirements by signing on to Powell's Base Force approach of keeping the relative size of the army, navy, and air force in roughly the same proportions they had been in during the cold war, despite the changes in likely enemies and combat terrain. (The army ended up bearing more than its share of force cuts, at least in part because Congress had legislatively blocked any significant cut in the size of the Marine Corps.) That bow to the service bureaucracies locked in an active-duty air force and navy too large and too expensive for current needs. Paying for them within the Clinton budget caps meant squeezing procurement.[7]

But instead of maximizing procurement savings by canceling expensive systems designed to meet cold war threats—like F-22 air combat fighters and a national ballistic missile defense system—Clinton and Aspin continued to waste scarce procurement dollars on these legacy systems at the expense of other purchases more suited to the post-cold-war era, like unpiloted drones, navy ships designed for close-to-shore combat and support of ground forces, and slower and lower-flying planes less prone to mistake civilians for military targets.

Nor did Clinton provide the procurement relief that could have come from negotiating further nuclear arms reductions with Moscow. No further bilateral nuclear arms reduction treaties were negotiated with Russia during Clinton's two terms. Strategically deployed nuclear weapons, which Bush had cut from nearly 15,000 to less than 9,500 in the course of his four-year term, fell by less than 800 in Clinton's eight years.

Maintaining such large standing forces with no clear mission created political pressures to justify the expense by using them, even when, as in Haiti or the Balkans, no vital national interests were at stake. As

Clinton's UN ambassador, Madeleine Albright, put it to Colin Powell in 1993, "What's the point of having this superb military you're always talking about if we can't use it?"[8]

With the Soviet Union and the Warsaw Pact dissolved and the United States not facing a globally menacing, technologically formidable foe for the first time in fifty years, Clinton and his advisers recognized that the American people might begin to question the continued necessity of an expensive, globally interventionist foreign policy that was feeding federal deficits, undermining American competitiveness, and creating more new enemies than friends abroad.

Clinton might have embraced this new mood. He had condemned George Bush for being too focused on foreign policy and for not paying enough attention to domestic needs and problems. Instead, Clinton chose to go with the Reagan presidential template, serving up yet another replay of the glory days of American cold war international leadership.

Rather than seriously taking on the expensive military icons of emergency state thinking, Clinton preferred to savage his own signature programs of stimulus spending, upgrading worker skills, and middle-class tax relief to meet his deficit-reduction targets.

Why?

In part, it was because Clinton had been a draft-evading McGovern Democrat and feared a public fight with military leaders, as he showed when he let Colin Powell, as chairman of the Joint Chiefs, roll back his policy of letting gay Americans serve openly in the armed forces. In part, it was because Clinton had won only 43 percent of the popular vote for president in 1992 (although that hadn't stopped Nixon from acting decisively after his 43 percent win in 1968). In part, it was because Clinton felt his chances for reelection in 1996 depended on showing he was not the wimp that he thought America had come to believe Jimmy Carter was. And in part, it was because Clinton failed to focus on foreign policy and defense budget issues, wrongly seeing them as a distraction from his campaign promises to fix the economy.[9]

As a self-styled "New Democrat," Clinton chose to leave those divisive issues of the 1960s, 1970s, and 1980s on autopilot.

• • •

Bill Clinton was the first American president born under the emergency state, and unlike one of his early mentors, Senator William Fulbright, Clinton had no personal experience or historical perspective to point him back toward pre-emergency-state constitutional democracy.

So instead of educating Americans on the benefits of dismantling the emergency state, Clinton sent out his national security adviser, Anthony Lake, to hector them into retaining it. While Les Aspin was repackaging the cold war military in his Bottom-Up Review, Lake offered a repackaged version of universal containment and Wilsonian millenarianism that he called "enlargement."

Lake's biggest anxiety was not about some new external threat but about the possibility that America might democratically decide to turn its attention inward toward domestic concerns. Recalling the foreign policy debates of the Truman years, Lake noted that "the internationalists won those debates, in part because they could point to a unitary threat to America's interests and because the nation was entering a period of economic security. Today's supporters of engagement abroad have neither of those advantages. The threats and opportunities are diffuse and our people are deeply anxious about their economic fate."

If Lake's "internationalists" lost the 1990s version of those old debates, the public might not be willing to fund the emergency state at the levels to which its institutions had grown accustomed: "At a time of high deficits and pressing domestic needs, we need to make a convincing case for our engagement or else see drastic reduction in our military, intelligence, peacekeeping and other foreign policy accounts."

Lake did his best to portray 1993 as a replay of 1947, the annus mirabilis for the peacetime emergency state. GATT and NAFTA would stand in for the Marshall Plan. NATO, not yet invented in 1947, was cast for reinvention in the 1990s, with new members drawn from the ranks of the former Warsaw Pact and new missions beyond its original European perimeters.

But where the Marshall Plan had revived markets for American industry, GATT and NAFTA mainly lubricated the continued migration of American factories and jobs abroad. And where NATO's original mission strengthened transatlantic unity, Clinton's calls on European NATO members to fight for American-designated causes "out of area" subjected that hard-won unity to gratuitous new strains.

To replace the Stalinist "unitary threat" of 1947, Lake conjured up a hypothetical danger that drew on old Wilsonian pieties, the newest fashions in popular political science, and the latest Pentagon planning documents.

From Wilson came the missionary assertion that "our own security is shaped" not just by the behavior but "by the character of foreign regimes," and that "to the extent democracy and market economics hold sway in other nations, our own nation will be more secure, prosperous and influential, while the broader world will be more humane and peaceful."

Then came the political science: "Those whose power is threatened by the spread of democracy and markets will always have a personal stake in resisting those practices with passionate intensity."

Then the link to Pentagon threat scenarios and plans for fighting two simultaneous regional wars: "When such leaders sit atop regional powers, such as Iran and Iraq, they may engage in violence and lawlessness that threatens the United States and other democracies. Such reactionary 'backlash' states are more likely to sponsor terrorism and traffic in weapons of mass destruction and ballistic missile technologies. They are more likely to suppress their own people, foment ethnic rivalries and threaten their neighbors."

In other words, America's security needs required it to expand democracy and markets everywhere, but doing so would likely provoke regional despots to threaten America's security and that of other democracies.

And never mind that Lake's description of backlash states fit Pakistan and China as well as or better than it fit Iran and Iraq. The force structure the Pentagon had decided to retain was configured for simultaneous regional wars in the Persian Gulf region and the Korean Peninsula, so the doctrinal rationale had to point to the appropriate "rogues" and not get distracted elsewhere, where different reasons of state dictated different American policies.

Lake's list of new security concerns did, however, have room for countries "with the potential to generate refugee flows into our own nation or into key friends and allies," a category that had already sent American Coast Guard cutters into the waters between Haiti and Florida and would soon bring more than 20,000 American troops into Haiti itself.

Despite its claims to define America's new foreign policy priorities, Lake's doctrine, like Aspin's Bottom-Up Review, deliberately kept open the option of American intervention in virtually any country or region and made no clear distinctions between vital American interests and actions that would "generate broader security benefits for the people and the region in question."[10]

Despite Lake's promise of coherent themes that the public could understand and believe in, Clinton's foreign interventions lacked any obvious coherence.

Six weeks before Clinton took office, George Bush had ordered 25,000 U.S. troops to Somalia in what he described as a "humanitarian" military intervention. Clan warfare was endangering the distribution of international famine relief. Bush explained that the American troops would have only one objective: to secure food supply routes. Then they would depart, turning security over to UN peacekeepers. America had no desire to "dictate political outcomes."[11]

Bush had refused to send American troops to halt the slaughter of unarmed Bosnian Muslims by Yugoslav army–equipped Bosnian Serbs because the issue divided NATO, because no direct American interests were at stake, and because, as Colin Powell, then serving as chairman of the Joint Chiefs, pointed out, no clean exit strategy was assured.[12]

Somalia seemed simpler to Bush and Powell. No direct American interests were at stake there either. But the Somali relief crisis seemed to offer an opportunity for the United States to show it could use its military forces in a humanitarian cause while getting its troops in and out quickly and cleanly. Like Kuwait, it could burnish the image, and justify the high cost and extraconstitutional methods, of the emergency state. But to keep it quick and clean, Washington would have to be careful to resist all temptations of "mission creep." Bush, Cheney, and Powell were careful. Clinton and Aspin were not, and Powell, still at the Joint Chiefs, unhappily watched it happen.[13]

Most of the original U.S. troop contingent did withdraw during the first half of 1993. But UN secretary-general Boutros Boutros-Ghali and his special representative for Somalia, retired American admiral Jonathan Howe (a former Kissinger aide), kept trying to dictate political outcomes. In particular, they targeted Somalia's most powerful warlord, Mohammed Farah Aideed. When Aideed fought back, Clinton agreed to bolster the UN peacekeepers with elite American special forces units.

With that fateful decision, Bush's humanitarian mission turned into a war of U.S. firepower against Aideed and his armed supporters—with nationalist Somalis rallying to the side of the local warlord in his battle with armed foreigners. Three days after Powell concluded his term at the Joint Chiefs, American special forces trying to grab two of Aideed's top aides were surrounded and ambushed by the warlord's supporters. Aideed's men (trained by Al Qaeda, as Washington later learned, in the use of rocket-propelled grenades) brought down two of the U.S. Black Hawk helicopters sent as part of the evacuation force and dragged the corpses of American soldiers through cheering Somali crowds lining the streets of Mogadishu.

That effectively ended Les Aspin's tenure as defense secretary. But it only marked a detour in the Clinton administration's benighted pursuit of enlargement.

Six months after the "Black Hawk Down" fiasco, militias led and armed by Rwanda's majority tribe, the Hutu, launched a swift and systematic genocide against the country's Tutsi minority. In just one hundred days that spring and summer, Hutu militiamen armed with machetes and other primitive weapons killed more than 800,000 Tutsis. Armed UN peacekeepers whose commander believed he could have stopped them stood by, on orders from the Security Council and the secretary-general in New York.

The Clinton administration, burned by Somalia, then voted to withdraw most of those UN peacekeepers. A month later, when the UN finally sent reinforcements, Washington did all in its power to withhold promised logistical assistance. A second set of American military casualties in Africa might have risked public support for enlargement elsewhere.

Washington sat by while the genocide played itself out. Finally a Tutsi guerrilla army overthrew Rwanda's Hutu government and chased the Hutu militia into the neighboring Congo, where they became a focal point for years of deadly inter-African wars.

No direct U.S. national security interests were at stake in Rwanda, just Tutsi lives and the credibility of those moralistic Wilsonian exhortations that Clinton, Aspin, and Lake had been so freely using to justify big defense budgets and a globally interventionist foreign policy.

From then on, enlargement in Africa largely consisted of Clinton administration officials bestowing unmerited praise on authoritarian African leaders friendly to American investment and foreign policy, just as a succession of previous American administrations had done during the cold war.

While genocide was raging unchecked in Rwanda, a different kind of crisis was developing in one of the two areas around which the Pentagon had built its regional war plans—the Korean Peninsula. North Korea had signed the Nuclear Nonproliferation Treaty in 1985 but refused to accept the international monitoring requirements that went with it. In 1993 the North gave notice of withdrawal from the treaty, and in the spring of 1994, after much back-and-forth negotiating finally broke down, North Korea blocked international inspectors from taking samples at its plutonium reprocessing plant at Yongbyon. The inspectors withdrew, and Clinton ordered the Pentagon to plan missile strikes against the Yongbyon plant.

The threat of another all-out war on the Korean Peninsula suddenly loomed.

Then, at the height of the crisis, former president Jimmy Carter accepted an invitation from the North Korean Communist leader. Though the visit was billed as private and unofficial, it had Clinton's approval. After two days of talks, Carter emerged with an agreement that defused the crisis and led to renewed international monitoring of the Yongbyon nuclear plant.

The issues in this crisis—chiefly North Korea's intentions with regard to nuclear weapons—affected American interests far more directly and seriously than events in Somalia or Rwanda. Invoking the possibility of U.S. military action was justified and probably helped move the diplomatic process forward.

But to have proceeded with a missile strike on Yongbyon, as Clinton had apparently intended to do before the Carter visit, would have been a serious mistake at a moment when all diplomatic options had obviously not yet been exhausted. American intelligence analysts believed that North Korea likely had other nuclear facilities tunneled deep beneath its mountains. A precision missile strike on Yongbyon would have left these other facilities intact and might well have led to a general war in which tens of thousands of American troops and millions of Korean civilians would have been killed. Fortunately good luck intervened.

In the other area that the Pentagon had marked as a potential regional war zone, Iraq, the Bush administration had passed on a policy time bomb. By demonizing Saddam Hussein but not removing him, and leaving key American policy aims, from closing down Iraqi weapons programs to regime change, for future resolution, Bush had effectively created an unsustainable situation of strong international sanctions with no obvious exit.

Just prior to his inauguration, Clinton had tried to create a little breathing room by suggesting that the sanctions could be lifted if Iraq fully cooperated with UN weapons inspectors. But he was quickly assailed in the media and on Capitol Hill for this alleged sign of weakness and had to clamber back to Bush's bequeathed orthodoxy that the sanctions would effectively remain in place as long as Saddam did.[14]

Clinton's initial position was a sign of shrewdness rather than weakness, but unfortunately he did not hold to it very long. Sanctions without an exit formula are generally self-defeating. They take away the targeted country's strongest incentive to comply with international demands (or as it turned out in Saddam's case, to acknowledge that they were complying): the prospect that sanctions will then be lifted. And they exhaust the will of countries suffering commercially from the sanctions to keep enforcing them.

That is exactly what happened in the case of Iraq during the Clinton years, increasingly isolating the United States and leaving Washington to choose between eroding sanctions and risky uses of military force. That narrowing set of policy options led Clinton to endorse a CIA-backed coup attempt that was headed by one American-backed exile leader, Ayad Allawi; opposed by another, Ahmed Chalabi; and routed after a third American-backed Iraqi, the Kurdish leader Massoud Barzani, invited Iraqi troops into Kurdistan, where many of the plotters were based, to help Barzani defeat his American-backed Kurdish rival Jalal Talabani. The emergency state was literally tripping over itself, with Saddam the main beneficiary.[15]

Two years later Clinton punished Iraq for interfering with international weapons inspectors by four days of punitive bombing that backfired even more disastrously. For their own safety, the inspectors left Iraq before the Anglo-American bombing offensive began. They never returned. That meant that from the end of 1998 onward, no Western intelligence agencies had any access to accurate information about whether Iraq was reconstituting its weapons programs. Three years later, when George W. Bush began pressing the CIA to provide information on this issue, they could offer no more than guesswork or secondhand intelligence from unreliable Iraqi émigrés.

But that was for the future. After the spring 1994 North Korea crisis, Clinton's next military adventure came later the same year in Haiti. The goal was to restore President Jean-Bertrand Aristide, ousted in a 1991 army coup. This was militarily far less dangerous terrain. Jimmy Carter, Colin Powell, and Sam Nunn had negotiated an uncontested entry by more than 20,000 American troops. There was no risk of regional war or needless casualties.

But neither was there much political or strategic coherence to the September 1994 military intervention, which brought U.S. troops back to a country they had occupied from 1915 to 1934, restored a ruler in whom the Clinton administration had little faith, and produced few lasting positive results. It isn't clear what international objectives Clinton had in mind. In domestic political terms, Haiti seemed to offer the prospect of a low-risk humanitarian intervention that might appeal to the pro-Aristide Democratic left, appease Democratic internationalist critics of Clinton's inaction in Rwanda and Bosnia, and relieve the anxieties of Democratic politicians in the swing state of Florida by turning back an unpopular tide of black Haitian refugees from the state's beaches.

By late 1994 Clinton was no longer able to ignore Bosnia. For months he had been trying to walk a narrow policy tightrope, hoping to deter Bosnian Serb attacks against Sarajevo and other Bosnian Muslim enclaves with NATO air strikes while refusing to commit any U.S. ground troops.

It didn't work, for several reasons. The most important was that two key NATO allies, Britain and France, did have ground troops in Bosnia as part of a UN peacekeeping mission, and the UN's mandate required neutrality between Bosnian Serb and Bosnian government forces. The UN had to sign off on all planned NATO air strikes, which it could do within the terms of its neutral mandate, provided the strikes were solely for the purpose of protecting civilians. But the UN also had to worry about Bosnian Serb forces retaliating against its vulnerable peacekeepers.

Those circumstances greatly limited the effectiveness of NATO air strikes as a means of bringing military pressure. And they led the Bosnian Serbs to step up their own pressure on the peacekeepers. By late 1994 UN secretary-general Boutros-Ghali was threatening to withdraw the peacekeepers. And Bill Clinton, who had refused to consider using U.S. ground troops to protect Bosnian Muslim civilians, pledged to send 25,000 U.S. ground troops if NATO was called on to evacuate the UN peacekeepers.[16]

Now the only way for Clinton to avoid sending ground troops was to try to force a peace settlement. And that was just what Clinton proceeded to do, though not in time to prevent the slaughter of some 8,000 Muslim men and boys in Srebrenica in July 1995. Two years earlier the UN Security Council had declared Srebrenica a safe area under UN protection. But the Dutch peacekeepers sent there to protect it felt overwhelmed and powerless when Bosnian Serb forces rounded up Srebrenica's Muslim men and boys and took them away to be murdered.

Washington increased pressure on the Serbs through stepped-up NATO air strikes, muscular American diplomacy, and covert U.S. military support to Croatian ground troops fighting the Serbs in other parts of the former Yugoslavia. In November 1995 the Clinton administration brokered the Dayton peace agreement, signed by Slobodan Milosevic, as president of Serbia, along with the presidents of Croatia and Bosnia. It gave the Bosnian Serbs their own ministate comprising almost half of Bosnia in return for leaving the other half alone.[17]

Clinton had belatedly stopped the slaughter in Bosnia. But the path that finally got him there was driven at least as much by expedience as by principle and brought no great coherence to the theme of "enlargement." Was America's mission to stop genocide or to preempt a call for ground troops? Was Milosevic a rogue threat or a legitimate bargaining partner? Those issues were kicked down the road till the next Balkan crisis in Kosovo, three and a half years later.

The Bosnian war had begun under George Bush, and much of Serbian "ethnic cleansing" of Muslim areas had already occurred when

Clinton took office. By then only two choices were realistically available to Washington. Either Clinton could have demanded that Britain and France, two of America's leading European allies, stop hiding behind the fiction of neutral peacekeeping and an arms embargo that made it almost impossible for Bosnia to defend itself and instead stand with the United States against genocide. Or, with no direct U.S. security interests at stake besides NATO, and with NATO divided, he could have continued George Bush's policy of deliberately looking away.

Clinton chose neither, only to end up sucked in by the back door two years later, after thousands more had died, transatlantic divisions had deepened, and America's moral reputation had been further tarnished. It was hardly a performance to gloat about. Yet that was just what the Clinton administration began to do, creating a new righteous mythology of humanitarian interventionism without having behaved very righteously when it had mattered most.

America became, in the words of Clinton's second secretary of state, Madeleine Albright, "the indispensable nation." "If we have to use force, it is because we are America," she told Matt Lauer on the *Today* show in early 1998, responding to critics of the administration's plans for punitive bombing of Iraq. "We are the indispensable nation. We stand tall. We see further into the future."[18]

This hubris found clear expression in the 1999 war over Kosovo, when NATO carried out seventy-seven days of air strikes against Serbian military targets, the first offensive military operation in its history. NATO acted without a mandate authorizing the use of force from the UN Security Council. No obvious vital interests of any NATO member were at stake. No one could claim to be acting in self-defense. And in terms of international law, the only aggression was NATO's, since Kosovo was legally Serbian territory.

Kosovo had been a central part of Serbian history and culture since the twelfth century. But starting in the 1700s, much of its original ethnic

Serb population had migrated to other parts of Serbia and a large influx of ethnic Albanians moving in from nearby Albania replaced them.

Slobodan Milosevic took up the cause of Kosovo's remaining Serb minority long before the Bosnian war. In 1989 he had used his power as president of Serbia to rescind Kosovo's administrative autonomy, fire thousands of ethnic Albanians from public jobs, close their schools, deny them public services, and subject them to police harassment and violence.

In response, the ethnic Albanian community rallied to a nonviolent political resistance movement, the Democratic League of Kosovo, led by Ibrahim Rugova. The league created its own parallel social service system but could not provide protection from Milosevic's police. That challenge was taken up in the mid-1990s by a very different group calling itself the Kosovo Liberation Army, which carried out armed attacks against Serbian police—and, occasionally, Serb civilians—in Kosovo.[19]

The KLA knew it had no realistic chance of driving the Serbs out of Kosovo on its own. Looking to replay the events of 1995 in Bosnia, it tried to enlist NATO on its side, even though the Clinton administration's special envoy to the region, Robert Gelbard, had described the KLA's methods as "terrorist" as late as 1998.[20]

In the end, KLA terrorism proved no great obstacle to winning NATO's support. The group continued to provoke Milosevic by killing Serbian police. Serbia responded with reprisal massacres of ethnic Albanian civilians. In the first months of 1999 an international conference presented Milosevic and the KLA with a take-it-or-leave-it offer backed by the threat of NATO military force. The terms restored autonomy for Kosovo under formal Serbian sovereignty but with 30,000 NATO troops policing the province. The KLA, wanting full independence, resisted, then agreed. Milosevic refused.

Encouraged by Albright, who assured him that Milosevic was just a "schoolyard bully" who would yield as soon as the first bombs fell, Clinton ordered NATO air strikes to begin on March 24, 1999. Instead of yielding, Milosevic responded with a reign of terror that sent some 800,000 ethnic Albanians, the overwhelming majority of Kosovo's Albanian population, fleeing for their lives across the Albanian and Macedonian borders. NATO's actions had precipitated the humanitarian crisis they had been intended to prevent. Now NATO had no choice but to fight to the finish.[21]

That was not going to be easy relying on airpower alone. Serbian forces held out against the NATO bombing for more than two months. As in Bosnia four years earlier, Clinton found himself in a difficult policy box—either risk a domestic political uproar by sending Americans to fight and die on the ground where no clear American national interests were at stake, or let NATO fail in its first military test. Either result would likely spell the end of Clinton's enlargement policy, whose formulator, Anthony Lake, had already left the administration.

Finally Russia's president, Boris Yeltsin, who had opposed the NATO bombing, sent his own special envoy, Viktor Chernomyrdin, to Belgrade to advise Milosevic to come to terms. Milosevic, realizing that he was now diplomatically isolated and that NATO would not give up, agreed to make peace.

Yeltsin had shown that Russia still counted for something in southeastern Europe. Milosevic accepted what he could not prevent. Clinton emerged with his hubris fully intact. And the UN Security Council, which voted to place Kosovo under postwar UN administration, moved farther down the road from providing the ultimate source of international legitimacy for military action to the much-diminished position it now occupies: an international service organization called in to provide diplomats and administrators only after the crucial decisions have been made elsewhere.

George W. Bush didn't have to invent the idea of bypassing the Security Council to wage war in Iraq. Bill Clinton had already tried it out in Kosovo.

Two weeks before the Kosovo war, NATO had admitted three new members from the former Warsaw Pact—the Czech Republic, Hungary, and Poland. Clinton had been pushing for NATO enlargement since 1994.

In a sense, it was a logical extension of Lake's enlargement doctrine and the post-cold-war military ambitions of Aspin's Bottom-Up Review.

NATO enlargement appealed to an American public opinion used to thinking in cold war terms. It had strong support from two politically important constituencies—Americans of Eastern European ancestry, and military contractors who stood to reap a bonanza in new orders as new members reequipped their armed forces to NATO standards.[22]

Central and Eastern European countries also pressed hard for enlargement, which would provide them with an explicit American military guarantee against a potentially revived and hostile Russia. And they felt NATO membership would smooth their path to early admission into the European Union. Western European NATO members had misgivings about diluting NATO's military strength and taking on risky new security guarantees, but they accepted enlargement as a necessary price of keeping the United States strongly committed to a transatlantic military alliance.[23]

In Washington, where expansion required Senate approval, few Democrats or Republicans were opposed, despite the warnings of Russia specialists from George Kennan to Michael Mandelbaum that expanding the former anti-Soviet alliance eastward toward Russia's shrunken frontiers would sour relations with Moscow and compromise the future of nuclear arms control.

The warnings of the Russia specialists proved prescient. NATO enlargement did not rekindle cold war tensions. Russia was too weak for that militarily and too dependent on maintaining good economic relations with Germany and other European NATO countries.

But Clinton's NATO enlargement, along with other Clinton policies that Moscow found threatening—like national missile defense, the military and economic wooing of former Soviet republics such as Georgia, Azerbaijan, and Uzbekistan, and Washington's promotion of new energy pipeline routes designed to bypass Russian territory—gradually contributed to a sour and defensive new mood in Moscow that eventually found expression in the chilly anti-Western nationalism of Vladimir Putin.

When the Bush administration had negotiated with Mikhail Gorbachev over the terms of German reunification and NATO membership in 1990, it had assured the Soviet leader that there would be a new post-cold-war NATO, with its role in European security issues thoroughly transformed. Clinton's NATO enlargement didn't look that way to Moscow. (Nor have two subsequent rounds of enlargement, which between them brought in all of the Kremlin's former Warsaw Pact allies along with three former Soviet Republics.)[24]

The line between expanding the sphere of democracy and markets and hemming in Russia proved a thin one. So did the line between the Pentagon's hedging against a hypothetical reconstituted Soviet military threat and Washington stoking Moscow's insecurities about shrinking security frontiers, reduced missile warning times, and the possibility that even a partial national missile defense would dilute the deterrent value of Russia's one remaining superpower military attribute, its strategic missile force.

Clinton's enlargement policy had replaced containment with a new paradigm of American global management, American global policing, and occasional American-directed regime change. The alternative was not, as Lake had feared, an American isolationist withdrawal from world affairs, but (as we will discuss in chapter 15) active American participation in new, postcontainment forms of international trade, global governance, and collective security that did not try to mechanically reproduce cold-war-style American leadership.

A Clinton administration that aspired to that kind of forward-looking internationalism would have recast NATO in a way that included rather than isolated Russia. It would have revised NAFTA to make it a vehicle for European Union–style economic integration rather than a shelter for runaway polluters and sweatshops. It would have strengthened the authority and reach of the Nuclear Nonproliferation Treaty by pushing for deeper great power nuclear arms cuts and putting more pressure on friendly nonsigner states like India, Pakistan, and Israel as well as on unfriendly ones like North Korea and Iran. And it would have looked for ways to reinforce the moral and legal authority of the UN Security Council rather than marginalizing it, as Clinton did on Kosovo.

Taking advantage of the end of the cold war to modernize American foreign policy along these lines would not have fit into the Reagan presidential template. But it would have better served America's late-twentieth-century needs. Clinton ran for reelection in 1996 urging Americans to build a "bridge to the twenty-first century." Instead, he built a bridge to nowhere.[25]

Lake's 1993 enlargement speech had offered four criteria for judging the success of Clinton's foreign policy vision:

> *Whether Americans' real incomes double every 26 years, as they did in the 1960s, or every 36 years, as they did during the late '70s and '80s.*
>
> *Whether the 25 nations with weapons of mass destruction grow in number or decline.*
>
> *Whether the next quarter century will see terrorism, which injured or killed more than 2000 Americans during the last quarter century, expand or recede as a threat.*
>
> *Whether the nations of the world will be more able or less able to address regional disputes, humanitarian needs and the threat of environmental degradation.*

By none of these measures could the eight years of the Clinton administration be judged a success.

Containment had been a calibrated response to a broadly perceived Communist threat, steering a middle course between hot war and appeasement. Enlargement was a deliberate search for threats that seemed impressive enough to justify the United States maintaining a superpower military and to require hegemonic American international leadership.

Enlargement was not aimed at any external danger but at America's supposed reflexive isolationism, even though real isolationists had been an endangered political minority in America since 1947 if not since Pearl

Harbor. By 1993 most Americans were politically addicted to the role of leader of the free world.

With Communism gone and no existential threats on the horizon, Lake redefined that leadership in far-reaching Wilsonian terms that paved the way for the later armed messianism of George W. Bush—making the worldwide expansion of democracy and markets the new precondition for America's security.

Clinton sent U.S. troops on more overseas peacekeeping missions where no direct American security interests were at stake than any previous president. These often-extended deployments took their toll on the readiness and operation tempos of the forces involved—a preview of what would happen when his successor sent wrongly sized and configured forces on extended combat missions to Afghanistan and Iraq.[26]

Mistaking 1993 for 1947, enlargement miscast open trade as creating U.S. jobs at a time when globalization was increasingly turning trade agreements into a tool for accelerating the export of U.S. jobs and capital.

Increasing global trade was a reality and a necessity, but Lake's speech cast it as a win-win bargain requiring nothing more of democratic governments than a laissez-faire policy of standing back and letting the invisible hand lead global corporations toward socially beneficent outcomes. The hard truth proved to be otherwise.

Without the firm regulatory hand of democratic governance, laissez-faire globalization can become an international race to the bottom on labor and environmental standards and a maldistributor of income that allows countries to grow richer while most of their inhabitants grow poorer.

Rather than shifting American resources and energy to the challenges of the future, enlargement followed the Reagan template of turning America's attention from present-day economic anxieties and social discontents to a Hollywood replay of the glory days of a triumphant post–World War II America rebuilding a broken world in its own image.

Whether in the liberal internationalist tones of Bill Clinton and

Barack Obama or the belligerent military neoconservatism of George W. Bush, the ideas behind Lake's enlargement speech became the new rationale for America's post-cold-war emergency state. They have left America less secure at home and abroad, our domestic economy less competitive, and our democracy less vibrant than they were in 1993.

Stated as a percentage of America's entire gross domestic product, as it usually is, military spending seems relatively small. In Clinton's first full fiscal year, FY 1994, it amounted to just 4.1 percent of GDP, falling to 3.0 percent of a significantly larger GDP eight years later.[27]

But that is not the best way to measure military spending's real effects on federal finances or on what government services people feel they are getting in return for their tax dollars.

During the Clinton years, military spending made up between 17 and 20 percent of all federal spending and between 46 and 53 percent of all discretionary federal spending—that is, of all spending not already obligated for entitlements like Social Security, Medicare, Medicaid, veterans benefits, food stamps, etc., or for interest payments on the national debt.

In other words, roughly fifty cents out of every federal dollar that Congress and the administration controlled went to the Pentagon or to nuclear weapons programs run by the Department of Energy. No wonder people didn't feel they were getting much in the way of tangible returns for the taxes they paid and turned back toward Republican candidates promising tax cuts.[28]

Further, in every fiscal year of Clinton's term, military spending exceeded the overall deficit. That means if Clinton had not shied away from deeper cuts in military spending, he could have achieved a budget surplus, and the accompanying low interest rates, years earlier and with less drastic surgery to his campaign platform of restoring the competitiveness of American workers and American products in an increasingly globalized marketplace through public investments in productivity-enhancing training and infrastructure programs.[29]

Clinton's failure to reconfigure the cold war force structure and to shift weapons procurement away from fabulously expensive cold war systems not only weakened America's military preparedness to meet post-cold-war threats. It also forced Clinton to abandon much of the economic strategy he ran on—a strategy based on the recommendations of his longtime friend and adviser on employment and competitiveness issues, Robert Reich.

"The American people have earned this peace dividend through forty years of unrelenting vigilance and sacrifice and an investment of trillions of dollars. And they are entitled to have the dividend reinvested in their future," Clinton had declared during the campaign.[30]

And he had spelled out how it should be reinvested: "Education is economic development. We can only be a high-wage, high-growth country if we are a high-skills country. In a world in which money and production are mobile, the only way middle-class people can keep good jobs with growing incomes is to be lifetime earners and innovators. Without world-class skills, the middle class will surely continue to decline. With them, middle-class workers will generate more high-wage jobs in America in the '90's."[31]

Instead, Clinton embraced a very different strategy, one urged on him by his conservative treasury secretary, Lloyd Bentsen; his deficit-hawk budget director, Leon Panetta; and his Wall Street–minted economic adviser, Robert Rubin. Their strategy, also supported by the Reagan-appointed Federal Reserve chairman, Alan Greenspan, aimed at bringing down interest rates through sharply lower deficits. And because Clinton shied away from deeper defense cuts, those lower deficits were achieved mainly through reductions in Clinton's promised investments in making the domestic economy more globally competitive.[32]

By hewing to the Reagan political template and carrying emergency state thinking and spending into the post-cold-war era—while simultaneously embracing the very un-Reagan-like Rubin-Greenspan commitment to deficit reduction—Clinton squeezed out the fiscal resources needed to deliver on his 1992 campaign promises. He doomed much of the planned public investment in worker retraining, education, and infrastructure and the planned progressive tax reform that had helped him win the votes of hard-pressed middle- and working-class Americans. His promised national health insurance program, too, would now have to be fashioned within even tighter fiscal constraints than he had originally hoped.

By cutting the deficit, moving ahead with Bush's NAFTA, and completing the Uruguay Round negotiations of GATT to establish the World Trade Organization, Rubin and the others assured Clinton, he could cut the deficit, win the confidence of the bond market, preside over a fall in interest rates, and increase the global profits of American businesses. And eventually, at least by his second term, these policies would reduce unemployment and reverse the income declines of American workers (though not the increasingly unequal distribution of income and wealth).[33]

Clinton's economic program achieved all of the goals Rubin promised it would, but at a heavy and lasting cost to the competitiveness of American industry and the vitality of American democracy.

Falling interest rates pumped up the financial sector of America's economy: international investment banks, stock and bond traders, marketers of financial derivatives, hedge funds, real estate lenders. But by doing nothing to make American workers stronger competitors in an increasingly globalized economy, Clinton's policies hollowed out the remaining competitive strengths of American industry.

Just as Clinton had predicted during the campaign, without world-class skills the American middle class did continue to decline into economic insecurity and downward social and income mobility. And although Clinton had sold his new trade agreements as adding jobs through expanding export markets, they also subtracted jobs, and not just at the low-skill, low-income end of the spectrum. They made it even easier for American businesses to move manufacturing and service jobs abroad to countries that decades of emergency state foreign policy had finally made safe for profitable American investment, rapidly widening America's trade deficits. In the 1990s world of integrated transnational production, the huge pool of high-skill, low-wage workers around the globe represented a far bigger profit center for American business than the much smaller number of new middle-class consumers.

And at home, in the absence of those promised public investments in education, skills, and infrastructure, the Clinton economic boom, when it came, left its mark not in more productive American workers and factories but in successive financial and asset bubbles that moved from the stock market, to the dot-coms, to real estate.

American democracy also found itself deeply discounted in the global marketplace.

Clinton's trade agreements did not just reduce or eliminate tariffs and other protective barriers and stop there. That worthy goal could have been achieved in agreements just a few pages long that would have benefited most American workers and consumers. These could have been freely published and openly debated before Congress voted on them.

Instead, these agreements ran to hundreds of pages of arcane text, which incorporated thousands of special interest deals negotiated by American businesses in closed-door negotiations. Most members of Congress voting on them, let alone the general public, had very limited information on what they were approving.

Even worse, it has become a general principle of trade negotiations that the resulting agreements consider goods and services only in the form in which they arrive in the final marketplace. Whether they were produced under freely negotiated labor conditions or in a police state, in a sweatshop or in a humane workplace, in a factory pouring toxic chemicals into the air and water or in one equipped with environmental safeguards, they are legally entitled to equal treatment.

These rules all but ensure a race to the bottom, stacked in favor of the countries with the lowest wages and the weakest environmental rules or enforcement. And this does not just affect the conditions of production abroad. When Congress accepts trade agreements incorporating this equal treatment principle, it makes it all but politically impossible to insist on strong environmental or labor laws in the United States, since these would now undermine the competitiveness of American-made products and lead to the export of still more industrial jobs overseas.

The Clinton economic boom was thus hollow in two senses. It was built on financial bubbles and soaring trade deficits. And it came at the cost of a serious erosion of American democracy—compromising the ability of Congress and the electorate to decide on environmental and working conditions and to rebuild and strengthen the Main Street economy.

Clinton was right that the jobs of millions of American workers in globalized industries could not be protected or retained. That is the nature of a globalized economy in which comparably productive labor can be found at far lower cost abroad. But Clinton was wrong to imagine that lowering trade barriers or even retraining Rust Belt workers in computer skills could preserve American wage and benefit levels at a time when hundreds of millions of skilled or readily trainable Chinese, Indian, and Eastern European workers were being added to the global capitalist labor market. And he was wrong again to assume that the resulting unemployment and displacement would be limited to low value-added industries in the rust belt. Software design can be outsourced just as easily as shoemaking.

Clinton's use of the formidable political and economic power of the U.S. government to pry open global capital markets only worsened the squeeze on the nonfinancial economy at home. American investment capital was now free to move almost anywhere. America's workforce was free only to figure out how to adjust itself to the resulting downward pressure on its job security and living standards.

A progressive American government in 1993 might have tried to formulate foreign and military policies that strengthened the domestic economy rather than undermined it. It might have tried to use tax policy to promote and reward productive domestic investment, to retrain displaced workers in fields where America still retained a comparative economic advantage, and to tax and redistribute some of the incremental gains that U.S.-based corporations and shareholders drew from expanded trade so that globalization left no, or very few, net losers in the American economy.

Such policies would have transgressed the Reagan template but not the laws of modern economics. If the $15 trillion U.S. economy as a whole gains 2 percent of annual GDP growth from trade, that amounts to nearly $1,000 more per year for every man, woman, and child in the United States, enough to spread the gains around far more widely than they are today.[34]

CHAPTER THIRTEEN

COME THE DESTROYER

George W. Bush, the first president to enter the White House with an MBA, planned to govern like a corporate CEO. He wouldn't micromanage domestic policy, like Bill Clinton, or foreign policy, like his father. Instead he would pick a strong and experienced team of advisers and function as "the decider," using his leadership instincts, rather than any detailed factual grounding, to choose among their recommendations.

Bush did assemble an experienced team. But he followed the advice of a favorite few, especially Vice President Dick Cheney and Defense Secretary Donald Rumsfeld, while barely listening to most of the rest.[1]

Cheney and Rumsfeld had both held top jobs in the Ford administration and had spent much of the intervening twenty-five years bitterly complaining about the damage the assertive Democratic Congresses of the 1970s had done to the presidency and the country by encroaching on what both believed to be the rightful and necessary executive privileges of the emergency state.

Following the presidential fiascoes of Vietnam and Watergate and the subsequent revelations of intelligence abuses at home and abroad, those Congresses had shaken off decades of deference to presidents of both parties on national security issues and had begun to reclaim some of the war powers, oversight responsibilities, and control over military and intelligence spending that the Constitution's framers had very deliberately placed in their hands.

But that wasn't the way Cheney, Rumsfeld, and their like-minded colleagues in the new Bush administration saw it. They believed that 1970s measures like the War Powers Act (1973), the new intelligence reporting and oversight laws (beginning in 1974), the expansion of the Freedom of Information Act (passed over Ford's veto in 1974), the open meetings law (1976), and the Foreign Intelligence Surveillance Act (1978) had imperiled the nation by weakening the commander in chief's powers in the permanent undeclared war against America's enemies. They had been outraged when Democratic congressional majorities voted to cut off funding for White House–directed military and intelligence operations in Indochina (1970–73), Angola (1976), and Nicaragua (1982–84).

For most Americans in 2001, those were long-ago, cold-war-era struggles. But they had been searing for people who had been at the center of the action like Cheney and Rumsfeld and who had felt powerless in the face of what they had seen as a destructive congressional onslaught.

It had been Rumsfeld, as White House chief of staff, and Cheney, as his deputy, who had persuaded Ford to veto those FOIA amendments in 1974, only to see Congress override Ford's veto. They feared damaging national security leaks and a weakened presidency. History, they believed, had proven them right, with countless national humiliations during the Carter and Clinton years flowing from what they saw as reckless and partisan congressional assaults on the virtually unlimited powers they felt American presidents needed to wield on national security questions.[2]

That had been Richard Nixon's view of the presidency. It was also Cheney's and Rumsfeld's. And it was shared by a younger generation of activist Republican lawyers who soon joined the new administration, like David Addington, who became Cheney's general counsel and later chief of staff, along with Jay Bybee and John Yoo, who became top figures at the Office of Legal Counsel, the Justice Department's in-house arbiter of constitutional law.

Cheney and Rumsfeld came back to office in 2001 determined to undo the damage they felt Congress had inflicted on presidential power a generation earlier, even if most Americans believed that the work of those Congresses had, rightly or wrongly, long ago been undone. As Senator John Sununu, the son of George H. W. Bush's former White House chief of staff, said of Cheney in 2005: "The vice president may be the only person I know of that believes the executive has somehow lost power over the last 30 years."[3]

After Congress chose not to mount a full-scale constitutional challenge to Ronald Reagan over Iran-Contra in the late 1980s, three successive administrations had not only reclaimed the executive powers that earlier Congresses had pruned back after Vietnam and Watergate in the 1970s but had gone on to assert new ones.

By 2001 emergency state powers had been flowing back toward the White House for well over a decade, helped along by a series of executive-friendly Supreme Court decisions and a loss of public and congressional appetite for challenging presidents on national security and civil liberties issues.[4]

George H. W. Bush had waged an undeclared war in Panama to arrest Manuel Noriega. He had persuaded the Supreme Court to uphold his forcible abduction of a Mexican citizen from Mexico to stand trial in the United States for killing an American drug enforcement agent. Bush had begun, and Clinton had continued, using the Coast Guard to intercept Haitian refugees on the high seas so that United States courts could not protect their rights under federal law and international treaty. Clinton had used emergency powers to lend Mexico $20 billion after Congress voted down a similar request.

The elder Bush had hailed America's victory in the 1991 Gulf War, a victory Cheney had shared in as secretary of defense, as marking the end of "the Vietnam syndrome." It also marked the end of the Vietnam-era struggles between Congress and the White House over national security powers.

For Cheney, Rumsfeld, and their like-minded colleagues, this decade-long accretion of White House powers wasn't enough. They were still determined to restore what they felt was the commanding authority that presidents had wielded before Watergate, along with the secrecy, arrogance, and lack of accountability to Congress and the courts that went with it. They were convinced, well before the 9/11 terrorist attacks, that only an almighty presidency could make allies and foes alike respect and fear the United States again and do what Washington demanded, thereby restoring the sense of purpose and security they believed America and Americans had lost.

Their pre-9/11 views were expressed in the June 1997 "Statement of Principles" of the Project for the New American Century. The statement was signed by, among others, Cheney, Rumsfeld, Paul Wolfowitz (who became Rumsfeld's deputy at the Pentagon), Scooter Libby (who became Cheney's first chief of staff), Elliott Abrams (the pardoned Iran-Contra defendant who became Bush's senior National Security Council staff director, first for democracy, human rights, and international organizations, then for the greater Middle East), Zalmay Khalilzad (who became successively Bush's ambassador to Afghanistan, Iraq, and the United Nations), and Paula Dobriansky (who became undersecretary of state for democracy and global affairs). The Project for the New American Century also posted a January 1998 letter to President Clinton, signed by many of the same people, urging him to brush aside opposition in the UN Security Council and prepare to use American military power to overthrow Saddam Hussein.[5]

The political circumstances of early 2001—Bush's loss of the popular presidential vote, the near dead heat in the Senate (which switched from Republican to Democratic control after Senator James Jeffords declared himself an independent in May), and the slim ten-vote Republican advantage in the House—complicated the new administration's bid for expanded executive powers. But none of that kept Cheney and Rumsfeld from pushing their long-sought agenda.

One of Cheney's first moves as vice president was to convene a behind-closed-doors task force on energy, heavily lobbied by invited industry executives. With their help, Cheney devised a new national energy policy that turned its back on international efforts to slow global warming and tossed aside even the mild environmental commitments of Bush's presidential campaign.[6]

Rumsfeld spent his pre-9/11 days at the Pentagon downgrading the power and prestige of the Joint Chiefs of Staff and asserting his own authority in the chain of command—twisting the doctrine of civilian control over the military into something the Constitution's framers never intended. For Rumsfeld, civilian control meant the right of the presidentially appointed secretary of defense to recommend military interventions that neither the public nor the military believed in.

Rumsfeld despised the senior officer corps, with its post-Vietnam resistance to fighting wars that were not clearly required by the national interest, that were not widely supported at home, and that were not shaped by well-defined military goals and exit strategies. In other words, Rumsfeld despised the service leadership and doctrines that had been shaped by Colin Powell when he headed the Joint Chiefs in the late 1980s and early 1990s.

Powell was now Bush's secretary of state and, nominally at least, Rumsfeld's equal in authority and public influence. But as Powell soon discovered, he was left outside the administration's inner Cheney-Rumsfeld-Rice power loop.[7]

Rumsfeld's least favorite service was the one Powell had come from, the army. The army is, by tradition, the biggest of America's armed services and the least elitist, its ranks most reflective of America as a whole. These were not the characteristics Rumsfeld most valued. He considered the army too slow, heavy, and tradition-bound to fight the kind of rapid, light-on-the-ground, technology-powered, presidentially ordered wars he anticipated.

Rumsfeld also waged war on the Pentagon's civilian bureaucracy. On September 10, 2001, he assailed that bureaucracy as "an adversary that poses a threat, a serious threat, to the security of the United States of America. This adversary is one of the world's last bastions of central planning. It governs by dictating five-year plans. From a single capital, it attempts to impose its demands across time zones, continents, oceans and beyond. With brutal consistency, it stifles free thought and crushes new ideas. It disrupts the defense of the United States and places the lives of men and women in uniform at risk."[8]

Others in the new administration had similar agendas for enhancing executive powers at the expense of congressional and public claims. Attorney General John Ashcroft began working on a new set of FOIA guidelines designed to more rigorously subordinate the public's right to information about the government to the claims of national security, law enforcement, protection of trade secrets, and lawyer-client privilege. Bybee and Yoo, at the Office of Legal Counsel, were strong advocates of almost unlimited presidential war powers.[9]

In Cheney's office, David Addington developed an all-encompassing theory of "unitary" executive power, which—as he later described it to Congress—holds that the first sentence of the Constitution's article 2 vests "in the president of the United States, one president, all of the executive power, not some of it, not part of it, not the parts Congress doesn't want to exercise itself."[10]

In these early months Ashcroft, Addington, Yoo, and others were building the legal foundations for later claims of almost unlimited presidential power to set aside the Constitution and exercise military and police powers found nowhere in that document. Meanwhile Bush's deep tax cuts and sweeping deregulatory program continued to strip the federal government of its ability to carry out the intent of the Constitution's opening sentence and "promote the general welfare" or for the president to carry out his requirement under article 2 "to take care that the laws be faithfully executed."

In other words, the presidency would be too powerful to be constitutionally restrained and the federal government would be too impoverished to expect the president to fulfill his domestic constitutional responsibilities.

Then came 9/11.

That day's terrorist attacks awakened Americans to a shocking new vulnerability at home that they had never anticipated. Nothing in recent American history prepared us for it. Nothing in the elaborate and expensive repertory of national security doctrines, forces, and weapons developed by the emergency state since 1940 had much power to defend us against it.

Since the time of Woodrow Wilson, America had been sending its armies and navies abroad in the certain faith that by doing so it would keep powerful enemy states from directly threatening its shores. War was "over there," not over here. Even before America had the worldwide armed strength to enforce such doctrines of forward defense, it had the doctrines. The Monroe Doctrine had proclaimed an American security frontier hundreds of miles south of our own borders. The Truman Doctrine had dug containment's frontline trenches against Soviet political and military advance along the northern frontiers of Greece and Turkey. Truman's successors had claimed that the security of Americans required friendly governments in Guatemala, Iran, Congo, Vietnam, Chile, and Angola.

Now a loose autonomous network of international terrorists had simply jumped over America's elaborate and expensive overseas network of forward defenses as if it were some latter-day Maginot Line. They infiltrated their unarmed commandos into the United States through our undefended airports and then used our own domestic passenger planes as devastatingly effective weapons of mass murder.

And while the Al Qaeda hijackers were not—like the British army that burned Washington in 1814 or the Japanese fleet that launched the attack on Pearl Harbor in 1941—the soldiers of a well-armed military empire capable of directly challenging America's own armed forces, their use of fuel-packed civilian airliners as piloted firebombs gave their deadly strikes the semblance of a wartime military attack by an enemy state. As it unfolded, 9/11 seemed perhaps only the opening salvo of an extended series of outrages against vulnerable American civilians.

Fortunately, it didn't turn out that way. But the fear was not easily or quickly shaken off (especially after envelopes containing deadly anthrax were mailed to political and media offices over the next few weeks).

An alarmed public demanded that the government find and punish the culprits responsible for 9/11 and act decisively to ward off further attacks. Any administration would have responded strongly to that public mood. Americans were prepared to trade civil liberties, privacy, and convenience for greater security.

But the particular trade-offs that took place over the next seven years owed less to the specific nature of 9/11 than to the exotic constitutional theories of Cheney, Rumsfeld, Ashcroft, and their administration allies.

Had Al Gore been president, he surely would have taken military action against Al Qaeda camps in Afghanistan and the Taliban government that gave them sanctuary. But he likely would also have made more use of the kind of aggressive law enforcement techniques that Tony Blair used after the July 2005 bomb attacks in central London.

Blair's methods, which included longer-than-usual periods of detention without charge, extraordinary methods of surveillance, and special forms of house arrest, clearly narrowed the scope of privacy and civil liberties. But unlike the Bush administration's strategy, they focused on uncovering and uprooting homegrown jihadis and sleeper cells rather than on overthrowing foreign regimes and uprooting overseas training camps. Blair tried to cast the suicide bombers as criminal terrorists, while Bush played into the martyrology of their sympathizers by casting them as enemy combatants. Tony Blair followed George W. Bush into Afghanistan and Iraq mainly for alliance reasons, not as Britain's main strategic response to terrorist threats in the U.K.

If George H. W. Bush had still been president, he likely would have worked hard to isolate Al Qaeda by building the broadest possible international coalition and then used it to impose tough financial and travel sanctions, take military action against specific Al Qaeda–related targets, and issue and enforce international arrest warrants.

There were other plausible responses. A different administration might have moved to reassure and protect an anxious nation through a crash program of securing vulnerable chemical plants near heavily populated areas, container seaports, nuclear power reactors, and passenger and freight rail lines.

Over time a different administration might also have rethought America's suddenly obsolete doctrine of forward defense and its corollary that the surest way to keep attackers away from American soil was by creating a dense worldwide network of foreign military bases, often secured through unsavory deals with unpopular dictators. The 9/11 attacks showed that such deals created dangerous enemies abroad who could ignore those bases and carry out attacks directly on the American homeland.

All of these responses would have addressed the specific circumstances of the 9/11 attacks. But none would have advanced the constitutional and political agenda of Bush, Cheney, Rumsfeld, Ashcroft, and other like-minded administration officials as effectively as the one they chose—declaring a permanent undeclared global war on terror and using the unreviewable presidential powers that Bush claimed as a "war president" to wage wars against selected "rogue states" abroad and waive basic constitutional protections at home.

The leading figures in the Bush administration understood, as the founding fathers understood, that nothing aggrandizes presidential power more than waging war abroad. That is why the founding fathers preached abstinence from foreign military quarrels and required a congressional declaration to trigger presidential war powers. Bush, Cheney, and Rumsfeld, their outlooks formed in the emergency state tradition of undeclared wars, devoted to notions of a strong presidency, and seeing congressional power as a threat to national security, had no compunctions about effectively cutting Congress out of the constitutional war powers formula.

The American tradition of enhanced presidential powers during wartime helps explain why the notion of a "global war on terrorism" appealed to Bush, Cheney, and Rumsfeld as the defining paradigm for fighting terrorism in general and Al Qaeda in particular. And it may have helped push them toward novel doctrines of preventive war when they proved unable to come up with convincing hard evidence that Iraq was still producing weapons of mass destruction.

The emergency state tradition also taught them to see war against another state as the strongest available tool in the foreign policy toolkit, even though no enemy state had sponsored the 9/11 attacks and Al Qaeda could easily survive the defeat of the Taliban and Saddam Hussein. When your toolbox has only hammers, everything starts looking like a nail.

Waging war in Afghanistan and Iraq also helped justify big increases in military spending. This was, of course, welcomed by the military-industrial complex, which was well represented in the Bush administration and the Republican Party electorate. But more specifically, post-9/11 increases in military spending fed the politically convenient notion that the 9/11 attacks had been the fault of a Clinton administration "procurement holiday," rather than G. W. Bush–era intelligence failures by the FBI and CIA, the G. H. W. Bush–era decision to base American troops in Saudi Arabia, or the Reagan-era links between the CIA and the Afghan mujahedeen.

Exactly how buying more aircraft carriers, stealth bombers, and ballistic missile interceptors might have stopped the 9/11 hijackers is hard to fathom. But it played into the deeply held political belief that the Democrats are dangerously weak on national security. By insinuating that America was attacked because the Democrats had slowed spending on cold war weapons, the Bush administration hit upon an argument that enormously helped Republican candidates in 2002 and 2004 and military contractors in every year since the September 11, 2001, attacks.

After 9/11 Americans no longer believed that the end of the cold war had brought lasting security or any realistic prospect of a "peace dividend." They were right about the first point. An America that uses its military and economic power to shape a world order in its own image will always face armed resistance. If that resistance isn't fueled by leftist ideologies, it will be fueled by nationalist or religious doctrines. If it isn't armed with multiple-warhead nuclear ICBMs, it will be armed with the kind of asymmetrical weapons and tactics to which America is in many ways more vulnerable.

But there is no obvious reason why defending against these post-cold-war enemies should be more costly than deterring a thermonuclear superpower. Additional ground troops might be required, at roughly $160,000 a year per added soldier. But that should be more than offset by a sharply reduced need for stealthy F-22 air combat fighters at $350 million per plane and DDG-1000 stealth destroyers at $3.2 billion per ship.[11]

The war paradigm didn't only boost presidential war powers and the Pentagon budget. It also gave Bush administration domestic law-enforcement and intelligence-surveillance officials wider scope to evade the constitutional restrictions and legal restraints that had previously defined their work. This applied especially to the far-ranging data-mining and communications-interception operations of the National Security Agency, which picked up the private communications of millions of innocent American citizens. Since these operations were for intelligence-gathering purposes, not for criminal prosecution, those carrying them out did not have to worry about the usual penalty for unconstitutional and illegal snooping—no cases would ever come to court, so no judge would ever throw out the government's evidence. Nor did administration officials worry much about judicial scrutiny of the interrogation and punishment techniques they authorized for use on other categories of people they never expected to face eventual trial in American civilian courts, from detained aliens to "illegal enemy combatants."

Congress made no serious attempt to challenge the war paradigm, to write restrictions into military funding, to investigate administration abuses, or to take advantage of every member's constitutionally protected right to put information into the public record—techniques that congressional Democrats and some Republicans had used to good effect during the Vietnam War.

Democrats during the G. W. Bush era no longer had the courage of their own policy convictions. They were still trying to live down their party's Vietnam-era reputation as weak on national security and years of Republican charges that congressional intelligence oversight had weakened the CIA and endangered the country. They had internalized the new third-way politics of Democratic survival under the Reagan template. They feared, perhaps accurately, that a still-traumatized American public would turn on them for defending the Constitution and their own, often more nuanced views of how to keep American lives and liberties secure.

For the next five years Congress left Bush, Cheney, and Rumsfeld free to operate the emergency state the way these lifetime devotees of presidential power had always longed to. The Bush administration's behavior during those years provided the clearest demonstration yet of the devastating consequences of emergency state thinking for American constitutional democracy.

After the 9/11 attacks, Bush styled himself a "war president" engaged in a global "war on terror" of indefinite duration. This, he felt, entitled him to exercise implicit executive powers found nowhere in the Constitution. In his view, these powers gave him full command authority over civilians as well as soldiers, and over U.S. citizens seized at home as well as enemy combatants detained on foreign battlefields. Bush also claimed the power to detain prisoners indefinitely, without charges or access to the courts.[12]

Within weeks of the attacks Bush easily persuaded a receptive Congress to pass the USA Patriot Act. Building on the Clinton-era precedent of the 1996 Antiterrorism and Effective Death Penalty Act—passed after the Oklahoma City domestic terrorist bombing—which had greatly expanded the surveillance authority of the federal government and sharply limited prisoners' access to the federal courts, the Patriot Act granted the federal government sweeping new powers to intercept private communications and to demand previously confidential library, education, and private business records.

Following the wartime precedents of Lincoln and FDR, Bush announced that people he declared enemy combatants would be tried by military commissions, without the due process and fairness safeguards of America's civilian court system or regular U.S. military courts.

Echoing the post–World War I Palmer raids and the World War II internment of Japanese Americans, Ashcroft's Justice Department required tens of thousands of adult male aliens in the United States from twenty-four predominantly Arab or Muslim countries to specially register their presence with the federal government. Hundreds were detained for periods of up to four months on minor immigration charges before being deported.[13]

Rumsfeld's Pentagon reopened the military detention facility at the U.S. naval base at Guantánamo Bay, Cuba, that Bush's father and Bill Clinton had used to detain Haitian refugees beyond the reach of American courts. He turned it into an internationally notorious prison camp for holding a motley mix of Al Qaeda members and innocent bystanders indefinitely and denying them any chance to challenge their detention or establish their innocence.

Building on the Clinton innovation of "rendition," in which American officials kidnapped individuals abroad and forcibly brought them to the United States to be tried with full legal rights in American civilian courts, Bush introduced "extraordinary rendition," in which American officials kidnapped individuals abroad and then delivered them into the hands of foreign torturers and jailers without court review, independent oversight, or public notice. In another variant, American officials transferred prisoners from nonbattlefield countries abroad to military detention facilities like those at Bagram air base in Afghanistan and Guantánamo Bay, where they were held as enemy combatants and denied access to American courts.

In a series of so-called torture memos, Bybee, Yoo, and their successors at the Justice Department's Office of Legal Counsel declared that CIA and Pentagon interrogators could subject prisoners to a litany of physical abuses and psychological terrors, including the simulated-drowning experience of "waterboarding," without violating U.S. laws and international treaties prohibiting torture.

And in a gratuitous swipe at the intelligence reforms of the 1970s that had so offended Cheney, the Bush administration bypassed the easily satisfied warrant requirements of the FISA law and instituted the Terrorist Surveillance Program, intercepting the private electronic communications of millions of law-abiding Americans.

"When the president does it," Richard Nixon had assured David Frost in a famous 1977 television interview, "that means that it is not illegal." Acting on that belief in Watergate had cost Nixon his presidency. Congress, the Supreme Court, and the public had insisted instead that presidents, even when exercising their executive powers, must follow the laws and obey the Constitution.

Nixon's rogue view of presidential powers made a spectacular comeback in a John Yoo memo of March 2003. By virtue of the president's constitutional authority as commander in chief of U.S. military forces, Yoo argued, he is entitled, even when no war has been constitutionally declared, to ignore the Bill of Rights and the law and act on his personal vision of national security. Writing for the Office of Legal Counsel, Yoo's memo represented the Bush administration's official interpretation of the Constitution.[14]

By the end of Bush's first term, the Supreme Court began setting some limits on Bush's constitutional innovations, but not before Bush had substantially infringed on at least five of the first ten amendments to the Constitution that make up America's Bill of Rights.[15]

Bush's second term saw only limited improvement. Alberto Gonzalez replaced Ashcroft as attorney general but proved no strong defender of American constitutional traditions. Bybee's and Yoo's successors at the Office of Legal Counsel discarded some of their more exotic findings but still found that the torture methods used by the CIA and Pentagon were legal. New leaders at the CIA and Pentagon ordered an end to those interrogation techniques, but there was no end to extraordinary rendition and no closing down of Bagram or other rule-bending detention centers beyond the reach of American courts. The Supreme Court recognized limited habeas corpus rights for detainees at Guantánamo, but that did not help those held in other overseas American military installations. The Court also threw out Bush's original version of military commissions, but Congress quickly relegalized them in only slightly altered form.

Democratic House and Senate victories in the 2006 midterm elections revived some appetite for congressional oversight. But the new Democratic majorities proceeded warily and cautiously, not sure whether public opinion would reward or punish serious challenges to Bush administration policies. Bush's failed military strategy in Iraq, more than any constitutionalist backlash, had brought the Democrats their victories. That was why Donald Rumsfeld announced his resignation the day after the midterm voting. The Democrats were not yet offering, and the public was not yet demanding, a decisive break with the familiar mindset of the emergency state.

CHAPTER FOURTEEN

HOPE ABANDONED

The 2008 elections registered a still-more-emphatic public rejection of Bush administration policies, this time domestic as well as foreign. The tidal wave of insolvencies that staggered America's biggest banks and insurance companies that autumn laid bare the dark side of Bush's policy of heedless, wholesale deregulation. The White House's late and inadequate response to a crisis that quickly escalated to threaten the credit, jobs, homes, and pensions of millions of Americans—and the economically incoherent flailings of Republican presidential candidate John McCain—sent voters fleeing to the Democrats, increasing their House and Senate majorities.

That year's Democratic presidential primaries also registered the voters' desire to turn a page. Barack Obama triumphed over Hillary Clinton because he promised more than a recycling of the policies and the people of the Clinton era. His opposition to the Iraq War was earlier and more clear-cut. He was not associated with the Democratic economic advisers and policies of the late 1990s who had helped launch the long orgy of speculation, leveraging, and asset bubbles that led up to the 2008 meltdown.

Obama's November victory thus seemed to signal a clear break from not just the Bush but also the Clinton model. The new president entered office with a strong mandate to extricate American troops from the Iraq War, roll back Bush's constitutional abuses, and nurture a more balanced American economy—one less dependent on Wall Street and more capable of producing goods and services that could successfully compete in world markets.

Obama's election was a moment of rare opportunity and high expectations. But those hopes were almost instantly deflated by the new administration's backward-looking appointments, timid and inadequate policies, and muddled political message.

As Obama begins his fourth year, he can point to solid achievements. He rescued America's biggest banks and insurance companies, bought time for the American auto industry, withdrew American combat troops from Iraq, and negotiated a new nuclear arms reduction treaty with Russia. He got Congress to expand health insurance coverage, toughen automobile fuel economy standards, and tighten supervision of financial markets. He brought better leadership, better policies, and better morale to key regulatory agencies, especially those enforcing labor, environmental, and civil rights laws.

After more than a quarter-century of mindless deregulation, fraying of the social safety net, and halting efforts to dismantle the cold war's nuclear legacy, Obama tried to point the government in new and more positive directions. That was more than Jimmy Carter or Bill Clinton achieved in his first three years, and in less demanding times that might be as much as anyone could reasonably expect.

But these are not ordinary times. Obama was elected at a moment when the emergency state's national security strategy was proving unable to cope with a new set of nonstate enemies and unconventional threats, when the emergency state's approach to international economics was undermining the economic security and prospects of most Americans, and when the emergency state's cumulative encroachments on the Constitution were threatening American democracy and the Bill of Rights.

None of those concerns has been adequately addressed.

America's armed forces are still being overstretched and squandered in counterproductive efforts to achieve military victories over "terrorism." They are still fighting undeclared wars on remote battlefields from Afghanistan to Yemen, arenas chosen by our enemies to neutralize our advantages and maximize theirs.

American special operations military units now carry out secretive intelligence-gathering and counterterrorism operations in at least seventy-five countries, fifteen more than when Obama took office. Their secrecy, intended to protect cooperating foreign governments from accountability to their own people, increases the risks of dangerous explosions of rage against the United States and its allies when the drone strikes and targeted killings that are the main purpose of these interventions inevitably give away the secret American military presence.[1]

The Obama administration sought and won court approval for continuing to transport people seized by special forces or CIA agents in these and other "nonbattlefield" countries to prisons on American military bases in Afghanistan. These and other detainees are still being held in American custody with no opportunity to try to prove their innocence before an American civilian or military court. Early on, the administration decided to indefinitely prolong the parallel, extraconstitutional legal system the Bush administration created to detain and try "unlawful combatants." Faced with domestic political opposition, Obama abandoned his early unequivocal pledge to shut down the notorious Guantánamo Bay prison camp.

Obama claims a presidential right to order the assassination of American citizens in countries like Yemen on the basis of his own conclusion that they are directly or indirectly involved in terrorism. No court will review Obama's assassination orders or the evidence behind the terrorist designation, violating the letter and the spirit of the Fifth Amendment's guarantee of due process.[2]

The Obama administration has been more aggressive than any of its predecessors in prosecuting government whistleblowers for speaking with the press. Such prosecutions have been very rare in American history, but the Obama administration has already pursued five of them, two more than the last seven presidents combined. And it has made a particularly chilling example of Bradley Manning, the army private charged with the capital offense of "aiding the enemy" for leaking classified Pentagon and State Department cables to Wikileaks. Without whistleblowers, the American people would never have learned about the Abu Ghraib prisoner abuse scandals or the National Security Agency warrantless wiretaps. Without leakers inside the national security bureaucracy, ordinary Americans would never have been able to read the Pentagon Papers.

The Obama administration has shown no such zeal in investigating and prosecuting possible crimes committed by senior officials in the Bush administration Justice Department and Pentagon, passing up the chance to make similarly placed officials think twice if asked to ignore the law and the Constitution. It has embraced its predecessor's expansive interpretation of the "state secrets" defense—an assertion that claims of illegal government conduct cannot proceed to trial because information bearing on national security might be disclosed—to head off court review of Bush's legally dubious national security wiretap program and its "extraordinary rendition" kidnappings. And in a case first argued by Elena Kagan when she was Obama's solicitor general, it won the right to use the Patriot Act's extremely broad "material support" language to prosecute constitutionally guaranteed free speech.[3]

Obama's Rubinesque economic policies, largely formulated by two leading alumni of Rubin's Treasury Department—Timothy Geithner and Larry Summers—produced an essentially jobless "recovery" that bailed out Wall Street while continuing to undermine the competitiveness of American workers. America's banking system is once again solvent and profitable but still not providing the credit that domestic employers need to power a jobs-driven recovery. The global economy is more imbalanced than ever. Wall Street's risky practices and risky practitioners are back. And as of June 2011, America had (on a seasonally adjusted basis) nearly 3 million fewer jobs than it had in January 2009 (and 14 million fewer than it needed to employ everyone actively seeking work).[4]

The hope and renewed democratic faith of the 2008 election have given way to disappointment, disillusionment, and anger.

Ignoring the crisis of the emergency state will not make it go away. It will make it even more dangerous. And if a president with the mandate for change that Obama had fails to tackle this challenge, it is very hard to see how any likely successor from either party will try. Until, that is, they find themselves compelled to act by increasingly desperate voters, in desperate circumstances, and with fewer promising alternatives than Obama had in 2009. Reviving our constitutional democracy in those conditions would be a far greater challenge.

The defining mistake of Obama's first-term foreign policy was his decision to escalate American military operations in Afghanistan. There were 35,000 American troops in Afghanistan when Obama was inaugurated. By the summer of 2011 there were roughly 100,000. The main national security rationale for their presence was to prevent the Taliban from regaining sufficient strength to invite Al Qaeda back to the Afghan training camps and sanctuaries it had operated from before 9/11. But since early 2002, seven years before Obama became president, Al Qaeda and Osama bin Laden himself—until he was tracked down and killed by U.S. commandos in May 2011—had been based in Pakistan, under the protection of a Pakistani army that continues to receive billions of dollars in American military aid.

Long before his presidential bid, Obama had called for an increased American military effort in Afghanistan. He repeated that position frequently during the 2008 campaign. Obama's strong opposition to the Iraq War led many supporters to imagine that he rejected the idea of defending America against terrorism by waging conventional military conflicts in distant Islamic lands. Some of the more philosophical passages in Obama's autobiographical books, writings, and speeches elaborating on his opposition to the Iraq War fed that misimpression.

In a widely noted November 2006 speech to the Chicago Council on Global Affairs, he emphasized his belief that the war had been not just a "failure of implementation" but "also a failure of conception," going on to argue that "the rationale behind the war," including an excessive faith that "we can impose democracy on a country through military force," was "misguided."[5]

Some thought they heard echoes of the Reverend Martin Luther King's famous 1967 speech declaring opposition not just to the war in Vietnam but to "a far deeper malady of the American spirit" that, if not confronted then, could lead to other misguided wars in other countries also waged in the name of guaranteeing liberty.[6]

But Obama had long made a clear distinction between the wars in Iraq and Afghanistan. He opposed the invasion and occupation of Iraq as an unnecessary war of choice and a diversion from the main battle against Osama bin Laden and Al Qaeda. He supported the war in Afghanistan as a justified response to the 9/11 terrorist attacks and necessary to America's future security. On that basis Obama had harshly criticized the Bush administration for diverting military resources from Afghanistan to Iraq after 2003. And during his presidential campaign Obama had talked about sending three to five more brigades to Afghanistan as he drew down U.S. combat forces in Iraq.

Within a month of taking office, Obama approved a 17,000-troop increase for Afghanistan. That was less than the top U.S. commander there, General David McKiernan, had requested. But it was within the range Obama had called for during the campaign. It amounted to a roughly 50 percent rise in troop strength.

Just two months later, with the military situation in Afghanistan continuing to deteriorate, Obama removed General McKiernan and replaced him with General Stanley McChrystal. McChrystal was favored by Admiral Mike Mullen, the chairman of the Joint Chiefs; General David Petraeus, the former Iraq commander then in charge of all U.S. troops in the Middle East and Central Asia; and Defense Secretary Robert Gates—all three of them Bush administration holdovers.

During the Bush years McChrystal had made his name as the leader of the elite Joint Special Operations Command for Afghanistan and Iraq—the same command that was later to dispatch Navy SEALs to kill bin Laden in Pakistan. In Iraq, McChrystal's JSOC commandos had been responsible for the capture of Saddam Hussein and for tracking down Abu Musab al-Zarqawi, the leader of Al Qaeda in Mesopotamia, and calling in the air strikes that killed him. JSOC units had also been investigated for abusing Iraqi prisoners, making McChrystal a surprising choice for someone with Obama's stated views on how and how not to fight Al Qaeda.

But Obama was looking for someone who could quickly turn around what was by then a faltering seven-and-a-half-year-old war effort. McChrystal's reputation as a tough, can-do commander and his endorsement by the Pentagon's top military and civilian leaders counted in his favor.

Instead of the rapid turnaround Obama was hoping for, McChrystal brought bad news that pointed to an even longer, less conclusive war. Soon after arriving in Afghanistan the new commander concluded, in an assessment that he improperly made public while Obama was still weighing it, that a further rapid infusion of 40,000 to 80,000 American troops was required. Otherwise, he argued, continuing Taliban gains would soon make the war unwinnable.

With those extra troops, McChrystal said, the military deterioration *might* be halted within a year, clearing the way for a long-term counterinsurgency struggle aimed at winning over Afghan civilian hearts and minds. Only at that point, McChrystal argued, could America begin safely drawing down its forces.

McChrystal the war-fighting commando leader had morphed into McChrystal the embodiment of the new counterinsurgency doctrine Petraeus had developed in Iraq. And as in Iraq, the doctrine glossed over the fundamental question of how American military forces could win over civilian hearts and minds in the absence of a credible, effective, and willing local partner.

Six-digit troop levels and a lengthy military commitment were not what Obama had originally had in mind when he had criticized Bush for diverting troops to Iraq in 2003 instead of clinching the victory he believed was then within America's grasp in Afghanistan. But whatever might have been possible in 2003 was no longer possible by 2009, with a resurgent Taliban operating from Pakistani sanctuaries and increasing numbers of Afghans disenchanted with President Karzai's government and with U.S. and NATO military operations.

Obama had unwisely ensnared himself in a trap with no obvious escape hatch. He could not easily deny his handpicked new commander, General McChrystal, the resources that the latter had publicly declared necessary to avert defeat. But even with those additional troops, McChrystal could not promise Obama eventual, let alone early, victory.

Meanwhile the American public was losing patience with the lengthening stalemated war. And with each passing month it became clearer that America was fighting on not so much in support of a viable Afghan government as in the vague hope that one day a viable Afghan government might emerge.

Obama's range of bad options was beginning to resemble those that had faced Lyndon Johnson in Vietnam. The whole cost-benefit equation had changed so drastically since Obama first called for more troops in Afghanistan that the U.S. military commitment now needed to be seriously reassessed and perhaps written off. But after all Obama had said and done, he seemed to feel, as Johnson had felt in regard to Vietnam in 1964, that he could not step back and risk the likely military result—in this case, a Taliban victory. It was the same falsely constrained emergency state decision making, the same implicit assumptions of universal containment, that had brought eight more years of war and more than 55,000 additional American fatalities in Vietnam.

Obama's decision to step forward—or as he presented it, to escalate in 2010 and hope to begin withdrawing in 2011—carries heavy strategic costs as well as potential political costs. The most important of these is extending and deepening Washington's commitment to an obsolescent and dangerously counterproductive strategy for protecting American security. That commitment only deepened when, after a second and even more embarrassing episode of McChrystal speaking out of turn—this time being quoted expressing scorn for top administration officials in an article in *Rolling Stone* magazine—Obama fired McChrystal and replaced him with Petraeus, stating more emphatically than he ever had before, "I have a responsibility to do what is—*whatever is necessary to succeed in Afghanistan,* and in our broader effort to disrupt, dismantle, and defeat al Qaeda."[7]

There is no question that Obama has that second responsibility. But an open-ended commitment to military "success" in Afghanistan could prove a very costly distraction from pursuing that broader strategic goal.

With bin Laden dead, and General John Allen succeeding Petraeus (who now runs the CIA), Obama has a fresh opportunity to redefine military success in Afghanistan in more limited and realistic ways.

Afghanistan was an inherited commitment. But in early 2011, when Libyan rebels requested international military help against Colonel Muammar al-Qaddafi's counterattacking forces, Obama had the chance to define his own criteria for the commitment of American forces. His initial preference, following the advice of veteran emergency state advisers like Defense Secretary Robert Gates, Joint Chiefs chairman Mike Mullen, and Secretary of State Hillary Clinton, was to try to avoid direct U.S. involvement. The resulting delay only succeeded in raising the threshold of potential intervention from the fairly low-risk no-fly zone—which might have sufficed when the rebels held much of coastal Libya—to higher-risk air strikes against the Qaddafi forces once these had rolled the rebels back to their last major stronghold in Benghazi.

By then, with the Arab League, France, and Britain pushing for intervention and Qaddafi promising to carry out wholesale slaughter once he retook Benghazi, first Clinton, then Obama, changed their minds. The United States would make an initial commitment of naval and air forces, but no ground troops—provided the UN Security Council authorized it and NATO, rather than Washington, took command. Once NATO was in charge, the United States would withdraw its fighter and tank-buster aircraft and let its NATO allies take over. Obama was determined to learn the right lessons from Iraq and avoid George W. Bush's unilateralist bypassing of the Security Council and the costly, divisive, and open-ended military commitment that led to. But when it came to meeting the constitutional and domestic political responsibilities of a president sending American forces into battle, Obama fell further short than any of his recent predecessors.

An American president has no constitutional obligation to consult with the UN Security Council, the Arab League, or any other international body before committing American troops to battle. But except in emergency cases of national self-defense, he has a clear legal obligation to consult with Congress and a moral and political obligation to state his case to the American people. Libya was clearly a war of choice, and by all accounts, Obama made his choice days before sending planes and cruise missiles against Libyan antiaircraft defenses. Surprise was not a military consideration. Colonel Qaddafi knew the attacks were coming, and there was nothing much he could do about it. Yet Obama failed to request congressional authorization before the attack and failed to explain his decision to the American people. That a former constitutional law professor (and former critic of George W. Bush's constitutional high-handedness) could behave so egregiously regarding his own constitutional responsibilities shows how completely emergency state norms have superseded constitutional norms in the presidential exercise of war powers.[8]

Equally disappointing has been Obama's failure to reverse some of the most dangerous encroachments on constitutional democracy of the Bush years. This is not an area where Obama supporters deluded themselves. It is an area where Obama deluded his supporters by clearly promising a return to constitutional legality and then not delivering.

To cite the most prominent example, he forthrightly declared on his first full day in office that the Guantánamo Bay prison camp would be closed within a year, but then he backed off quickly in the face of congressional and political opposition. He has since distanced himself from those early declarations and from his own appointees in the Justice Department and White House counsel's office who made the mistake of taking them too seriously. In March 2011 Obama ordered the resumption of military commission trials at Guantánamo and issued an executive order formalizing the Bush practice of indefinite detention there.[9]

Imposing constitutional limits on the emergency state takes political courage. Voters have been told for years, and continue to be told by most Republicans and many Democrats, that bringing terrorist cases to court endangers their personal safety and that subjecting presidential actions taken in the name of national security to legislative and judicial oversight weakens America in the face of its enemies. Nothing weakens America more than panicky and unwarranted abandonment of the core values of American constitutional democracy.

Bowing to political expediency on these questions, while at the same time continuing to wage wars like Afghanistan and worldwide military special operations, invites repetition of the same kind of abuses that happened at Abu Ghraib, Guantánamo, and Bagram air force base. Specific responsibility for these most recent abuses belongs to the Bush administration. But more broadly, they are inevitable by-products of emergency state governance, like Japanese detention during World War II and the My Lai massacre during the Vietnam War.

By refusing to pursue issues of legal accountability from the Bush years, and by blocking victims of possible criminal wrongdoing by the government from seeking legal redress, Obama is not just closing the door on an ugly past. He is opening the door to an ugly future. In the absence of any serious effort to reestablish high-level legal accountability for the Bush policies that enabled and encouraged torture, extraordinary rendition, and the indefinite detention of innocent people never given a chance to establish their innocence, we will almost certainly see more horrific scandals and more horrific damage to America's good name in the future.

In economic policy, Obama failed to seize the opportunity he had during 2009 to reorient the banking system away from reckless derivatives trading toward its core function of providing credit for the production of competitive American goods and services. That function had been partially subordinated to competing foreign policy objectives of the emergency state and was increasingly ignored in the scramble for paper trading profits that followed post-cold-war banking deregulation.

Obama's decision to invest public money to keep the biggest banks from failing in early 2009 was correct and necessary—the alternative would have been a sudden freeze-up of the entire economy. Obama's mistake was not using those public loans and equity shares to insist on badly needed banking reforms—reforms that would have modernized and restored those parts of the New Deal bank regulatory system that served the nation extremely well from the 1930s through the early postwar decades, until lobbyists for the financial sector banks got the Reagan, G. H. W. Bush, Clinton, and G. W. Bush administrations to dismantle it and leave vast new areas of high-risk derivatives trading largely unregulated.[10]

By 2010 Obama had returned most of the big banks to private ownership, with their reckless trading philosophies and perverse salary incentive structures largely intact. The financial regulation bill that followed, too weak to begin with and then further weakened by financial lobbyists, strengthened some consumer protections but left regulatory loopholes wide enough to permit another devastating financial crash.

But by then, most of the public leverage for change created by the crisis, Obama's election, and the government loans and equity shares had been dissipated.

The regression of Obama's foreign policy thinking from dreams, audacity, and change to the old dysfunctional emergency state norm resembles the trajectories of Carter and Clinton before him. Both also moved from preelection criticism to postelection subservience to the mind-set and methods of the permanent emergency state.

Does this reflect harsh presidential education in the realities of geopolitics and the American political system? Is it simply socialization by the emergency state bureaucracy, with its closed culture of classified secrets, permanent danger, and rarefied detachment from the lives of ordinary Americans? Or does it just tell us something about the Democratic Party's underlying attitudes toward the emergency state—critical about its operation when the other party is in office, but defending and extending its power when it occupies the White House itself?

After all, the Democrats invented and institutionalized the emergency state. It was a Democratic administration that formulated universal containment, scared hell out of the American people, created the CIA and the NSC, adopted NSC-68, and intervened in Korea. It was another Democratic administration that turned an advisory mission into the commitment of over half a million American troops to Vietnam.

The emergency state cohabits comfortably with the modern Democratic Party's core beliefs—activist presidents, broad and flexible constitutional interpretation, big and free-spending government, and belief in the possibility and desirability of social engineering on a global scale.

The two most enthusiastic emergency state Republicans, Richard Nixon and George W. Bush, borrowed many of these core beliefs from the Democratic playbook, adapting them to appeal to the Republican electoral base. Nixon was a Keynesian; Bush, a Wilsonian. Neither shared William McKinley's belief in sound and strong money, Calvin Coolidge's distaste for foreign intervention and national police spying, or even Dwight Eisenhower's ambivalence about the military-industrial complex.

Nor is any future Republican likely to return to the limited-government, putting-American-domestic-interests-first philosophy of Robert Taft.

Both parties now maintain deep benches of national security specialists, all of them thoroughly imbued with an emergency state worldview, one that flatteringly casts their own roles and advice as essential to national survival. However much Democratic and Republican national security specialists may disagree on specific points, their belief in the overriding importance of their specialty and its arcane and obsolescent dogmas is truly bipartisan.

Members of the Democratic Party's quasi-permanent foreign policy establishment are not very different in their educational or social backgrounds or in their geopolitical worldviews from their Republican counterparts. When the Republicans are in office, Democratic foreign policy mandarins bide their time in Washington foreign policy think tanks like the Brookings Institution, high-profile academic deanships, the Council on Foreign Relations, Wall Street banking houses like Goldman Sachs, and corporate law and lobbying firms. And when the Democrats are in office, Republican mandarins do the same. Nor is there that much difference anymore in the two parties' partially overlapping corporate fundraising bases, which include defense contractors, international businesses, and others with a heavy investment in the foreign policy status quo.

Yet voters looking for a real alternative to the emergency state generally rally around Democratic Party presidential candidates. They do so not because they are hopelessly gullible but because they see no realistic alternative and hope against hope that this time around a Democratic president will deliver on the rhetoric that got him or her elected, and will not write off core Democratic voters in a vain attempt to appease Republican hawks and the national security establishment.

That could happen, especially if those Democratic voters started insisting on greater responsiveness and accountability from those they help to get elected. Democratic voters are not politically powerless. Without their support there would be no victories for Democratic presidential candidates and hence no jobs for Democratic Party national security specialists. And perhaps the most important difference between a centrist Democratic national security specialist like Ashton Carter and a centrist Republican one like Richard Haass is which party each needs to help elect before he can claim a top foreign policy position.

CHAPTER FIFTEEN

BEYOND THE EMERGENCY STATE

After nearly a century of looking at the world primarily through the lens of Wilsonian liberal internationalism, we now find ourselves trapped in a national security dead end. We consume our political and military energies in the addictive pursuit of chronic crisis management, leaving our own, and the planet's, most serious challenges largely unaddressed.

Before Wilson, the mainstream American view was that entangling foreign alliances should be carefully avoided, especially those that might ensnare the United States in the armed quarrels of Europe. But with World War I raging, freedom of the seas menaced by German U-boats, and American war loans to the Allies and postwar trade with Europe at risk, Wilson found continued American self-restraint untenable. To break through the nonintervention taboo and defend what he saw as fundamental American national interests, Wilson chose to speak instead about abstract international principles like making the world safe for democracy. And so it has been ever since.

Wilson replaced America's founding foreign policy parameters with new Wilsonian parameters. Turning the traditional nineteenth-century doctrine on its head, he set out to make the wider world safe for American democracy by transforming that world. Instead of a post–World War I return to the American tradition of no entangling alliances, Wilson sought the opposite—permanent, institutionalized American engagement with a new world order built around a new League of Nations that would be open to all countries and be bound by pledges of mutual collective security. Had he succeeded, the transformation of American constitutional democracy into the emergency state that began in 1940 might have begun twenty years earlier.

But emergency state Wilsonianism is not the only possible form of American internationalism. Theodore Roosevelt stood for a more realist version that melded frank pursuit of American national interests with an active and constructive participation in international affairs. Franklin Roosevelt, though in many ways a pioneer of the emergency state, offered another variant—closer to Wilsonianism, but more confident of American strength and therefore more willing to acknowledge that other countries might have legitimate national interests.

For a country that likes to think of itself as exceptionalist, and is uncomfortable fighting only in the name of national self-interest, emergency state Wilsonianism is a familiar and comfortable brand. But it has outlived its era and its usefulness and become dangerous to our security, to our democracy, and to international cooperation itself. It no longer keeps America secure. It no longer keeps America prosperous and free. And it no longer uses American power to the best international effect.

Returning to the narrow insularity of nineteenth-century American foreign policy is not a viable alternative. We live in a globalized world and cannot prosper, or even survive, without constructively engaging it. And because of America's disproportionate power and wealth, its engagement, constructive or not, will always have decisive consequences.

Our challenge now is to move forward from emergency state Wilsonianism to a twenty-first-century internationalism more suited to our economic and security needs, more suited to our democratic constitutional traditions, and more suited to our increasingly permeable twenty-first-century world. We can move toward a less cramped and crisis-driven form of internationalism. With a more open, forward-looking American internationalism, American presidents would feel less need to dress up the pursuit of legitimate national interests, like ensuring energy supplies and protecting American lives, as the pursuit of abstract principles like stability or quasi-religious crusades against incarnated evil. Such masquerades make it harder to democratically debate appropriate policy responses, enlist suitable allies, and devise exit strategies once our most important interests have been achieved.

An internationalism no longer defined by crisis management and ideological crusades would make essential global problems like halting climate degradation, curbing nuclear weapons proliferation, and combating preventable infectious diseases the central themes of American foreign policy. Such issues may not bring presidents the political glory achievable through military muscle flexing. But applying the kind of material and technological resources America squandered in Iraq to these problems would have a far greater positive impact on international society and on America's own security. And it would not require turning over our constitutional democracy to a permanent peacetime emergency state.

With more to lose than any other society, America has the biggest stake in guaranteeing the planet's environmental sustainability, in steering it away from nuclear self-destruction, and in preventing its polarization between an increasingly rich minority of haves and a desperately poor majority of have-nots. And America can make the most critical contributions toward overcoming those challenges.

These challenges are subtly interrelated. Rich countries like the United States are the biggest per capita consumers of nonrenewable resources and the biggest per capita emitters of greenhouse gases. But without better answers for those struggling at the margins of subsistence, the land hunger of the poor will lead to more clearing of rain forests, more washing away of arable land, and more millions of rural refugees squatting in toxic, disease-spawning urban slums. Political leaders who cannot deliver sustainable development will build their power on military prowess and flaunt nuclear weapons. And nuclear war would be the ultimate environmental disaster.

Even modest global progress in these three areas would make more of a difference in the lives of most Americans, and most people everywhere, than such second-order questions as who will lead the next governments of Iraq and Afghanistan and with which regional powers they will align their foreign policies. Yet these second-order questions continue to consume most of America's foreign policy attention, talent, and resources and burden its diplomatic efforts in more fundamentally important arenas.

And modest global progress is achievable, if the United States reorders its priorities.

Deeper American and Russian nuclear weapons cuts would help—effective deterrence requires no more than a few hundred warheads each. Retaining three or four times that many advertises to other countries that Washington and Moscow still think nuclear weapons are valuable military assets to have, making their calls on others to renounce them reek of great power hypocrisy.

America further undermines its persuasive power on nonproliferation issues by granting credibility-destroying exceptions to supposedly universal international rules for allies like India and Israel while rightly demanding strict compliance from Iran and North Korea.

And in America's own self-interest, the Obama administration should follow through on its pledges to provide increased funding to the International Atomic Energy Agency so that it can hire additional technical experts and inspectors.[1]

Atmospheric concentrations of carbon dioxide, the most important greenhouse gas, are already dangerously high and rising rapidly. If nothing is done to limit emissions, average global temperatures could rise by as much as 5°C (9°F) by the end of this century, with catastrophic effects on climate, sea levels, and agriculture. If that could somehow be reduced to the more manageable 2°C target proposed by the 2009 Copenhagen accords, the damage could be significantly limited. Doing so would require reducing worldwide per capita emissions of carbon dioxide and other greenhouse gases by more than 70 percent over the next forty years, from today's average of 7 metric tons per person to only 2 metric tons. Any conceivable deal will depend on huge reductions by the United States, which, though no longer the world's biggest overall emitter of greenhouse gases (China took over that title in 2006), is still one of the biggest per capita emitters, spewing out over 20 metric tons per person per year—double the per capita rate of Europe, triple that of China, and more than ten times that of India.[2]

Of the world's nearly 7 billion people, about one in four still live on less than $1.25 per day and nearly half on less than $2.50 a day. Reducing those numbers costs money, but usually less money than dealing with the multiple consequences of neglecting this problem, including wars, destabilizing flows of unwanted refugees, and fast-spreading epidemics. For the past three decades, developed countries have had a target of spending 0.7 percent of their gross national income on official development assistance, but they have actually spent less than half of that. The United States has been one of the worst performers in percentage terms, at roughly 0.2 percent—although in dollar terms it is still by far the biggest aid giver, spending roughly $30 billion per year. Raising U.S. aid spending to 0.7 percent would bring it to roughly $100 billion a year, less than the 2010 cost of the wars in Afghanistan and Iraq.[3]

It has been decades since Americans dared to dream of a better society and a better world. But they once did, and not all that long ago. Franklin Roosevelt promised a post–World War II world "attainable in our time and generation" where people everywhere would enjoy freedom of speech, freedom of religion, "freedom from want," and "freedom from fear." Martin Luther King, Jr., dreamed of an America living up to its founding promises of life, liberty, and the pursuit of happiness for all its people. Lyndon Johnson, before he let the Vietnam War consume his presidency, exhorted Americans to use their wealth to build a great society "where progress is the servant of our needs."[4]

In 2008 Americans dared to dream again. Barack Obama consciously evoked America's long tradition of hope and promise. Nearly 70 million people voted for him, hoping and believing that his would be a transformative presidency. Those hopes have been terribly disappointed.

The circumstances in which Obama took office, marked by two seemingly endless wars and a failing economy, presented him with a classic opening for transformative change—but also with a classic excuse for bipartisan caution, bureaucratic inertia, and a return to the tired policy playbooks of the past. He chose the latter.

Change is still possible. The circumstances still cry out for it. But it will require an aroused electorate insisting on it.

For a long time, this country's racial divisions seemed an insuperable obstacle to realizing the American dream. Roosevelt's New Deal reforms were hemmed in by his unwillingness to face up to racial inequality. Johnson did face up to it, costing the Democrats millions of white votes over the next forty years. Obama's historic 2008 electoral victory suggested those divisions may at last be diminishing.

But another, similarly daunting obstacle remains—the obsessive national security fears described in this book. One has only to recall how the onset of the cold war blighted Franklin Roosevelt's hopes for the postwar era and how the Vietnam War incinerated the Great Society.

For the first four postwar decades, life-and-death nuclear rivalry between the two superpowers pushed America into zero-sum foreign policies, destructive global economic rivalries, and a stunted security state democracy.

That superpower rivalry, with its ever-looming threat of nuclear Armageddon, ended two decades ago. America still faces deadly threats in today's world, but they are less existential and more manageable. Today's threats do not preclude a shift to more enlightened policies that could improve the quality of our lives and the prospects for our children. They demand it. What stands in our way is fear itself—not the economic panic of 1933 but the national security obsession of 2012.

Transformative change must begin by weaning the American people away from that addiction to fear and replacing it with a more realistic sense of America's position in the twenty-first-century world.

Throughout seven decades of the emergency state, Washington has reflexively believed that the surest way to keep Americans safe at home is to fight potential foes abroad. To that end, we have built the world's most powerful and most expensive armed forces. During the cold war that belief translated into policing the front lines of universal containment. Since the Soviet collapse, Washington has taken on the even-more-demanding mission of policing the entire planet, managing every crisis, denying our nonstate enemies any sanctuary anywhere. We have specialized in military power, letting our economic power and the attractive power of our democratic example erode. Over the past ten years we have expanded, not contracted, the ranks of those with the motive and the means to harm us. And we continue to expand them.

Al Qaeda, its allies, and its imitators are at war with the United States. They have attacked us and will likely keep attacking us. This is not a fight we could walk away from if we wanted to. But we simply cannot afford to keep fighting pointless fights for territory with internationally mobile nonstate terrorist groups who can find sanctuary and support as easily in one country as in another. Nor can we afford to keep staking our international reputation on long-shot nation-building efforts carried out on inhospitable terrain with unsuitable, unreliable, or uncommitted local partners.

We need to move beyond the dirty little wars of the cold war and decolonization eras. These limited military interventions, fought to contain the advance of Communism or slow the pace of decolonization, rarely ended in any decisive military victories for the West. At best, they were successful holding actions, preventing defeat, establishing a military stalemate, buying some time.

Afghanistan and Iraq, while neither cold war nor anticolonial conflicts, fall into the same general pattern. George W. Bush may have thought he was fighting a new kind of global war on terrorism. But after toppling the Taliban and Saddam Hussein from power, the only kind of war the Pentagon knew how to fight was an old-fashioned counterinsurgency campaign, based on the lessons the American military believes it finally learned in Vietnam.

However improved the model, counterinsurgency warfare plays to our greatest vulnerabilities and our enemies' greatest strengths. Al Qaeda can base its operations in Yemen, Somalia, or Sudan as easily as in Afghanistan. To score military victories and attract new recruits, it needs us to stir up the hornet's nests of societies that we do not understand and that likely will see our heavy-handed presence as the latest incarnation of foreign colonialism and occupation. We would do better by trying to geographically contain Al Qaeda's dangers than by metastasizing them through war making.

We need to relearn the difference between endless cold-war-style crisis management and a proactive approach to keeping America secure in a globalized world. We need to learn how to discover and play to our strengths and fight on our own terms. And we need to stop strengthening the hands of weaker foes by acting like what they say we are, modern-day successors of the colonial empires so recently evicted from the greater Middle East and South Central Asia.

These aren't the easiest times for Americans to dream again about a better, freer, more just world. Roosevelt made his Four Freedoms speech to a nation that was finally pulling out of the Depression; Johnson and King offered their visions at a time of unprecedented prosperity and full employment. By contrast, today's Americans are still struggling to dig themselves out from the wreckage of the 2008 financial crash. Yet for all that, the world's *potential* output, and the overall productivity of its inhabitants, is higher than ever before in human history.

With crisis also comes opportunity, if it can be seized, and powerful new arguments for long-overdue changes. An overleveraging of credit in an underregulated global financial system triggered the 2008 financial meltdown. Thoughtful proposals for reinvigorating, reregulating, and rebalancing the global economy have since been put forth by eminent and experienced economists and bankers, like the Nobel Prize winners Joseph Stiglitz and Paul Krugman and the former chief economist of the International Monetary Fund Simon Johnson. Unfortunately, the Obama administration chose to ignore them in favor of those—like Larry Summers, Timothy Geithner, and Ben Bernanke—who missed the warning signs and then the long-term lessons of the 2008 crash.

Not surprisingly then, the political response by the Obama administration and Congress has been timid, anemic, and in some cases retrograde, carving out huge speculative loopholes at the behest of financial lobbyists and punching new holes in an already patchwork and ineffective regulatory structure. Reviving Wall Street has been the main thrust of public policy. Reviving Main Street, nurturing new jobs, and rebuilding an internationally competitive American economy have not gotten nearly as much attention from Washington.

Some of the most important features underlying today's economic ills can be traced directly back to the decisions Washington did and did not make in the 1970s, when the problems of a weakening dollar, declining American industrial competitiveness, and growing trade and budget deficits first became evident.

As we saw in chapters 6 to 9, these problems reflected a growing gap between the waning competitiveness of America's underinvesting domestic economy and the limitless global ambitions of the American emergency state. For all the anguished self-examination triggered by Vietnam and Watergate, America never faced up to this gap, in the 1970s or later. We preferred to live in the familiar world built by and for the postwar emergency state.

Instead of addressing these growing international imbalances through changes in our relations with a changing world, we displaced them into the financial system through massive international borrowing. With American real incomes stagnating, American industry increasingly uncompetitive, and American trade and fiscal deficits rising, Main Street decayed into the Rust Belt while Wall Street built a thriving two-way financial superhighway.

The resulting system reflected not only the costs of emergency state economics to American workers, but also the benefits to American consumers and investors. Factories shut down, but malls proliferated. Dollars flowed outward to buy imports, but the rest of the world's factory products flowed in to stock American homes and businesses. Mobile investment capital fled abroad in search of cheaper labor and environmental costs, confident that American power could protect it anywhere from nationalization or other political risks.

America created the Pax Americana it had set out to create. American economic, political, and military power helped forge a global consensus for lowering trade barriers and capital controls, paving the way for international capital mobility and transnational assembly lines.

Meanwhile, thanks to the dollar's special role as an international reserve currency and America's sterling reputation for political and financial stability, foreign savings and surpluses kept flowing inward to pay the bills for America's government and private consumption.

Thus arose a new, finance-driven American economy whose main business was not making and selling things but creating the intricate financial instruments required to keep the money flowing in both directions and deliver big trading profits to Wall Street banks. These financial vehicles had to be complex because they had to attract the money needed to pay America's growing international bills despite shifting exchange rates, fluctuating economic cycles, and changing investment strategies by countries running trade surpluses. Being complex, these vehicles were often opaque to all but the specialists who created and traded them. And being international, they generally escaped national regulatory oversight.

But for a surprisingly long time, it all seemed to work. Reagan's military reinvestment was financed by domestic deficits covered by international borrowing; George W. Bush's, even more so. If American industry could no longer finance American military ambitions, Chinese industry could. And if Chinese industry was built on a low-wage, low-consumption model, its resulting dollar surpluses could be lured back into Treasury bills. Or so Robert Rubin, Larry Summers, and Alan Greenspan kept assuring us.

Sure, an SUV in every driveway meant more money flowing out to OPEC, but that money too could be lured back through Arab purchases of expensive American warplanes and dollar-denominated financial instruments. If foreign borrowers then sought higher returns to compensate for a depreciating dollar, they could be sold Fannie Mae and Freddie Mac bonds and more exotic new forms of financial paper packaged into derivatives. These, in turn, rested on arcane mathematical formulas that promised to make all risk safely manageable by quantifying it and appropriately pricing it. Major international banks declared these mortgage-backed derivatives safe. So did nominally independent rating agencies. So did the U.S. government.

The American economic policy makers who relied on this system to balance the books of an increasingly imbalanced international economy convinced themselves that it could keep working indefinitely. And until the tremors that began in the subprime mortgage market in 2007 abruptly revealed the fallacies behind the risk models and nearly brought down the whole financial system, nobody really wanted to question the magic that kept paying the bills for an America that was no longer earning its way in the world.

Then came the crash, and the 2008 presidential election. And for a time in 2009 almost everyone was prepared to acknowledge that mistakes had been made and that fundamental changes were needed. And just about everyone—even Alan Greenspan—seemed prepared to put aside a generation's worth of free-market ideology in the hope of reviving an economy desperately gasping for credit.

Obama let that rare opportunity pass. Where Franklin Roosevelt had used a similar moment to rationalize and regulate the nation's financial system, Obama limited himself to injecting public cash into the old unreformed system. Once the big banks began paying back their government loans, Washington largely set them free to resume their old risky ways. Financial lobbyists regained their budgets and their nerves, and Republicans and conservative Democrats returned to the deregulatory faith. The political moment and the financial leverage for fundamental reform were squandered.

What the moment demanded was a new regulatory system that covered all derivatives trading; that provided for the mandatory splitting up or downsizing of financial institutions deemed too big to fail; and that reprivatized the risks of speculative trading by banks by moving them into separate institutions without the explicit and implicit public guarantees that cover the classical banking functions of deposit taking and credit creation. It also demanded tax reforms that favored investments in competitive industries over financial speculation and capital exports.

Not all of this might have been achievable in 2009 or 2010. But enacting even a partial installment of these reforms would have done America a lot more good than merely lending out hundreds of billions of dollars, free of meaningful conditions, to resuscitate the old overleveraged financial structures and the unbalanced model of globalization they fed.

We live in a global economy. But globalization, like internationalism, can take different forms. And just as America can pursue an internationalism that isn't shaped by Wilsonianism and the emergency state, it can pursue a different kind of globalization than the neoliberal model promoted by Reagan, George H. W. Bush, Clinton, George W. Bush, and Obama.

A globalization more actively shaped and regulated by democratic civil society would be better all around—more financially balanced, more broadly beneficial, and thus more politically sustainable. That double-barreled formula of market economics and democratic civil society brought the United States, Western Europe, and Japan three exemplary decades of prosperity, mobility, and social security between 1945 and 1975.

The specific global market conditions that shaped those golden decades for the first world cannot be reestablished; nor should they be—development ought not to be a monopoly privilege of a few rich countries. But a better balance between the economic power of capital markets and the political power of democratic governments can and should be restored, this time on a much broader geographic basis.

Stronger U.S. financial reregulation is not enough. The New Deal and postwar financial regulatory systems operated most effectively in a Keynesian world that combined increasingly free trade in goods and services with enough residual control over capital flows to let national governments manage effective demand and create incentives for productive investment. Attempting that kind of regulation today in just one country, even the United States, would not achieve the desired effects and might even prove counterproductive.

What is needed is a contemporary version of the 1944 Bretton Woods global financial agreement. Its purpose would be to build the same kind of financial architecture for decades of largely uninterrupted prosperity and sustainable, equitable growth that the original Bretton Woods created for the developed world of North America, Western Europe, and Japan back then. Helping to design such a system would mark a return to the creative American internationalism of the mid-1940s that later ceded ground to the more shortsighted military and economic nationalism of the emergency state.

The original Bretton Woods system depended on the printing and export of U.S. dollars to increase global liquidity as the world economy grew. It collapsed in the early 1970s, when a financially overstretched America could no longer sustain its assigned role. The system would have eventually broken down anyway, since America's abnormally large 1945 share of world production and trade necessarily contracted as the rest of the world rebuilt from wartime devastation. Or at least the system's exclusive reliance on dollars would have broken down, replaced by an international reserve currency not tied to any one single economy.

That would not have been a simple transition, since the original Bretton Woods system was not just a technical financial agreement but an international political agreement as well. The resulting system registered the economic results of World War II, and an economically dominant Washington overrode the objections of Lord Keynes himself to make sure it had an American stamp.

A new Bretton Woods system would have to be more internationally diversified, like today's world economy. It would need to provide for other means of expanding international reserves than printing and exporting dollars. To accommodate rising economic powers like China, it would probably have to hark back to the original Bretton Woods formula favoring open world trade but allowing limited national capital controls. Though that would be a departure from the free-market fundamentalism of the past three decades, limited capital controls might turn out to be good for the United States as well. Without some such restraint on panicky capital flight and exchange rate speculation, no country can safely reflate its way out of recession with standard Keynesian demand-management tools.

A reformed, sustainable international economic system should not just address currencies and exchange rates. It also needs to renegotiate international trade rules to let countries take some account of the environmental and labor conditions under which goods are produced. Otherwise, trade can only mean a race to the bottom for poor and rich countries alike.

Governments that have based their growth models on cheap labor and loose environmental rules, like China and India, will howl. But new trade arrangements like these, by linking these countries' future growth rates to higher labor and environmental standards, will provide those governments with strong market incentives to change their practices in the ways most consistent with the nature of their own societies and their special economic needs.

One approach to doing this would be to amend the rules of the World Trade Organization to allow voluntary coalitions of the virtuous—built around countries willing to abide by stricter standards on labor rights, product safety, and environmental emissions, and to grant each other enhanced trading access for doing so.

That could help restore the lost balance between market expansion and democratic accountability and could help narrow, rather than widen, economic inequalities at home and abroad. Some goods might cost more at Walmart, but there would be trade-offs like better-paying, more secure jobs in the West and lower public health and environmental cleanup costs in the newly industrializing world.

Such arrangements would help raise living and social standards around the world. They would make it possible to replace the current model of globalization—based on transferring work to low-wage countries while sustaining continued high levels of consumption in deindustrializing countries with deficits and foreign borrowing—with a more sustainable one: a new model based on expanding production and rising living standards everywhere.

This second-generation model for globalization lacks the theoretical simplicity of the current neoliberal model. But it has the decided advantage of being more economically and environmentally sustainable, more humane, and more capable of mobilizing broad public support.

Market-driven economic growth never distributes its material rewards with mathematical equality. Economic incentives and disincentives spur hard work, innovation, and risk taking. Open markets encourage efficiency and growth. But there can be no excuse for resuscitating a flawed version of globalization that produced tens of millions of absolute losers in job security and living standards among the middle and working classes of Western countries—despite the steady expansion of GDP per capita in these countries.

The essential precondition for a wiser approach to globalization is moving away from the obsolete American worldview that nourishes and is nourished by our emergency state. Our relations with the rest of the world will need to become less militarized and managerial, our sense of national identity less rooted in a Wilsonian sense of moral mission and American exceptionalism.

No American government of either party will ever explain that to us. It undercuts their brand identities. The American people will have to assert their interests through the democratic process and thereby make the political parties change their ways to survive. It can be done. But it will require innovative approaches like those described in the concluding chapter.

CONCLUSION

A better future will not arrive on its own; nor can it be miraculously delivered by a transformational president. We will have to bring it into being ourselves, reviving the spirit and the institutions of American democracy and recharging them with grassroots energy.

We do not need to change our Constitution. It was well designed by the framers to provide accountable government and checks on executive power with a view to avoiding the endless wars that had eroded Europe's finances and its freedoms. It can achieve the same ends today.

Seven decades of the emergency state have created a shadow constitution of presidential precedents, lapsed oversight, and deferential court decisions that permit the very practices the framers tried to prevent. But our real democratic Constitution remains intact.

That Constitution's provisions have been interpreted in different ways by different Supreme Court justices over the past two and a quarter centuries. But today's conservative Court majority, whose watchword is deference to the political branches, and its liberal minority, which generally takes a more expansive view of civil liberties and individual rights, might both look with favor on reforms enacted by Congress in response to a grassroots democratic revival.

The bigger problem may be getting the people's elected representatives to do the people's bidding, rather than follow the bad habits of a cocooned political class and the agendas of big contributors and lobbyists.

Without a democratic revival, our foreign policy will consist of endless crisis management, with none of America's enormous creative energy addressed to real problem solving. We will continue to live out our lives knowing that we are leaving our children a damaged planet, an inhumane society, and a legacy of physical and economic insecurity, feeling that the best we can do for them is to try to tweak the lengthening odds that they will somehow individually make it through unscathed.

A revitalized democracy would insist on debating other ways America can engage the world, its problems, and its opportunities.

The ten proposals that follow are intended to spark just that kind of democratic debate. All are within Congress's constitutional power to enact or enforce. Presidents can put some of them (for example, classification reform) into effect on their own by executive order. All must be able to withstand court review. But none will make any headway until an aroused and educated public opinion begins challenging the self-perpetuating emergency state in the name of American constitutional democracy.

WAR AND PEACE—ENDING THE PERMANENT EMERGENCY

1. Presidential war powers come only with a congressional declaration of war.

Peacetime presidents have plenty of power. The Constitution makes them commander in chief of the armed forces and gives them the authority to respond to imminent threats with military force. If they want to exercise the enhanced constitutional powers of a war president, such as sending troops into extended combat, convening military commissions, diluting habeas corpus, or keeping legitimate cases out of court for reasons of national security, they should be required to seek and obtain a congressional declaration of war.

Wartime presidential powers alter the normal constitutional balance. They strengthen the presidency and diminish the role of Congress, the courts, and individual citizens. Such constitutional departures should not be a matter for the president alone to decide. They should require the approval of both elected branches of our government, by means of a congressional declaration of war.

No new legislation would be required to achieve this reform—just a return to pre-emergency-state constitutional practice. Congress declared war against Britain in 1812, against Mexico in 1846, against Spain in 1898, against Germany and Austria-Hungary in 1917, against Japan, Germany, and Italy in 1941, and against Bulgaria, Hungary, and Romania in 1942.

Since then, all of America's wars have been decided upon by presidents. They have usually sought and obtained some form of congressional authorization, before or after the fact. But they have simply ignored the requirements of article 1, section 8, of the Constitution that all presidents swear to "preserve, protect and defend." And Congress has generally been happy to let these presidents go on ignoring their constitutional responsibilities. If the voters began insisting on it, Congresses would cease shirking their constitutional responsibilities.

This is not some archaic formality. It is the constitutional mechanism by which the nation, not just the president, decides whether to go to war and whether to grant the president extraordinary wartime powers.

Following this constitutional procedure will not alone protect our freedoms from all wartime abuses. Congress passed the speech-suppressing Espionage Act of 1917 and the Sedition Act of 1918 during a declared war. Nor will it necessarily protect us from unwise wars. But it will make it harder for presidents to take the country to war and limit our constitutional freedoms without adequate democratic scrutiny and debate. And it will undercut the momentum of, and the rationale for, the peacetime emergency state.

2. Members of congressional military authorization and appropriations committees should recuse themselves from voting on military contracts in their districts.

Military contracts aren't the only part of the federal budget distorted by earmarks and pork. But they are the part with perhaps the greatest impact on the emergency state.

The iron triangle of military contractors, congressional appropriators, and uniformed service chiefs is shaped as much by its civilian base as by its military apex. Successive secretaries of defense have found it almost impossible to shift spending from no-longer-needed weapons systems to newly needed ones in the face of contractors and appropriators fighting to protect highly profitable, job-creating contracts. This not only swells deficits and starves real military needs; it distorts military strategy and national security planning as well.

For example, our out-of-date attachment to short-range fighter jets makes us overly dependent on foreign dictators who can barter air bases near our shifting battle zones for unwise and undeserved American accolades and hefty payouts to support their repressive regimes and family bank accounts. Over the long run, these deals feed regional instability and popular animosity toward the United States.

The simplest path to procurement recusal would be for the congressional leaders of both parties, who control committee appointments, to include this reform in their parties' congressional election platforms. In the case of senators, recusal would apply to contracts in their home states. Recusal would not completely eliminate the pork and earmarks problem—members could still privately agree to vote for each other's projects. But making recusal a part of both parties' congressional platforms would shine a public spotlight on the high military costs of pork-driven procurement and help disperse the now-often-insurmountable power of contractor lobbying.[1]

3. Supplement the all-volunteer military with a new version of Harry Truman's plan for universal military training.

Universal military training is a logical extension of the constitutional scheme for national defense, based on the Second Amendment right of citizens to keep and bear arms and the well-regulated militias that that amendment was meant to sustain.

The all-volunteer military we have had since 1973 is an improvement on the socially pernicious selective service system that preceded it. Selective service made it easier for the educated and the affluent to win indefinite deferments. The sense of unfairness that that system created helped undermine military discipline, morale, and cohesion during the Vietnam War and sparked protest and evasion at home.

But the all-volunteer military has also turned out to have serious military and political deficiencies. The armed forces it has produced are not demographically representative of the larger American population. Democrats and affluent households are underrepresented; southerners are overrepresented. Military families in some ways resemble a caste apart.[2]

That cuts against the constitutional concept of a broad-based citizen army whose misuse in an unwise, unnecessary, or poorly managed war would lead to quick electoral retribution against those responsible. The problem is made worse by the bad constitutional habit of presidential war making, since presidents run only every four years and second-term presidents know they will never have to face the voters again. Instead of biannual congressional coaccountability for the prudent use of a citizen army, we have a professional army, subject to egregious presidential misuse, often without any effective electoral recourse.

The present system causes military problems, too. Our military forces, especially our ground forces, are both too small and too large to fit our military needs. Too small, because throughout the Afghanistan and Iraq wars, the Pentagon has strained to put adequate ground forces in the field and has generally managed to do so only by sending troops back into combat for repeat tours without adequate rest and training. That has made it harder to attract the high-quality recruits the army needs.

And too large, because for a decade before the Afghanistan and Iraq wars, and most likely in the years ahead, the active-duty military force structure has been based on future combat contingencies rather than on present combat needs.

One year of universal military training of all Americans between the age of eighteen and nineteen, with pacifists permitted to choose alternative service and all trainees guaranteed that—unless they choose to enlist in the all-volunteer military or ready reserves—they will not be sent into combat without a congressional declaration of war, would better serve our military needs and constitutional principles.[3]

A host of practical issues, including cost, would have to be solved. But they should not be insurmountable. Other countries have successfully adopted even more demanding systems: Israel, for example, drafts all Jewish men and women into the armed forces at age eighteen, deferring college students and granting permanent exemptions to those whose religious faith bars military service. Of course, no president will propose this, and no Congress will approve it, until the American public faces up to its own mixed feelings about the kind of military power it wants to project and the kind of military obligation it is prepared to demand from all citizens.

CHECKS AND BALANCES—RIGHTING THE CONSTITUTIONAL BALANCE

4. No branch of the federal government should exercise unreviewable powers.

The executive branch in particular has a built-in bias for making the wheels of government turn freely, even if they ride over the rights of individuals and the interests of justice. The president, and those who answer to his or her orders, should not have the sole power to decide whether the country goes to war, whether detainees seized on or off the military battlefield are entitled to the protections of the Geneva Conventions, what treaties ratified by the Senate mean, and whether presidential decisions are governed by federal law. The contrary view is an affront to our constitutional system and to the idea that we are governed by the rule of law, not by the whims of individuals.

Giving the courts, the Congress, and independent review panels within the executive branch the right to review, and if necessary overturn, initial executive decisions is the remedy most in keeping with our constitutional design. Congress, through the power of the purse, and the federal courts, through the power of judicial review, have the means to insist on the principle of universal review.

Congress would likely be eager to do so if an aroused and enlightened public opinion demanded it. The courts, however, could prove a major obstacle. Most of today's judicial conservatives believe in deferring to the executive branch when it claims national security is involved. And most of today's judicial liberals tend to be broadly permissive toward executive power in general.

It wasn't always so, on either end of the judicial spectrum. Judges are citizens, too, and their judicial views tend to be shaped by the national political experience. If a call for universal oversight emerged not just from would-be congressional overseers but from a broader revival of democratic citizenship, it might eventually find greater judicial favor.

5. Congress should be more assertive about exercising its oversight powers on national security and international economic issues.

The principle of universal review should govern not just particular executive branch decisions but overall policies as well. Throughout the period of the emergency state, with the notable exception of the 1970s and early 1980s, Congresses have been reluctant to challenge the rationale and the effectiveness of American foreign, military, and international economic policies formulated by the executive branch. As a result, committees that should be watchdogs for the national interest have evolved into passive clients of the cabinet departments and federal agencies they are supposed to monitor, especially when the president's party has a congressional majority.

Formulating day-to-day policies is the prerogative of the executive in our system. Congress is far too large and diverse a body to step into that day-to-day role. But like a board of directors, Congress has a fiduciary duty to the American people to inquire into those policies, to hold public hearings on them, and to make sure they are producing the desired results.

And when presidents resist sharing necessary information and sending appropriate officials to testify and be questioned on the grounds of executive privilege, Congress should be prepared to challenge those claims in court. Executive privilege appears nowhere in the Constitution. When the Supreme Court addressed the issue in the Watergate case *United States v. Nixon* in 1974, it recognized only a qualified privilege, not an absolute one.

The Court ruled in that case that Nixon could not use a blanket claim of executive privilege to shield himself from legitimate criminal prosecution. The same principle should apply to legitimate congressional oversight. The validity of any specific presidential claim of privilege that Congress contests should be decided by the federal courts. The Nixon case did not result in an endless stream of court cases, and most likely the extension of the principle to oversight won't either, once a definitive court ruling clarifies the ground rules that both elective branches must observe.

6. All chiefs of operational departments and agencies in the executive branch should be subject to Senate confirmation and congressional oversight.

This would overcome a constitutional and historical anomaly that makes it much harder for Congress to exercise effective oversight of foreign, military, and international economic policy.

The text of the Constitution does not provide much explicit guidance. Article 2, section 2, requires the president to seek the advice and consent of the Senate in the appointment of "all other Officers of the United States, whose Appointments are not herein otherwise provided for, and which shall be established by Law: but the Congress may by Law vest the Appointment of such inferior Officers, as they think proper, in the President alone, in the Courts of Law, or in the Heads of Departments."

"Heads of Departments" refers to what we now call cabinet members. There were only four of these in George Washington's day—there are fifteen today. They, and some of their principal deputies, must be confirmed by the Senate and are regularly summoned to testify before congressional oversight committees. The national security adviser, often a more powerful policy maker than the secretary of state or defense, is not subject to Senate confirmation. That's because the job is not classified as an officer, or a department head, but merely as a presidential assistant, and one whose advice is often shielded from Congress by claims of executive privilege.

The perverse effects of this arbitrary distinction on effective oversight became clear during the Iran-Contra affair, when the national security adviser's office was used to run a foreign policy operation that Congress had explicitly prohibited cabinet departments and the CIA from carrying out. That probably wasn't the only time the National Security Council staff had functioned as an operational department.

Making the national security adviser's job confirmable, and lifting the veil of executive privilege from his or her advice when such secrecy gets in the way of legitimate oversight, won't guarantee wiser policies. But it will ensure more widely debated ones and will allow congressional oversight to function as it was meant to function, as a check by one elected branch on the appointees and policies of the other.

ACCOUNTABILITY TO THE PEOPLE—PROVIDING THE INFORMATION NEEDED FOR DEMOCRATIC DECISION MAKING

7. **Declassify all information held by the U.S. government that is directly germane to debating and deciding foreign and international economic policy issues—omitting only information that would compromise intelligence sources and methods, the security of military operations, ongoing treaty negotiations, the privacy of private citizens, and proprietary trade secrets revealed to the government for regulatory or negotiating purposes.**

   Documents containing such sensitive information should be partially declassified, with only the sensitive portions redacted. In the case of documents and other materials that cannot be declassified at all without compromising such information, a broadly descriptive catalog list of the kinds of information contained in these materials should be declassified, so that the public can have some idea of what it is not allowed to know.

If the commonsense guidelines listed above were put into effect, probably more than 90 percent of what is now classified information would be opened to scrutiny. The public would be able to learn how our government arrived at its policy decisions, what those policies were intended to achieve, whether the information our government had at its disposal proved accurate or inaccurate, and what kind of commitments were made to foreign governments. This kind of information is today routinely classified for decades, not to protect national security but to protect the professional reputations of American policy makers and to keep the public from learning things that might turn them against policies the executive branch favors. In other words, they are classified to shield questionable policies from legitimate public debate.

8. **The annual intelligence budget of the United States should be published, redacting only properly classified information as defined above. Intelligence programs should be subjected to regular audits by Congress's Government Accountability Office, in the same way that classified Defense Department programs now are.**

Article 1, section 9, of the Constitution stipulates that "no Money shall be drawn from the Treasury, but in Consequence of Appropriations made by Law; and a regular Statement and Account of the Receipts and Expenditures of all public Money shall be published from time to time."

Since the CIA was created in 1947, this required statement and account has been published in only two budget years, 1997 and 1998. No adverse consequences for America's security are known to have resulted from these two constitutional disclosures. But this healthy practice was discontinued after 1998. It should be resumed. No enemy will conclude we are wimps when it sees the actual numbers. But Americans will be able to engage in informed debate about whether we are getting the best possible value for our intelligence dollars.

GAO monitoring of intelligence projects, as advocated by House Minority Leader Nancy Pelosi, would help uncover and remedy the waste and corruption that inevitably come with unaudited secret spending.[4]

9. Establish a statutory charter for the FBI, enforceable by Congress.

The CIA has had a legislative charter spelling out its jurisdictional authority and limits since it was founded in 1947. When press reports revealed in the 1970s that it had repeatedly violated this charter, remedial action was taken. Regrettably, the FBI, founded in 1908 and with a long history of seriously abusing constitutional rights, has never had such a charter. Attempts to enact one after the disclosures of the 1970s fell short.

That piece of unfinished business needs to be seen through. There is no place for a secret, above-the-law national police force in America. That should be something on which the small-government right and the civil libertarian left should be able to agree. A legislative charter will not prevent FBI abuses, but it will set a lawful standard for detecting and correcting them.

REGULATING FOREIGN COMMERCE—PROMOTING THE GENERAL WELFARE

10. Trade agreements submitted and approved under fast-track authority should contain no clauses overriding Congress's right to enact and enforce environmental and labor laws.

Article 1, section 8, of the Constitution assigns Congress the right "to regulate Commerce with foreign Nations." But since 1974 Congress has delegated much of that authority to the executive branch under a procedure known as "fast-track negotiating authority."

Fast-track authority, which periodically lapses unless Congress renews it, gives presidents the power to negotiate trade agreements and then send them to Congress for expedited up-or-down votes, with no possibility of amendments or filibusters. Most recent U.S. free trade agreements, along with the Uruguay Round Agreements Act of 1994 that helped pave the way for the World Trade Organization the following year, were approved under fast-track authority.

Congress's partial delegation of its tariff-setting authority has long constitutional precedents and has been upheld by the Supreme Court. What is more novel about fast track in the modern era is the way it has been used to limit Congress's authority to legislate in other areas, especially those related to environmental protection.

Because current international trade law generally considers only the final form in which a product enters international trade, not the conditions under which it is produced, laws that attempt to regulate those conditions for imported goods—like laws requiring that tuna sold in America be caught in dolphin-free nets—can be overruled by trade agreements. And laws that attempt to regulate labor and environmental conditions at home can make American products uncompetitive against imports produced without such regulations.

The second problem will be harder to solve than the first. Congress cannot legislate minimum wage laws or environmental protection standards for other countries. But it can ask U.S. trade negotiators to take the strength or weakness of those laws into account in writing the details of trade agreements, much the way patent evasion, copyright piracy, and other infringements of intellectual property rights are now taken into account. Congress should be able to penalize imports made by slave or child labor and to favor dolphin-free tuna.

Tying Congress's hands on these issues under fast track runs counter to at least one of the six chief purposes for which the Constitution was created, according to its preamble: to promote the general welfare. Whatever else this vague phrase may or may not embrace, protecting the environment, enacting fair labor standards, and protecting the health and safety of American workers on the job ought to qualify. Or at least Congress should be required to specifically decide on these issues.

With that in mind, the next grant of fast-track authority by Congress should specify that whenever a president submits a trade agreement under fast track, he or she will be required to certify that nothing in the agreement can negate Congress's ability to enact and enforce environmental or labor laws—as long as these do not directly discriminate against foreign products on the basis of where they are produced.

If that certification is later found to be false, any provisions of the trade agreement that negate Congress's ability in those areas shall be immediately voided and have no legal effect. If other parties to the agreement do not accept such selective voiding, Congress should repudiate the whole agreement and invite the president to negotiate a better one.

Presidents have certified a lot of things in recent years that turned out to be wishful or untrue. But by penalizing an incorrect certification in this way, Congress will give presidents a strong incentive to certify accurately. Doing so will also make it easier for senators and representatives with strong labor and environmental constituencies to vote for future trade agreements.

These proposals deliberately focus on how the branches of our government relate to each other and to the sovereign people. Not at all coincidentally, those are the central themes of America's democratic Constitution. Rolling back the emergency state requires returning to and revitalizing that Constitution, not rewriting or overturning it. Readers persuaded by the arguments in these pages would do well to demand that their elected representatives, from state legislatures to the White House, explain why they have allowed, and continue to allow, America's actual governance to stray so far from the constitutional system that served the country so well for the century and a half up to 1940. The Constitution's formulas for representative democracy, for checks and balances, and its guarantees for political and individual liberties were well designed to "provide for the common defence" and "secure the Blessings of Liberty," neither at the expense of the other. They can still do so today. The emergency state cannot.

ACKNOWLEDGMENTS

I owe an enormous debt of gratitude to the large number of people who helped me develop, test out, and refine the ideas in this book. Whatever merit it has owes much to them; its shortcomings are mine alone. There is not enough space here to list them all. But these deserve special mention.

My father, Myron Unger, first planted in my mind many of the questions this book sets out to answer. A lifelong challenger of conventional wisdom, he knowingly and deliberately passed on this uncomfortable habit to his only son. My mother, Leona Unger, set an example of clear writing I have always tried to follow. Both passed away as this book was being written. I hope they would recognize in the finished product a proud memorial to their love and example.

Among my academic mentors, Walter Lafeber, David Brion Davis, G. B. Kay, E. J. Hobsbawm, Roger Louis, and the late W. W. Rostow, M. M. Postan, and Ed Hewett awakened my lifelong interests in American foreign policy, intellectual history, economic history, and economics.

At *The New York Times* I have had the good fortune to work for a succession of editors who have believed in me and challenged me with the successive foreign policy writing assignments that became my continuing education: Max Frankel, Jack Rosenthal, Howell Raines, Gail Collins, and Andrew Rosenthal. Of my many colleagues there over the years, special thanks to Daniel Altman, Ethan Bronner, Lincoln Caplan, Francis X. Clines, Adam Cohen, Roger Cohen, Helene Cooper, Leslie H. Gelb, Bob Herbert, Nicholas Kristof, Anthony Lewis, John P. MacKenzie, Karl Meyer, Alison Mitchell, Floyd Norris, Peter Passell, Eduardo Porter, Frank Rich, Dorothy Samuels, John Schwartz, Robert B. Semple,

Jr., Leon V. Sigal, Brent Staples, Teresa Tritch, Matthew Wald, and Roger Wilkins.

Special thanks to Rand Beers, Stephanie Blankenburg, Adrienne Clarkson, James P. Cole, Carole Corcoran, Bart Drakulich, David Greeley, Roya Hakakian, Mira Kamdar, Dimitris Kyriakou, Florence Madsen, Jocelyn McCalla, Silvano Nova, Piero and Hanne Ottone, Dan Plesch, John Ralston Saul, Craig Seligman, Laura Silber, Robert Silvers, and Markus Wiedemeier for their penetrating questions and steady support.

Thanks also to Kofi Annan, David P. Calleo, David Cole, Gary Hart, Larry Korb, Andrew Krepinevich, Michael Mandelbaum, Jeffrey Sachs, Charles Schumer, Richard Ullman, and Richard C. Wald, who generously shared their thoughts and wide-ranging expertise. And thanks to Farnaz Fassihi, Tim O'Brien, Zainab Salbi, Jayne Lyn Stahl, Masaro Tamamoto, and Marilyn Young for their repeated expressions of interest and encouragement.

My teaching colleagues at the SAIS Bologna Center of the Johns Hopkins University have been extremely supportive and helpful, especially Ken Keller, Erik Jones, and Romano Prodi. A special thanks to all my graduate students in the "Politics and Policies of the American Emergency State" and "Crises in Context" courses there—especially Romulo Cabeza, Matthew Carroll, Peter Christeleit, Samuel George, Klaas Hinderdael, Deane Hinton, Joan Kato, Anthony Mansell, Sarah Mercadante, Valerie Mock, Joshua Nickell, Niraj Patel, Matt Sollenberger, Emilie Greenhalgh Stammer, Elizabeth Wente, and Eleanor Wylie.

Jack Gerson, Gerry Lantz, the Markels (Jeff, Joy, and David), Jenny Nordberg, and Nicholas X. Rizopolous all read early versions of the manuscript and offered very helpful comments and suggestions. Douglas T. Stuart of Dickinson College reviewed and gave good advice on several early chapters. John L. Harper of the SAIS Bologna Center read and critiqued the entire final manuscript and saved me from uncounted minor and major embarrassments.

My two talented and resourceful research assistants—Anthony Halley and Davide Scigliuzzo—carefully tracked down and verified facts and notes and, where necessary, challenged my insufficiently grounded opinions. This book is theirs as well as mine.

Finally, thanks to my excellent and companionable literary agent, Andrew Stuart, who often understood what I meant to say before I did, and my extraordinary editor at Penguin, Laura Stickney, who "got" the book from the beginning and made it far more readable and more rigorous than it ever could have been without her.

NOTES

CHAPTER 1: LOSING OUR WAY

1. Madison wrote in 1795: "Of all the enemies to public liberty war is, perhaps, the most to be dreaded, because it comprises and develops the germ of every other. War is the parent of armies; from these proceed debts and taxes; and armies, and debts, and taxes are the known instruments for bringing the many under the domination of the few. In war, too, the discretionary power of the Executive is extended; its influence in dealing out offices, honors, and emoluments is multiplied; and all the means of seducing the minds, are added to those of subduing the force, of the people. The same malignant aspect in republicanism may be traced in the inequality of fortunes, and the opportunities of fraud, growing out of a state of war, and in the degeneracy of manners and of morals engendered by both. No nation could preserve its freedom in the midst of continual warfare." James Madison, "Political Observations," April 20, 1795, in *Letters and Other Writings of James Madison,* vol. 4, 1829–1836 (Philadelphia: J. P. Lippincott, 1867), pp. 491–92.

He wrote in 1793: "In war, a physical force is to be created; and it is the executive will, which is to direct it. In war, the public treasuries are to be unlocked; and it is the executive hand which is to dispense them. In war, the honors and emoluments of office are to be multiplied; and it is the executive patronage under which they are to be enjoyed. It is in war, finally, that laurels are to be gathered; and it is the executive brow they are to encircle. The strongest passions and the most dangerous weaknesses of the human breast; ambition, avarice, vanity, the honorable or venial love of fame, are all in conspiracy against the desire and duty of peace." James Madison, Letter of Helvidius no. 4, in *The Writings of James Madison,* ed. Gaillard Hunt (New York: G. P. Putnam's Sons, 1900–1910), 6:174.

Alexander Hamilton wrote in *Federalist* 8: "Safety from external danger is the most powerful director of national conduct. Even the ardent love of liberty will, after a time, give way to its dictates. The violent destruction of life and property incident to war, the continual effort and alarm attendant on a state of continual danger, will compel nations the most attached to liberty to resort for repose and security to institutions which have a tendency to destroy their civil and political rights. To be more safe, they at length become willing to run the risk of being less free. The institutions chiefly alluded to are STANDING ARMIES and the correspondent appendages of military establishments. Standing armies, it is said, are not provided against in the new Constitution; and it is therefore inferred that they may exist under it. Their existence, however, from the very terms of the proposition, is, at most, problematical and uncertain. But standing armies, it may be replied, must inevitably result from a dissolution of the Confederacy. Frequent war and constant apprehension, which require a state of as constant preparation, will infallibly produce them. The weaker States or confederacies would first have recourse to them, to put themselves upon an equality with their more potent neighbors. They would endeavor to supply the inferiority of population and resources by a more regular and effective system of defense, by disciplined troops, and by fortifications. They would, at the same time, be necessitated to strengthen the executive arm of government, in doing which their constitutions would acquire a progressive direction toward monarchy. It is of the nature of war to increase the executive at the expense of the legislative authority." *Federalist* 8, http://www.constitution.org/fed/federa08.htm.

Hamilton took up the theme again in *Federalist* 26: "The legislature of the United States will be *obliged*, by this provision, once at least in every two years, to deliberate upon the propriety of keeping a military force on foot; to come to a new resolution on the point; and to declare their sense of the matter, by a formal vote in the face of their constituents. They are not *at liberty* to vest in the executive department permanent funds for the support of an army, if they were even incautious enough to be willing to repose in it so improper a confidence." *Federalist* 26, http://www.constitution.org/fed/federa26.htm.

2. Ronald Steel, *Walter Lippmann and the American Century* (Boston: Little, Brown, 1980), p. 124.

3. It is of course impossible to quantify a *what if*. But by staying out of World War I until April 1917, and out of serious combat until far later, the United States missed most of the deadly trench warfare that destroyed the youth of France, Britain, Russia, and Germany. The final World War I death toll for the United States was 116,708. For the U.K. it was 885,138, for France 1,397,800, for Russia 1,811,000, and for Germany 2,050,897. In World War II the U.S. military death toll of 416,800 was well below what it might have been had U.S. troops entered the European war when Germany and Russia attacked Poland in September 1939 rather than after Pearl Harbor.

4. Frank J. Rafalko, *A Counterintelligence Reader,* October 4, 2004, http://www.fas.org/irp/ops/ci/docs/index.html, p. 157; U.S. Congress, Senate, Select Committee to Study Governmental Operations with Respect to Intelligence Activities, *Final Report—Book II, Intelligence Activities and the Rights of Americans*, 94th Cong., 2nd sess., 1976, hereinafter cited as *Church Committee Report,* CD-ROM available from Assassination Archives and Research Center, http://www.aarclibrary.org.

CHAPTER 2: THE GODFATHER

1. *Church Committee Report,* 2:30, 158, http://www.aarclibrary.org/publib/contents/church/contents_church_reports_book2.htm.

2. Robert David Johnson, *The Peace Progressives and American Foreign Relations* (Cambridge, Mass.: Harvard Historical Studies, 1995), quoted in Charles Chatfield, "American Insecurity, Dissent from the Long War," in Andrew J. Bacevich, ed., *The Long War: A New History of U.S. National Security Policy Since World War II* (New York: Columbia University Press, 2007), p. 459.

3. Bruce E. Fein, *Constitutional Peril: The Life and Death Struggle for Our Constitution and Democracy* (New York: Palgrave Macmillan, 2009), pp. 60–61.

4. *Church Committee Report,* 2:30, 158.

5. Ibid., 2:29.

6. Ibid.

7. John M. Crewdson, "FBI Lists 1,200 as Security Risks," *New York Times*, October 23, 1975; *Church Committee Report,* 2:29.

8. *Church Committee Report,* 2:146, 244, 259.

9. Ibid., 2:27.

10. Ibid., 2:31–32.

11. Richard Polenberg, *War and Society: The United States 1941–1945* (Westport, Conn.: Greenwood Press, 1980), p. 38.

12. Ibid., p. 48.

13. U.S. Congress, House of Representatives, Naval Affairs Subcommittee to Investigate Congested Areas, 78th Cong., 1st sess., hearing, testimony of John L. DeWitt, April 13, 1943.

14. Francis Biddle, *In Brief Authority* (Garden City, N.Y.: Doubleday, 1962), pp. 212–13.

15. Ibid., p. 223.

16. Polenberg, *War and Society,* pp. 5–8; diary entry for August 26, 1940, quoted in Henry L. Stimson, *On Active Service in Peace and War* (New York: Harper & Bros., 1948), p. 353.

17. Alan Brinkley, *The End of Reform: New Deal Liberalism in Recession and War* (New York: Alfred A. Knopf, 1995), pp. 190, 192.

18. Ibid., p. 199; Polenberg, *War and Society,* p. 237.

19. Brinkley, *The End of Reform,* p. 172.

20. Benjamin O. Fordham, "Paying for Global Power: Costs and Benefits of Postwar U.S. Military Spending," in Bacevich, ed., *The Long War,* p. 378.

21. Ibid., pp. 385–95.

22. "The Pentagon Meets the Real World," *New York Times,* editorial, March 1, 2009.

CHAPTER 3: THE FRAMING OF THE PERMANENT EMERGENCY STATE

1. United Nations, Statistical Office, *International Trade Statistics, 1900–1960,* May 1962, http://unstats.un.org/unsd/trade/imts/Historical%20data%201900-1960.pdf; Lloyd C. Gardner, *Architects of Illusion: Men and Ideas in American Foreign Policy, 1941–1949* (Chicago: Quadrangle, 1970), p. 122.

2. "Four policemen" because Roosevelt had added China to the list for diplomatic and political reasons, despite its obvious military incapacities. The North Atlantic Treaty of 1949 was the first peacetime mutual defense treaty to bind the United States since the dissolution of the Revolutionary War alliance with France in 1800.

3. Office of European Affairs and Office of Far Eastern Affairs memoranda, in U.S. Department of Defense, *Report of the Office of Secretary of Defense Vietnam Task Force,* also known as the Pentagon Papers (Washington, D.C.: GPO, 1971), part VB2a, pp. 5–21, http://www.archives.gov/research/pentagon-papers/.

4. Benjamin O. Fordham, "Paying for Global Power: Costs and Benefits of Postwar U.S. Military Spending," in Andrew J. Bacevich, ed., *The Long War: A New History of U.S. National Security Policy Since World War II* (New York: Columbia University Press, 2007) p. 384.

5. Truman quoted in "National Affairs: Anniversary Remembrance," *Time,* July 2, 1951, http://www.time.com/time/magazine/article/0,9171,815031,00.html.

6. Serhii Plokhy, *Yalta: The Price of Peace* (New York: Viking, 2010), p. 217.

7. Ibid., pp. 152–80, 196–206, 241–51.

8. Ibid., pp. 143–51, 289–90.

9. Ibid., pp. 167–80, 394–98.

10. Ibid, p. 411.

11. Charles L. Mee, *Meeting at Potsdam* (New York: M. Evans, 1975), pp. 237–38.

12. Ibid., pp. 238, 289.

13. U.S. Department of Defense, Defense Manpower Data Center, Statistical Information Analysis Center, *Selected Manpower Statistics for FY 2005,* http://siadapp.dmdc.osd.mil/personnel/M01/fy05/m01fy05.pdf, p. 47; U.S. Department of Defense, Office of the Under Secretary of Defense (Comptroller), *National Defense Budget Estimates for FY2004,* March 2003, http://comptroller.defense.gov/defbudget/fy2004/fy2004_greenbook.pdf.

14. U.S. Department of Defense, Directorate for Information Operations and Reports, *Selected Manpower Statistics, Fiscal Year 2003,* http://siadapp.dmdc.osd.mil/personnel/M01/fy03/m01fy03.pdf.

U.S. MILITARY SPENDING, FISCAL YEARS 1945–2008
(billions of constant 2004 dollars)

1945–1959	**1960–1974**	**1975–1989**	**1990–2004**	**2005–2008**
1945 871.0	*1960* 331.6	*1975* 292.8	*1990* 431.2	*2005* 421.5
1946 444.6	*1961* 332.8	*1976* 281.8	*1991* 376.6	*2006* 430.0
1947 120.3	*1962* 348.6	*1977* 279.4	*1992* 397.2	*2007* 438.5
1948 93.5	*1963* 342.6	*1978* 280.6	*1993* 381.4	*2008* 455.5
1949 132.4	*1964* 348.6	*1979* 287.9	*1994* 362.0	
1950 138.5	*1965* 321.9	*1980* 297.6	*1995* 342.6	
1951 225.9	*1966* 354.7	*1981* 314.6	*1996* 323.1	
1952 427.6	*1967* 421.5	*1982* 342.6	*1997* 321.9	
1953 451.9	*1968* 460.4	*1983* 370.5	*1998* 315.8	
1954 414.2	*1969* 438.5	*1984* 375.4	*1999* 317.1	
1955 346.2	*1970* 411.8	*1985* 402.1	*2000* 329.3	
1956 321.9	*1971* 375.4	*1986* 430.0	*2001* 335.3	
1957 328.0	*1972* 343.8	*1987* 438.5	*2002* 374.1	
1958 324.3	*1973* 309.8	*1988* 443.4	*2003* 447.1	
1959 325.6	*1974* 297.6	*1989* 449.5	*2004* 475.3	

Source: Office of the Under Secretary of Defense (Comptroller), *National Defense Budget Estimates for FY2004,* March 2003, tables 7-2 and 5-9, http://comptroller.defense.gov/defbudget/fy2004/fy2004_greenbook.pdf.

15. Gardner, *Architects of Illusion,* p. 93.

16. John Lewis Gaddis, *Strategies of Containment: A Critical Appraisal of American National Security Policy During the Cold War* (New York: Oxford University Press, 2005), p. 19.

17. Ibid., p. 29.

18. Ibid., p. 25.

19. Ronald Steel, *Walter Lippmann and the American Century* (Boston: Little, Brown, 1980), pp. 438–39.

20. American Presidency Project. John Woolley and Gerhard Peters, "Presidential Job Approval, F. Roosevelt (1941) to Obama," http://www.presidency.ucsb.edu/data/popularity.php; U.S. Congress, Senate, Committee on Foreign Relations, 80th Cong., 1st sess., Executive Session Hearings on S. 938, "A Bill to Provide Foreign Assistance to Greece and Turkey," held March 13, 28, April 1, 2, 3, 7, 1947, http://www.archive.org/stream/legislativeorigi00unit/legislativeorigi00unit_djvu.txt/.

21. Stephen E. Ambrose and Douglas Brinkley, *Rise to Globalism: American Foreign Policy Since 1938* (New York: Penguin, 1997), p. 82.

22. Senate Committee on Foreign Relations, Executive Session Hearings on S. 938, pp. ix–xi.

23. Douglas T. Stuart, *Creating the National Security State: A History of the Law That Transformed America* (Princeton, N.J.: Princeton University Press, 2008), pp. 1–73.

24. The National Security Act authorizes the director of central intelligence to "perform such other functions and duties related to intelligence affecting the national security as the President or the Director of National Intelligence may direct." National Security Act, 1947, sec. 104A, "Director of the Central Intelligence Agency," clause D, "Responsibilities," http://intelligence.senate.gov/nsaact1947.pdf.

25. U.S. National Security Council, "United States Objectives and Programs for National Security," April 14, 1950, NSC-68, Sec. IV(A), "Nature of Conflict," http://www.fas.org/irp/offdocs/nsc-hst/nsc-68.htm.

26. Gaddis, *Strategies of Containment*, p. 123.

27. Ibid., pp. 87–124.

28. Athan Theoharis, "The Rhetoric of Politics: Foreign Policy, Internal Security, and Domestic Politics in the Truman Era, 1945–1950," in Barton J. Bernstein, ed., *Politics and Policies of the Truman Administration* (Chicago: Quadrangle, 1970), pp. 214, 256, 260, 264.

CHAPTER 4: RUNAWAY TRAIN

1. Senator Robert A. Taft, Speech on the North Atlantic Treaty, July 26, 1949, http://teachingamericanhistory.org/library/index.asp?document=857; William L. O'Neill, *A Democracy at War* (New York: Free Press, 1993), p. 232.

2. Klaus Larres, *Churchill's Cold War: The Politics of Personal Diplomacy* (New Haven, Conn.: Yale University Press, 2002), pp. 188–91; Mark Kramer, "The Early Post-Stalin Succession Struggle and Upheavals in East-Central Europe: Internal-External Linkages in Soviet Policy-Making (Part 1)," *Journal of Cold War Studies* 1, no. 1 (Winter 1999): 3–56; Michael R. Beschloss, *The Crisis Years: Kennedy and Khrushchev, 1960–1963* (New York: HarperCollins, 1991), 39.

3. Melvyn P. Leffler, *For the Soul of Mankind: The United States, the Soviet Union, and the Cold War* (New York: Hill & Wang, 2007), pp. 84–150.

4. John Foster Dulles, speech at Iowa State College, June 9, 1956, quoted in Gaddis, *Strategies of Containment*, p. 151.

5. "Statement of Policy by the National Security Council on Basic National Security Policy," October 30, 1953, in *The Pentagon Papers: The Defense Department History of United States*

Decisionmaking on Vietnam, "Senator Gravel Edition" (Boston: Beacon Press, 1971), vol. 1, doc. 18, pp. 412–29.

6. Peter R. Lavoy, "The Enduring Effects of Atoms for Peace," *Arms Control Today,* December 2003, http://www.armscontrol.org/act/2003_12/Lavoy.

7. John Lewis Gaddis, *Strategies of Containment: A Critical Appraisal of American National Security Policy During the Cold War* (New York: Oxford University Press, 2005), p. 149.

8. U.S. Office of Management and Budget, *The Budget of the United States Government, Fiscal Year 2010,* table 3-1, "Outlays by Superfunction and Function: 1940–2014," pp. 47–48, http://www.gpoaccess.gov/usbudget/fy10/hist.html.

9. Douglas T. Stuart, *Creating the National Security State: A History of the Law That Transformed America* (Princeton, N.J.: Princeton University Press, 2008), p. 216.

10. John Foster Dulles, Speech to the Council on Foreign Relations, New York, January 12, 1954, in Department of State *Bulletin* 30 (January 25, 1954), p.108, http://www.freerepublic.com/focus/f-news/1556858/posts.

11. James Shepley, "How Dulles Averted War," *Life,* January 16, 1956, pp. 70–80.

12. U.S. Department of Defense, Office of the Under Secretary of Defense (Comptroller), *National Defense Budget Estimates for FY2012,* March 2011, pp. 141, 142, 232, 238, http://comptroller.defense.gov/defbudget/fy2012_Green_Book.pdf.

13. National Security Act, 1947, sec. 104A, "Director of the Central Intelligence Agency," clause D, "Responsibilities," para. 4.

14. Stuart, *Creating the National Security State,* p. 270; David Wise and Thomas B. Ross, *The Invisible Government* (New York: Random House, 1964), p. 264.

15. Wise and Ross, *Invisible Government.*

16. *Church Committee Report,* 2:134–35, http://www.aarclibrary.org/publib/contents/church/contents_church_reports_book2.htm.

CHAPTER 5: BELATED REALISM

1. Theodore C. Sorensen, *Counselor: A Life at the Edge of History* (New York: Harper, 2008), pp. 310–40.

2. Ibid., pp. 353–59; David E. Kaiser, *American Tragedy: Kennedy, Johnson, and the Origins of the Vietnam War* (Cambridge, Mass.: Belknap Press of Harvard University Press, 2000), pp. 286–90; David E. Kaiser, *The Road to Dallas: The Assassination of John F. Kennedy* (Cambridge, Mass.: Belknap Press of Harvard University Press, 2008), pp. 415–17.

3. John F. Kennedy, Inaugural Address, January 20, 1961, http://www.jfklibrary.org/Research/Ready-Reference/JFK-Miscellaneous-Information/Inaugural-Address.aspx.

4. Ivo H. Daalder and I. M. Destler, *In the Shadow of the Oval Office: Profiles of the National Security Advisers and the Presidents They Served; From JFK to George W. Bush* (New York: Simon & Schuster, 2009), pp. 7–8, 12–14.

5. Michael R. Beschloss, *The Crisis Years: Kennedy and Khrushchev, 1960–1963* (New York: HarperCollins, 1991), pp. 27–29.

6. *Church Committee Reports, Interim Report on Alleged Assassination Plots Involving Foreign Leaders*, pp. 138–41, http://www.aarclibrary.org/publib/contents/church/contents_church_reports_ir.htm.

7. Ernest R. May and Philip D. Zelikow, eds., *The Kennedy Tapes: Inside the White House During the Cuban Missile Crisis* (Cambridge, Mass.: Belknap Press of Harvard University Press, 1997).

8. Ibid., p. 100.

9. Ibid., p. 61.

10. Anatoly Dobrynin, *In Confidence: Moscow's Ambassador to America's Six Cold War Presidents, 1962–1986* (New York: Random House, 1995), p. 44.

11. President John F. Kennedy, Statement on Cuba, September 4, 1962, in Department of State *Bulletin* 47, no. 1213 (September 24, 1962), http://www.mtholyoke.edu/acad/intrel/jfkstate.htm.

12. May and Zelikow, eds., *Kennedy Tapes*, pp. 60, 100.

13. Natural Resources Defense Council (NRDC), Archive of Nuclear Data, http://www.nrdc.org/nuclear/nudb/datainx.asp.

14. May and Zelikow, eds., *Kennedy Tapes*, pp. 89–91.

15. Ibid., p. 92.

16. Ibid., p. 84.

17. Ibid., pp. 98, 120, 163.

18. Ibid., p. 182.

19. John Lewis Gaddis, *Strategies of Containment: A Critical Appraisal of American National Security Policy During the Cold War* (New York: Oxford University Press, 2005), p. 203.

20. Ibid. pp. 205–6.

21. Ibid., p. 206.

22. Ibid., p. 215; John F. Kennedy, Televised Address on the Berlin Crisis, July 25, 1961, http://www.presidentialrhetoric.com/historicspeeches/kennedy/berlincrisis.html.

23. Gaddis, *Strategies of Containment*, p. 215.

24. Lawrence M. Greenberg, *The Hukbalahap Insurrection: A Case Study of a Successful Anti-Insurgency Operation in the Philippines, 1946–1955*, Historical Analysis Series, U.S. Army Center of Military History, Analysis Branch (Washington, D.C.: GPO, 1987), pp. 94–97.

25. Kaiser, *American Tragedy*, p. 346.

26. Gaddis, *Strategies of Containment*, p. 217.

27. NRDC, Archive of Nuclear Data.

CHAPTER 6: TUNNEL VISION

1. *The Pentagon Papers: The Defense Department History of United States Decisionmaking on Vietnam,* "Senator Gravel Edition," (Boston: Beacon Press, 1971), vol. 2, p. 201; David E. Kaiser, *American Tragedy: Kennedy, Johnson, and the Origins of the Vietnam War* (Cambridge, Mass.: Belknap Press of Harvard University Press, 2000), pp. 230–34.

2. Kaiser, *American Tragedy,* pp. 307–9; Robert S. McNamara and Brian VanDeMark, *In Retrospect: The Tragedy and Lessons of Vietnam* (New York: Times Books, 1995), p. 119.

3. Kaiser, *American Tragedy,* pp. 289–90.

4. Dwight D. Eisenhower, news conference, April 7, 1954, http://www.h-net.org/~hst306/documents/domino.html.

5. Kaiser, *American Tragedy,* pp. 321–23, 327, 329; McNamara and VanDeMark, *In Retrospect,* pp. 147–48, 154–55, 167–68.

6. Edward J. Marolda, *Summary of Tonkin Gulf Crisis of August 1964,* July 13, 2005, U.S. Department of the Navy, Navy History and Heritage Command, http://www.history.navy.mil/faqs/faq120-1.htm.

7. Lyndon Johnson, "Report on the Gulf of Tonkin Incident," August 4, 1964. http://millercenter.org/scripps/archive/speeches/detail/3998.

8. Lyndon Johnson, Message to Congress, August 5, 1964, http://www.pbs.org/wgbh/amex/presidents/36_l_johnson/psources/ps_tonkin.html.

9. U.S. Congress, Gulf of Tonkin Resolution, Joint Resolution of Congress, H.J. Res. 1145, August 7, 1964.

10. Lyndon Johnson, speech before the American Bar Association, New York City, August 12, 1964, http://www.presidency.ucsb.edu/ws/index.php?pid=26434#axzz1SNlHvKUD.

11. McNamara and VanDeMark, *In Retrospect,* pp. 205–6; *Pentagon Papers,* Gravel Edition, 3:2.

12. McNamara and VanDeMark, *In Retrospect,* p. 205.

13. Doris Kearns Goodwin, *Lyndon Johnson and the American Dream* (New York: St Martin's Press, 1991), pp. 251–52.

14. David Wise, *The American Police State: The Government Against the People* (New York: Random House, 1976), p. 289.

15. Ibid., pp. 288–92; *Church Committee Report,* 2:293, http://www.aarclibrary.org/publib/contents/church/contents_church_reports_book2.htm.

16. Bill Moyers, "LBJ and the FBI," *Newsweek,* March 10, 1975, p. 84.

17. Wise, *American Police State,* p. 287.

18. *Church Committee Report,* 2:86–96, http://www.aarclibrary.org/publib/contents/church/contents_church_reports_book2.htm.

CHAPTER 7: EMERGENCY REPAIRS

1. Richard M. Nixon, "Asia After Viet Nam," *Foreign Affairs* 46, no. 1 (October 1967): 121–25.

2. Michael R. Beschloss, *Taking Charge: The Johnson White House Tapes, 1963–1964* (New York: Simon & Schuster, 1997), p. 162.

3. McGeorge Bundy, memo of conversation with Ambassador Dobrynin, May 17, 1963, National Security Archive, http://www.gwu.edu/~nsarchiv/NSAEBB/NSAEBB38/; Igor Sutyagin, *The Role of Nuclear Weapons and Its Possible Future Missions,* chap. 2, sec. 3, NATO Research Fellowship Report, 1996, http://www.nato.int/acad/fellow/94-96/sutyagin/index.htm.

4. Richard M. Nixon, Remarks to the Nation Announcing Acceptance of an Invitation to Visit the People's Republic of China, July 15, 1971, http://www.presidency.ucsb.edu/ws/?pid=3079#axzz1aCNNFWRM.

5. Henry Kissinger and William Burr, *The Kissinger Transcripts: The Top-Secret Talks with Beijing and Moscow* (New York: New Press, 1999), pp. 61, 65.

6. Washington's cold war triangulating with China brought other Orwellian moments as well. Presidents Ford and Reagan funneled aid to Jonas Savimbi's Beijing-sponsored UNITA movement in Angola to fight against the Soviet- and Cuban-backed MPLA government. Presidents Carter and Reagan supported the Beijing-backed Zimbabwean Marxist, Robert Mugabe, over the Moscow-backed Zimbabwean Marxist, Joshua Nkomo. President George H. W. Bush fought to keep Cambodia's UN seat in the hands of the defeated pro-Beijing Khmer Rouge, rather than let it fall into the hands of the Vietnamese-backed Hun Sen government.

7. John Lewis Gaddis, *Strategies of Containment: A Critical Appraisal of American National Security Policy During the Cold War* (New York: Oxford University Press, 2005), p. 292.

8. Connally quoted in "The Burden of Saving the World Economy," *Global Times,* June 23, 2010, http://opinion.globaltimes.cn/editorial/2010-06/544381.html.

9. Thomas S. Blanton, ed., "The Pentagon Papers: Secrets, Lies, and Audiotapes," National Security Archive, Electronic Briefing Book no. 48, June 5, 2001, telephone conversation with Kissinger, June 13, 1971, at 3:09 p.m., http://www.gwu.edu/~nsarchiv/NSAEBB/NSAEBB48/nixon.html.

10. Ibid., telephone conversations with Alexander Haig, June 13, 1971, at 12:18 p.m.; Kissinger, June 13, 1971, at 3:09 p.m.; John Ehrlichman, June 14, 1971, at 7:13 p.m.; and John Mitchell, June 14, 1971, at 7:19 p.m.

11. Ibid., telephone conversation with John Mitchell, June 14, 1971, at 7:19 p.m.

12. U.S. Supreme Court, *United States v. Nixon,* 418 U.S. 683 (1974), http://caselaw.lp.findlaw.com/scripts/getcase.pl?court=us&vol=418&invol=683; Richard Nixon, interview by David Frost, May 20, 1977, http://www.guardian.co.uk/theguardian/2007/sep/07/greatinterviews1.

CHAPTER 8: DAMAGE CONTROL

1. Bernard J. Firestone and Alexej Ugrinsky, *Gerald R. Ford and the Politics of Post-Watergate America* (Westport, Conn.: Greenwood Press, 1993), p. 39.

2. Tim Weiner, *Legacy of Ashes: The History of the CIA* (New York: Anchor, 2008), p. 394; David W. P. Elliott, *The Vietnamese War: Revolution and Social Change in the Mekong Delta, 1930–1975* (Armonk, N.Y.: M. E. Sharpe, 2006), p. 339; *Church Committee Report,* book 1, http://www.aarclibrary.org/publib/contents/church/contents_church_reports_book1.htm, book 2, http://www.aarclibrary.org/publib/contents/church/contents_church_reports_book2.htm; R. Manning, ed., *War in the Shadows: The Vietnam Experience* (New York: Time-Life Education, 1988), pp. 72, 55–65.

3. Gerald Ford et al., memorandum of White House conversation with Bipartisan Congressional Leadership, February 3, 1975, http://www.history.state.gov/historicaldocuments/

frus1969-76v30/d211; Gerald R. Ford, statement on signing the Foreign Assistance Act of 1974, December 30, 1974, http://www.presidency.ucsb.edu/ws/index.php?pid=4660.

4. Gerald Ford, Proclamation 4311, Granting a Pardon to Richard Nixon, September 8, 1974, http://watergate.info/ford/pardon-proclamation.shtml.

5. Senator Harry F. Byrd of Virginia, not up for election that year, was an Independent.

6. Douglas F. Garthoff, *Directors of Central Intelligence as Leaders of the U.S. Intelligence Community, 1946–2005* (Washington, D.C.: Center for the Study of Intelligence, Central Intelligence Agency, 2005), chap. 6, https://www.cia.gov/library/center-for-the-study-of-intelligence/csi-publications/books-and-monographs/directors-of-central-intelligence-as-leaders-of-the-u-s-intelligence-community/dci_leaders.pdf.

7. Thomas S. Blanton, ed., "The CIA's Family Jewels: Agency Violated Charter for 25 Years, Wiretapped Journalists and Dissidents," National Security Archive, Electronic Briefing Book no. 222, June 21, 2007, http://www.gwu.edu/~nsarchiv/NSAEBB/NSAEBB222/index.htm.

8. Kenneth Kitts, "Commission Politics and National Security: Gerald Ford's Response to the CIA Controversy of 1975," *Presidential Studies Quarterly* 26, no. 4 (Fall 1996): 1081–98; David Wise, *The American Police State: The Government Against the People* (New York: Random House, 1976), p. 211.

9. Wise, *American Police State,* p. 212.

10. Gerald K. Haines, "The Pike Committee Investigation and the CIA: Looking for a Rogue Elephant," *Studies in Intelligence,* Winter 1998–99, https://www.cia.gov/library/center-for-the-study-of-intelligence/csi-publications/csi-studies/studies/winter98_99/art07.html.

11. Ibid.

12. Ibid.; Kitts, "Commission Politics."

CHAPTER 9: A DIFFERENT PATH

1. Tip O'Neill, *Man of the House* (New York: Random House, 1987), p. 311; Michael J. Towle, *Out of Touch: The Presidency and Public Opinion* (College Station: Texas A&M University Press, 2004), p. 70; Jimmy Carter, *Our Endangered Values: America's Moral Crisis* (New York: Simon & Schuster, 2005), p. 8.

2. U.S. Department of Commerce, Census Bureau, *Demographic Trends in the 20th Century,* Census 2000 Special Reports, November 2002, http://www.census.gov/prod/2002pubs/censr-4.pdf.

3. Jimmy Carter, Address at the Commencement Exercises at the University of Notre Dame, May 22, 1977, http://www.presidency.ucsb.edu/ws/index.php?pid=7552#axzz1Q84NnO7G.

4. Jimmy Carter, Televised Speech on Energy Policy, April 18, 1977, http://www.pbs.org/wgbh/americanexperience/features/primary-resources/carter-energy/.

5. Brent D. Yacobucci and Robert Bamberger, *Automobile and Light Truck Fuel Economy: The CAFE Standards,* Congressional Research Service, CRS Report for Congress R40166, January 19, 2007, http://ncseonline.org/NLE/CRSreports/08Jun/RL33413.pdf; James K. Jackson, *U.S. Trade Deficit and the Impact of Rising Oil Prices,* Congressional Research Service, CRS Report for Congress RS2204, November 14, 2006, http://fpc.state.gov/documents/organization/77719.pdf.

6. Penny Lernoux, *Cry of the People: The Struggle for Human Rights in Latin America—The Catholic Church in Conflict with U.S. Policy* (New York: Penguin, 1983), p. 81.

7. Anthony Lake, *Somoza Falling: The Nicaraguan Dilemma; A Portrait of Washington at Work* (Boston: Houghton Mifflin, 1989), pp. 115–16.

8. Ibid., p. 25.

9. Gary Sick, "Iran: A View from the White House," *World Affairs* 149, no. 4 (1987): 210; Farah Pahlavi, *An Enduring Love: My Life with the Shah* (New York: Miramax, 2004), pp. 272–73.

10. Tim Weiner, *Legacy of Ashes: The History of the CIA* (New York: Anchor, 2008), p. 92.

11. Loch K. Johnson, *The Oxford Handbook of National Security Intelligence* (New York: Oxford University Press, 2010), p. 368.

12. William J. Daugherty, "Jimmy Carter and the 1979 Decision to Admit the Shah into the United States," AmericanDiplomacy.org, March 16, 2003, http://www.unc.edu/depts/diplomat/archives_roll/2003_01-03/dauherty_shah/dauherty_shah.html.

13. Zbigniew Brzezinski, "The CIA's Intervention in Afghanistan: Interview with Zbigniew Brzezinski," trans. Bill Blum, *Le Nouvel Observateur,* January 15–21, 1998.

14. Jimmy Carter, Crisis of Confidence Speech, July 15, 1979, http://www.pbs.org/wgbh/americanexperience/features/primary-resources/carter-crisis/.

15. "Carter's Crisis of Confidence Speech," *American Experience,* WGBH, n.d., http://www.pbs.org/wgbh/amex/carter/peopleevents/e_malaise.html.

CHAPTER 10: THE PRESIDENT WE WANTED

1. David E. Hoffman, *The Dead Hand: The Untold Story of the Cold War Arms Race and Its Dangerous Legacy* (New York: Anchor, 2009), pp. 60–71.

2. Caspar W. Weinberger, "The Uses of Military Power," National Press Club, Washington, D.C., November 28, 1984, http://www.airforce-magazine.com/MagazineArchive/Pages/2004/January%202004/0104keeper.aspx.

3. Frank Newport, Jeffrey M. Jones, and Lydia Saad, "Ronald Reagan from the People's Perspective: A Gallup Poll Review," Gallup.com, June 7, 2004, http://www.gallup.com/poll/11887/Ronald-Reagan-From-Peoples-Perspective-Gallup-Poll-Review.aspx; Richard A. Brody and Catherine R. Shapiro, "Policy Failure and Public Support: The Iran-Contra Affair and Public Assessment of President Reagan," *Political Behavior* 11, no. 4 (December 1989): 353–69, http://www.jstor.org/stable/586163.

4. Lawrence E. Walsh, *Final Report of the Independent Counsel for Iran/Contra Matters,* August 4, 1993, vol. 1, chap. 28, p. 1, http://www.fas.org/irp/offdocs/walsh/.

5. Ibid., vol. 1, chap. 27, p. 1.

6. "Reports of the Iran-Contra Committees: Excerpts from the Minority View," *New York Times,* November 17, 1987.

7. Frances FitzGerald, *Way Out There in the Blue: Reagan, Star Wars, and the End of the Cold War* (New York: Simon & Schuster, 2000), pp. 224, 234, 236.

8. Steven Hildreth, *Ballistic Missile Defense: Historical Overview,* January 5, 2007, Congressional Research Service, CRS Report for Congress RS22120, http://www.fas.org/sgp/crs/weapons/RS22120.pdf (updated through FY2011 budget by Center for Strategic and Budgetary Assessments); U.S. Congress, House of Representatives, Committee on Armed Services, Sub-

committee on Strategic Forces, 111th Cong., 1st sess., hearing on "The Future of Missile Defense Testing," prepared remarks of Philip E. Coyle III, February 25, 2009, p. 11, http://www.cdi.org/pdfs/CoyleHASCfull2_25_091.pdf.

9. FitzGerald, *Way Out There,* pp. 366–69.

10. Barry Bluestone and Bennett Harrison, *The Deindustrialization of America: Plant Closings, Community Abandonment, and the Dismantling of Basic Industry* (New York: Basic Books, 1982), p. 189.

CHAPTER 11: SOFT LANDING

1. Robert Ajemian, "Where Is the Real George Bush?" *Time,* January 26, 1987.

2. James Addison Baker and Thomas M. DeFrank, *The Politics of Diplomacy: Revolution, War, and Peace, 1989–1992* (New York: Putnam, 1995), pp. 234, 235.

3. Ibid., pp. 230–59.

4. George H. W. Bush, Statement on the Chinese Government's Suppression of Student Demonstrations, June 3, 1989, http://www.presidency.ucsb.edu/ws/index.php?pid=17101#axzz1Q84NnO7G.

5. James Mann, *About Face: A History of America's Curious Relationship with China, from Nixon to Clinton* (New York: Vintage, 2000), p. 193.

6. Ibid., pp. 221, 223.

7. U.S. Department of Commerce, Census Bureau, *Foreign Trade Statistics,* http://www.census.gov/foreign-trade/balance/c5700.html#1989.

8. Herbert S. Parmet, *George Bush: The Life of a Lone Star Yankee* (New Brunswick, N.J.: Transaction, 2001), p. 204.

9. Marlin Fitzwater, statement, December 20, 1989, in *Public Papers of the Presidents of the United States: George H. W. Bush, 1989* (Washington, D.C.: GPO, 1990).

10. Cynthia Arnson, *Crossroads: Congress, the President, and Central America, 1976–1993* (University Park: Pennsylvania State University Press, 1993), p. 33; Jim McGee and Bob Woodward, "Noriega Arms Indictment Stalled in '80," *Washington Post,* March 20, 1988; Eytan Gilboa, "The Panama Invasion Revisited: Lessons for the Use of Force in the Post Cold War Era," *Political Science Quarterly* 110, no. 4 (1995): 541.

11. Bob Woodward, *The Commanders* (New York: Simon & Schuster, 1991), pp. 92–93.

12. William A. Owens and Edward Offley, *Lifting the Fog of War* (New York: Farrar, Straus & Giroux, 2000), pp. 32–34; Michael Klare, *Rogue States and Nuclear Outlaws: America's Search for a New Foreign Policy* (New York: Hill & Wang, 1995), pp. 12–14, 28–32.

13. George H. W. Bush, Remarks at the Aspen Institute Symposium in Aspen, Col., August 2, 1990, http:www.presidency.ucsb.edu/ws/index.php?pid=18731#ixzz1aBnsgfTN

14. U.S. Department of Energy, Energy Information Administration, "World Proved Crude Oil Reserves, January 1, 1980–January 1, 2009," www.eia.doe.gov/pub/international/iealf/crudeoilreserves.xls.

15. George H. W. Bush, Remarks at a Fundraising Breakfast for Representative Stan Parris, Alexandria, Va., October 31, 1990, http://bushlibrary.tamu.edu/research/public_papers.php?id=2376&year=1990&month=10.

16. Mark T. Clark, "The Trouble with Collective Security," *ORBIS: A Journal of World Affairs* 39, no. 2 (Spring 1995): 237–58.

17. U.S. General Accounting Office, *Operation Desert Storm: Evaluation of the Air War,* July 1996, GAO/PEMD-96–10, pp. 4, 17, http://www.gao.gov/archive/1996/pe96010.pdf; Barton Gellman, "Allied Air War Struck Broadly in Iraq: Officials Acknowledge Strategy Went Beyond Purely Military Targets," *Washington Post,* June 23 1991.

18. Klare, *Rogue States,* pp. 120–23; R. Jeffrey Smith, "U.S. Urged to Cut 50% of A-Arms; Soviet Breakup Is Said to Allow Radical Shift in Strategic Targeting," *Washington Post*, January 6, 1992.

19. Patrick E. Tyler, "U.S. Strategy Calls for Insuring No Rivals Develop in a One-Superpower World," *New York Times,* March 8, 1992.

20. Patrick E. Tyler, "Senior U.S. Officials Assail Lone Superpower Policy," *New York Times,* March 11, 1992; Barton Gellman, "Keeping the U.S. First: Pentagon Would Preclude a Rival Superpower," *Washington Post,* March 11, 1992.

21. Tyler, "U.S. Strategy."

CHAPTER 12: BRIDGE TO NOWHERE

1. David Halberstam, *War in a Time of Peace: Bush, Clinton, and the Generals* (New York: Touchstone, 2002), p. 117.

2. Bill Clinton to Colonel Eugene Holmes, December 3, 1969, http://www.pbs.org/wgbh/pages/frontline/shows/clinton/etc/draftletter.html.

3. U.S. Department of Defense, *Report on the Bottom-Up Review,* section III, "Forces to Implement the Defense Strategy," Secretary of Defense Les Aspin, October 1993, p. 3, http://www.fas.org/man/docs/bur/index.html; Andrew F. Krepinevich, Jr., "Assessing the Bottom-Up Review," *Joint Forces Quarterly* (Winter 1993–94): 24.

4. Bill Clinton, "A New Covenant for American Security," Remarks to Students at Georgetown University, December 12, 1991, http://www.dlc.org/ndol_ci.cfm?kaid=128&subid=174&contentid=250537.

5. Department of Defense, *Report on the Bottom-Up Review,* section II, "A Defense Strategy for the New Era," http://www.fas.org/man/docs/bur/part02.htm.

6. Michael Klare, *Rogue States and Nuclear Outlaws: America's Search for a New Foreign Policy* (New York: Hill & Wang, 1995), pp. 109–10.

7. Eric V. Larson, David T. Orletsky, and Kristin J. Leuschner, *Defense Planning in a Decade of Change: Lessons from the Base Force, Bottom-Up Review, and Quadrennial Defense Review,* RAND Corporation Monograph MR-1387-AF (RAND, 2001), p. 61.

8. Quoted in Colin L. Powell and Joseph E. Persico, *My American Journey: Colin Powell* (New York: Random House, 1995), p. 576.

9. Halberstam, *War in a Time of Peace,* p. 282.

10. Anthony Lake, "From Containment to Enlargement," remarks at Johns Hopkins University, School of Advanced International Studies, Washington, D.C., September 21, 1993, http://www.mtholyoke.edu/acad/intrel/lakedoc.html.

11. George H. W. Bush, Address on Somalia, December 4, 1992, http://millercenter.org/scripps/archive/speeches/detail/3984.

12. Halberstam, *War in a Time of Peace,* p. 34; Samantha Power, *A Problem from Hell: America and the Age of Genocide* (New York: Basic Books, 2002), p. 285.

13. Halberstam, *War in a Time of Peace,* p. 251.

14. William Safire, "Stumbling into the Oval Office," *New York Times*, January 18, 1993; Thomas L. Friedman, "The New Presidency: Clinton Backs Raid but Muses About a New Start," *New York Times,* January 14, 1993; Thomas L. Friedman, "Clinton Affirms U.S. Policy on Iraq," *New York Times,* January 15, 1993.

15. Dexter Filkins, "Where Plan A Left Ahmad Chalabi," *New York Times,* November 3, 2006; Tim Weiner, "Iraqi Offensive into Kurdish Zone Disrupts U.S. Plot to Oust Hussein," *New York Times,* July 25, 1998; James Risen, "U.S. Welcomes Kurdish Leader Who Betrayed C.I.A. in Iraq," *New York Times,* December 9, 1994.

16. Douglas Jehl, "25,000 U.S. Troops to Aid U.N. Force If It Quits Bosnia," *New York Times,* December 9, 1994.

17. Alan Cowell, "U.S. Builds Influence in Croatia," *New York Times,* August 1, 1995; Roger Cohen, "U.S. Cooling Ties to Croatia After Winking at Its Buildup," *New York Times,* October 28, 1995; Halberstam, *War in a Time of Peace,* p. 293.

18. Madeleine Albright, on *Today,* NBC, February 19, 1998. http://www.fas.org/news/iraq/1998/02/19/98021907_tpo.html.

19. Chris Hedges, "In New Balkan Tinderbox, Ethnic Albanians Rebel Against Serbs," *New York Times,* March 2, 1998; Chris Hedges, "Albanian Rebels Take to the Hills in Kosovo," *New York Times*, March 14, 1998; Chris Hedges, "A New Tactic for Kosovo Rebels: Attacks on Isolated Civilians," *New York Times,* June 24, 1998.

20. Chris Hedges, "Fog of War—Coping with the Truth About Friend and Foe; Victims Not Quite Innocent," *New York Times,* March 28, 1999.

21. Anthony Lewis, "Ends and Means," *New York Times*, April 10, 1999; Tom Carver, "Madeleine Albright: Haunted by History," BBC News, April 9, 1999, http://news.bbc.co.uk/2/hi/special_report/1999/03/99/kosovo_strikes/315053.stm; Dusko Doder and Louise Branson, *Milosevic: Portrait of a Tyrant* (New York: Free Press, 1999), p. 7.

22. Chalmers A. Johnson, *The Sorrows of Empire: Militarism, Secrecy, and the End of the Republic* (New York: Henry Holt, 2005), p. 280.

23. R. W. Apple, Jr., "Road to Approval Is Rocky, and the Gamble Is Perilous," *New York Times,* May 15, 1997; Alison Mitchell, "NATO Debate: From Big Risk to Sure Thing," *New York Times*, March 20, 1998.

24. John Addison Baker and Thomas M. DeFrank, *The Politics of Diplomacy: Revolution, War, and Peace, 1989–1992* (New York: Putnam, 1995), pp. 231–32, 257, 259.

25. Bill Clinton, Acceptance Speech to the Democratic National Convention, Chicago, August 29, 1996, http://www.4president.org/speeches/clintongore1996convention.htm; see also Bill Clinton, Second Inaugural Address, January 20, 1997, http://www.american-presidents.com/bill-clinton/1997-inaugural-address.

26. Larson, Orletsky, and Leuschner, *Defense Planning in a Decade of Change,* pp. 59–60.

27. U.S. Office of Management and Budget, *The Budget of the United States Government, Fiscal Year 2009,* Historical Tables, p. 137, http://www.gpoaccess.gov/usbudget/fy09/pdf/hist.pdf.

28. Ibid., Historical Tables, pp. 124, 125, 134, 137.

29. Ibid., Historical Tables, p. 25.

30. Bill Clinton, "A New Covenant for American Security."

31. Bill Clinton, "A New Covenant for Economic Change," Remarks to Students at Georgetown University, November 20, 1991, http://www.dlc.org/ndol_ci.cfm?contentid=250528&kaid=128&subid=174.

32. Bob Woodward, *The Agenda: Inside the Clinton White House* (New York: Simon & Schuster, 1994), pp. 80–107.

33. Ibid., pp. 81–82.

34. GDP taken from U.S. Department of Commerce, Bureau of Economic Analysis, *Gross Domestic Product, First Quarter 2010,* June 24, 2011, estimate, http://www.bea.gov/newsreleases/national/gdp/gdpnewsrelease.htm; population taken from U.S. Census Bureau, July 16, 2011, estimate, http://factfinder2.census.gov/faces/nav/jsf/pages/index.xhtml.

CHAPTER 13: COME THE DESTROYER

1. Ron Suskind, *The Price of Loyalty: George W. Bush, the White House, and the Education of Paul O'Neill* (New York: Simon & Schuster, 2004), pp. 70–86.

2. Dan Lopez, Thomas Blanton, Meredith Fuchs, and Barbara Elias, eds., "Veto Battle 30 Years Ago Set Freedom of Information Norms: Scalia, Rumsfeld, Cheney Opposed Open Government Bill," National Security Archive, Electronic Briefing Book no. 142, November 23, 2004, http://www.gwu.edu/~nsarchiv/NSAEBB/NSAEBB142/index.htm.

3. Quoted in Peter Baker and Jim VandeHei, "Clash Is Latest Chapter in Bush Effort to Widen Executive Power," *Washington Post,* December 21, 2005.

4. Bruce Fein, *Constitutional Peril: The Life and Death Struggle for Our Constitution and Democracy* (New York: Palgrave Macmillan, 2008), pp. 87–90.

5. Project for the New American Century, Statement of Principles, June 3, 1997, http://www.newamericancentury.org/statementofprinciples.htm; letter to President Clinton on Iraq, January 26, 1998, http://www.newamericancentury.org/iraqclintonletter.htm.

6. Suskind, *Price of Loyalty,* p. 124.

7. Bob Woodward, *State of Denial* (New York: Simon & Schuster, 2006), pp. 17–27.

8. Donald H. Rumsfeld, "DOD Acquisition and Logistics Excellence Week Kickoff—Bureaucracy to Battlefield," remarks at the Pentagon, September 10, 2001, http://www.defense.gov/speeches/speech.aspx?speechid=430.

9. John Ashcroft, "The Freedom of Information Act," memorandum, October 12, 2001, http://www.fas.org/sgp/foia/ashcroft.html.

10. U.S. Congress, House of Representatives, Judiciary Committee, Subcommittee on the Constitution, Civil Rights, and Civil Liberties, 110th Cong., 2nd sess., June 26, 2008, hearing, "From the Department of Justice to Guantanamo Bay: Administration Lawyers and Ad-

ministration Interrogation Rules," p. 45, http://judiciary.house.gov/hearings/printers/110th/43152.pdf.

11. Stephen Daggett, *Long-Term Trends in the Defense Budget,* Congressional Research Service, May 5, 2010, p. 7, http://www.cdi.org/files/CRSDDeficitCommission.ppt.; Winslow Wheeler, "What Does an F-22 Cost?" Military.com, March 28, 2009, http://www.military.com/opinion/0,15202,187737,00.html; U.S. Congress, Senate, Committee on Armed Services, Subcommittee on Seapower, 110th Cong., 2nd sess., *Defense Acquisitions: Cost to Deliver Zumwalt-Class Destroyers Likely to Exceed Budget,* GAO Report, GAO-08-804, July 2008, http://www.gao.gov/new.items/d08804.pdf.

12. Fein, *Constitutional Peril,* p. 7.

13. U.S. Department of Justice, Office of the Inspector General, *The September 11 Detainees: A Review of the Treatment of Aliens Held on Immigration Charges in Connection with the Investigation of the September 11 Attacks,* April 2003, http://www.usdoj.gov/oig/special/0306/full.pdf.

14. John Yoo, memo to William J. Haynes II, March 14, 2003, http://www.aclu.org/pdfs/safefree/yoo_army_torture_memo.pdf.

15. U.S. Constitution; First Amendment: freedom of speech; Fourth Amendment: freedom from unwarranted search; Fifth Amendment: due process of law; Sixth Amendment: trial by jury; Eighth Amendment: prohibition of cruel and unusual punishment.

CHAPTER 14: HOPE ABANDONED

1. Karen DeYoung and Greg Jaffe, "U.S. 'Secret War' Expands Globally As Special Operations Forces Take Larger Role," *Washington Post,* July 24, 2010.

2. Dana Priest, "U.S. Military Teams, Intelligence Deeply Involved in Aiding Yemen on Strikes," *Washington Post,* July 24, 2010.

3. Scott Shane, "Obama Steps Up Prosecution of Media Leaks," *New York Times,* June 12, 2010; John Schwartz, "In a Federal Case over 'State Secrets,' a Question of Whether Evidence Is Too Secret," *New York Times,* December 16, 2009; James Risen and Charlie Savage, "Court Ruling on Wiretap Is a Challenge for Obama," *New York Times,* April 2, 2010; Josh Gerstein, "Despite Openness Pledge, President Obama Pursues Leakers," Politico.com, March 7, 2011, http://www.politico.com/news/stories/0311/50761.html.

4. U.S. Department of Labor, Bureau of Labor Statistics, *Labor Force Statistics (CPS),* July 2011, http://www.bls.gov/webapps/legacy/cpsatab1.htm.

5. Barack Obama, "A Way Forward in Iraq," Remarks to Chicago Council on Global Affairs, November 20, 2006, http://obamaspeeches.com/094-A-Way-Forward-in-Iraq-Obama-Speech.htm.

6. Reverend Martin Luther King, Jr., "Beyond Vietnam: A Time to Break Silence," April 4, 1967, http://www.hartford-hwp.com/archives/45a/058.html.

7. Barack Obama, Statement in the Rose Garden, June 23, 2010 [emphasis added], http://www.whitehouse.gov/the-press-office/statement-president-rose-garden.

8. Helene Cooper and Steven Lee Myers, "Shift by Clinton Helped Persuade President to Take a Harder Line," *New York Times,* March 19, 2011.

9. Executive Order, "Periodic Review of Individuals Detained at Guantánamo Bay Naval Sta-

tion Pursuant to the Authorization for Use of Military Force," March 7, 2011, http://www.whitehouse.gov/sites/default/files/Executive_Order_on_Periodic_Review.pdf.

10. Joseph E. Stiglitz, *Freefall: America, Free Markets, and the Sinking of the World Economy* (New York: W. W. Norton, 2010), p. 12; Paul R. Krugman, *The Return of Depression Economics* (New York: W. W. Norton, 1999), p. 65.

CHAPTER 15: BEYOND THE EMERGENCY STATE

1. U.S. Department of State, Briefing on the Nonproliferation Treaty Review Conference, April 30, 2010, Ellen Tauscher, Susan E. Rice, and Susan F. Burk, http://www.state.gov/t/us/141271.htm.

2. Nicholas Stern, "Climate: What You Need to Know," *New York Review of Books,* June 24, 2010.

3. Poverty estimates from World Bank, *World Development Report 2008, Agriculture for Development* (Washington, D.C.: World Bank, 2007), http://siteresources.worldbank.org/INTWDR2008/Resources/WDR_00_book.pdf, and from United Nations, *The Millennium Development Goals Report 2010* (New York: United Nations, 2010), http://unstats.un.org/unsd/mdg/Default.aspx.

4. Franklin D. Roosevelt, "The Four Freedoms," Annual Address to Congress, January 6, 1941, http://docs.fdrlibrary.marist.edu/od4frees.html; Martin Luther King, Jr., "I Have a Dream" Speech, August 28, 1963, http://www.usconstitution.net/dream.html; Lyndon B. Johnson, "Great Society" Speech, Remarks at the University of Michigan, May 22, 1964, http://www.lbjlib.utexas.edu/johnson/archives.hom/speeches.hom/640522.asp.

CONCLUSION

1. Barring all members with any military contracting in their district would be impractical, especially in the Senate, since virtually no state is, or should be, completely without military contractors or subcontractors. National party platforms for congressional elections are unusual in America, but the Republicans' 1994 "Contract with America" demonstrated the political effectiveness of this approach.

2. Donald S. Inbody, "Grand Army of the Republic or Grand Army of the Republicans? Political Party and Ideological Preferences of American Enlisted Personnel," Ph.D. diss., Texas State University, August 1, 2009, http://ecommons.txstate.edu/polsfacp/51/.

3. Those who did volunteer could be temporarily deployed on presidential authority to meet emergencies, but they too would not face extended combat tours without a congressional declaration of war.

4. Massimo Calabresi, "Pelosi Faces Off with Obama on CIA Oversight," *Time,* June 25, 2010.

BIBLIOGRAPHY

BOOKS

Ambrose, Stephen E., and Douglas Brinkley. *Rise to Globalism: American Foreign Policy Since 1938*. New York: Penguin, 1997.

Arnson, Cynthia. *Crossroads: Congress, the President, and Central America, 1976–1993*. University Park: Pennsylvania State University Press, 1993.

Bacevich, Andrew J., ed. *The Long War: A New History of U.S. National Security Policy Since World War II*. New York: Columbia University Press, 2007.

Bacevich, Andrew. *The New American Militarism: How Americans Are Seduced by War.* New York: Oxford University Press, 2005.

Baker, James Addison, and Thomas M. DeFrank. *The Politics of Diplomacy: Revolution, War, and Peace, 1989–1992*. New York: Putnam, 1995.

Bernstein, Barton J., ed. *Politics and Policies of the Truman Administration*. Chicago: Quadrangle, 1970.

Beschloss, Michael R. *The Crisis Years: Kennedy and Khrushchev, 1960–1963*. New York: HarperCollins, 1991.

———. *Taking Charge: The Johnson White House Tapes, 1963–1964*. New York: Simon & Schuster, 1997.

Biddle, Francis. *In Brief Authority.* Garden City, N.Y.: Doubleday, 1962.

Bluestone, Barry, and Bennett Harrison. *The Deindustrialization of America: Plant Closings, Community Abandonment, and the Dismantling of Basic Industry*. New York: Basic Books, 1982.

Brinkley, Alan. *The End of Reform: New Deal Liberalism in Recession and War*. New York: Alfred A. Knopf, 1995.

Bush, George W. *We Will Prevail: President George W. Bush on War, Terrorism, and Freedom*. New York: Continuum, 2003.

Carter, Jimmy. *Our Endangered Values: America's Moral Crisis*. New York: Simon & Schuster, 2005.

Clifford, Clark. *Counsel to the President: A Memoir*. New York: Random House, 1991.

Coll, Steve. *Ghost Wars: The Secret History of the CIA, Afghanistan, and bin Laden, from the Soviet Invasion to September 10, 2001*. New York: Penguin, 2004.

Daalder, Ivo H., and I. M. Destler. *In the Shadow of the Oval Office: Profiles of the National Security Advisers and the Presidents They Served: From JFK to George W. Bush*. New York: Simon & Schuster, 2009.

Daalder, Ivo, and James M. Lindsay. *America Unbound: The Bush Revolution in Foreign Policy.* Rev. ed. New York: John Wiley & Sons, 2005.

Dobrynin, Anatoly. *In Confidence: Moscow's Ambassador to America's Six Cold War Presidents, 1962–1986*. New York: Random House, 1995.

Doder, Dusko, and Louise Branson. *Milosevic: Portrait of a Tyrant*. New York: Free Press, 1999.

Elliott, David W. P. *The Vietnamese War: Revolution and Social Change in the Mekong Delta, 1930–1975*. Armonk, N.Y.: M. E. Sharpe, 2006.

Fein, Bruce E. *Constitutional Peril: The Life and Death Struggle for Our Constitution and Democracy*. New York: Palgrave Macmillan, 2009.

Firestone, Bernard J., and Alexej Ugrinsky. *Gerald R. Ford and the Politics of Post-Watergate America*. Westport, Conn.: Greenwood Press, 1993.

FitzGerald, Frances. *Way Out There in the Blue: Reagan, Star Wars, and the End of the Cold War*. New York: Simon & Schuster, 2000.

Fordham, Benjamin O. "Paying for Global Power: Costs and Benefits of Postwar U.S. Military Spending." In Andrew J. Bacevich, ed., *The Long War: A New History of U.S. National Security Policy Since World War II*. New York: Columbia University Press, 2007.

Gaddis, John Lewis. *Strategies of Containment: A Critical Appraisal of American National Security Policy During the Cold War*. New York: Oxford University Press, 2005.

Gardner, Lloyd C. *Architects of Illusion: Men and Ideas in American Foreign Policy, 1941–1949*. Chicago: Quadrangle, 1970.

Ginsborg, Paul. *Democracy: Crisis and Renewal*. London: Profile Books, 2008.

Goodwin, Doris Kearns. *Lyndon Johnson and the American Dream*. New York: St. Martin's Press, 1991.

Halberstam, David. *War in a Time of Peace: Bush, Clinton, and the Generals*. New York: Touchstone, 2002.

Halperin, Morton H., et al. *The Lawless State: The Crimes of the U.S. Intelligence Agencies*. New York: Penguin, 1976.

Harper, John Lamberton. *American Visions of Europe: Franklin D. Roosevelt, George F. Kennan, and Dean G. Acheson*. New York: Cambridge University Press, 1996.

Hoffman, David E. *The Dead Hand: The Untold Story of the Cold War Arms Race and Its Dangerous Legacy*. New York: Anchor, 2009.

Inbody, Donald S. "Grand Army of the Republic or Grand Army of the Republicans? Political Party and Ideological Preferences of American Enlisted Personnel." Ph.D. diss., Texas State University, August 1, 2009. http://ecommons.txstate.edu/polsfacp/51/.

Johnson, Chalmers A. *The Sorrows of Empire: Militarism, Secrecy, and the End of the Republic*. New York: Henry Holt, 2005.

———. *Nemesis: The Last Days of the American Republic*. New York: Henry Holt, 2006.

Johnson, Loch K. *The Oxford Handbook of National Security Intelligence*. New York: Oxford University Press, 2010.

Johnson, Robert David. *The Peace Progressives and American Foreign Relations*. Cambridge, Mass.: Harvard Historical Studies, 1995.

Kaiser, David E. *American Tragedy: Kennedy, Johnson, and the Origins of the Vietnam War*. Cambridge, Mass.: Belknap Press of Harvard University Press, 2000.

———. *The Road to Dallas: The Assassination of John F. Kennedy*. Cambridge, Mass.: Belknap Press of Harvard University Press, 2008.

Katzenbach, Nicholas de B. "The Constitution and Foreign Policy." In Burke Marshall, ed., *A Workable Government?: The Constitution After 200 Years*. New York: W. W. Norton, 1987.

Kissinger, Henry, and William Burr. *The Kissinger Transcripts: The Top-Secret Talks with Beijing and Moscow*. New York: New Press, 1999.

Klare, Michael. *Rogue States and Nuclear Outlaws: America's Search for a New Foreign Policy.* New York: Hill & Wang, 1995.

Krugman, Paul R. *The Return of Depression Economics*. New York: W. W. Norton, 1999.

Lake, Anthony. *Somoza Falling: The Nicaraguan Dilemma; A Portrait of Washington at Work.* Boston: Houghton Mifflin, 1989.

Larres, Klaus. *Churchill's Cold War: The Politics of Personal Diplomacy*. New Haven, Conn.: Yale University Press, 2002.

Larson, Eric V., David T. Orletsky, and Kristin J. Leuschner. *Defense Planning in a Decade of Change: Lessons from the Base Force, Bottom-Up Review, and Quadrennial Defense Review*. RAND Corporation Monograph MR-1387-AF. RAND, 2001.

Leffler, Melvyn P. *For the Soul of Mankind: The United States, the Soviet Union, and the Cold War*. New York: Hill & Wang, 2007.

Lernoux, Penny. *Cry of the People: The Struggle for Human Rights in Latin America—The Catholic Church in Conflict with U.S. Policy.* New York: Penguin, 1983.

McLellan, David S. *Dean Acheson: The State Department Years*. New York: Dodd, Mead, 1976.

McNamara, Robert S., and Brian VanDeMark. *In Retrospect: The Tragedy and Lessons of Vietnam*. New York: Times Books, 1995.

Madrick, Jeffrey. *The End of Affluence: The Causes and Consequences of America's Economic Dilemma*. New York: Random House, 1997.

Mann, James. *About Face: A History of America's Curious Relationship with China, from Nixon to Clinton*. New York: Vintage, 2000.

Manning, R., ed. *War in the Shadows: The Vietnam Experience*. New York: Time-Life Education, 1988.

Marshall, Burke. *A Workable Government?: The Constitution After 200 Years*. New York: W. W. Norton, 1987.

Marshall, Will. *With All Our Might: A Progressive Strategy for Defeating Jihadism and Defending Liberty.* Lanham, Md.: Rowman & Littlefield, 2006.

May, Ernest R., and Philip D. Zelikow, eds. *The Kennedy Tapes: Inside the White House During the Cuban Missile Crisis*. Cambridge, Mass.: Belknap Press of Harvard University Press, 1997.

Mee, Charles L. *Meeting at Potsdam*. New York: M. Evans, 1975.

O'Neill, Tip. *Man of the House*. New York: Random House, 1987.

O'Neill, William L. *A Democracy at War.* New York: Free Press, 1993.

Owens, William A., and Edward Offley. *Lifting the Fog of War*. New York: Farrar, Straus & Giroux, 2000.

Pahlavi, Farah. *An Enduring Love: My Life with the Shah*. New York: Miramax, 2004.

Parmet, Herbert S. *George Bush: The Life of a Lone Star Yankee*. New Brunswick, N.J.: Transaction, 2001.

Plokhy, Serhii. *Yalta: The Price of Peace*. New York: Viking, 2010.

Polenberg, Richard. *War and Society: The United States 1941–1945*. Westport, Conn.: Greenwood Press, 1980.

Powell, Colin L., and Joseph E. Persico. *My American Journey: Colin Powell*. New York: Random House, 1995.

Power, Samantha. *A Problem from Hell: America and the Age of Genocide*. New York: Basic Books, 2002.

Prestowitz, Clyde V. *Rogue Nation: American Unilateralism and the Failure of Good Intentions*. New York: Basic Books, 2003.

Skoblic, Peter. *U.S. Versus Them: How a Half-Century of Conservatism Has Undermined American Security.* New York: Viking, 2008.

Sorensen, Theodore C. *Counselor: A Life at the Edge of History*. New York: Harper, 2008.

Soros, George. *The Bubble of American Supremacy: The Costs of Bush's War in Iraq*. New York: PublicAffairs, 2004.

Steel, Ronald. *Walter Lippmann and the American Century*. Boston: Little, Brown, 1980.

Stiglitz, Joseph E. *Freefall: America, Free Markets, and the Sinking of the World Economy*. New York: W. W. Norton, 2010.

Stimson, Henry L. *On Active Service in Peace and War.* New York: Harper & Bros., 1948.

Stuart, Douglas T. *Creating the National Security State: A History of the Law That Transformed America*. Princeton, N.J.: Princeton University Press, 2008.

Suskind, Ron. *The Price of Loyalty: George W. Bush, the White House, and the Education of Paul O'Neill*. New York: Simon & Schuster, 2004.

Towle, Michael J. *Out of Touch: The Presidency and Public Opinion*. College Station: Texas A&M University Press, 2004.

Tucker, Robert W., and David C. Hendrickson. *The Imperial Temptation: The New World Order and America's Purpose*. New York: Council on Foreign Relations, 1992.

Weiner, Tim. *Legacy of Ashes: The History of the CIA*. New York: Anchor, 2008.

Wise, David. *The American Police State: The Government Against the People*. New York: Random House, 1976.

Wise, David, and Thomas B. Ross. *The Invisible Government*. New York: Random House, 1964.

Woodward, Bob. *The Commanders*. New York: Simon & Schuster, 1991.

———. *The Agenda: Inside the Clinton White House*. New York: Simon & Schuster, 1994.

———. *State of Denial*. New York: Simon & Schuster, 2006.

Yergin, Daniel. *The Prize: The Epic Quest for Oil, Money, and Power*. New York: Simon & Schuster, 1991.

PERIODICALS AND WEB SITES

Ajemian, Robert. "Where Is the Real George Bush?" *Time*, January 26, 1987.

American Presidency Project. John Woolley and Gerhard Peters, "Presidential Job Approval, F. Roosevelt (1941) to Obama." http://www.presidency.ucsb.edu/data/popularity.php.

Apple, R. W., Jr. "Road to Approval Is Rocky, and the Gamble Is Perilous." *New York Times*, May 15, 1997.

Baker, Peter, and Jim VandeHei. "Clash Is Latest Chapter in Bush Effort to Widen Executive Power." *Washington Post*, December 21, 2005.

Baum, Dan. "Madison on the Dangers of War." *Harper's Magazine*, July 7, 2007. http://harpers.org/archive/2007/07/hbc-90000432.

Blanton, Thomas S., ed. "The Pentagon Papers: Secrets, Lies, and Audiotapes." National Security Archive, Electronic Briefing Book no. 48, June 5, 2001. http://www.gwu.edu/~nsarchiv/NSAEBB/NSAEBB48/nixon.html.

———, ed. "The CIA's Family Jewels: Agency Violated Charter for 25 Years, Wiretapped Journalists and Dissidents." National Security Archive, Electronic Briefing Book no. 222, June 21, 2007. http://www.gwu.edu/~nsarchiv/NSAEBB/NSAEBB222/index.htm.

Brody, Richard A., and Catherine R. Shapiro. "Policy Failure and Public Support: The Iran-Contra Affair and Public Assessment of President Reagan." *Political Behavior* 11, no. 4 (December 1989): 353–69. http://www.jstor.org/stable/586163.

Brzezinski, Zbigniew. "The CIA's Intervention in Afghanistan: Interview with Zbigniew Brzezinski." Translated by Bill Blum. *Le Nouvel Observateur,* January 15–21, 1998.

"The Burden of Saving the World Economy." *Global Times,* June 23, 2010. http://opinion.globaltimes.cn/editorial/2010-06/544381.html.

Calabresi, Massimo. "Pelosi Faces Off with Obama on CIA Oversight." *Time*, June 25, 2010.

Carver, Tom. "Madeleine Albright: Haunted by History." BBC News, April 9, 1999. http://news.bbc.co.uk/2/hi/special_report/1999/03/99/kosovo_strikes/315053.stm.

Clark, Mark T. "The Trouble with Collective Security." *ORBIS: A Journal of World Affairs* 39, no. 2 (Spring 1995): 237–58.

Cohen, Roger. "U.S. Cooling Ties to Croatia After Winking at Its Buildup." *New York Times*, October 28, 1995.

Cooper, Helene, and Steven Lee Myers. "Shift by Clinton Helped Persuade President to Take a Harder Line." *New York Times,* March 19, 2011.

Cowell, Alan. "U.S. Builds Influence in Croatia." *New York Times*, August 1, 1995.

Crewdson, John M. "FBI Lists 1,200 as Security Risks." *New York Times*, October 23, 1975.

Daugherty, William J. "Jimmy Carter and the 1979 Decision to Admit the Shah into the United States." AmericanDiplomacy.org, March 16, 2003. http://www.unc.edu/depts/diplomat/archives_roll/2003_01-03/dauherty_shah/dauherty_shah.html.

DeYoung, Karen, and Greg Jaffe. "U.S. 'Secret War' Expands Globally as Special Operations Forces Take Larger Role." *Washington Post,* July 24, 2010.

Filkins, Dexter. "Where Plan A Left Ahmad Chalabi." *New York Times*, November 3, 2006.

Friedman, Thomas L. "The New Presidency: Clinton Backs Raid but Muses About a New Start." *New York Times*, January 14, 1993.

———. "Clinton Affirms U.S. Policy on Iraq." *New York Times*, January 15, 1993.

Gellman, Barton. "Allied Air War Struck Broadly in Iraq: Officials Acknowledge Strategy Went Beyond Purely Military Targets." *Washington Post*, June 23, 1991.

———. "Keeping the U.S. First: Pentagon Would Preclude a Rival Superpower." *Washington Post,* March 11, 1992.

Gerstein, Josh. "Despite Openness Pledge, President Obama Pursues Leakers." Politico.com, March 7, 2011. http://www.politico.com/news/stories/0311/50761.html.

Gilboa, Eytan. "The Panama Invasion Revisited: Lessons for the Use of Force in the Post Cold War Era." *Political Science Quarterly* 110, no. 4 (1995): 539–62.

Haines, Gerald K. "The Pike Committee Investigation and the CIA: Looking for a Rogue Elephant." *Studies in Intelligence,* Winter 1998–99. https://www.cia.gov/library/

center-for-the-study-of-intelligence/csi-publications/csi-studies/studies/winter98_99/art07.html.

Hedges, Chris. "In New Balkan Tinderbox, Ethnic Albanians Rebel Against Serbs." *New York Times*, March 2, 1998.

———. "Albanian Rebels Take to the Hills in Kosovo." *New York Times*, March 14, 1998.

———. "A New Tactic for Kosovo Rebels: Attacks on Isolated Civilians." *New York Times*, June 24, 1998.

———. "Fog of War—Coping with the Truth About Friend and Foe; Victims Not Quite Innocent." *New York Times*, March 28, 1999.

Jehl, Douglas. "25,000 U.S. Troops to Aid U.N. Force If It Quits Bosnia." *New York Times*, December 9, 1994.

Kitts, Kenneth. "Commission Politics and National Security: Gerald Ford's Response to the CIA Controversy of 1975." *Presidential Studies Quarterly* 26, no. 4 (Fall 1996): 1081–98.

Kramer, Mark. "The Early Post-Stalin Succession Struggle and Upheavals in East-Central Europe: Internal-External Linkages in Soviet Policy-Making (Part 1)." *Journal of Cold War Studies* 1, no. 1 (Winter 1999): 3–56.

Krepinevich, Andrew F., Jr. "Assessing the Bottom-Up Review." *Joint Forces Quarterly* (Winter 1993–94): 23–24.

Lavoy, Peter R. "The Enduring Effects of Atoms for Peace." *Arms Control Today,* December 2003. http://www.armscontrol.org/act/2003_12/Lavoy.

Lewis, Anthony. "Ends and Means." *New York Times*, April 10, 1999.

Lopez, Dan, Thomas Blanton, Meredith Fuchs, and Barbara Elias, eds. "Veto Battle 30 Years Ago Set Freedom of Information Norms: Scalia, Rumsfeld, Cheney Opposed Open Government Bill." National Security Archive, Electronic Briefing Book no. 142, November 23, 2004. http://www.gwu.edu/~nsarchiv/NSAEBB/NSAEBB142/index.htm.

McGee, Jim, and Bob Woodward. "Noriega Arms Indictment Stalled in '80." *Washington Post*, March 20, 1988.

Mitchell, Alison. "NATO Debate: From Big Risk to Sure Thing." *New York Times*, March 20, 1998.

Moyers, Bill. "LBJ and the FBI." *Newsweek,* March 10, 1975, p. 84.

"National Affairs: Anniversary Remembrance." *Time*, July 2, 1951. http://www.time.com/time/magazine/article/0,9171,815031,00.html.

Natural Resources Defense Council. Archive of Nuclear Data. http://www.nrdc.org/nuclear/nudb/datainx.asp.

Newport, Frank, Jeffrey M. Jones, and Lydia Saad. "Ronald Reagan from the People's Perspective: A Gallup Poll Review." Gallup.com, June 7, 2004. http://www.gallup.com/poll/11887/Ronald-Reagan-From-Peoples-Perspective-Gallup-Poll-Review.aspx.

Nixon, Richard M. "Asia After Viet Nam." *Foreign Affairs* 46, no. 1 (October 1967): 121–25.

"The Pentagon Meets the Real World." Editorial. *New York Times*, March 1, 2009.

Priest, Dana. "U.S. Military Teams, Intelligence Deeply Involved in Aiding Yemen on Strikes." *Washington Post,* July 24, 2010.

Project for the New American Century. Statement of Principles, June 3, 1997. http://www.newamericancentury.org/statementofprinciples.htm.

———. Letter to President Clinton on Iraq, January 26, 1998. http://www.newamericancentury.org/iraqclintonletter.htm.

Rafalko, Frank J. *A Counterintelligence Reader,* October 4, 2004. http://www.fas.org/irp/ops/ci/docs/index.html.

"Reports of the Iran-Contra Committees: Excerpts from the Minority View." *New York Times,* November 17, 1987.

Risen, James. "U.S. Welcomes Kurdish Leader Who Betrayed C.I.A. in Iraq." *New York Times*, December 9, 1994.

Risen, James, and Charlie Savage. "Court Ruling on Wiretap Is a Challenge for Obama." *New York Times*, April 2, 2010.

Safire, William. "Stumbling into the oval Office." *New York Times,* January 18, 1993.

Schwartz, John. "In a Federal Case over 'State Secrets,' a Question of Whether Evidence Is Too Secret." *New York Times*, December 16, 2009.

Shane, Scott. "Obama Steps Up Prosecution of Media Leaks." *New York Times,* June 12, 2010.

Shepley, James. "How Dulles Averted War." *Life,* January 16, 1956, pp. 70–80.

Sick, Gary. "Iran: A View from the White House." *World Affairs* 149, no. 4 (1987): 209–13.

Smith, R. Jeffrey. "U.S. Urged to Cut 50% of A-Arms; Soviet Breakup Is Said to Allow Radical Shift in Strategic Targeting." *Washington Post*, January 6, 1992.

Stern, Nicholas. "Climate: What You Need to Know." *New York Review of Books*, July 24, 2010.

Tyler, Patrick E. "U.S. Strategy Calls for Insuring No Rivals Develop in a One-Superpower World." *New York Times*, March 8, 1992.

———. "Senior U.S. Officials Assail Lone Superpower Policy." *New York Times,* March 11, 1992.

Weiner, Tim. "Iraqi Offensive into Kurdish Zone Disrupts U.S. Plot to Oust Hussein." *New York Times*, July 25, 1998.

Wheeler, Winslow. "What Does an F-22 Cost?" Military.com, March 28, 2009. http://www.military.com/opinion/0,15202,187737,00.html.

GOVERNMENT DOCUMENTS AND PUBLIC COMMUNICATIONS

Albright, Madeleine. *Today*, NBC, February 19, 1998. http://www.fas.org/news/iraq/1998/02/19/98021907_tpo.html.

Ashcroft, John. "The Freedom of Information Act." Memorandum, October 12, 2001. http://www.fas.org/sgp/foia/ashcroft.html.

Bundy, McGeorge. Memo of conversation with Ambassador Dobrynin, May 17, 1963. National Security Archive. http://www.gwu.edu/~nsarchiv/NSAEBB/NSAEBB38/.

Bush, George H. W. Statement on the Chinese Government's Suppression of Student Demonstrations, June 3, 1989. http://www.presidency.ucsb.edu/ws/index.php?pid=17101#axzz1Q84NnO7G.

———. Remarks at a Fundraising Breakfast for Representative Stan Parris, Alexandria, Va., October 31, 1990. http://bushlibrary.tamu.edu/research/public_papers.php?id=2376&year=1990&month=10.

———. Address on Somalia, December 4, 1992. http://millercenter.org/scripps/archive/speeches/detail/3984.

Carter, Jimmy. Televised Speech on Energy Policy, April 18, 1977. http://www.pbs.org/wgbh/americanexperience/features/primary-resources/carter-energy/.

———. Address at the Commencement Exercises at the University of Notre Dame, May 22, 1977. http://www.presidency.ucsb.edu/ws/index.php?pid=7552#axzz1Q84NnO7G.

———. Crisis of Confidence Speech, July 15, 1979. http://www.pbs.org/wgbh/americanexperience/features/primary-resources/carter-crisis and http://www.pbs.org/wgbh/amex/carter/peopleevents/e_malaise.html.

Clinton, Bill. Letter to Colonel Eugene Holmes, December 3, 1969. http://www.pbs.org/wgbh/pages/frontline/shows/clinton/etc/draftletter.html.

———. "A New Covenant for Economic Change." Remarks to Students at Georgetown University, November 20, 1991. http://www.dlc.org/ndol_ci.cfm?contentid=250528&kaid=128&subid=174.

———. "A New Covenant for American Security." Remarks to Students at Georgetown University, December 12, 1991. http://www.dlc.org/ndol_ci.cfm?kaid=128&subid=174&contentid=250537.

———. Acceptance Speech to the Democratic National Convention, Chicago, August 29, 1996. http://www.4president.org/speeches/clintongore1996convention.htm.

———. Second Inaugural Address, January 20, 1997. http://www.american-presidents.com/bill-clinton/1997-inaugural-address.

Daggett, Stephen. *Long-Term Trends in the Defense Budget,* May 5, 2010. Congressional Research Service, http://www.cdi.org/files/CRSDeficitCommission.ppt.

Dulles, John Foster. Speech to the Council on Foreign Relations, New York, January 12, 1954. In Department of State *Bulletin* 30 (January 25, 1954), p. 108. http://www.freerepublic.com/focus/f-news/1556858/posts.

———. Speech at Iowa State College, June 9, 1956. Department of State *Bulletin* 30, no. 886 (June 20, 1956).

Eisenhower, Dwight D. News conference, April 7, 1954. http://www.h-net.org/~hst306/documents/domino.html.

Fitzwater, Marlin. Statement, December 20, 1989. In *Public Papers of the Presidents of the United States: George H. W. Bush, 1989.* Washington, D.C.: GPO, 1990.

Ford, Gerald. Proclamation 4311, Granting a Pardon to Richard Nixon, September 8, 1974. http://watergate.info/ford/pardon-proclamation.shtml.

———. Statement on signing the Foreign Assistance Act of 1974, December 30, 1974. http://www.presidency.ucsb.edu/ws/index.php?pid=4660.

Ford, Gerald, et al. Memorandum of White House conversation with Bipartisan Congressional Leadership, February 3, 1975. http://www.history.state.gov/historicaldocuments/frus1969-76v30/d211.

Garthoff, Douglas F. *Directors of Central Intelligence as Leaders of the U.S. Intelligence Community, 1946–2005.* Washington, D.C.: Center for the Study of Intelligence, Central Intelligence Agency, 2005. https://www.cia.gov/library/center-for-the-study-of-intelligence/csi-publications/books-and-monographs/directors-of-central-intelligence-as-leaders-of-the-u-s-intelligence-community/dci_leaders.pdf.

Greenberg, Lawrence M. *The Hukbalahap Insurrection: A Case Study of a Successful Anti-Insurgency Operation in the Philippines, 1946–1955.* Historical Analysis Series. U.S. Army Center of Military History, Analysis Branch. Washington, D.C.: GPO, 1987.

Hamilton, Alexander. "The Consequences of Hostilities Between States" (November 20, 1787), *Federalist* 8. http://www.constitution.org/fed/federa08.htm.

———. "Idea of Restraining the Legislative Authority in Regard to the Common Defense Considered" (December 22, 1797), *Federalist* 26. http://www.constitution.org/fed/federa26.htm.

Hildreth, Steven. *Ballistic Missile Defense: Historical Overview,* January 5, 2007. Congressional Research Service, CRS Report for Congress RS22120. http://www.fas.org/sgp/crs/weapons/RS22120.pdf.

Jackson, James K. *U.S. Trade Deficit and the Impact of Rising Oil Prices,* November 14, 2006. Congressional Research Service, CRS Report for Congress RS2204. http://fpc.state.gov/documents/organization/77719.pdf.

Johnson, Lyndon B. "Great Society" Speech. Remarks of the University of Michigan, May 22, 1964. http://www.lbjlib.utexas.edu/johnson/archives.hom/speeches.hom/640522.asp.

———. Message to Congress, August 5, 1964. http://www.pbs.org/wgbh/amex/presidents/36_l_johnson/psources/ps_tonkin.html.

———. "Report on the Gulf of Tonkin Incident," August 4, 1964. http://millercenter.org/scripps/archive/speeches/detail/3998.

———. Speech before the American Bar Association, New York City, August 12, 1964. http://www.presidency.ucsb.edu/ws/index.php?pid=26434#axzz1SNlHvKUD.

Kennedy, John F. Inaugural Address, January 20, 1961. http://www.jfklibrary.org/Research/Ready-Reference/JFK-Miscellaneous-Information/Inaugural-Address.aspx.

———. Statement on Cuba, September 4, 1962, in Department of State *Bulletin* 47, no. 1213 (September 24, 1962). http://www.mtholyoke.edu/acad/intrel/jfkstate.htm.

———. Televised Address on the Berlin Crisis, July 25, 1961. http://www.presidentialrhetoric.com/historicspeeches/kennedy/berlincrisis.html.

King, Martin Luther, Jr. "I Have a Dream" Speech, August 28, 1963. http://www.usconstitution.net/dream.html.

———. "Beyond Vietnam: A Time to Break Silence," April 4, 1967. http://www.hartford-hwp.com/archives/45a/058.html.

Lake, Anthony. "From Containment to Enlargement." Remarks at Johns Hopkins University, School of Advanced International Studies, Washington, D.C., September 21, 1993. http://www.mtholyoke.edu/acad/intrel/lakedoc.html.

Madison, James. Letter of Helvidius no. 4 (September 14, 1793). In *The Writings of James Madison,* ed. Gaillard Hunt. New York: G. P. Putnam's Sons, 1900–1910. http://press-pubs.uchicago.edu/founders/documents/a2_2_2-3s15.html.

———. "Political Observations" (April 20, 1795). In *Letters and Other Writings of James Madison,* vol. 4, 1829–1836. Philadelphia: J. P. Lippincott, 1867. http://www.archive.org/stream/cu31924024263505#page/n557/mode/2up.

Marolda, Edward J. *Summary of Tonkin Gulf Crisis of August 1964,* July 13, 2005. U.S. Department of the Navy, Navy History and Heritage Command. http://www.history.navy.mil/faqs/faq120-1.htm.

National Commission on Terrorist Attacks upon the United States. *The 9/11 Commission Report.* Washington, D.C.: GPO, 2004. http://govinfo.library.unt.edu/911/report/index.htm.

National Security Act, 1947. Sec. 104A, "Director of the Central Intelligence Agency," clause D, "Responsibilities." http://intelligence.senate.gov/nsaact1947.pdf.

Nixon, Richard M. Remarks to the Nation Announcing Acceptance of an Invitation to Visit the People's Republic of China, July 15, 1971. http://www.presidency.ucsb.edu/?pid=3079#axzz1aCNNFWRM.

———. Interview by David Frost, May 20, 1977. http://www.guardian.co.uk/theguardian/2007/sep/07/greatinterviews1.

Obama, Barack. "A Way Forward in Iraq." Remarks to Chicago Council on Global Affairs, November 20, 2006. http://obamaspeeches.com/094-A-Way-Forward-in-Iraq-Obama-Speech.htm.

———. Executive Order, "Periodic Review of Individuals Detained at Guantánamo Bay Naval Station Pursuant to the Authorization for Use of Military Force," March 7, 2011. http://www.whitehouse.gov/sites/default/files/Executive_Order_on_Periodic_Review.pdf.

———. Statement in the Rose Garden, June 23, 2010. http://www.whitehouse.gov/the-press-office/statement-president-rose-garden.

The Pentagon Papers: The Defense Department History of United States Decisionmaking on Vietnam. "Senator Gravel Edition." 5 vols. Boston: Beacon Press, 1971.

Roosevelt, Franklin D. "The Four Freedoms." Annual Address to Congress, January 6, 1941. http://docs.fdrlibrary.marist.edu/od4frees.html.

Rumsfeld, Donald H. "DOD Acquisition and Logistics Excellence Week Kickoff—Bureaucracy to Battlefield." Remarks at the Pentagon, September 10, 2001. http://www.defense.gov/speeches/speech.aspx?speechid=430.

Sutyagin, Igor. *The Role of Nuclear Weapons and Its Possible Future Missions*. NATO Research Fellowship Report, 1996. http://www.nato.int/acad/fellow/94-96/sutyagin/index.htm.

Taft, Robert A. Speech on the North Atlantic Treaty, July 26, 1949. http://teachingamericanhistory.org/library/index.asp?document=857.

United Nations. *The Millennium Development Goals Report 2010*. New York: United Nations, 2010. http://unstats.un.org/unsd/mdg/Default.aspx.

United Nations, Statistical Office. *International Trade Statistics, 1900–1960*. May 1962. http://unstats.un.org/unsd/trade/imts/Historical%20data%201900-1960.pdf.

U.S. Congress. Gulf of Tonkin Resolution, Joint Resolution of Congress, H.J. Res. 1145, August 7, 1964.

U.S. Congress. House of Representatives. 78th Cong., 1st sess. Naval Affairs Subcommittee to Investigate Congested Areas. Hearing. Testimony of John L. Dewitt, April 13, 1943.

———. House of Representatives. 110th Cong., 2nd sess. Judiciary Committee. Subcommittee on the Constitution, Civil Rights, and Civil Liberties. Hearing on "From the Department of Justice to Guantanamo Bay: Administration Lawyers and Administration Interrogation Rules," June 26, 2008. http://judiciary.house.gov/hearings/printers/110th/43152.pdf.

———. House of Representatives. 111th Cong., 1st sess. Committee on Armed Services, Subcommittee on Strategic Forces. Hearing on "The Future of Missile Defense Testing." Philip E. Coyle III, prepared remarks, February 25, 2009. http://www.cdi.org/pdfs/CoyleHASCfull2_25_091.pdf.

U.S. Congress. Senate. 80th Cong., 1st sess. Committee on Foreign Relations. Executive

Session Hearings on S. 938, "A Bill to Provide Foreign Assistance to Greece and Turkey," March 13, 28, April 1, 2, 3, 7, 1947. http://www.archive.org/stream/legislativeorigi00unit/legislativeorigi00unit_djvu.txt/.

U.S. Congress. Senate. 94th Cong., 1st sess. Select Committee to Study Governmental Operations with Respect to Intelligence Activities. Interim Report on Alleged Assassination Plots Involving Foreign Leaders. Also known as part of the *Church Committee Reports*. Available from Assassination Archives and Research Center, http://www.aarclibrary.org.

———. Senate. 94th Cong., 2nd sess. Select Committee to Study Governmental Operations with Respect to Intelligence Activities. *Final Report—Book II, Intelligence Activities and the Rights of Americans*. 1976. Also known as the *Church Committee Reports*. CD-ROM available from Assassination Archives and Research Center, http://www.aarclibrary.org.

———. Senate. 110th Cong., 2nd sess. Committee on Armed Services. Subcommittee on Seapower. *Defense Acquisitions: Cost to Deliver Zumwalt-Class Destroyers Likely to Exceed Budget*. GAO Report, GAO-08-804, July 2008. http://www.gao.gov/new.items/d08804.pdf.

U.S. Constitution. 1787.

U.S. Department of Commerce. Bureau of Economic Analysis. *Gross Domestic Product, First Quarter 2010*. June 24, 2011, estimate. http://www.bea.gov/newsreleases/national/gdp/gdpnewsrelease.htm.

———. Census Bureau. American FactFinder, U.S. Population Clock, July 17, 2011. http://factfinder2.census.gov/faces/nav/jsf/pages/index.xhtml.

———. Census Bureau. *Demographic Trends in the 20th Century*. Census 2000 Special Reports, November 2002. http://www.census.gov/prod/2002pubs/censr-4.pdf.

———. Census Bureau. *Foreign Trade Statistics*. http://www.census.gov/foreign-trade/.

U.S. Department of Defense. Defense Manpower Data Center, Statistical Information Analysis Center. *Selected Manpower Statistics for FY 2005*. http://siadapp.dmdc.osd.mil/personnel/M01/fy05/m01fy05.pdf.

———. Directorate for Information and Operations Reports. *Selected Manpower Statistics, Fiscal Year 2003*. http://siadapp.dmdc.osd.mil/personnel/M01/fy03/m01fy03.pdf.

———. Office of the Under Secretary of Defense (Comptroller). *National Defense Budget Estimates for FY2004*. March 2003. http://comptroller.defense.gov/defbudget/fy2004/fy2004_greenbook.pdf.

———. Office of the Under Secretary of Defense (Comptroller). *National Defense Budget Estimates for FY2009*. March 2008. http://comptroller.defense.gov/defbudget/fy2009/fy2009_greenbook.pdf.

———. Office of the Under Secretary of Defense (Comptroller). *National Defense Budget Estimates for FY2012*. March 2011. http://comptroller.defense.gov/defbudget/fy2012_Green_Book.pdf.

———. *Report of the Office of Secretary of Defense Vietnam Task Force*. Also known as the Pentagon Papers. Washington, D.C.: GPO, 1971. http://www.archives.gov/research/pentagon-papers/.

———. *Report on the Bottom-Up Review*. http://www.fas.org/man/docs/bur/index.html.

U.S. Department of Energy. Energy Information Administration. "World Proved Crude Oil Reserves, January 1, 1980–January 1, 2009." http://www.eia.doe.gov/pub/international/iealf/crudeoilreserves.xls.

U.S. Department of Justice. Office of the Inspector General. *The September 11 Detainees: A Review of the Treatment of Aliens Held on Immigration Charges in Connection with the Investigation of the September 11 Attacks.* April 2003. http://www.usdoj.gov/oig/special/0306/full.pdf.

U.S. Department of Labor. Bureau of Labor Statistics. *Labor Force Statistics (CPS).* http://www.bls.gov/webapps/legacy/cpsatab1.htm.

U.S. Department of State. Briefing on the Nonproliferation Treaty Review Conference, April 30, 2010. Ellen Tauscher, Susan E. Rice, and Susan F. Burk. http://www.state.gov/t/us/141271.htm.

U.S. General Accounting Office. *Operation Desert Storm: Evaluation of the Air War,* July 1996. GAO/PEMD-96-10. http://www.gao.gov/archive/1996/pe96010.pdf.

U.S. National Security Council. "United States Objectives and Programs for National Security," April 14, 1950, NSC-68. Sec. IV(A), "Nature of Conflict." http://www.fas.org/irp/offdocs/nsc-hst/nsc-68.htm.

U.S. Office of Management and Budget. *The Budget of the United States Government, Fiscal Year 2009.* Historical Tables. http://www.gpoaccess.gov/usbudget/fy09/pdf/hist.pdf.

———. *The Budget of the United States Government, Fiscal Year 2010.* Table 3-1, "Outlays by Superfunction and Function: 1940–2014." http://www.gpoaccess.gov/usbudget/fy10/hist.html.

———. *Mid-Session Review, The Budget of the United States Government, Fiscal Year 2004,* July 15, 2003. http://www.gpoaccess.gov/usbudget/fy09/pdf/09msr.pdf.

U.S. Supreme Court. *United States v. Nixon,* 418 U.S. 683 (1974). http://caselaw.lp.findlaw.com/scripts/getcase.pl?court=us&vol=418&invol=683.

Walsh, Lawrence E. *Final Report of the Independent Counsel for Iran/Contra Matters,* August 4, 1993. http://www.fas.org/irp/offdocs/walsh/.

Weinberger, Caspar W. "The Uses of Military Power." National Press Club, Washington, D.C., November 28, 1984. http://www.airforce-magazine.com/MagazineArchive/Pages/2004/January%202004/0104keeper.aspx.

World Bank. *World Development Report 2008, Agriculture for Development.* Washington, D.C.: World Bank, 2007. http://siteresources.worldbank.org/INTWDR2008/Resources/WDR_00_book.pdf.

Yacobucci, Brent D., and Robert Bamberger. *Automobile and Light Truck Fuel Economy: The CAFE Standards.* Congressional Research Service CRS Report for Congress R40166, January 19, 2007. Update, April 23, 2010. http://ncseonline.org/NLE/CRSreports/08June/RL33413.pdf.

Yoo, John. Memo to William J. Haynes II, March 14, 2003. http://www.aclu.org/pdfs/safefree/yoo_army_torture_memo.pdf.

INDEX

Abrams, Creighton, 134
Abrams, Elliott, 190, 255
Abu Ghraib prison, 3, 269–70, 277
Acheson, Dean, 62, 70, 79, 81, 216
Adams, John, 21
Adams, John Quincy, 21
Addington, David, 253, 257
Afghanistan, 9, 16, 51, 142, 180, 214, 245, 259, 261, 283
  Communist regime in, 177, 178
  Soviet invasion of, 162, 176–79, 184
  U.S. support for mujahedeen in, 177, 178–79, 189, 261
Afghanistan War, 134, 268, 272, 277, 285, 287–88, 300
  Obama and, 271–75
Africa, 142, 184
Aideed, Mohammed Farah, 233
Alamogordo, N.Mex., 64
Albania, 240–41
Albright, Madeleine, 229, 239, 240
Alien and Sedition Acts, 21
Allawi, Ayad, 236
Allen, Richard, 189
Allende, Salvador, 172
Al Qaeda, 9–10, 178, 220, 233, 258–60, 261, 264, 271, 272, 274, 287–88
alternative energy, 168
America First Committee, 30–32, 34, 149
American Communist Party, 43
Amin, Hafizullah, 177
anarchists, 25
Anglo-Iranian Oil Company, 96–97
Angola, 141, 189, 253, 258
anthrax, 259
anti-Americanism, 5, 16
anti-Communist insurgencies, Reagan Doctrine and, 185, 188–90
anti-Semitism, 30
Antiterrorism and Effective Death Penalty Act (1996), 263–64
antiwar movement, 133–34
  CIA surveillance of, 153–54
Arab-Israeli conflict, 164
Arab League, 275
Árbenz, Jacobo, 97
Argentina, 189
Aristide, Jean-Bertrand, 237
arms control, 164
arms control agreements, 91, 140–41
Arms Control and Disarmament Agency, 116
army, U.S., 256
Articles of Confederation, 19
Ashcroft, John, 257, 259, 260, 264, 265
Aspin, Les, 212, 225–26, 227–28, 234
  Bottom Up Review of, 227–28, 230, 232, 242
assassinations, 269
  foreign, 192
Atlantic Charter, 56
atomic bomb, *see* nuclear weapons
Atoms for Peace plan, 90, 91
Austria-Hungary, 298
automobiles, fuel efficiency of, 169–70
Azerbaijan, 242

Bagram air base, 264, 266, 277
Baker, James, 203, 204, 205, 207, 217
balance of power, 84
  as foreign policy, 69–70
Balkans, 228
Bani-Sadr, Abulhassan, 176
banking system, 270, 277–78, 291–92
  reforms and, 278
Barzani, Massoud, 236
Base Force plan, 212–13, 214, 215, 221, 225, 228
Bayh, Birch, 160

Bay of Pigs invasion, 86, 97, 99, 101, 103–4, 107, 147, 189
Beard, Charles A., 31
Belgium, 215
Benghazi, 275
Bentsen, Lloyd, 247
Beria, Lavrenty, 88, 89
Berlin, 58, 66, 106
  blockade of, 66, 78, 106
Berlin crisis (1961), 107, 112
Berlin wall, 107, 208, 209
Bernanke, Ben, 288
Biddle, Francis, 41, 42, 43, 44, 45
Biden, Joe, 221
Big Three alliance, 55, 59, 66, 68
  Poland and, 58
Bill of Rights, 20, 44, 82, 265–66
bin Laden, Osama, 10, 178, 271, 272
Bissell, Richard, 104
Black, Hugo, 44
Blair, Tony, 259
Bohlen, Charles, 86–87
Boland amendments, 190, 191, 210
Borah, William, 31
Bosnia, 220, 232, 237–39, 241
Boutros-Ghali, Boutros, 233, 238
Bowles, Chester, 31
Bretton Woods, 59, 76, 142, 199, 293–94
Brewster, Kingman, 31
Brezhnev, Leonid, 140–41, 142, 171
Britain, Battle of, 36
Brookings Institution, 279
Brownell, Herbert, 98
Brunei, 190
Brzezinski, Zbigniew, 103, 166, 175, 178, 189
Bulgaria, 208, 298
Bundy, McGeorge, 101, 103
Bush, George H. W., 7–8, 144, 156, 192, 193, 203–23, 224, 229, 233, 238, 254–55, 259, 264, 278, 292
  administration, 91
  China policy of, 206–8
  Gulf War and, 214–15
  legacy of, 222–23
  military spending under, 213–14
  nuclear reductions by, 228
  Panama invasion of, 210–12
  realist statecraft of, 203–4
  rogue states doctrine of, 219–20
  Somalia and, 232–33
  START agreements and, 218–19
Bush, George W., 3, 73, 75, 144, 220, 221, 236, 241, 245, 246, 252–66, 273, 275, 276, 278, 279, 287, 290, 292
  domestic law enforcement of, 262
  expansion of presidential power by, 263–65
  management style of, 252
  tax cuts under, 257
  trials by military commission authorized by, 45, 264, 266
Bush, George W., administration, 10, 16, 40, 134
  military spending under, 261–62
  national security policies of, 3–4, 262
  Obama and lack of legal accountability for, 270, 277
  public rejection of policies of, 267
  wiretaps of, 41, 270
Bybee, Jay, 253–54, 257, 264–65
Byrd, Robert, 221
Byrnes, James, 62

cabinet members, 303–4
Caddell, Patrick, 180
Cambodia, 94, 149, 150–51, 152
Camelot legend, 100–101
Camp David summit (1959), 92
capital flows, government control over, 182–83
carbon dioxide, 284
Carlucci, Frank, 192
Carter, Ashton, 280
Carter, Jimmy, 144, 156, 157, 189, 229, 235, 237, 268, 278
  administration, 140
  aid to mujahedeen approved by, 177, 178
  Congress and, 160–62, 166
  "crisis of confidence" speech of, 180–81
  developing nations and, 164, 166
  economic policy of, 180–83
  energy policy of, 163, 167–70, 181, 186
  foreign policy of, 163–65, 170–81
  free speech and, 164
  human rights and, 164, 165–66
  Iranian hostage crisis and, 158, 162, 175–76, 183
  leadership failures of, 162–63, 165, 171, 175, 181, 185, 186
  Panama Canal treaties and, 170, 171, 172
  return to founding principles urged by, 158–60, 164, 166–67
  Soviet grain embargo ordered by, 177
Carville, James, 224
Case-Church amendment, 152

Casey, William, 189–90, 197
Castro, Fidel, 97, 103, 172
  assassination plots against, 105
CBS Evening News, 154
CENTO, 95
Central America, 205
Central Asia, 177
Central Europe, 60, 61, 62, 63, 78
Central Intelligence Agency (CIA), 2, 9, 10, 74, 75, 85–86, 105, 141, 146, 149, 156, 160, 190, 195, 210, 261, 263, 265, 266, 269, 279, 304, 305, 306
  Bay of Pigs and, 97, 101, 103–4
  congressional investigation of, 153
  covert operations of, 95–96
  destabilization operations of, 13
  domestic surveillance of, 153–54, 159
  Iraq coup attempt backed by, 236
  mujahedeen supported by, 178, 189, 261
  in 1953 Iranian coup, 95, 96–97, 104, 173, 175
  in 1954 Guatemalan coup, 3, 95, 97, 104
  oversight lacking for, 148
  Phoenix program of, 149
  Reagan Doctrine and, 189–90
  reform of, 149
  Rockefeller Commission investigation of, 154
  SAVAK and, 174
  Watergate scandal and, 147–48, 191
Chalabi, Ahmed, 236
Chamberlain, Neville, 62, 63, 65
Chamorro, Pedro Joaquín, 173
Chamorro, Violeta, 205
checks and balances, 5, 20, 27, 82, 160, 301–4
Cheney, Dick, 156, 209, 213, 221, 233, 252–53, 254, 255, 256, 259, 260, 261, 263, 265
  task force on energy of, 256
Chernomyrdin, Victor, 241
Chiang Kai-shek, 78, 81, 136, 137
Chicago Council on Global Affairs, 271
Chile, 13, 172, 258
China, 10, 13, 14, 54, 198, 231, 284, 285, 290, 293, 294
  Communist victory in, 78, 81, 209
  Cultural Revolution in, 136
  economic power of, 11
  G. H. W. Bush's policy toward, 206–8
  Johnson and, 136
  Korean War and, 79–80, 81
  Nixon's opening to, 130, 135–40
  nuclear weapons of, 94, 124, 136
  Soviet relations with, 136–37, 139, 171
  Taiwan and, 137–38
  Tiananmen Square and, 206–8
  U.S. relations with, 89, 130, 135–40, 164
  Vietnam invaded by, 140
Church, Frank, 154, 160
Churchill, Winston, 34, 36, 57, 58, 59–61, 70, 86, 140
  "Iron Curtain" speech of, 66
civil liberties, 20, 118, 205, 259, 296
  FDR's violations of, 38–45
  Wilson-era abuses of, 25
civil rights, 118–19, 125–26, 296
Civil War, U.S., 21
Clark, William, 189
classified information, 304–5
climate change, 283
Clinton, Bill, 3, 23, 144, 161, 224–51, 252, 254, 255, 261, 264, 268, 278, 292
  Africa policy of, 234
  Bosnia and, 237–39
  budgets of, 247–48
  draft deferment of, 224–25
  emergency powers used by, 254
  Haiti and, 237
  Iraq and, 235–36
  and Kosovo, 240–41
  military spending under, 225–27, 246–47
  and NATO enlargement, 241–43
  North Korea and, 234–35
  Somalia and, 232–33
  trade agreements of, 249–50
Clinton, Hillary, 267, 275
coalitions of the willing, 221
Coast Guard, U.S., 254
Colby, William, 149, 153, 154, 156
cold war, 1, 5, 6, 7, 8–9, 14, 86, 126, 165, 166, 176, 179, 183, 190, 203–4, 205, 210, 261, 287
  beginning of, 66–67
  defense spending in, 48
  détente and, 130, 140–42, 166, 171, 177, 184
  nuclear arms race in, 64–65, 89, 90–91, 99, 101, 108, 116–17, 140–42, 188
  presidential power and, 51
  Stalin's death as chance for peace in, 86–88, 89
  Truman and, 67–68
Communications Act (1934), 41
communications interception, 262

Communism, Communists, 1, 11, 13, 40, 42–43, 54, 76, 77
McCarthyism and, 80–82
U.S. containment of, *see* universal containment, doctrine of
Congo, 258
Congress, U.S., 137, 149, 252–53, 262–63, 265, 266, 297
and appointments process, 303–4
Boland amendments passed by, 190, 191
Bush (G. W.) administration and, 4
Carter and, 160–62, 166
China policy in, 207–8
Clinton's trade agreements in, 249–50
and constitutional authority to declare war, 28
Constitution's delegation of foreign policy role to, 51–52
Contra funding and, 194, 205
in declaration of war on Germany and Japan, 37–38
draft and, 65
and FDR's domestic surveillance programs, 42
and FDR's expansion of presidential power, 28
intelligence abuses investigation of, 153, 154–55, 160, 161
intelligence oversight role of, 75, 153, 161, 189
Iran-Contra and, 254
Korean War and, 79
military and security spending by, 2, 17–18, 226, 298–99
presidential power and, 5–6, 135, 151–52, 156–57, 160–61, 167, 183–84, 254–55, 257, 276, 297–98, 301–3
Tiananmen Square and, 206
Tonkin Gulf Resolution passed by, 3, 122
Tonkin Gulf Resolution repealed by, 135, 152
trade agreements and, 306–8
Truman and, 71
and Vietnam endgame, 150, 151–52
war-making powers and, 5–6, 17, 19, 28, 135, 151–52, 159, 260, 276, 297–98
Connally, John, 143
Constitution, U.S., 2, 4, 5, 21, 82, 296, 303, 305, 306, 307, 308
checks and balances in, 20, 82, 160
Congress granted foreign policy role by, 51–52
government accountability in, 17, 20
presidential duties under, 191, 298
presidential power in, 27–28, 29, 32, 257, 296
Tonkin Gulf Resolution as evasion of, 123
Constitutional Convention, 19
containment, *see* universal containment, doctrine of
Coolidge, Calvin, 25, 158, 279
Cooper-Church amendment, 152
Copenhagen accords (2009), 284
corporations:
political power of, 32
see also multinational corporations
cost-plus contracts, 46, 47
Council on Foreign Relations, 85, 279
counterinsurgency programs, 100, 105, 113–15, 287–88
counterterrorism, 269
Croatia, 238
Cuba:
Bay of Pigs invasion of, 97, 103–4, 147
Operation Mongoose and, 105
Cuban missile crisis, 100, 101, 105–6, 107–11, 113, 116, 117, 194
U.S. credibility as issue in, 109
Cultural Revolution, 136
Cummings, Homer, 42
Czechoslovakia, 203, 208
Communist coup in, 66, 78
Czech Republic, 241–42

Daoud, Mohammad, 177
data-mining, 262
Davies, Joseph, 59
Dayton peace agreement, 238
DDG-1000 stealth destroyers, 262
Declaration of Independence, 160
decolonization, 53, 56
defense contractors, 92
cost-plus contracts of, 46, 47
Defense Department, U.S., 2, 9, 74, 102, 103, 105, 190, 192, 193, 195, 196, 212, 231–32, 246, 264, 265, 266, 270, 287, 300
Aspin in, 227–28
civilian bureaucracy of, 257
contracting policies of, 47–48
deficit spending in, 16
new strategic narrative for, 220–21
Rumsfeld at, 256–57
Defense Intelligence Agency, 174

Defense Planning Guide, 220–22
deficits, 51, 214, 246, 247
as positive economic tool, 48
trade, 143, 186, 187
deficit spending, 16, 100, 186, 187
deindustrialization, 198–99, 201
Dellums, Ron, 160
DeLoach, Deke, 127
democracy, American, 17
traditional tenets of, 5–6
Democratic Convention (1964), FBI surveillance of, 41, 126–27
Democratic League of Kosovo, 240
Democratic National Committee, 145
Democratic Party, 192, 205, 209, 213, 261, 263, 278–79, 286, 291
China policy and, 207–8
defense spending and, 48, 225–26
defensive posture of, 82
foreign policy establishment of, 279–80
presidential politics and, 161–62
traditional base of, 162, 183
Deng Xiaoping, 207
Depression, Great, 7, 31, 33, 35, 46, 54
and expansion of presidential powers, 27
deregulation, 257, 267, 268, 291
derivatives trading, 278
Desert Storm, Operation, 214–18, 219
détente, 130, 140–42, 156, 164, 166, 171, 177, 184
deterrence, 196, 284
developing nations, Carter and, 164, 166
development assistance, 285
Dewey, Thomas E., 84
DeWitt, John, 44
Dien Bien Phu, battle of, 94, 115
Dirksen, Everett, 127
diseases, infectious, 283
Dobriansky, Paula, 255
dollar, U.S., 293
gold convertibility ended for, 143, 182, 187
as international reserve currency, 76, 129, 142, 182, 290, 293
dollar-a-year men, 47, 48
domestic spying, 192
domino theory, 115, 121, 136
draft, 63, 65, 123, 124, 133, 301
Clinton's opposition to, 225
lottery in, 132
peacetime, 84, 113, 130, 132–33
due process, 20, 269
Dulles, Allen, 85–86, 96, 97, 103, 104
Dulles, John Foster, 84, 85, 87–88, 91, 94–95, 96, 102
bipolar worldview of, 90
nuclear brinkmanship of, 94, 112, 186

Eagleburger, Lawrence, 207
Eastern Europe, 67, 198, 209
Soviet control of, 86, 141
East Germany, 106–7, 208
workers' revolt in, 88, 94
economy, international, 53, 76
Bretton Woods and, 59, 76, 142
competition in, 128–29, 130, 143, 182
economy, U.S., 247–48, 288–94
bubbles in, 15, 249, 250
Carter and, 180–83
Chinese influence on, 11
deficit spending in, 16, 100, 186, 187
deregulation and, 257, 267, 268, 291
finance-driven, 290
financial crisis of 2008 and, 15–17, 288–89, 291
impact of U.S. foreign policy on, 11–12
inflation in, 142–43, 162, 181, 183, 186
international competition and, 128–29, 130, 143, 182
under Johnson, 127–28
Keynesianism and, 48, 100, 102, 128, 129, 143, 182, 183
under Nixon, 142–44
Obama and, 270, 277–78, 288, 291
postwar, 11–12, 77
under Reagan, 185, 186, 199–200
unemployment in, 181–82, 183, 270
World War II and, 33–34, 45–49
education, 247
Eighth Amendment, 20
Eisenhower, Dwight, 3, 43, 45, 48, 58, 80, 83–85, 103, 107, 121, 132, 140, 186, 189, 197, 200, 205, 279
Atoms for Peace plan of, 90, 91
bipolar worldview of, 90
"Chance for Peace" speech of, 87
containment policy of, 93, 95, 112, 139–40
counterinsurgency policies of, 114
on dangers of "military-industrial complex," 92, 102, 187
institutionalization of emergency state under, 98
military spending under, 92–95, 99, 112, 187

Eisenhower (*cont.*)
national security policy of, 89, 90–91, 93–99
New Look policy of, 93–94, 95
Open Skies proposal of, 91
in summit meetings, 91–92
elections, U.S.:
of 1940, 35, 36
of 1964, 121, 123
of 1968, 125–26
of 1974, 152–53
of 1976, 157
of 1980, 183
of 1984, 186
of 2008, 267, 272, 285
Ellsberg, Daniel, 144, 145
enemy combatants, 264
energy:
dependence on, 15
U.S. consumption of, 167–70, 186
Energy Department, U.S., 248
energy independence, Carter and, 163, 167–68
Enlightenment, 6
environmental conditions, 294
environmental protection, 307
Espionage Act (1917), 23, 25, 43, 298
euro, 13
Eurodollar market, 129, 182
Europe, 182, 204, 285
economic unification and, 14
Eisenhower's policy on, 94
Marshall Plan and, 76–78
postwar division of, 66
postwar economic devastation of, 53
postwar economic revival of, 128, 130
see also specific countries
European Union, 13, 242
ExComm, 194
executive branch, 306–7
review of, 301–2
Executive Order 9066, 43
executive power, *see* presidential power
executive privilege, 75, 146, 147, 252–53, 302–3, 304
Export-Import Bank, 199
extraordinary rendition, 3, 264, 266, 269, 270, 277

F-22 stealth fighter, 49, 262
Fair Deal, 57
Fascists, 40, 43
fast-track negotiating authority, 306–7
Federal Bureau of Investigation (FBI), 82, 146, 147, 154, 160, 261
Custodial Detention List (Security Index) of, 40, 42
domestic surveillance by, 39, 41, 42, 98, 126–27, 159
statutory charter for, 306
in surveillance of FDR's political opponents, 29, 38, 39–40
federal courts, 301–2
federal government:
control of money supply and capital flows by, 182–83
domestic surveillance by, 7, 23, 39, 41–42, 75, 98, 153–54, 262, 263–64, 265, 270
secrecy of, 23
Federalist Papers, The, 5, 111
Federal Reserve, U.S., 182, 199
Fifth Amendment, 20, 82, 269
financial crisis (2008–), 15–17, 288–89, 291
financial sector, 270
financial system, global, 76, 199, 248–49, 289–90
financial system, U.S., 289–90
regulation of, 291–92
reregulation of, 292–93
First Amendment, 6, 20, 28, 39
FOIA, 257
Ford, Gerald, 31, 144, 148–49, 193, 253
administration, 155–56
Nixon pardoned by, 152–53
Foreign Affairs, 135
Kennan's "Mr. X" article in, 70
foreign aid, U.S., "loyalty tests" and, 13
Foreign Intelligence Surveillance Act (FISA; 1978), 161, 253, 265
foreign policy, U.S., 17, 278–80
American public as ignorant of, 97
America's founding, 281
balance of power as, 69–70
of Carter administration, 163–65, 170–81
CIA covert operations as, 96
Communist containment as goal of, 13
crisis management in, 296–97
of FDR administration, 59–61, 119
as granted to Congress under Constitution, 51–52
impact on U.S. economy of, 11–12

intelligence vetting in, 193–94
internationalism and, 281, 282–83
of Reagan administration, 190, 198
third world and, 13–14
of Truman administration, 54–59, 65–67, 68–69, 80, 119; *see also* Truman Doctrine
Forrestal, James, 62
Fourth Amendment, 20, 39, 75, 160
FDR's subversion of, 40–42
intelligence agency abuses of, 154
Fourth Amendment rights, 6
France, 89, 136, 204, 237, 239, 275
imperialism of, 32
in Indochina, 94, 114
Franklin, Benjamin, 6, 19
Freedom of Information Act, 161, 253
free speech, 6, 20, 270
Carter and, 164
Friedman, Milton, 132
Frost, David, 146, 265
Fulbright, William, 230

Gates, Robert, 197, 209, 272, 275
GATT, 230, 248, 321
Geithner, Timothy, 270, 288
Gelbard, Robert, 240
Geneva summit (1955), 92
Georgia, 242
Germany, 217, 222, 242, 298
postwar division of, 66, 67
reunification of, 204, 209, 243
Germany, Nazi, 1, 215, 219
atrocities of, 32
in declaration of war on U.S., 37
nuclear weapons and, 64
Soviet Union invaded by, 30, 36, 59–60
submarine attacks by, 37, 215
as threat to U.S., 32, 38
in World War II, 59, 62, 64
Gilpatric, Roswell, 110
globalization, 14, 144, 183, 198, 245, 248–49, 250, 292–93, 294–95
labor and, 1, 14, 182
multinational corporations and, 143–44
neoliberal model of, 16
second-generation model for, 294–95
global warming, 256, 284–85
global war on terror, 10, 223, 260, 261, 263, 268–69, 287
Goldman Sachs, 279
Goldwater, Barry, 123, 127
Gonzalez, Alberto, 265
Goodwin, Doris Kearns, 124
Gorbachev, Mikhail, 88, 185, 195, 197, 203, 204, 207, 208, 209, 218, 242–43
Gore, Al, 259
Government Accountability Office, 305
government whistleblowers, 269–70
Gravel, Mike, 152
Gray, L. Patrick, 147
Great Britain, 136, 204, 237, 239, 275, 298
Greece and, 70, 73
imperialism of, 32
postwar economic weakness of, 53
Turkey and, 70
U.S. relationship with, 58
U.S. World War II aid to, 32
in World War II, 27, 28, 33, 47
Great Depression, *see* Depression, Great
Great Game, 177
Great Society, 124, 285, 286
Greece, 13, 70–73, 76, 258
greenhouse gases, 283, 284–85
Greenland, 37
Greenspan, Alan, 247, 290, 291
Grenada, 212
Gruening, Ernest, 122
Guantánamo Bay, 3, 264, 266, 269, 276, 277
Guatemala, 13, 189, 258
1954 CIA-backed coup in, 3, 95, 97, 104
Gulf War (1991), 214–18, 254

Haass, Richard, 280
habeas corpus, 6, 20, 39, 266
Haig, Alexander, 144–45, 149
Haiti, 228, 232, 237
Haitian refugees, 264
Haldeman, H. R., 147–48
"Halloween Massacre," 155–56
Harding, Warren, 83
Harriman, W. Averell, 61, 62
Hatch Act (1939), 43
Hatfield, Mark, 151, 160
Hawaii, Japanese Americans in, 44
Heller, Walter, 112
Helms, Richard, 104–5, 147, 153
Hersh, Seymour, 153, 154
Hezbollah, 191
Hiroshima, atomic bombing of, 64
Hiss, Alger, 80
Hitler, Adolf, 30, 33, 37, 38, 215, 219
Ho Chi Minh, 38, 56, 89, 131
Hong Kong, 198

Hoover, Herbert, 183
Hoover, J. Edgar, 25, 44, 126–27
blackmail files of, 98
domestic surveillance and, 28
FDR's relationship with, 39–40, 42
Hopkins, Harry, 59
House of Representatives, U.S., 255, 266
Armed Services Committee of, 227
Pike Committee of, 154–55, 160, 161
Tonkin Gulf Resolution passed by, 122
Howe, Jonathan, 233
Hue, Vietnam, 125
Hughes-Ryan Act (1974), 153, 161, 189
Hukbalahap insurgency, 114
human rights, 208
Carter and, 164, 165–66
Humphrey, Hubert, 125
Hungary, 241–42, 298
1956 revolution in, 92, 94, 203, 208
Hunt, E. Howard, 145
Hussein, Saddam, 8, 214–15, 219, 235–36, 255, 261, 272, 287
Hutchins, Robert Maynard, 31
Hutus, 233–34
Hu Yao Bang, 207

Iceland, 37
indefinite detention, 276, 277
India, 14, 198, 243, 284, 285, 294
Indochina, 94, 114, 253
Indonesia, 13
inflation, 142–43, 162, 181, 183, 186
intelligence budget, 305
intelligence data, misuse of, 3, 5
Intelligence Oversight Act (1980), 161
Intelligence Reform Act (1980), 189
Internal Revenue Service (IRS), 154
International Atomic Energy Agency, 90–91, 284
internationalism, 281, 282–83, 292, 293
International Monetary Fund, 288
Iran, 13, 90, 161, 173–76, 179, 190, 215, 217, 231, 243, 258, 284
CIA-backed coup in, 95, 96–97, 104, 173, 175
Iran, shah of, 96, 170, 171, 173–74, 175
Iran, U.S. arms embargo against, 195
Iran-Contra affair, 161, 190–91, 193, 195, 197, 254, 304
Iranian hostage crisis, 158, 162, 175–76, 183, 191
Iran-Iraq War, 190
Iraq, 3, 8, 9, 16, 51, 193, 213, 214–15, 216, 235–36, 245, 259, 261, 266, 275, 283
sanctions on, 235–36
Iraq War, 10, 73, 134, 267–68, 272, 273, 283, 285, 287, 300
Obama's strong opposition to, 271, 272
Islamic fundamentalism, 178–79, 180
isolationism, isolationists, 9, 30, 34, 43, 244, 281
honest critics characterized as, 38
Israel, 243, 284, 301
Italy, U.S. missile deployments in, 108, 110

Jackson, Henry, 99
Jackson, Robert, 41, 42
Jackson-Vanik amendment, 171
James, William, 168
Japan, 56, 141, 182, 198, 217, 222, 298
Pearl Harbor attack by, 30, 36, 37, 43–44, 74, 215
postwar devastation of, 53
postwar economic revival of, 128, 130
in World War II, 64
Japanese Americans, World War II internment of, 29, 38, 43–45, 84, 264, 277
Jefferson, Thomas, 5, 6, 19, 21, 160
Jeffords, James, 255
Jenkins, Walter, 127
Johnson, Hiram, 32
Johnson, Lyndon, 3, 35, 48, 73, 100, 101, 102, 105, 115, 118, 140, 144, 160, 170, 285, 286, 288
China and, 136
containment policy of, 121, 124, 126, 139–40, 186
domestic agenda of, 119–20, 124, 125–26
domestic surveillance authorized by, 126–27
economic policies of, 127–28
isolation of, 119
political spying by, 126–27
presidential power expanded by, 119
Tonkin Gulf incident and, 38, 121–22
Vietnam War and, 119–25, 131, 133, 134, 152, 158, 159, 186, 274
Johnson, Simon, 288
Joint Chiefs of Staff, 74, 101, 104, 105, 109, 110, 114, 120, 188, 256
Joint Special Operations Command, 272
Jordan, Hamilton, 160
judicial review, 6

jury trial, right to, 20
Justice Department, U.S., 205, 254, 264, 270, 276
  General Intelligence Division of, 25

Kabul, 177, 178
Kagan, Elena, 270
Karzai, Hamid, 273
Keating, Kenneth, 106, 107, 108
Kennan, George F., 61, 62, 69, 242
  selective containment policy of, 69–70, 135–36, 209
Kennedy, John F., 31, 73, 97, 99, 100, 119, 130, 140, 144
  administration, 86, 101–2
  American University speech (June 1963) of, 101, 116
  assassination of, 101, 119
  Bay of Pigs fiasco and, 97, 101, 103–4, 189
  Camelot legend and, 100–101
  containment as basic tenet of, 102, 139–40
  counterinsurgency policies of, 100, 105, 113–15
  in Cuban missile crisis, 100, 101, 105–6, 107–11, 113, 116, 194
  expansion of presidential power by, 102–3
  military spending under, 102, 113
  opportunism of, 118–19
  test ban agreement and, 116–17
  at Vienna summit, 106–7, 113
  Vietnam War and, 120–21
Kennedy, Robert, 101, 105, 109, 127
Kennedy, Ted, 160
Kennedy Tapes, The, 106
Keynesian economics, 48, 100, 102, 112, 129, 143, 144, 182, 183
Keyserling, Leon, 48
Khalilzad, Zalmay, 221, 255
Khmer Rouge, 150
Khomeini, Ayatollah Ruhollah, 97, 174–75
Khrushchev, Nikita, 88, 92, 112, 113
  Cuban missile crisis and, 105–6, 107–8, 110, 111, 117
  test ban agreement and, 116–17
  in Vienna summit, 106–7, 113
Kim Il Sung, 89–90, 219
King, Martin Luther, Jr., 118, 271–72, 285, 288
  FBI surveillance of, 41, 127
Kissinger, Henry, 103, 137, 138, 140–41, 144–45, 149, 154, 156, 166, 175, 208
Knudsen, William, 47
Korean War, 55, 65, 66, 79–80, 81, 85, 86, 87, 88, 90, 92, 95, 101, 115, 121, 124, 132, 142, 186, 205, 225, 279
Korematsu, Fred, 45
Kosovo, 239–41, 244
Kosovo Liberation Army, 240
Krugman, Paul, 288
Kurdistan, 217, 236
Kuwait, 214–16, 217, 218, 220, 221, 233

labor, 307
  globalization and, 1, 14, 182
labor conditions, 294
labor unions, 186
La Follette, Robert, Jr., 31–32
La Follette, Robert, Sr., 31
Lake, Anthony, 172, 230–32, 234, 241, 242, 243, 244–46
Lansdale, Edward, 105, 114–15
Laos, 94, 152
Lauer, Matt, 239
League of Nations, 24, 55, 66, 281–82
Leahy, William, 61
Lebanon, U.S. hostages in, 191
LeMay, Curtis, 110
Lend-Lease Act (1941), 36–37, 47
  Soviet Union and, 61, 62, 65, 66
Lewis, Sinclair, 31
Libby, I. Lewis "Scooter," 221, 225
Libya, 275–76
Liddy, G. Gordon, 145
Life, 94
Limited Test Ban Treaty (1963), 117
Lincoln, Abraham, 21, 22, 264
Lindbergh, Charles, 30
Lippmann, Walter, 69, 70, 71, 78
Lodge, Henry Cabot, Jr., 84
Long Telegram, 69–70
Los Angeles Chamber of Commerce, 41
loyalty programs, 82, 98
Lusitania, 35

MacArthur, Douglas, 79, 124
McCain, John, 267
McCarthy, Joseph, 43, 80–81, 98, 130
McCarthyism, 80–82
McChrystal, Stanley, 272–74
McCloskey, Pete, 160
McCone, John, 104–5, 107
McFarlane, Robert "Bud," 189

McGovern, George, 151, 156, 224
McGrath, J. Howard, 82
McKiernan, David, 272
McKinley, William, 83, 279
McNamara, Robert, 101, 102, 109–10, 113
Maddox, USS, 121
Madison, James, 5, 6, 19, 20, 160
Magsaysay, Ramón, 114
Malaysia, 198
Malenkov, Georgy, 87
Mandelbaum, Michael, 242
Manifest Destiny, 22
Manning, Bradley, 269
Mao Zedong, 54, 66, 78, 89, 136, 137
Marines, U.S., 172, 228
Marshall, George, 76
Marshall Plan, 11, 55, 66, 76–78, 189, 230, 231
Mathias, Charles, 160
Matsu, 94
Mayaguez incident, 150–51
Mesopotamia, 272
Mexico, 198, 254, 298
Middle East, 9
  U.S. influence in, 8
military, Soviet:
  postwar level of, 63–64
  see also Red Army
military, U.S., 256
  as all-volunteer, 65, 130, 132, 134, 299
  buildups of, 48
  force requirements of, 228
  overseas deployment of, 133, 142–43
  peacetime levels of, 65, 92
  postwar level of, 63
  reserves in, 134
  selective service in, 299–300
  special forces of, 113–14, 269
  see also draft
military commissions, 45, 264, 266, 276
military-industrial complex, 7, 99, 102, 279
  Eisenhower on, 92, 102, 187
  FDR and beginnings of, 29, 45–49
military spending, 6, 17–18, 48, 54, 65, 209–10, 212–14, 224, 298–99
  under Clinton, 225–27, 246–47
  under Eisenhower, 92–95, 99, 112, 187
  under Kennedy, 102, 113
  misplaced priorities in, 9–10, 49
  under Nixon, 187
  post-9/11 increase in, 261–62
  under Reagan, 185, 186–88
  under Truman, 65, 92, 95
militias, 133
Milosevic, Slobodan, 220, 238, 240
missile gap, 99, 108, 112, 117
mission creep, 233
Mitchell, George, 208
Mitchell, John, 144–45
Mogadishu, 233
Molotov, Vyacheslav M., 62, 65, 89
money supply, government control over, 182–83
Mongoose, Operation, 105, 107
Monroe Doctrine, 21, 172, 258
Morse, Wayne, 122
mortgage-backed derivatives, 290–91
Mossadegh, Mohammad, 90, 96, 175
Moyers, Bill, 127
mujahedeen, U.S. support of, 177, 178–79, 189, 261
Mullen, Mike, 272, 275
multilateralism, 221
multinational corporations, 14
  tax-avoidance strategies of, 143–44
Munich conference, 9, 38, 55, 62, 220
Murphy, Frank, 39, 42
mutually assured destruction (MAD), 196, 197
My Lai massacre, 277

NAFTA, 230, 231, 243, 248
Nagasaki, atomic bombing of, 64
Nasser, Gamal Abdel, 90
Nation, The, 31
National Guard, Nicaraguan, 172
national security, 17, 52, 212–13
  constitutional limits on, 6
  and expansion of presidential power, 75
  misplaced priorities in, 9–10
  politics and, 6, 7, 9
  prior restraint and, 145
  as underminded by permanent emergency state, 3, 4, 8–9
  see also specific agencies and presidents
National Security Act (1947), 74–75, 78
national security adviser, 102–3, 192, 303–4
  lack of oversight of, 103
National Security Agency, 154, 160
  domestic surveillance by, 75, 262, 270

National Security Council (NSC), 2, 74, 78, 166, 172, 279, 304
Iran-Contra affair and, 190, 191, 193, 195
Report 68 of, *see* NSC-68
national security establishment, 2, 9, 17
congressional oversight of, 75, 153, 161, 189
FDR and growth of, 28
National Security Act and, 74–75, 78
political spying and, 7, 21, 29, 38, 39, 41, 42, 118, 126–27, 130, 146, 148
presidential oversight and, 104–5
secrecy culture of, 5, 75
Nazism, 40
Nedzi, Lucien, 154
Nehru, Jawaharlal, 90
Nelson, Donald, 47
neoconservatives, 176
neutrality, 23, 28
Neutrality Acts, 32, 34, 35–36, 37
New Deal, 32, 48, 50, 80, 278, 286, 292
New York Times, 25, 39, 144–45, 153, 155, 220–21
Ngo Dinh Diem, 114, 120, 172
Ngo Dinh Nhu, 120
Nguyen Van Thieu, 134
Nicaragua, 170, 172–73, 190, 205, 211, 253
Nicaraguan Contras, 189, 190–91, 194, 210
Nicaraguan National Guard, 172
1984 (Orwell), 140
Nitze, Paul, 62, 112
Nixon, Richard, 3, 35, 75, 80, 103, 105, 125–26, 130, 160, 170, 186, 199, 200, 205, 216–17, 229, 253, 265, 279
administration, 25, 41, 91
all-volunteer military and, 130, 132, 134
as anti-Communist, 135
China opening and, 130, 135–40
constitutional accountability avoided by, 138–39
détente and, 130, 140–42
dollar-gold convertibility ended by, 143, 182, 187
economic policies of, 142–44, 158
executive privilege claims of, 146, 147, 303
expansion of presidential power by, 138–39, 160
Ford's pardon of, 152–53
military spending under, 187
Pentagon Papers and, 144–45
political spying by, 130, 145
"Saturday Night Massacre" of, 156
secrecy and paranoia of, 130, 146
Vietnam War and, 122, 130–32, 134–35, 137, 144, 150
Watergate scandal and, 130, 135, 145–46, 147–48, 158, 159, 191, 192
Nixon Doctrine, 173, 174
Noriega, Manuel, 8, 210, 212, 219, 254
North, Oliver, 190, 192
North Atlantic Treaty Organization (NATO), 11, 56, 78, 83, 84, 93, 95, 113, 197, 204, 222, 230, 232, 275
Bosnia and, 237–39
enlargement of, 230, 231, 241–43, 244–46
and Kosovo, 239–41
North Korea, 79, 81, 89–90, 196, 213, 219, 234–35, 237, 243, 284
North Vietnam, 123, 125, 131, 145, 171
Nouvel Observateur, 178
NSC-68 (National Security Council Report 68), 55, 65, 78–79, 85, 92, 121, 164, 279
nuclear brinkmanship, 94, 112, 186
nuclear deterrence, 108
nuclear freeze movement, 188
Nuclear Nonproliferation Treaty, 234, 243
nuclear power, 168
nuclear weapons, 53, 58, 59, 66, 67, 78, 93–94, 116, 124, 136, 210, 228, 242, 283, 284, 286
arms race and, 64–65, 89, 90–91, 99, 101, 108, 116–17, 140–42, 185, 188
Cuban missile crisis and, 105–6, 107–11
test ban agreement on, 116–17
World War II and, 64
Nunn, Sam, 212, 237
Nye, Gerald, 31

Obama, Barack, 4, 161, 248, 267–80, 285–86, 292
administration, 4, 15, 17, 268, 284
Afghanistan and, 271–75
constitutional failures of, 276–77
defining mistake in first term of, 271–75
economic policies of, 270, 277–78, 288, 291
Iraq War opposed by, 271, 272
lack of legal accountability for Bush administration under, 270, 277
Libya and, 275–76

Office of Legal Counsel, 254, 257, 265–66
Office of Strategic Services (OSS), 56, 85, 189
oil, 215, 220
1973 Arab embargo of, 167
prices of, 12, 14
U.S. dependence on, 167–70, 180
Oklahoma City bombing (1995), 263
O'Neill, Tip, 160
OPEC, 12, 14, 173
open meetings law, 253
Operation Mongoose, 105, 107
Orwell, George, 140
Overseas Private Investment Corporation, 199

Pacific Rim, U.S. interests in, 54
Pakistan, 137, 177, 231, 243, 271, 273
ISI of, 178, 179
Palmer, A. Mitchell, 25
Palmer Raids, 25, 31, 264
Panama, 8, 210–12, 254
Panama Canal, 172
Panama Canal treaties, 170, 171, 172, 211–12
Panetta, Leon, 225–26, 247
Paris Peace Accords, 132, 135, 150, 152
Pastor, Robert, 172
Patriot Act, 3, 39
Peace Corps, 118
peace dividend, 247, 261
Pearl Harbor, Japanese attack on, 30, 36, 37, 43–44, 74, 133, 215
Pelosi, Nancy, 208, 305
Pentagon, *see* Defense Department, U.S.
Pentagon Papers, 25, 144–45, 152, 160, 270
Pérez, Carlo Andrés, 173
Persian Gulf, 173, 177
Petraeus, David, 272, 273, 274
Philippines, 13
Hukbalahap insurgency in, 114
U.S. annexation of, 21
Pike, Otis, 154, 160
plausible deniability, 148
Poindexter, John, 189
Poland, 58, 60, 61–62, 94, 141, 208, 215, 241–42
police actions, 225
politics, national security and, 6, 7, 9
Polk, James, 21
Potsdam conference, 66, 209
Powell, Colin, 134, 188, 192, 220, 221, 225, 228, 229, 232, 233, 237, 256
presidential power, 205, 256, 257, 260–61, 263, 265
Cheney's view on, 194–95
CIA and, 96–97, 148
cold war and, 51
congressional oversight of, 5–6, 135, 151–52, 156–57, 160–61, 167, 254–55, 257, 276, 301–3
in Constitution, 27–28, 29, 257, 396
constitutional limits on, 32
executive privilege and, 75, 146, 147
expansion of, 21–23
"fast-track negotiating authority" and, 306–7
FDR's expansion of, 27–29, 32–38, 50
G. W. Bush's expansion of, 263–65
international commerce and, 23
JFK's expansion of, 102–3
Johnson's expansion of, 119
Korean War and, 79
and lack of accountability, 75
and national security decisions, 75, 104–5
national security establishment and, 104–5
Nixon's expansion of, 138–39, 160
political spying and, 7, 21, 29, 38, 39, 41, 42, 118, 126–27, 130, 146, 148, 153–54, 191
review of, 301–2
theory of "unitary" executive power and, 257–58
Truman's postwar expansion of, 68
war making and, 2, 3, 5–6, 7, 10, 134, 135, 151–52, 260–61, 275–76, 297–98, 300
wartime expansion of, 27–29, 32–38, 260–61, 262
presidents, 21
accountability of, 5
as commander in chief, 19
public image of, 158
preventive war, 261
prior restraint, 145
privacy, right to, 259
Progressive movement, 31
Project for the New American Century, 255
public, American, as ignorant of U.S. foreign policy, 97
Putin, Vladimir, 242–43

Qaddafi, Muammar al-, 275, 276
Quemoy, 94

racial inequality, 286
Reagan, Ronald, 15, 144, 170, 183, 192, 205, 209, 212, 217, 278, 290, 292
  administration, 161
  anti-Communist insurgencies supported by, *see* Reagan Doctrine
  anti-labor stance of, 200
  approval ratings of, 192
  economic policy of, 185, 186
  foreign policy of, 190
  international economic policies of, 199
  Iran-Contra affair and, 161, 190–91, 193, 254
  labor unions and, 186
  legacy of, 201–2
  military spending under, 185, 186–88, 199
  personal confidence of, 185
  SALT talks and, 196
  SDI proposal of, 185, 195–97
  tax cuts of, 186, 187, 198–99
Reagan Democrats, 199
Reagan Doctrine, 178, 185, 188–90
  CIA and, 189–90
Red Army, 53, 58, 62, 86, 177
  size of, 113
Reich, Robert, 247
Republican Party, 32, 192, 211, 261, 263, 279, 291
  anti-Communism and, 80–81
  defense spending and, 48
Reserve Officer Training Corps (ROTC), 225
Reuben James, USS, 37
Rice, Condoleezza, 103, 256
Roberts, Owen, 44
Rockefeller, David, 175
Rockefeller, Nelson, 154, 156
rogue states, 212, 219–20, 232, 260
Rolling Stone, 274
Romania, 208, 298
Roosevelt, Franklin D., 3, 23, 26, 52, 56, 127, 130, 133, 140, 141, 172, 202, 215, 223, 264, 282, 291
  in assault on civil liberties, 38–45
  and beginnings of military-industrial complex, 29, 45–49
  business-friendly policies of, 46–47
  domestic surveillance authorized by, 28–29
  emergency state created by, 4, 6–7, 29
  expansion of presidential power by, 27–29, 32–38, 50
  foreign policy of, 59–61, 119
  "Four Freedoms" speech of, 288
  and growth of national security establishment, 28
  J. Edgar Hoover's relationship with, 39–40, 42
  military preparedness and, 63
  postwar intentions of, 58–59, 61, 66, 285, 286
  and surveillance of political opponents, 29, 38, 39–40
  trials by military commission authorized by, 45
  wiretaps and intercepts authorized by, 40–41
Roosevelt, Kermit, 96
Roosevelt, Theodore, 22, 24, 31, 32, 52, 170, 211, 282
Ross, Thomas, 97
Rubin, Robert, 247, 248, 290
Rugova, Ibrahim, 240
Rumsfeld, Donald, 150, 156, 252–53, 254, 255, 256–57, 259, 260, 261, 263, 264, 266
  civilian control and, 256
Rusk, Dean, 101–2, 109, 112
Russia, 10, 66, 228, 241, 242–43
  see also Soviet Union
Rwanda, 233–34, 235, 237
Ryan, Leo, 160

Saigon, 125
  fall of, 150, 165
Saipan, 198
Samuelson, Paul, 112
Sandinistas, 172–73, 179, 205
Sandino, Augusto, 172
Sarajevo, 220, 237
satellites, surveillance by, 91
"Saturday Night Massacre," 156
Saudi Arabia, 190, 215, 217, 261
SAVAK, 174
Savimbi, Jonas, 189
Schlesinger, James, 149, 153, 156
Schorr, Daniel, 154
Schultze, Charles, 182
Scowcroft, Brent, 103, 156, 207, 208, 209
SEATO, 95, 122
Second Amendment, 133, 299

Security Council, UN, 55, 58, 67, 215, 238, 239, 241, 244, 275
Sedition Act (1918), 23, 25, 298
selective service, 299–300
Senate, U.S., 242, 255, 266
  Church committee of, 154, 160, 161
  confirmation hearings in, 303–4
  Tonkin Gulf Resolution passed by, 122
September 11, 2001, terrorist attacks of, 1, 9, 10, 17, 43, 220, 255, 258–59, 260, 261, 272
  increased military spending in wake of, 261–62
Serbia, 239–41
Shanghai Communiqué, 137–39
Shiites, 217
Shriver, Sargent, 31
Shultz, George, 191, 197
Singapore, 198
Sixth Amendment, 20
smart bombs, 217–18
Smith, Walter Bedell, 96
Smith Act (1940), 43
Socialist Party, 31
Solidarity, 208
Somalia, 232–33, 235, 287
Somoza Debayle, Anastasio, 170, 171, 172
Somoza García, Anastasio, 172
Sorensen, Theodore, 101
South Africa, 189
Southeast Asia, 115
  in World War II, 56
South Korea, 198
South Vietnam, 94, 100, 120, 124, 125, 131, 135, 145, 150, 172
Soviet expansionism, 55
Soviet Union, 13, 173, 201, 203–4, 207–9, 218, 220, 221, 229, 258, 287
  Afghanistan invaded by, 162, 176–79, 184
  Chinese relations with, 136–37, 139, 171
  in Cuban missile crisis, 100, 101, 105–6, 107–8, 110–11
  Eastern Europe and, 86, 141
  expansionist policies of, 59–61, 66, 69, 132
  German invasion of, 30, 36, 59–60
  Lend-Lease and, 61, 62, 65, 66
  national liberation wars supported by, 112, 113
  nuclear weapons of, 64–65, 66, 67, 78, 94
  Pacific war and, 58, 59, 60, 64
  Poland and, 60, 61–62
  post-Stalin era in, 86–88
  and postwar Europe, 53
  SDI and, 195–97
  in space race, 98
  U.S. relations with, 58–59, 63, 64, 66, 67, 86, 130, 139, 140–42, 164, 171; *see also* cold war
  in World War II, 42, 47
Spain, 298
Srebrenica, 238
stagflation, 144, 182, 183, 199–200, 201
Stalin, Joseph, 53, 57, 69, 140, 141, 209
  death of, 86
  expansionist policies of, 59–61, 62–63, 66, 69
  Pacific war and, 64
  Truman's push-back against, 55–56, 57, 61–62, 88
START I agreement, 218
START II agreement, 219
Star Wars, *see* Strategic Defense Initiative
State Department, U.S., 56, 74, 75, 103, 105, 137, 166, 172, 193
  McCarthy's attacks on, 80–81
  Nixon's bypassing of, 138–39
"Statement of Principles," 255
state secrets defense, 270
statutory charter, 306
Stettinius, Edward, 47
Stiglitz, Joseph, 288
Stimson, Henry L., 43, 46, 65
Stone, Harlan Fiske, 25–26
Strategic Arms Limitation talks (SALT), 196
Strategic Defense Initiative (SDI), 185, 195–97
strategic petroleum reserve, 169
student protests, 130, 132, 133–34
subprime mortgage market, 291
Sudan, 287
Sukarno, 90
Sullivan, William, 126–27
Summers, Larry, 270, 288, 290
summit meetings, 91–92
  Camp David (1959), 92
  Geneva (1955), 92
  Vienna (1961), 106–7, 113
Sununu, John, 254
supply-side economics, 187
Supreme Court, U.S., 22, 205, 254, 265, 266, 296, 307
  Japanese American internments upheld by, 44–45

and Nixon's executive privilege claims, 146, 147, 303
Pentagon Papers and, 145
wiretap rulings of, 41
sustainable development, 283

Taft, Robert, 83–84, 279
emergency state opposed by, 84
Taft, William Howard, 83, 84
Taiwan, 136, 137–38, 190, 198
Talabani, Jalal, 236
Taliban, 179, 259, 261, 271, 273, 274, 287
tax cuts, 246
under G. W. Bush, 257
under Reagan, 185, 186, 187, 198–99
Taylor, Maxwell, 105, 110, 112, 114
Tehran, 175, 176
terrorism, 201, 220, 231, 240, 258–59, 261, 268–69, 271, 276–77, 287
Terrorist Surveillance Program, 265
Tet offensive, 125, 152
Thomas, Norman, 31
Thompson, Llewellyn, 110
Tiananmen Square massacre, 206–8
Tito, Josip Broz, 89
Tonkin Gulf incident, 38, 121–22
Tonkin Gulf Resolution (1964), 3, 122, 135, 152
as evasion of Constitution, 123
torture, 266, 277
torture memos, 264–65
Tower, John, 193
trade agreements, 306–8
trade deficits, 143, 186, 187, 250
Trading with the Enemy Act, 23
transatlantic trade, 33
Truman, Harry, 3, 31, 43, 48, 82, 96, 124, 133, 197, 209, 216, 223, 299
administration, 11, 48
Congress and, 71
domestic policy of, 57, 119
economic policies of, 54
foreign policy of, 54–59, 65–67, 68–69, 80; *see also* Truman Doctrine
as inheritor of FDR's emergency state, 50–51
Korean War and, 79, 186
"losing China" charge against, 81, 104, 119, 135, 136
military preparedness and, 65
military spending under, 65, 92, 95
national security policies of, 52, 54–56, 57, 63–65, 67–68, 74–75
peacetime emergency state created by, 51–53
Poland and, 61–62
presidential power expanded by, 68
in push-back against Stalin, 55–56, 57, 61–62, 88
Truman Doctrine, 15, 55, 66, 69, 70–74, 76, 81, 102, 104, 108, 122, 130, 139–40, 258
Turkey, 13, 70–72, 76, 258
U.S. missile deployments in, 108, 110
Tutsis, 233–34

U-2 surveillance, 92, 99, 106, 107, 112
unemployment, 181–82, 183, 200, 248, 270
UNITA, 189
unitary executive, 3, 156, 257–58
United Fruit, 97
United Nations, 55, 61, 66, 67, 68, 71, 79, 141, 221
and Bosnia, 237–39
founding of, 58–59, 60, 62
and Rwanda, 233–34
and Somalia, 232–33
weapons inspectors of, 235
see also Security Council, UN
United States:
as Arsenal of Democracy, 47
avoidance of alliances as traditional peacetime policy of, 56
balance-of-payments deficits of, 142
balance of trade and, 51
Chinese relations with, 89, 130, 135–40, 164
containment policy of, *see* universal containment, doctrine of
deficit of, 51
deindustrialization of, 198–99, 201
energy consumption in, 167–70, 186
energy dependence of, 15
Great Britain's relationship with, 58
Greece and, 71, 76
influence in Middle East of, 8
isolationism in, 30, 281
military power of, 1, 8, 12–13
Nazi threat to, 32, 38
neutrality of, 23, 28, 30
new social contract in, 11
nuclear weapons of, 58, 59, 64, 67, 93–94, 108, 116

United States (*cont.*)
  Pacific Rim interests of, 54
  as sole superpower, 8, 68
  Soviet expansionism and, 55
  Soviet relations with, 58–59, 63, 64, 66, 67, 86, 130, 139, 140–42, 164, 171; *see also* cold war
  trade balance of, 14, 15, 16
  trade deficits of, 143, 186, 187
  transatlantic trade of, 33
  Turkey and, 71, 76
  in World War I, 33, 35
United States v. Nixon, 146, 147, 303
universal containment, doctrine of, 15, 69–70, 74, 76, 93, 95, 99, 100, 102, 104, 108, 111–12, 115, 121, 124, 126, 131, 135, 136, 139, 141, 142, 165, 186, 209, 222, 223, 230, 243, 244, 258, 287
  see also NSC-68; Truman Doctrine
Universal Military Training, 65, 299–301
unlawful combatants, 269
unreasonable searches, 39, 41
unwarranted searches, 6, 20
Uruguay Round Agreements Act (1994), 306
USA Patriot Act, 3, 39, 263–64, 270
Uzbekistan, 242

Vance, Cyrus, 166, 176
Vandenberg, Arthur, 71
Velvet Revolution, 208
Versailles, Treaty of (1919), 24
Vienna summit (1961), 106–7, 113
Vietnam, 9, 13, 89, 95, 114, 164, 252, 258, 279
  Chinese invasion of, 140
Vietnam syndrome, 220, 254–55
Vietnam War, 15, 38, 65, 73, 101, 118, 142, 149, 165, 183, 184, 194, 205, 215, 220, 225, 263, 271, 277, 285, 286, 289, 300
  Americanization of, 115, 121, 123
  antiwar movement and, 133–34
  escalation of, 123–24, 131, 133
  JFK and, 120–21
  Johnson and, 119–25, 131, 133, 134, 152, 158, 159, 186, 274
  Nixon and, 122, 130–32, 134–35, 137, 144, 150
  Pentagon Papers and, 144–45
  Tet offensive in, 125, 152
  "Vietnamization" of, 130, 132, 134, 144
Village Voice, 155
Villard, Oswald Garrison, 31
Volcker, Paul, 143, 183

Wallace, George, 125–26, 130, 158
Wallace, Henry, 69
Wall Street, political power of, 32
Walsh, Lawrence, 193
Walters, Vernon, 147
war:
  civil liberties and, 20
  founders' views of, 19–21
  of ideological choice vs. war of necessity, 68, 188
  preventive, 261
War Industries Board (World War I), 45–46
war on terror, 10, 260, 261, 268–69, 287
War Powers Act (1973), 135, 149, 151, 152, 253
Warren, Earl, 43
Warsaw Pact, 93, 113, 218, 221, 229, 230, 241
Washington, George, 5
  Farewell Address of, 20
Washington Post, 145
waterboarding, 265
Watergate scandal, 130, 135, 145–46, 147–48, 151, 158, 159, 160, 183, 184, 191, 192, 194, 252, 255, 289, 303
Wayne, John, 170
weapons of mass destruction, 261
Weinberger, Caspar, 188, 191, 192, 193
Weinberger-Powell Doctrine, 213, 216, 217
Western Europe, 54, 182
Westmoreland, William, 125
Wheeler, Burton K., 32
White House Plumbers, 145–46
Wikileaks, 269
Willkie, Wendell, 35
Wilson, Charles, 47
Wilson, Woodrow, 15, 21, 30, 31, 46, 52, 56, 83, 164, 215, 231, 258, 281–82
  administration, 25, 39
  deceptive rhetoric of, 24–25, 34
  and expansion of presidential powers, 22–23

wiretaps, 40–41, 270
Wirthlin, Richard, 195
Wise, David, 97
Wolfowitz, Paul, 221, 255
World Trade Organization, 248, 294, 306
World War I, 23–24, 30, 33, 35, 39, 46, 215, 281
  as disillusioning experience, 31, 32, 34
World War II, 4, 6, 7, 17, 27, 35–38, 42–44, 140, 189, 215, 225
  aftermath of, 52–53
  commando units in, 114
  Japanese American internment in, 29, 38, 43–45, 84, 264, 277
  nuclear weapons and, 64
  in, Southeast Asia, 56
  U.S. anti-interventionist movement and, 30–31
  U.S. economy and, 33–34, 45–49

Yalta conference, 57, 58–59, 60, 61, 62, 66, 70, 141, 142, 209
Yeltsin, Boris, 218, 219, 241
Yemen, 268, 269, 287
Yongbyon nuclear plant, 234–35
Yoo, John, 253–54, 257, 264–65
Yugoslavia, 89, 220, 232, 238

Zarqawi, Abu Musab al-, 272
Zhou Enlai, 137